IN SEARCH OF

British Injustice and Collusion in Northern Ireland

THE TRUTH

WITHDRAWN
FROM
STOCK

MICHAEL O'CONNELL, from Nottingham, has divided his time between Ireland and England since childhood. He specialised in criminal law in England, Wales and Ireland from 1966 and was legal adviser to the Catholic Social Services for Prisoners, a charity helping prisoners and their families. The author of several books on the criminal justice system, he jointly edited nine editions of *Blackstone's Statutes on Evidence* (Oxford University Press).

Stay up to date with the author on Facebook at:
michael.oconnell.5076

This book is dedicated with love to my wife, Eileen, to my two sisters, Mary and Patricia, and my brother, Charles. Also to the memory of my parents, James and Mary O'Connell.

IN SEARCH OF
British Injustice and Collusion in Northern Ireland
THE TRUTH

MICHAEL O'CONNELL

The Collins Press

FIRST PUBLISHED IN 2017 BY
The Collins Press
West Link Park
Doughcloyne
Wilton
Cork
T12 N5EF
Ireland

A CIP record for this book is available from the British Library.

Paperback ISBN: 978-1-84889-300-9
PDF eBook ISBN: 978-1-84889-635-2
EPUB eBook ISBN: 978-1-84889-636-9
Kindle ISBN: 978-1-84889-637-6

Typesetting by Patricia Hope
Typeset in AGaramond
Printed in Poland by Drukarnia Skleniarz

CONTENTS

Acknowledgements

I wish to thank the many people who helped me write this book. Special thanks go to my two old friends and colleagues, Professor Terence Walters BL, LLB, LLM and Phil Huxley LLB LLM. Their knowledge of criminal law and procedure and the law of evidence is immense. The views expressed in this book, the conclusions drawn, and any errors are mine alone.

Abbreviations

CCRC	Criminal Cases Review Commission
CID	Criminal Investigation Department
CPS	Crown Prosecution Service
DC	detective constable
DCI	detective chief inspector
DCS	detective chief superintendent
DPP	Director of Public Prosecutions
Det Sgt	detective sergeant
Det Supt	detective superintendent
ESDA	electrostatic detection apparatus
HET	Historical Enquiries Team
INLA	Irish National Liberation Army
IRA	Irish Republican Army
MOD	Ministry of Defence
NCO	Non-commissioned Officer
NG	nitroglycerine
NICRA	Northern Ireland Civil Rights Association
PACE	Police and Criminal Evidence Act 1984
PC	police constable
PCA	Police Complaints Authority

PIRA   Provisional Irish Republican Army

PSNI   Police Service of Northern Ireland

QC   Queen's Counsel

RARDE   Royal Armament Research Development Establishment

RMP   Royal Military Police

RUC   Royal Ulster Constabulary

SLR   self-loading rifle

SSU   Special Support Unit (RUC)

TLC   thin-layer chromatography

UDA   Ulster Defence Association

UDR   Ulster Defence Regiment

UVF   Ulster Volunteer Force

Introduction

BETWEEN 14 AUGUST 1969 and 31 July 2007 the British army ran an operation in Northern Ireland in support of the civil power. Codenamed Operation Banner, it was the longest continuous campaign in the history of that army. In response to a Freedom of Information request the Ministry of Defence (MOD) disclosed that 1,441 members of the UK armed forces died as a result of operations in Northern Ireland or Irish terrorism in other countries.[1] There were many more civilian casualties. The figures are both daunting and haunting. One casualty, however, was the truth. There are some who call for the establishment of a truth commission, claiming that there can be no reconciliation and forgiveness without truth. I believe that will never happen. The British state has concealed the truth about the past in a bodyguard of lies for too long to allow the world to know exactly how it fought its carefully selected enemy. Britain was a colonial power, Northern Ireland its last colony. It has always operated on the basis of purchasing one part of the population and intimidating the other. For a country of its geographical size and population, the United Kingdom of Great Britain and Northern Ireland has had a disproportionate influence on world events. That influence has not always been beneficial to the people of these islands, but for some at the top echelons in society, colonialism has meant wealth, power and prestige, often at the cost of the lives of others.

Chapter 1 of this book is an overview of past events, the consequences of which still resound today. Northern Ireland was created in 1922 as a sectarian wilderness designed by its political architects as a one-party state. That was foolish in the extreme. It was bound to lead to conflict, with each side claiming the high moral ground. In 1973 Britain demonstrated its inability to understand the source of the latest conflict in Northern Ireland, often referred to as 'the Troubles', by inducing the Ulster Unionists, led by

1

the late Brian Faulkner, to form a power-sharing assembly with the Social Democratic and Labour Party (SDLP), led by Gerry Fitt. Britain seemed not to know it, but the real power-brokers were the late Ian Paisley and his Democratic Unionist Party (DUP) on the one hand, and Gerry Adams of Provisional Sinn Féin, closely allied to the Provisional IRA, on the other. One senior civil servant, Oliver Wright, was indiscreet enough to put in writing in 1972 what he and many of his colleagues thought of the host population of the North at that time. He described many of the Protestant people being 'driven by a desire for hatred and vengeance and too many looked to the one man with charisma in Ulster, a man of God, the Rev. Ian Paisley, to give it to them'.[2] In that regard Paisley did not let them down. If only he had publicly made known then his long-nursed ambition to be the political head of Northern Ireland, how many individuals on both sides of the sectarian divide who went to their graves violently and prematurely would instead have led a long and peaceful life? As for the Catholic minority community in the North, Oliver Wright wrote, 'in true Irish fashion the Micks have enjoyed provoking the Prods as much as the Prods have enjoyed retaliating. It makes the Prods' blood boil – and Irish blood boils at a very low temperature – to see the Micks enjoying the superior material benefits of the British connection while continuing to wave the Tricolour at them'.[3] The document containing these quotations was released by the British government in 2002 under the '30-year rule', which allows public access in the National Archives to documents of state. Some politicians and members of the legal establishment immensely dislike that rule and would like to safeguard secrets of the state for ever. In one of the cases described below, that of the Guildford Four, many of the documents were originally sealed for 30 years, but did it become apparent to someone that they contained material that contained the suppressed truth, so a decision was made that they should be sealed for 75 years? This will ensure that those who have an interest in uncovering that truth will no longer be around to do so.

During this time of sectarian strife in the early 1970s, efforts were made to preserve the rule of law, but the fact is that the legal system in Northern Ireland was not detached and impartial, but had long, since the inception of the Province of Ulster, directly reflected the sectarian politics of a very confused society.

The decision-makers at the top echelons of British society have always acted, so they allege, in the name of bringing democratic principles to those not fortunate to be able to acquire them for themselves. Behind the colonial administrators and civil servants who introduced the native population to the rule of law was the British army, soldiers of which fought and died in foreign fields without knowing exactly why they were there. They manned the concentration camps in the Boer War in South Africa at the beginning of the twentieth century, without asking why. It is said that 20,000 women and children died in these camps after an outbreak of measles. In the First World War, thousands of Irishmen fought alongside their English, Welsh and Scottish comrades for the freedom of small nations, not realising that in their own homeland others were fighting and dying for the same principle.

It has long been my view that it was the Easter Rising in Dublin in April 1916 that spelled the beginning of the end of the British Empire. There was no public support for those who considered it a great and glorious thing to die for Ireland until the military blunders of courts martial and summary executions, followed by the desecration of the dead leaders by dumping their bodies in a pit so revolted the country that the Empire started to fall asunder from then on. There was no going back after that.

During the Second World War the British armed the Communists in their fight against the Japanese in Malaya. When the Japanese surrendered in 1945 the Communists turned on the British, using the very armaments provided for their own armed struggle, killing many young British servicemen. No one will ever discover, or even want to discover, the truth about the killings by the Scots Guards of unarmed men in Batang Kali in December 1948, any more than they want to find out the truth about similar actions in Northern Ireland.

Chapter 2 illustrates the links between the legal process in Great Britain and Northern Ireland. It is a reminder that the law of Northern Ireland is closely bound up with that of England and Wales, even though some seek to deny that connection. I describe events in a criminal case that shows the abuse of power, corruption on an industrial scale, and hypocrisy of the worse possible kind. The case involved the brutal murder of the daughter of a High Court judge in Country Antrim in 1952 that remains unsolved to this day.

The third chapter deals with the case of the 14 men detained in August 1971 when internment was introduced into Northern Ireland. The Catholic/nationalist people in the North saw the principle of 'the enemy of my enemy is my friend' being put into effect. Imprisonment without trial was directed against only one section of the population. The 14 hooded men were selected for special treatment under interrogation. They were blindfolded, starved, deprived of sleep, subjected to intolerable noise, and forced to stand in stress positions against a wall. The European Court did not consider that the 14 were tortured, merely ill-treated. The Irish government has recently invited the European Court to reopen the case on the basis of evidence that on two material issues the British government misled the Court. That has yet to be resolved. The RTÉ television programme *The Torture Files*, broadcast on 4 June 2014, discovered a letter dated 1977 indicating that it was ministers in the UK, not the Northern Ireland prime minister Brian Faulkner, who had authorised internment. The letter contains a handwritten note, 'this could grow into something awkward if pursued'. That means 'if the truth were ever found out'.

If the European Court had been more robust, it may be that the people of Iraq would have been spared the ill-treatment they received at the hands of the British army. The army had apparently and conveniently 'forgotten' that the United Kingdom's attorney general had told the European Court in 1998 that in future prisoners would not be treated in the same shameful way, and in particular that the sensory deprivation techniques that had been used on the 14 hooded men would not be employed again.

The fourth chapter, 'The Window Cleaners', describes the murder of Peter Johnson in Belfast in 1976. He was an innocent Catholic, chosen at random for sectarian assassination. Two young boys confessed to that murder. They were innocent; their confessions were false. The prime suspect was a member of a gang known as the Window Cleaners. The BBC Northern Ireland *Spotlight* programme identified him as Thomas McCreery, the leader of a UDA gang in north Belfast, and named him as the killer. He was arrested for the murder, but never charged. He now lives in southern Spain and is believed to have organised the murder of a London drug dealer outside his home. There are substantial suspicions that he was a police informer, given immunity from prosecution, even for murder. In his case, like others, the truth cannot be allowed to be established – too many others fear the consequences if it is.

Chapter 5 discusses the paramilitary police force in Northern Ireland, the Royal Ulster Constabulary (RUC), and the willingness of that force to follow the lead of the politicians in a one-party state. In the early days the RUC's basic training was haphazard, their skills and morale were poor, their powers of detection were limited. Even when one of their own officers was brutally murdered with the wife of one of his friends, his death was treated as suicide until the killer confessed to the double murder, which would otherwise have gone unsolved. There is also the disquieting disclosure of the army's efforts to obtain preferential treatment for its soldiers, so that they would face a military court martial, rather than a criminal court, if accused of criminal offences. Those efforts failed, but the fact that they were made at all must give cause for concern.

In Chapter 6 there is a reminder that a basic legal principle in any criminal justice system is that the rules of practice, evidence and procedure are clear, unambiguous and easily ascertainable in advance. There should also be clearly defined limits to the powers of the police in the investigation of crime. Those suspected of committing criminal offences have the right to fair treatment in custody and the right to a fair trial. But victims of crime also have the right to the truth. They must be told what happened, or did not happen, in their case.

This is a crucial index of a state's commitment to human rights and its ability to make reparations where breaches have occurred, most especially in criminal cases. But for the parents, brothers and sisters of those victims, many of them only in their late teens, who died in public house bombings in Birmingham, Guildford and Woolwich in October and November 1974 there has been no explanation why those who confessed to those bombings while in police custody were set free on appeal, while those who openly and repeatedly admitted those offences in open court on oath were never charged and thus not convicted in respect of the deaths of their children. That cannot be right.

But there is another, more fundamental problem. The UK is a secretive society with a tradition, especially among some elements in the political establishment, of concealing the truth without actually telling a lie. The Freedom of Information Act 2000 promised that the public would know more, not less, about what is being done in the British state in the name of all its citizens. That has not happened. The political and legal establishment that makes up the state will go to extreme lengths not just to avoid fair criticism of the prosecuting authorities but also to seek to conceal the truth from both the victims and those charged with and frequently convicted of crimes they did not commit. When the state convicts and imprisons the innocent, and justice is shown to have miscarried, the state response is not to seek out the truth and punish the wrongdoers, but too often to reconvict the innocent all over again.

Chapter 7 deals with two of the most scandalous miscarriages of justice in British legal history: the cases of the Guildford Four and the Maguire Seven. The Four were convicted on the evidence that they provided against themselves – their confessions in custody. They complained of the use of force and of the threat of force, directed not only against themselves but also against their families. One of them, Paul Hill, said that when he was held at Guildford police station a police officer pushed a gun through the flap on the cell door and 'dry fired' the gun. No one believed him at the time. They do now. We also know about the regrettable conduct of Sir Michael Havers QC, prosecuting counsel, in distributing photographs of the mutilated bodies of the dead soldiers from the Guildford pub bombing to members of the press at the start of the Guildford Four's case. That information is confirmed by the BBC journalist Paul Reynolds.[4] That simply cannot be right and should not have happened. It was highly prejudicial and must have caused immense grief to the families of the deceased if they ever discovered what he had done.

The case of the Maguire Seven was another dreadful case of the conviction of the innocent. Like the Guildford Four, six of the Seven complained about vicious and sustained violence while they were in police custody. They stood strong and confessed to nothing. I contend that they did not receive a fair trial; the trial was more political than legal. The forensic evidence against them was false and misleading from the start. Anne Maguire, who had been named frequently in the Guildford Four trial press reports only some months previously, fought fiercely to establish her innocence and that of her children, but to no avail. The law was unrelenting and unbending and totally wrong.

Chapter 8 describes the trial of three former Surrey police officers who were alleged to have perverted the course of justice by putting forward interview notes which they said were made at the time of the interview, but were not. I pose the question: does it matter if the police did not make contemporaneous interview notes, provided the officers told the truth about what the accused said in interviews, and in reply to questions? What really counted, in my view, was whether the content of those notes was the truth. In my view there was more than enough prima facie evidence to charge a number of other Surrey police officers with perjury. That was not done, and my view is that if they had been convicted they would not have gone to prison without disclosing who else was involved in the shameful conviction of the innocent.

Chapter 9, 'Covering up the Truth', describes the circumstances leading up to the murder of the Belfast solicitor Pat Finucane. The wartime slogan 'Careless Talk Costs Lives' comes to mind here. One careless talker was the Tory politician Douglas Hogg, whose words in the House of Commons shocked some and terrified others. He was apparently told, and he certainly repeated in the Commons, that some solicitors in Northern Ireland were unduly sympathetic to the IRA.[5] Within weeks of that statement, which Hogg refused to withdraw, Pat Finucane was savagely shot down in front of his wife and young children.

Chapter 10 is inspired by the suggestion of a former judge, Michael Argyle, that women who supported terrorism should be shot. The article in which he made this claim implied that he would dispense with trial by jury and simply select the candidates for assassination. The death squads operating in Northern Ireland at the time did exactly that when they murdered two women, Máire Drumm and Miriam Daly, in Belfast.

Mairéad Farrell and two colleagues were shot dead by the SAS in Gibraltar on 6 March 1988. It is now known that there were at least two highly placed informers in the IRA at that time. Did either of them betray Mairéad Farrell and two others? Does that explain why the SAS soldiers were flown to Gibraltar three days before Farrell was shot dead? Did the soldiers know exactly what plans she and the others had to place a bomb near an army unit? Did they know that on the day they shot them dead, there was no bomb and that all three were unarmed? If they did, does that mean that they were guilty of unlawful killing? Is the state that sent them to Gibraltar likely to put them on trial to find out?

Chapter 11 describes the murder trials of members of the security forces who killed two children, Kevin Heatley and Majella O'Hare, both only 12 years of age. The two cases provide an insight into the criminal justice process in Northern Ireland at that time. The two cases are linked, not only because both victims were children, but because the initial reaction of the authorities was to lie. Only the soldiers who were there and saw everything knew the plain unvarnished truth about the killings.

The results of the cases indicate why the nationalist people of Northern Ireland had no confidence in the administration of justice and those who tried to uphold the criminal law. The full and complete truth was not told in either of those cases. In 2011 the MOD formally apologised to Majella O'Hare's mother for the death of her young daughter, admitting that the army's version of the incident in which Majella died, and the account in court of the soldier who shot her, were 'unlikely'. However that may be, the trial judge at the time chose to believe that account, disregarding the evidence of credible eyewitnesses at the crime scene. The reality of life is that judges believe who and what they want to believe.

The shooting dead of Kevin Heatley and Majella O'Hare should cause some pause for thought. Describing them as 'collateral damage in time of war', as I have heard them described, is cruel, offensive and unforgivable.

Chapter 12 describes the series of incidents in 1982 when the RUC were accused of operating a 'shoot to kill' policy.

John Stalker, the assistant chief constable of the Greater Manchester

Police, tried in vain to establish the truth about the deaths of Seamus Grew and Roderick Carroll, and about the killings in two other linked cases. Rather than allow him access to the truth, he was removed from the inquiry into the three cases by the chief constable of the RUC, Sir John Hermon. Evidence at recent inquests has disclosed much more of the truth than was ever known at the time.

1 Past Events

COLONIAL POWERS DO not embrace the truth. On the contrary, they try to suppress it until those involved are dead, too old to remember, or too feeble to care. In addition, the political classes have an unlimited capacity to hide the truth. The legal and political establishment is too often prepared to conceal the truth on grounds of 'national security'.

When it became apparent that 18 innocent people – the Birmingham Six, the Maguire Seven, the Guildford Four and Judith Ward – had been wrongly convicted, some of the highest-ranked members of Britain's judiciary simply refused to accept that fact. How could these people be innocent? They were members of a suspect community – the ungrateful Irish.

There is a long history of troubles between these two nations, which share a common language but not much else. The old common law traditions in both jurisdictions no longer co-exist, and the Irish Free State (and later the Republic of Ireland) has enacted its own statutory provisions since 1922. Many of the differences, especially since that year, have led to communal violence, loss of life and damage to property. But did they do more than that? Did they cause irreparable damage to the reputation of the criminal justice system in England and Northern Ireland? Above all, was the system in both jurisdictions fair and impartial in its treatment of those accused of crime who were outsiders, 'not one of us', as Margaret Thatcher might have put it?

Britain's policy in Northern Ireland was based on one simple principle: total opposition to the reunification of the island of Ireland. In order to counter nationalist aspirations, Britain concentrated on the management of the civil conflict and control of political unrest and was prepared to do that ad infinitum.

The first Irish Republican Army (IRA) bombing campaign was launched in Britain in November 1920, when incendiary attacks on 19 buildings in Liverpool caused substantial damage. In the following year there were attacks on property on some 12 separate occasions in the north and northwest of England. Again the damage caused was very substantial.

The final act of violence attributed to the IRA prior to 1939 was the assassination of Field Marshal Sir Henry Wilson on 22 June 1922. A native of County Longford, he considered himself Anglo-Irish, and was treated as Irish in England and English in Ireland.

He had been appointed Chief of the Imperial General Staff in February 1918 but was not reappointed in 1922. Utterly disillusioned, Wilson left the army and went into politics. He was elected unopposed as MP for North Down in February 1922. A passionate supporter of the unionist cause, he became chief security adviser to the newly formed Northern Ireland government. He was suspected of failing to prevent, if not actually encouraging, sectarian violence against the minority Catholic population in Ulster, and he is also believed by some to have been involved in the Curragh Mutiny of 1914.

He was shot dead in the doorway of his house on Eaton Square in London by Reginald Dunne and Joseph O'Sullivan, both members of the IRA, who were tried at the Old Bailey on 2 July 1922. They did not deny what they had done, and the jury took only three minutes to arrive at their verdict. They were hanged side by side by the public executioner John Ellis at Wandsworth Prison on 10 August of that year. Forty-nine days from an indefensible murder to judicial execution. There was no delay in the law in those times.

Joseph O'Sullivan had fought on the Western Front and had lost a leg at the first battle of Ypres. The two men had walked to Eaton Square, and after the murder they tried to escape on foot. They had also shot and wounded three other men, including a detective and a uniformed constable and were detained a few hundred yards from the scene. O'Sullivan had no realistic chance of getting away because of his handicap; Dunne stayed with him, knowing that capture was inevitable. Their motive for killing a fellow Irishman will never now be known. Their execution may have had a deterrent effect, because the IRA did not make a violent return to the British mainland for 17 years.

In 1939 and 1940 the IRA renewed their campaign in England, causing deaths and damage throughout the country. On 24 July 1939 the home secretary, Sir Samuel Hoare, introduced the Prevention of Violence

(Temporary Provisions) Bill, telling the House of Commons that to date 66 members of the IRA had been convicted of serious crime; there had been 127 terrorist outrages, 57 in London and 70 in the provinces; an enormous amount of explosives had been seized by the police; there had been three explosions at electricity plants in the London area; and in the north and the Midlands many gas and electricity mains were damaged by bombing. In his book on the Provisional IRA, Gary McGladdery records that there were no fewer than 291 explosions in England during 1939, and even after the outbreak of the Second World War in September of that year the IRA continued to bomb shops in the West End of London.

On 25 August 1939 the IRA bombed Coventry. Five people were killed; 70 others were injured, 12 of them grievously. Two men, Peter Barnes, aged 32, a native of County Offaly, and 29-year-old Westmeath man James McCormack, who used the surname Richards, were charged with the murder of one of the five victims, Elsie Ansell. She was aged 21, newly engaged and worked as a shop assistant near the scene of the bomb. She was so badly mutilated that she could only be identified by her engagement ring and her shoes. Her marriage had been arranged for the following week, and she was buried in her wedding dress.

In the dock with Barnes and McCormack (Richards), jointly charged with murder, were Joseph and Mary Hewitt and Mary's mother, Brigid O'Hara. Their junior counsel, Thomas Tempest Dineen, a native of Bandon, County Cork, told me some years ago that when prosecuting counsel Richard O'Sullivan QC opened the case to the jury he said that the bomb had been made at the 'premises of *Joseph* and *Mary*', stressing those names with their biblical connotation, before adding, '. . . Hewitt at their premises at 25 Clara Street, Coventry'. O'Sullivan was an eccentric character who after this case convinced himself, but few others, that the IRA were determined to kill him in a revenge attack for his participation in the trial. He died peacefully in his own bed many years later.

The bomb involved in the fatal explosion was concealed in the carrier of a bicycle that was being wheeled along the Broadgate Centre in Coventry when the person wheeling the bicycle suddenly abandoned it. It exploded shortly afterwards.

Peter Barnes had transported potassium chlorate from London to Coventry. He believed that the intended target of the bombing was an electricity substation and he never intended or foresaw that anyone would be killed or injured. His aim was solely to damage property. If it was true that he did not intend to kill or cause serious injury to anyone, one has to question the basis on which he was convicted of murder. He was in London on the day the bomb exploded, so he knew nothing of how the bicycle had come to be abandoned in a crowded public place.

James McCormack (Richards) had bought the bicycle and saw the bomb, but it was another man who constructed it, and yet another who left it on the bicycle in the Broadgate Centre. They were never charged with any offence arising out of this incident.

At the end of the trial Joseph and Mary Hewitt and Mrs O'Hara were acquitted by the jury. Peter Barnes and James Richards were convicted of murder and sentenced to death by Mr Justice Singleton.[1] They were hanged side by side in Winson Green Prison on 7 February 1940. Two Catholic priests accompanied them to the gallows.

According to Tim Pat Coogan's widely acclaimed book *On the Blanket*, public opinion in Ireland was inflamed against Britain by the execution of the two men, no doubt on the grounds that they never intended to kill anyone but only to damage property. It may be worthy of note that in the course of the Troubles in Northern Ireland from 1970 onwards, in cases where a bomb was planted on premises, if the bomber fully and accurately informed the police and/or the army of the presence of that bomb, claiming that it was planted only for the purpose of damaging property, then in the event of someone being killed in a subsequent explosion, the bomber would be convicted of manslaughter, not murder, the assumption being that passing accurate information indicated that there was no intention to kill, only an intention to damage property. If this is correct, does that at least suggest the possibility that Peter Barnes was hanged for a murder of which, as he told the court, 'I would like to say as I am going before my God, as I am condemned to death, I am innocent and later I am sure it will all come out that I had neither hand, act or part in it. That is all I have to say'?[2] James Richards thanked the gentlemen who defended him during his trial and said, 'As a soldier of the Irish Republican Army I am not afraid to die, as I am doing it for as just cause. I say in conclusion, God bless Ireland and God bless the men who have fought and died for her. Thank you, my Lord.'[3]

That trial and those executions solved nothing. The IRA continued its bombing campaign in Liverpool, London, Southampton and Birmingham. Property was damaged, but there were no fatal injuries. Seven people were injured when a bomb placed in a rubbish bin exploded in Oxford Street, London on 28 November 1940. By this date the authorities in Britain had turned their attention to the war against Germany.

Within a day of internment without trial being introduced into

Northern Ireland on 9 August 1971, men claiming to be members of the Provisional IRA held a press conference in Dublin in which they warned that they would bring their campaign to Britain in the coming months. They began by bombing the Post Office Tower in London on 31 October 1971. No one was injured in that bombing, but damage was extensive. A telephone caller claimed that the Kilburn battalion of the IRA was responsible. That may not have been entirely true. This incident was the first act of unlawful violence in England after the Troubles began in Northern Ireland in 1968 and Britain's military response – Operation Banner – from August 1969 to July 2007 placed the criminal justice system under the spotlight as never before.

There were many civilian casualties on both sides of the sectarian divide in Northern Ireland and among the security forces, and many acts of wanton brutality, but did the state cover up the truth and resort to outright lying in criminal cases arising from the IRA's 'armed struggle'? Did the criminal justice system in the UK and Northern Ireland simply break down because of inherent failings, or was there a rush to judgement that blinded even the most careful and dispassionate participant in that system?

A Catalogue of Death and Lies; England, Ireland and Overseas

The year 1974 saw a terrible catalogue of horrendous acts of violence in Northern Ireland: 166 civilians and 50 members of the security forces were murdered in that year alone. The violence was no less brutal in England or in the Republic of Ireland. On 4 February 12 people died and 14 were seriously injured when members of the Provisional IRA placed an explosive device in the boot of a coach used by soldiers and their families returning from their homes in the Manchester area to Catterick military camp in Yorkshire. Among the dead were Corporal Clifford Houghton, aged 23, serving in the Royal Regiment of Fusiliers, his wife Linda, also 23, and their two children, Lee, aged five, and Robert, aged two. The family were Catholics. Bombs do not discriminate against victims on religious grounds.

It is my view that, in revenge and retaliation for that most dreadful and unforgivable massacre, some elements in the security forces in Northern Ireland colluded with loyalist paramilitaries to bomb the city of Dublin and the town of Monaghan on 17 May 1974. On that day Northern Ireland was in the grip of sectarian threats and violence. The Ulster Workers' Council had called a strike to undermine, perhaps even destroy, the Sunningdale Agreement, which envisaged power-sharing between nationalists and loyalists. The strike was savagely enforced by armed and heavily disguised men standing by road blocks on the streets. British politicians failed to order the army to confront the loyalists, perhaps fearing that the army might refuse to do so. (The situation was so serious that on 19 May the new Labour government declared a state of emergency in Northern Ireland.)

Around 5.30 in the afternoon of Friday 17 May three car bombs exploded in the centre of Dublin. All the vehicles bore Northern Ireland registration numbers and two had been hijacked in loyalist areas of Belfast earlier that day. Eyewitnesses saw two of the vehicles in the car park near the Catholic Church in the Whitehall district of Dublin, where a number of men were apparently tinkering with the cars. It is likely that they were arming the bombs. Twenty-two people died instantly and over 100 were injured, four of whom died. Among the dead were four members of the same family, John and Anna O'Brien and their two young children. Anna was wheeling her two little girls in a buggy when they were hit by the full blast of the first car bomb on Parnell Street. She was so badly mutilated that her sister was only able to identify her by one of her earrings.

Of the 26 people who died in the streets of Dublin on that day, 19 were women. One of them was 21-year-old Colette O'Doherty. She was killed in the second explosion in Talbot Street. She was expecting to go into hospital that evening for the birth of her second child. That unborn child died with her. Her first child, her two-year-old daughter Wendy, by some miracle survived the explosion and was found weeping in her pram some distance along Talbot Street, covered in the debris that cluttered the entire area. A young woman, still in shock, saw her, lifted her from the pram, and took her to a nearby hospital, where she was treated for what turned out to be minor injuries.

About 90 minutes after those explosions in Dublin, five others were killed instantly and 25 were injured when another bomb exploded outside a public house in the centre of Monaghan town, which lies about six miles from the border with Northern Ireland. Two other people, a man and a woman, later died of their injuries.

The final total death toll on that most dreadful day was 33. The killings led to the biggest unsolved murder inquiry in Ireland since independence. Anecdotal evidence from the time suggested that a Cabinet meeting called within two hours of the Dublin bombing by Liam Cosgrave, the Taoiseach in the Fine Gael/Labour coalition government, decided to relay a message to the British government, saying in effect, 'We've got the message; we will crack down on the IRA.' That is exactly what they did. Very little enthusiasm was shown by the politicians or the police to discover the identities of those who carried out the bombings. Media reports show that both Liam Cosgrave and the attorney general, Declan Costello SC, said that the IRA were morally responsible for the bombings. One wonders whether it might have been better to try to establish who was legally responsible, and bring them to justice, before apportioning 'moral' blame.

The Garda investigation, such as it was, was not a success. It is claimed that the names of some of those responsible are known, but there is insufficient evidence to put anyone on trial for murder on a massive scale. No one has ever been charged, let alone convicted, of any offence committed on 17 May 1974.

A judicial inquiry chaired by the retired Irish Supreme Court judge Mr Justice Henry Barron concluded in its report published in December 2003:

> [T]here are grounds for suspecting that the bombers have had assistance from members of the security forces . . . The involvement of individual members in such activity does not of itself mean the bombings were either officially or unofficially state-sanctioned . . . ultimately a finding that there was collusion between the perpetrators and the authorities in Northern Ireland is a matter of inference.

When the journalist Peter Taylor interviewed the loyalist politician David Ervine, a senior member of the Ulster Volunteer Force (UVF), which was widely believed to have carried out both bombings, he was told that the loyalists were 'returning the serve', which presumably means giving the people in the south of Ireland an insight into how it felt to be on the receiving end of the IRA terror bombing campaign.[4] Like so many others, David Ervine misunderstood that the main source of political grievance was vested, not in the south of Ireland, but in the North, among those who felt themselves excluded and marginalised by a one-party state that allowed nothing short of unconditional loyalty to the British Crown.

Some take the view that it was those Irish who fired the first shots of the Easter Rising in Dublin in April 1916 who shattered the myth of invincibility and eventually led to the break-up of the British Empire upon which the sun never set. The Rising showed that it was possible to force the British to enter into negotiation with the very people responsible for the use of armed struggle for political ends. Moreover, it broke the appearance of over-whelming superiority that seemed to surround the military guardians patrolling those countries whose only link was their enforced allegiance to the Crown.

The Rising lasted only six days before Patrick Pearse surrendered to the Crown Forces at the scene of the heaviest fighting at the General Post Office on O'Connell Street, Dublin. The public response may have been hostile at the outset, but the summary trials and swift executions of the leaders of the Rising changed everything. The British had won the battle but lost the war. In the space of nine days, 14 men gave their lives for the political and economic freedom of their country, When the news of the executions by firing squad became public, and the way in which the bodies of the dead were initially dumped into a pit without coffins and covered with quicklime rather than given a decent Christian burial, a sense of outrage completely enveloped the island of Ireland. After that, there was no going back from the road to full national independence.

The government in London, with the help of informers, knew the forthcoming War of Independence in Ireland had to be contained, and it was, between January 1919 and July 1921. The Irish Republican Army (IRA) had inflicted heavy casualties on the Royal Irish Constabulary (RIC), killing more than 50 of its officers, and the British response was to create a counter-insurgency force that included the RIC, the regular army, officers of the Secret Service, and two completely new forces, both despised in equal measure by the Irish, the Auxiliaries and the Black and Tans. The former were almost exclusively recruited from demobilised British army veterans. Their reputation, based on their propensity to carry out reprisals against a host population, was fully justified during their time in Ireland. The Black and Tans likewise had fought in the war and had returned to discover that the political promise that they would find themselves in a land fit for heroes was an empty one. Faced with long-term unemployment, they accepted the offer to take on a rough and dangerous task in Ireland for ten shillings a day plus board and lodgings. At the time the average private soldier's pay in the British army was just over one shilling a day.

The Tans regularly engaged in savage reprisals against civilians with the approval of the Prime Minster, David Lloyd George. In November 1920 he claimed, 'we have murder by the throat. We struck the terrorists and now the terrorists are complaining of terror.' Within ten days of that statement, on Sunday 21 November, the Tans and the Auxiliaries opened fire on the crowd watching a Gaelic football match between Tipperary and Dublin in Croke Park, Dublin, killing 14 people, among them three schoolchildren.

This attack was a calculated act of retaliation for the killing of 14 British undercover agents in various parts of the city of Dublin earlier that Sunday morning. The Tans and the Auxiliaries later claimed that they were fired on first, and only returned fire against identified targets. That claim is echoed by the soldiers of the 1st Battalion of the Parachute Regiment who shot 14 people dead in the Bogside in Derry on 30 January 1972. Like the Auxiliaries and the Tans, the paratroopers suffered not one single casualty, even though they said they were fired on first. Perhaps their superior field craft and training protected them. The alternative view, that they were collectively lying in their version of events and were not, as they claimed, subjected to hostile gunfire from a number of unidentified individuals, is perhaps too awful to contemplate.

The executions in Dublin marked the beginning of the end of the British Empire. The one politician who understood that above all others was Winston Churchill, and it explains his hatred for the Irish and for Ireland and his hostile and overbearing attitude towards the Irish government during the Second World War. He had been one of the signatories to, and perhaps the driving force behind, the Anglo-Irish Treaty that ended the War of Independence in December 1921. It was calculated to cause trouble and it did. The pro-treaty forces, led by Michael Collins, accepted an Irish Free State within the Commonwealth. Éamon de Valera rejected the treaty, calling it a betrayal of the Republic that had been declared after the 1918 general election and of the men who died in the Rising. A part of the settlement was the requirement that elected national politicians should take an oath of allegiance to the British Crown, something which Churchill knew would not be acceptable to many in Ireland, even those worn down by the ravages of the recent war. In signing the treaty, Michael Collins said that he was signing his own death warrant. He was right. On 22 August 1922 he was shot dead in an ambush in his own native County Cork, the one place where he thought he was safe.

The upshot of the conflict between Collins and de Valera was the Civil War, fought between those who favoured the Irish Free State and those who wanted nothing short of an independent republic. That war, which turned brother against brother and father against son, with many atrocities on both sides, dragged on for two years. British politicians watching from the sidelines, with only a limited interest, had other irons in the fire.

The British solution to the Irish problem was the imposition of partition, which satisfied no one on the island of Ireland. There was violence and bloodshed in the newly created Northern Ireland, especially in Belfast, and the unionist government started as they intended to go on, with discrimination and hatred directed towards their Catholic neighbours that they intended should never end.

From the establishment of Northern Ireland until the end of the Second World War, the one-party state in Northern Ireland continued on its way, basking in the praise of the soon-to-be-defeated prime minister, Churchill, but making no effort to explain why the Stormont politicians had refused to allow conscription into the British armed forces during the whole of the Second World War.

To the British, Northern Ireland was a problem shelved, if not solved. There were many other problems to be faced both domestically and internationally. There had been no general elections between 1935 and 1945. The defeat of the Churchill government and the election of the Labour Party in July 1945 brought about no change in Northern Ireland. There was, however, no time for post-war rest for British politicians even after the defeat of Nazi Germany and the surrender of Japan in 1945.

In the mid-1950s the British government was embroiled in the Suez when the Egyptian president nationalised the Suez Canal. Encouraged by the British and the French governments the Israelis invaded Egypt, followed shortly afterwards by troops from Britain and France. On 23 December 1956 both countries withdrew their troops from the canal zone.

On 20 December, the prime minister, Anthony Eden, lied to the House of Commons when he denied that the British had colluded with the Israelis in their invasion of Egypt. He said:

> [W]e have been accused of being, ever since the Israeli attack on Egypt, and indeed long before that, in collusion with the Israelis. My Right Hon and Learned Friend, the Foreign Secretary [Selwyn Lloyd] emphatically denied that charge on 31 October . . . But to say – and that is what I want to repeat to the House – that Her Majesty's government were engaged in some dishonourable conspiracy is completely untrue and I must emphatically deny it.[5]

No one, nationally or internationally, contradicted this brazen lie by producing the Protocol of Sevres, which had been signed by the British, French and Israeli governments. In spite of Eden's categorical denial, there had been a conspiracy between the three governments in 1956 over the invasion of Egypt. It was dishonourable and probably illegal. To learn that a prime minister lied to the House of Commons will not surprise those who know the thinking behind it. Manufacturing a lie is as good as telling the truth, provided someone is prepared to believe the lie.

Eight days before Anthony Eden's deceitful statement, the IRA began what is commonly called its Border Campaign – Operation Harvest – which ran from 12 December 1956 until 26 February 1962. Its objective was to put an end to the partition of the island. It failed. It commanded virtually no support either north or south of the border. The Stormont government and the Dublin government brought into law internment without trial. Six members of the RUC died and 11 republicans were killed in action. The British government, with its attention directed elsewhere, barely noticed.

Events elsewhere were also troubling the politicians. The Conservative and Unionist government, led by Harold Macmillan, which was facing a general election in 1959, found itself under international fire for its policies in Kenya and central Africa. There was substantial trouble, also in March 1959, in the African state of Nyasaland (now Malawi), where over 50 Africans had been killed in rioting, leading the governor general, Sir Robert Armitage, to declare a state of emergency. At that time Macmillan was attending a summit meeting in Russia, and the cabinet decided to set up a royal commission, which would be headed by Mr Justice Patrick Devlin. On 24 July 1959 the commission's report was published. Alan Lennox-Boyd, colonial secretary, had insisted that it should be sanitised before its publication, but the Colonial Office's censor had catastrophically missed a phrase that was extremely embarrassing for the government and indeed might have brought it down: 'Nyasaland is – no doubt temporarily – a police state, where it is not safe for anyone to express approval of the policies of the Congress Party . . . and where it is unwise to express any but the most restrained criticism of government policy'.[6]

As for public reaction at home to the bloody events in the UK's African colonies, was it best expressed in its support for Macmillan's government at the general election in October 1959? The Conservatives won the election with a majority of exactly 100 seats.

In December 1961 the Conservative government, headed by Harold Macmillan, gave Kenya its independence. Its first president, Jomo Kenyatta, long imprisoned by the British in his own country for daring to want that country's independence from its colonial rulers, elected to stay within the British Commonwealth.

In more recent UK colonial history, in March 1970 the defence secretary in the Labour government, Denis Healey, arranged with the Director of Public Prosecutions (DPP) for Detective Chief Superintendent (DCS) Frank Williams of Scotland Yard to carry out inquiries into the horrendous 1948 killings of rubber plantation workers in Malaya. A total of 24 unarmed men were shot dead by a 16-man patrol of the Scots Guards.

The army claimed at the time that the victims were trying to escape into the jungle. Then the *Sunday People* newspaper published two articles in February 1970 challenging the official version of events. That was not well received by the political establishment.

Malaya was at the time a British protectorate. The British had colonised the area and introduced the rubber tree, and eventually Malaya produced almost half of the world's supply of rubber. It was a highly profitable industry and the profits were repatriated to the ruling elite in the UK.

During the Second World War the British had trained and armed members of the Communist Party in Malaya to fight the Japanese invading army. When the war ended, the Communists turned on the British. In 1948 the local Communist Party, mostly made up of people of Chinese origin, attempted to overthrow the government by force. Politicians in the UK were not prepared to allow others to take what they regarded as their own. A state of emergency was declared and British troops were sent to Malaya in September 1948 in support of the civil power. Troops were sent into Northern Ireland in exactly the same way, to keep public order, some 21 years later.

Of the Scots Guards who were sent to Malaya, many were semi-trained, inexperienced young men doing their National Service, not full-time career soldiers. Shortly after their arrival word spread among the troops that three soldiers in the Royal Hussars had been captured, soaked in petrol and set alight by the insurgents. According to the later confessions of some of the soldiers, they were ordered on 11 December 1948 to 'wipe out' the village of Batang Kali, about 45 miles northwest of Kuala Lumpur, because the villagers had been supporting and feeding the terrorists in their area. The incident ended with the village being burned to the ground. The insurgents claimed that the men in the village were separated from the women and children, divided into groups and shot in cold blood. There was no escape attempt, they said, by any of them. It was later claimed that many of the victims' bodies had been mutilated. One victim had been beheaded.

In 1970 some of the former soldiers who had taken part in this incident admitted that they had been ordered to execute the men in the village and were later coached to put forward the false explanation that all this had happened during a mass escape attempt.

The Scotland Yard inquiry, which might have discovered the truth among all the conflicting claims and counter-claims, was terminated by the attorney general Sir Peter Rawlinson QC on 30 June 1970, 12 days after the election of the Conservative and Unionist government led by Edward

Heath. Not discovering the truth was clearly high on the list of priorities of the incoming government, which two years later appointed Lord Widgery to conduct his now discredited inquiry into the shootings in Derry on 30 January 1972 when 14 innocent people were killed.

The Malaya attorney general, Sir Stafford Foster Sutton (later a QC), did carry out some kind of investigation into the killings in December 1948. It did not take long and it found nothing. He did not interview any of the survivors from Batang Kali, and there was no scientific or forensic investigation of any kind. He was satisfied that evidence of bullet wounds in the back was sufficient evidence to establish that the victims were running away from the soldiers when they were shot down. His private view was apparently that there was 'something to be said for public executions'. No copy of the report of his investigations has ever been found. Many documents relating to the Malayan Emergency were destroyed under the provisions of Section 6 of the Public Records Act 1958 as 'not being worthy of permanent preservation', This was the fate of many documents relating to law and order in the Empire after the end of the Second World War.

According to *The Guardian*,[7] the British Foreign Office intervened in 1993 to stop a further investigation by Malaysian police officers into the deaths of the villagers.[8] Currently, four relations of the victims are seeking a court order to overturn the British government's refusal to investigate the killings. While they lost their case before two judges in the High Court, and lost again in the Civil Division of the Court of Appeal, they were encouraged by the ruling that they had 'forged the first link in the chain' in their campaign for an independent inquiry. The judges said that precedent (rulings in other cases which are binding on the court) forced them to dismiss the appeal, but that the initial British investigations into the killings were woefully inadequate and that later investigations by the Malaysian and British police cast doubt on the claims that the plantation workers were trying to escape. They noted also that the confessions of the soldiers in 1969 and 1970 were potentially significant, especially since the investigation in which they emerged was brought to an abrupt halt. Those confessions have never been tested or discredited. The appeal court judges indicated their view that the Supreme Court might well decide the case differently, in accordance with the current European Court of Human Rights jurisprudence.

On 22 April 2015 in the Supreme Court in London Michael Fordham QC, counsel for the four relations of the dead, told the five judges that the Batang Kali massacre was and remains the responsibility of the UK.

The relations of the dead contended that the killings in December 1948 amounted to unjustified murder, and that the UK authorities have subsequently refused to hold a public inquiry, and have sometimes deliberately kept back relevant evidence. The case turned on whether there was a duty on the state to investigate the deaths when the families sought a public inquiry into those killings, and whether the secretary of state had reasonably exercised his discretion when he decided not to hold an inquiry. The Supreme Court dismissed the appeal on 25 November 2015, holding that the UK was not obliged to hold such a public inquiry on the following grounds. First, the lapse of time since the killings meant there was no requirement under Article 2 of the European Convention on Human Rights and Fundamental Freedoms, which came into force for the UK on 3 September 1953, to hold such an inquiry. Second, a duty to hold an inquiry could not be implied into the common law under the principles of customary international law. Third, a decision not to hold an inquiry under the Inquiries Act 2005 was not open to challenge on ordinary judicial review principles.

The court was not, of course, examining the merits of the evidence and whether it supported a case for prosecuting the soldiers involved in the killing. Lord Kerr, the former Lord Chief Justice of Northern Ireland before his translation to the Supreme Court in London, said in his ruling:

> The shocking circumstances in which, according to the over-whelming preponderance of currently available evidence, wholly innocent men were mercilessly murdered and the failure of the authorities of this State to conduct an effective inquiry into their deaths have been comprehensively reviewed by Lord Neuberger in the course of his judgment and require no further emphasis or repetition.[9]

The burning factual question in this case is, in the light of the confessions to murder, why were those who so freely confessed not charged and tried for the murders?

The cover-up started immediately after the crime. Part of a telegram from the High Commissioner in Malaya to the Colonial Office in London claimed that the soldiers did everything possible to stop the escaping Chinese before resorting to force. That simply did not happen. The Commissioner then added the following words of warning: 'Moreover, we feel that it is most damaging to the morale of the security forces to feel that every actions of theirs, after the event, is going to be examined with the most meticulous care'.[10] That was a sentiment later frequently shared by senior officers serving in Northern Ireland during the Troubles.

The judgment continues:

> On 26 January 1949 the Colonial Secretary, Arthur Creech Jones, told the House of Commons in London that 'the Chinese in question were detained for interrogation . . . after careful consideration of the evidence and a personal visit to the places concerned the [Malayan] attorney general was satisfied that had the Security Forces not opened fire, the suspect Chinese would have made good an attempt at escape which had obviously been pre-arranged.'[11]

Although Mr Creech Jones, a dedicated trade unionist who had served prison time as a conscientious objector in the First World War, probably would not have known that his statement was a lie, it undoubtedly was.

The Scotland Yard officer appointed to carry out the inquiry said that he would need two months to interview the Scots Guardsmen in the UK and a further six weeks to interview 36 witnesses in Malaya. He further considered that the bodies of the victims might need to be exhumed for forensic examination. He had access to the sworn statement made to the *Sunday People* by Guardsman William Cootes. He claimed that the victims at Batang Kali had been murdered in cold blood. Sworn affidavits from three other guardsmen, Alan Tuppen, Robert Brownrigg and Victor Remedios, claimed that the victims had been murdered on the order of two sergeants on the patrol. They suggested that they had been ordered by their superior officers to say that the victims had been killed while trying to escape. A fifth guardsman, George Kydd, did not make a written statement on oath or on affidavit, but told the Sunday newspaper that the killings were 'sheer bloody murder . . . these people were shot down in cold blood. They were not running away. There was no reason to shoot them.'[12] The two sergeants involved both maintained that the victims of the massacre were shot while trying to escape.

The police interviewed Guardsmen Cootes, Tuppen, Brownrigg and Kydd under caution. Each man admitted that Sergeant Hughes had ordered them to shoot the victims, who were not trying to escape. They were suspected bandits or sympathisers, although some may consider that insufficient grounds to justify a summary execution. Another guardsman, Keith Wood, admitted that the victims were murdered. Guardsman Victor Remedios declined to answer any of the questions put to him by the police, but he did not withdraw his earlier admission of murder that he had made to the Sunday newspaper. Brownrigg and Kydd admitted that they had been instructed by the army to say that the men had been trying to run away. They had not made up the false explanation – this was the invention of the state's army. The two sergeants were not interviewed by the police, but two other non-commissioned officers, Lance Corporals George Power and Roy Gorton, said the victims had been shot while attempting to escape.

In the light of this confession evidence to the police by those directly involved in shooting down innocent men, it might be expected that a criminal prosecution for murder would follow. It was admittedly 22 years after the event, but as a matter of law there is no limitation on the time within which a prosecution can be instituted for the offence of homicide.

When the Conservative government won the general election on 18 June 1970, the newly appointed attorney general Sir Peter Rawlinson QC met the DPP, Sir Norman Skelhorn, eight days later. Rawlinson had clearly lost no time in reading the papers and coming to a decision about the case. But he had not seen the report of DCS Williams, for he had not yet submitted it to his senior officers. Why was that? Did the attorney general not wish to make an informed, impartial decision, based on the evidence, about whether to institute proceedings for murder? Skelhorn told the MOD on 29 June that the institution of criminal proceedings would not be justified on the evidence so far obtained (which some may find incomprehensible in the light of the confession statements to the police) and the possibility of obtaining further evidence was remote, so the police inquiry would not continue. The next day, 30 June, the public announcement was made. We now know that the case was closed because the truth was concealed.

Frank Williams nonetheless put forward his report into the case to his senior officers at Scotland Yard a month later, on 30 July 1970. The Supreme Court notes that he wrote:

> Cootes, Tuppen (with solicitor), Brownrigg and Kydd admitted in statements, after caution, that murder had been committed . . . At the outset this matter was politically flavoured and it is patently clear that the decision to terminate inquiries in the middle of the investigation was due to a political change of view when the new Conservative government came into office after the General Election of 18 June 1970.[13]

Was this a polite way of saying that one set of politicians sought the truth, while another set decided it should be suppressed?

The Williams Report notes (page 7) that according to Guardsman Cootes, four days after returning to the base camp the patrol was called together either by one of the sergeants who had been on the patrol or their acting company commander, Captain Ramsay, and told of the impending inquiry into the incident, at government offices in Kuala Lumpur. They were 'told to get together and fabricate a story and between them they decided to say that the villagers were shot while trying to escape into the jungle'. The report also notes (page 5) that the Scots Guardsmen knew about the brutal killing of the three members of the Royal Hussars, and because of that incident the soldiers were told that they were going to wipe out the village, 'as terrorists were being fed there'. Was this a clear admission that the soldiers knew that the 24 men they killed were not terrorists? And how could it be proved that any individual supported the terrorists by feeding them?

As a preliminary to the violence that lay over the horizon, the Williams Report cites (page 6) the evidence of Guardsman Cootes that Sergeant Douglas shot a young man in the back. All the villagers, about 80 in number, witnessed this. The victim did not die instantly, so Sergeant Hughes, the second NCO, finished him off with a bullet to the head. That was nothing short of cold-blooded murder, committed in front of witnesses, many of whom had to be permanently silenced.

In the light of this, does the decision of the attorney general seem justified and lawful? DCS Williams did record (page 17) that on 10 June 1970 he was called to see John Wood, then the deputy DPP. He told the police officer, 'now the initial police enquiries had been completed as far as possible, a decision would be made by the attorney general, Elwyn Jones, as to further enquiries being made in Malaysia. When the expected decision was reached a request would be made through diplomatic channels to the Malaysian government for their co-operation and assistance.' Williams was further told that no covering report was necessary (in itself a very unusual instruction) and he handed over the statements and documents obtained so far. Wood told him that no decision could be expected until after the general election on 18 June 1970 – eight days after their meeting in London.

Frank Williams was told on 29 June that following a conference between the DPP and the new attorney general, Peter Rawlinson, Rawlinson had decided that 'it was unlikely that sufficient evidence would be obtained to support a prosecution, therefore the investigation must terminate forthwith' (page 17).

Why the word 'unlikely' in Rawlinson's decision? Did he not want to know the view of DCS Williams about how many of the women and children who had witnessed the killings would be willing to give evidence of murder? Did he not want the police officer's assessment of the quality of the confession evidence of murder made by four guardsmen? Why should they lie about what they had done and incriminate themselves in such a way as to face a prosecution for murder? Was it not likely that they were telling the unpalatable truth? Or was the attorney general setting the scene for events that were about to unfold in Northern Ireland, where disputed killings by the British army had to be surrounded by dissemination of false information and outright lies by the state?

The majority decision in the Supreme Court states that the duty to investigate effectively cases such as this dates back to 1966 when the right of individual petition to the European Court of Human Rights was introduced by the British government's agreement to allow those petitions under the European Convention, and thereafter when the Human Rights Act 1998 adopted the Convention Rights, which are binding, not only in international law, but also in UK law.

In the present climate, will the European Court of Human Rights, if the appeal of the relatives of the dead goes there, direct the British government to carry out a public inquiry in an attempt to establish the truth about the Batang Kali killings? In the event of the UK withdrawing from the European Union the rulings of the European Court of Human Rights will no longer have effect in the UK. That withdrawal is expected to take some two years from March 2017, so one wonders whether the European Court will have the case in its list for decision before that event occurs.

2　Justice for Iain?

THE CRIMINAL JUSTICE system in England and Wales is identical in all respects. Not so in Northern Ireland, which had its own independent judicial system headed by its own lord chief justice. The final court of appeal in both jurisdictions, however, is the Supreme Court in London. Members of the judiciary are appointed by the state, but are independent of that state. That is the theory, at least, because from the formation of the Northern Ireland state in 1922 judicial appointments reflected the concept that those who were loyal to the state would be rewarded by promotion from the bar to the bench. As Professor Paddy Hillyard has noted, of the first 20 High Court judges appointed after 1921, no fewer than 15 had been members of, or associated with, the Unionist Party. There is reason to believe that at least one part of the population, namely the Catholic, nationalist people, had little or no faith in the judiciary. They had very little faith in the criminal justice system either.

At about the time of the outbreak of the Troubles in 1968 two of the three judges in the Court of Appeal in Belfast were not only members of the Unionist Party but had previously served as attorneys general and thus legal advisers to the unionist government. This is in contrast to the present situation; at the time of writing (late 2016), the three most important legal posts in Northern Ireland – lord chief justice, attorney general and DPP – are held by Catholics.

There is one area where jurisdiction is jointly exercised between Northern Ireland and England and Wales: criminal appeals in cases of alleged wrongful convictions.

In 1995 the Criminal Cases Review Commission (CCRC) was established by Part II of the Criminal Appeal Act 1995. The commission is tasked with the responsibility to review and investigate possible miscarriages of justice in England and Wales, and Northern Ireland. As a consequence, wrongful convictions in Northern Ireland were identified and referred on appeal to the High Court in Belfast by the CCRC, based in Birmingham.

One particular case stands out as an illustration of how rotten and corrupt the legal and political system was in Northern Ireland in the early 1950s, when the bench, the bar, the prosecutors, the police and even the defence lawyers not merely failed in their duty to achieve justice, but dispensed with it entirely.

In 1998 Iain Hay Gordon, who had been convicted of murder in March 1953 (he had been found guilty but insane), applied to the CCRC asking that they carry out an investigation and then, if there were grounds to do so, to refer his case to the Court of Appeal in Belfast.

The commission first asked the court to decide whether they had the power to refer the case. On 30 June 1998 the appeal court in Belfast ruled that the CCRC had no such power to refer the case back to the appeal court. There was no provision in law for the commission to go behind a verdict of guilty but insane and refer it to the appeal court. At the time of the legislation in 1995 someone had overlooked this rather important, if somewhat obscure, point.

On 10 July 1998 the distinguished judge Lord Desmond Ackner introduced a Criminal Appeal (Amendment) Bill into the House of Lords with the purpose of dealing with a lacuna in the Criminal Appeal Act 1995. That Act empowered the CCRC to deal with a case in which the verdict of the jury was not guilty by reason of insanity. That finding had been introduced into law by the Criminal Procedure (Insanity) Act 1964. No one apparently considered in 1995 that there might be the possibility of any outstanding case where the verdict had been guilty but insane, a special verdict under the Trial of Lunatics Act 1883. There was at least one. It related to a conviction for the murder of Patricia Curran in Northern Ireland in 1953 when a young Scottish serviceman, Iain Hay Gordon, was committed to Holywell psychiatric hospital in County Antrim where he remained for seven years following a criminal trial which was a travesty of justice. In the language of the time he was treated as a 'lunatic' and a murderer. In fact he was neither.

During the Second Reading of Lord Ackner's Bill the Home Office minister, the late Lord Gareth Williams of Mostyn, indicated that the government agreed with the intention of the Bill. He accepted that the commission's powers should be extended to cover the verdict of guilty but insane but because of the lack of Parliamentary time the Criminal Appeal (Amendment) Bill could not proceed any further.

Iain Hay Gordon was not in custody while this was going on. In 1960 he had been quietly released and put on a plane back to Scotland. That had been arranged by the Northern Ireland minister for home affairs, Brian Faulkner. His release was subject to two conditions: that he should never talk about his case; and that he should change his name. He did as he was told. Freedom was more important than challenging either condition. He returned to Glasgow to live quietly with his mother. At the same time as Hay Gordon's release from custody was being arranged, Patricia Curran's brother, Desmond, who had given up his practice as a barrister in Belfast, was being ordained as a Catholic priest at the Vatican.

Iain Hay Gordon stayed well away from the public eye for 31 years. By 1995, when the CCRC was established, he had become aware of cases like those of Judith Ward and the Guildford Four, whose false and fabricated confessions in police custody had led to their imprisonment until their eventual release when the truth was disclosed. Representations were made on his behalf, but the CCRC was unable to take up the case until there was a change in the law.

On 11 March 1999, after the lapse of the first Bill, Lord Ackner introduced another Bill into the House of Lords; the Criminal Cases Review (Insanity) Bill. It contained only four clauses. Lord Ackner said that 'the omission of a verdict of guilty but insane from the 1995 appeal Act was an error that has created a long-standing and tragic absurdity in the case of Iain Hay Gordon'. At the third reading of the Bill in the House of Commons on 23 July 1999, the then MP Chris Mullin said that Mr Gordon had long protested his innocence and was, at this date, frail and elderly. The Bill went speedily through the parliamentary process and received the Royal Assent four days later, on 27 July 1999.

There was a very good reason for haste. The stimulus behind the Act, as Lord Ackner told their Lordships in the House, was the case of Iain Hay Gordon. He was at that time 67 years of age and in failing health. Hay Gordon had been convicted, after a trial at the County Antrim Spring Assizes in Northern Ireland in March 1953, of the murder of 19-year-old Patricia Curran.

I consider that trial was a travesty of justice. It is significant that, at that time, murder was a capital offence. It is clear in this case that the senior law officer of the Crown, the attorney general, was deliberately involved in the suppression of the truth, and perverting the course of justice. There are grounds for believing that the murderer was a member of Patricia Curran's family, who killed her in her own home. Rather than face up to the reality and the real possibility that the person responsible would be charged, tried and convicted of a capital offence and sent to the gallows, an entirely innocent young man was scapegoated by the establishment and wrongly convicted of a crime in which he took no part.

The murder trial took place between 2 and 7 March 1953. The trial judge, the Lord Chief Justice, Lord MacDermott, began his summing-up to the jury at 6.20 p.m. on its final day, a Saturday. The jury retired to consider their verdict at 8.45 p.m. The judge told them that they could not have any food or drink once they retired (although he could have directed otherwise), and after two hours the jury came back with a unanimous verdict of guilty but insane. Concluding the summing-up so late in the evening and allowing the jury to retire at such a late hour is contrary to modern practice, but at that time the judge was within his rights to do what he did. Whether he should have exercised them in the way he did in such a serious case is open to question. It cannot be right that the jury had to undertake such an onerous task without refreshment of any kind. How long was it since they had had something to eat or drink? Was it during the lunch adjournment at about 1 p.m.? The jury must have found this pressure intolerable. Was this anything other than an attempt to ensure that the jury brought in the verdict that the state wanted – guilty but insane?

Patricia Curran was the only daughter of Doris and Mr Justice Lancelot Ernest Curran, the Chancery Division judge of the High Court in Belfast and former Unionist MP for the Carrick Division of County Antrim. He had been attorney general from 1947 to 1949, the youngest holder of that office in the history of the Stormont parliament. He was also a personal friend of the trial judge, Lord MacDermott.

Patricia lived with her parents and two older brothers, Desmond, then a 26-year-old barrister, and Michael, 24, an estate agent. The family home was Glen House in Whiteabbey, an attractive coastal village overlooking Belfast Lough about five miles north of Belfast. Iain Gordon Hay, then aged 20, was doing National Service in the RAF and was stationed with the 67 Air Force Group at Edenmore camp, half a mile from the Curran home. He was a rather lonely and isolated individual who felt far removed from his home and family in Scotland. He had met Desmond Curran, a member of the Moral Rearmament movement, at a local church, and was invited on a number of occasions to dinner at Desmond's family's home. There he met Patricia Curran.

On Wednesday 12 November 1952 Patricia spent the day in Belfast where she was a first-year social sciences student at Queen's University. She had afternoon tea with a fellow student, John Steel, who walked with her to the Smithfield bus station, where she took the five o'clock bus to Whiteabbey. Other passengers saw her get off the bus in Whiteabbey at about 5.20 p.m. and turn to walk home. An 11-year-old boy, George Chambers, who was doing his newspaper delivery round, saw her walking towards the gateway that opened on to a dark drive, some 600 yards long, that led to a small number of houses, including Glen House. George walked in the same direction shortly afterwards. He did not see Patricia again. He was, however, startled by a sound like birds in the leaves and a rustling noise in the bushes from the dark wooded area; frightened, he ran down the Glen towards the main road. Coinciding with that sound was the noise of a nearby factory horn, signalling the end of the working day. It was 5.45 p.m. That incident was later used to fix the time of the murder, but it does not necessarily follow that that was the case.

It was never established whether Patricia Curran reached the safety of her house on that Wednesday evening. The police assumed she did not. Her brother Michael did not arrive home until after her body was found. Her father got home by taxi at 7.20 p.m., having been sitting that day in court. Her mother's movements are more difficult to establish but it was thought that she may have spent the evening playing bridge with the family solicitor, Malcolm Davison and his wife, before driving home. Neither Lord Justice Curran nor his wife testified at the murder trial. If Patricia had arrived home in the early evening, there was therefore, apparently, no family member there to see her.

In the early hours of the following morning, at either 1.35 a.m. or 1.40 a.m., Lancelot Curran phoned the home of Malcolm Davison, his solicitor and a long-standing friend. His wife, Doreen, answered the phone and the judge told her that Patricia had caught the bus for home at about 5 p.m. but had not been seen since. Some minutes later, at about 1.45 a.m., Curran rang the local RUC barracks at Whiteabbey and told them that he had phoned some friends and had learned that his daughter had been left to the bus station at about 5 p.m. He asked if there had been any reports of an accident involving a bus. There had not. Five minutes later, Patricia's mother, Doris, rang the RUC barracks and told an officer that Patricia had been left to the bus station in Belfast at about 5 p.m. Lady Curran was now in a very distressed state. Neither parent seems to have told the police that their daughter had actually taken the bus home, simply that she had been at the bus station.

It might be thought unusual that the parents of a missing daughter should call a family friend and solicitor before the police. However that may be, a more interesting question is how did the judge and his wife know that their daughter had been at the bus station at 5 p.m.? The Davisons did not know anything about Patricia Curran's movements in Belfast that day. On the contrary, it was Patricia's father who gave them that information.

PC Edward Rutherford left the RUC barracks on his bicycle and arrived at the Glen shortly after 2 a.m. He saw Lancelot Curran in the driveway and as he walked towards him he heard shouting from the wooded area nearby. Both men ran towards the area, guided by the light of a torch. They saw Desmond Curran with the torch, kneeling or leaning over the body of his sister, Patricia. She was lying on her back at the foot of a tree, some 40 feet from the driveway. She had two facial injuries and bruising and abrasions to the neck. They did not know it at the time, but she had been stabbed 37 times. There was very little blood in the area in which the body was lying, indicating that Patricia might have been murdered elsewhere and her body taken to the spot where she was found.

The brilliant investigative journalist Frank White, who studied the case papers in depth, wrote in the *Carlow Nationalist* newspaper in May 2014 that the driveway to the Curran house was 600 yards long. That would surely mean that the area to be searched must have been very extensive. Desmond Curran was fortunate to have found the body so speedily, in such a large area, in utter darkness, aided only by the light of a hand-held torch. Or did he already know where to find the body?

Within moments of the discovery, Malcolm and Doreen Davison arrived at the crime scene. Desmond Curran thought his sister seemed to be breathing and it was decided – by a judge, a barrister, a solicitor and a police officer – that she should be put on the back seat of the Davisons' car and taken to the village, where the family doctor, Dr Wilson, lived. They lay Patricia on the back seat, but because rigor mortis had set in and her legs would not bend, they could not close the door on the rear passenger side. The car travelled the short journey with Patricia's legs protruding from the partially opened door. It is astonishing that four men who were involved in the law and the criminal process did exactly what good practice says should not be done at a crime scene.

The body was found some 260 yards from the road and about 40 feet from the edge of the driveway. There were indications that it had been dragged from the driveway and through the shrubbery. Patricia's handbag, books and papers were found close to the edge of the driveway.

Dr Wilson saw the body at 2.20 a.m. He considered that Patricia had been dead for between four and 12 hours. His initial diagnosis was that she had been shot with a shotgun in the chest and abdomen. Dr Wells, a registrar in pathology, arrived at Dr Wilson's surgery at 5 a.m. on Thursday 13 November. In his opinion Patricia had died about 12 hours previously. He concluded that she had been, not shot, but stabbed 37 times with a stiletto-type weapon, a paper knife or a lancet. She had not been robbed; the contents of her handbag were still intact. Her underclothes were still in place; she had not been sexually assaulted. But the position and number of wounds, 21 to the front of the chest, eight of them so serious that any one of them could have been fatal, indicated the ferocity of the assault. One blow was delivered with such force that it fractured one of her ribs. Her face was wounded in two places. Dr Wells later considered that these wounds were caused by a fist or a boot. She must have been lying on the ground when those blows were delivered. There was also some bruising and abrasions on her neck. Had her assailant approached her from behind, choking her to prevent her screaming?

If she had died at about 5 p.m. on the Wednesday, rigor mortis would have set in by about 2 a.m. and the likelihood of the body giving the impression of breathing would have been very remote. (It was, of course, known that Patricia was still alive at 5 p.m. She was in Belfast at the bus station at that time, and she was seen to get off the bus in Whiteabbey at about 5.20 p.m.) There was no post-mortem.

The police began a murder investigation. They interviewed all the airmen attached to the nearby 67 Group RAF base, including Iain Hay Gordon. In several interviews he gave an account of his movements on 12 November. In advance of one such interview his commanding officer, Pilot Officer Popple, said that Hay Gordon should have an RAF officer with him during the interview. That never happened, then or at any other time. The police said that Hay Gordon did not wish anyone else to be present at the interviews. That suited them rather than him.

Within a week of the murder, Lancelot and Doris Curran left their Whiteabbey home for a holiday in Edinburgh, but not before their daughter's bedroom had been completely repainted and decorated – within three days of her death. The judge refused to allow a search of the family home for eight days. He and his wife never returned to live in Glen House, which was later sold. It is easy to understand why; being there would bring back memories of their daughter. But was the most painful memory that Patricia Curran had actually died in the house, and someone who lived there with her was responsible for her death?

The RUC investigation got nowhere. They needed outside assistance.

Two officers from the London Metropolitan Police, Det. Supt Capstick and Det. Sgt Hawkins, were seconded to Northern Ireland to participate in the inquiry.

On Monday 15 January 1953, Capstick interviewed Hay Gordon. No caution was given. No other person was present. The police officer later said that the interview began with questions about Hay Gordon's sexual proclivities and particularly about an incident of homosexual conduct with another man in the Belfast area. (Such conduct was unlawful at that time.) There was some suggestion, according to Hay Gordon, that his mother would be told of that incident. He says now that if she had been, the shock would have killed her. Iain Hay Gordon confessed to murdering Patricia Curran that Monday afternoon and signed a statement written out for him by Det. Supt Capstick. In it he claimed to have stabbed Patricia once or twice (not 37 times) with his service knife. No RAF personnel, and certainly not those working in a clerical position, as Hay Gordon was, were issued with a service knife, or any knife at all.

The accused man was returned for trial. Leading counsel at his trial was Herbert McVeigh QC. It is said that McVeigh only accepted the brief on the understanding that he would not be required to cross-examine his friend and colleague Lancelot Curran or any member of the Curran family. Clearly he should not have imposed such conditions; he should not have been involved in the case at all. (Incidentally, the junior counsel for the defence was the unionist politician Basil Kelly, who became attorney general of Northern Ireland and later a High Court judge, and whose name appears with some frequency elsewhere in this book.)

The record shows that in 1957, when Sir Lancelot Curran was appointed as a lord justice in the Northern Ireland Court of Appeal, his successor as Chancery judge was his friend and colleague Herbert McVeigh.

The trial opened on Monday 2 March 1953. Leading counsel for the prosecution was the attorney general, John Edmund Warnock QC. He had been minister for home affairs from 1946 to 1949, during which time Sir Lancelot Curran had served as attorney general.

McVeigh tried to have the evidence of the confession excluded at a *voir dire* (a trial within a trial that decides matters of law in the absence of the jury). The issue of whether a confession is admissible is a matter of law for the trial judge. Whether the confession is true is a matter of fact to be decided by the jury. The evidence on which Lord MacDermott had to rule came exclusively from the prosecution witnesses. Det. Supt Capstick denied the defence suggestion that the confession statement had been obtained in a question-and-answer format; it had been, he claimed, dictated by the accused to him without question or interruption save for one minor matter of spelling a word. The accused did not give evidence either during the *voir dire* or at the trial proper in front of the jury. Some may find that extraordinary: if he were to claim that the way he was questioned so affected him that he caved in and confessed when otherwise he would not have done, the trial judge might have liked to hear his evidence on that point.

It is now clear that Capstick had been told by someone, probably Desmond Curran, that Iain Hay Gordon had admitted a homosexual encounter with another man, and that the police officer used his information to weaken and then dissolve Iain's resistance to admitting the murder, especially when the officer suggested that in the absence of a confession his mother would be told of that homosexual incident. He then made the confession statement.

Even more extraordinary was the decision not to challenge the truthfulness of the confession evidence in front of the jury. Capstick did not give evidence a second time, in full open court, in the presence of the jury, so they had no opportunity of deciding whether he was a truthful witness on the fundamental question of whether Hay Gordon's confession was true.

After the admission of the confession evidence it is clear that the defence no longer disputed that Iain Hay Gordon had murdered Patricia Curran. They called a number of witnesses whose evidence was directed at establishing the defence of insanity. One of them, Dr Rossiter Lewis, a consultant psychiatrist, told the jury that after he had administered the drug sodium thiopentone, a barbiturate, to Hay Gordon, he had confessed to assaulting Patricia Curran with his fist on the grass verge in the Glen on the night she died. That placed him at the crime scene and indicated that he had used violence against the young woman. As the death penalty was still in force at that time, it seems that the defence's sole purpose at that stage was to save Iain Hay Gordon from hanging. Should they not have focused primarily on whether the charge of murder was proved against him?

Hay Gordon was convicted and the court ordered that he be detained at the Holywell psychiatric hospital in County Antrim until Her Majesty's pleasure be known. This was in effect a life sentence. He stayed at the Holywell for seven years, until 1960. Iain's family had long campaigned on his behalf, believing in his innocence, and by 1960 the civil liberties group Justice had taken an interest in his case. They were all no doubt encouraged by the fact that Iain received no medical treatment at Holywell, for one simple reason: he was not suffering from any mental illness.

The Northern Ireland authorities were reluctant to release him, but after representations made by the distinguished British criminal lawyer Frederick Lawson QC (later a lord justice of appeal) to Brian Faulkner, the minister for home affairs in Belfast, Iain Hay Gordon was released on condition that no publicity was given to his release.

Iain returned to Scotland, where he had lived for most of his life. He found a job working in the warehouse of a publishing company in Glasgow. He changed his name and did not discuss his case with anyone.

As recent events and other cases have shown, the truth cannot be suppressed for ever. The media began to take a more intense interest in his case until such time as the CCRC was able, after Lord Desmond Ackner's Bill became law in 1999, to refer Iain Hay Gordon's case to the Court of Appeal in Belfast.

The case was listed for hearing in October 2000. Sir Louis Blom-Cooper QC, a distinguished and popular member of the bar of England and Wales, was briefed to lead for the appellant. He was the first lawyer outside the political and sectarian influences in the legal profession in Northern Ireland to have conduct of the case. He had first appeared in the case when efforts were made to get the court to sanction a reference to the Appeal Court by the CCRC against the finding that Iain Hay Gordon was guilty but insane.

In the month before the appeal hearing began, the *Sunday Mirror* reported that a faded brown envelope had been found during a clear-out of the Musgrave Street RUC station in Belfast, with the words 'To be opened only by County Inspector Kennedy' written on the front. This is clearly Albert Kennedy, who in 1953 was the head of the Northern Ireland CID and the senior investigating officer in the Patricia Curran case. Some six officers had interviewed Iain Hay Gordon over three days. County Inspector Kennedy was one of them. The notes inside the envelope, which were unsigned, were thought to be have been written by John Warnock QC, the attorney general who had prosecuted the case at trial. The newspaper reported that the notes 'reveal that the authorities had deep concerns about the evidence used to convict . . . Iain Hay Gordon . . . Legal sources said the notes highlight differences in evidence about phone calls relating to the time the teenager arrived home.'

The appeal hearing began on 24 October 2000, some 47 years after Patricia Curran's brutal killing. Sir Louis Blom-Cooper told the Lord Chief Justice, Lord Carswell, that the original trial was unfair, that there were material irregularities that went to the very heart of the case and that the verdict was not just unsatisfactory but unsafe. Sir Louis accused Det. Supt Capstick of lying when he claimed that the confession statement was voluntarily dictated and he was permitted to adduce expert evidence from Professor Malcolm Coulthard, Professor Gisli Gudjonsson and Dr J.P. French (whose evidence was obtained and submitted by the Crown) that throws doubt on this claim. Professor Gudjonsson said:

> [T]he confession Mr Gordon made to the police on 15 January 1953 is very vague, lacks much specific detail, and descriptions are prefaced by indefinite remarks suggesting that Mr Gordon was not confessing to an event of which he a clear recollection. The content of the confession is consistent with a false confession of the 'coerced internalised type'. The confession reads as if it was elicited by questioning rather than being a free narrative account, which contradicts the testimony of Detective Superintendent Capstick during the trial.

Sir Louis was highly critical of what he described as the prosecution's 'fixation' with putting the time of death at 5.45 p.m. when the evidence was that although the time was likely to have been around 6 p.m. it could have been up to four hours later. He also commented on the failure of defence counsel Herbert McVeigh to cross-examine Capstick about the truthfulness and accuracy of the confession statement in the presence of the jury, after the trial judge had admitted it into evidence during the *voir dire*. That would now be unthinkable in the conduct of a criminal case. Sir Louis stated openly and courageously that Iain Hay Gordon had not been well defended, something that might not have been well received in the court of the lord chief justice of Northern Ireland.

The transcript of the judgment of the appeal court refers to a report dated 17 October 2000 by Brian Craythorne, a document examiner, who proved that the notes found in Musgrave Street police station were written by the attorney general. There is little information in the transcript about the content of the notes, but it does refer to a discrepancy about the time of death that was of some concern to County Inspector Kennedy, that the attorney general was aware of that concern, and that Kennedy was reluctant to subject Lancelot Curran or his wife to further distress by asking them to give evidence at the trial. Although that is quite understandable, it is not for a police officer to decide who should give evidence in a criminal case. Nothing is said by the appeal court about any understanding, if it was arrived at, that Herbert McVeigh would not accept the brief if he was required to cross-examine Lancelot Curran.

What is most disturbing, however, and in my view this was glossed over by the appeal court, was the disclosure of evidence that led the CCRC and Blom-Cooper to suggest that the murder took place later than 5.45 p.m. and that the Curran family knew more about the circumstances in which Patricia died before the phone call to the family solicitor Malcolm Davison at either 1.35 a.m. or 1.40 a.m. on 13 November. (The solicitor gave one time, his wife gave another.)

Most significant and sinister was the concealment of the evidence of the statements of Sydney Steel and his wife, and part of the evidence of their son John, the student who had accompanied Patricia Curran to the Belfast bus station on 12 November. All three told the police that Lancelot Curran had phoned their house between 2.05 and 2.10 a.m. on Wednesday 13 November. The parents were adamant about the time and refused to accept that it was before 2 a.m. Patricia Curran's body had been found shortly after 2 a.m. and Dr Wilson had examined her body at 2.20 a.m. It would have been fairly easy to resolve the matter; if Lancelot Curran had accompanied his daughter's body from the wood to the village, he would have had no opportunity to use the telephone. My view is that there was not enough room for him in the Davisons' car and he returned to Glen House. In any event someone would have had to tell Doris Curran that Patricia's body had been found.

John Steel told the police that Curran had asked him on the telephone (which had been answered by his father) about Patricia and which bus she had caught. John said that he had left her at the bus station at 5 p.m. Curran told the police in a statement that this news had come as a great shock to him. Could this be true? In his phone calls to the Davisons at 1.35/1.40 a.m. and the RUC barracks at 1.45. a.m. he said that he had phoned some friends and had learned that his daughter had been left to the 5 p.m. bus. He did not receive that information from the Steel family until after 2 a.m. If he did not get it from them, who had told him? Could it have been Patricia herself? Had she in fact returned home and been murdered in her own bedroom?

Although Mr and Mrs Steel could not be shifted from their timings of the phone call, even after being interviewed at length by the police, their son John, after initially confirming the time, admitted to the possibility of some doubt. That was, however, only after a long interview with Capstick and Kennedy. Had he succumbed to pressure from the police? Why were two police officers interviewing a witness at length for any reason other than to change his evidence to suit the prosecution case?

The prosecution at the trial concealed from the defence the existence of the Mr and Mrs Steel's statements. They simply hid them away. Their evidence would not have advanced the case for the prosecution, but it would have greatly assisted the defence and for that reason it was not disclosed.

The prosecution served an edited statement of John Steel's evidence upon the defence at the trial in 1953. They left in the statement the reference to him accompanying Patricia to the bus station in Belfast. They suppressed the evidence relating to the phone call and the conversation between him and Mr Justice Curran. One is bound to ask why. Who edited the statement? Was it the police or the prosecuting lawyers? What was there to hide? That phone call and its time puts a worrying gloss on the events. If the defence had known of it, they surely would have investigated the source of Mr Justice Curran's knowledge of the facts provided to Malcolm Davison and his wife prior to speaking to the Steels. That would have involved the judge giving evidence in court as a witness. Had someone decided that must be avoided at any cost? If the Steel family had been the sole source of information about Patricia Curran being at the bus station and catching the five o'clock bus, and they were correct about the time of that telephone conversation, then Mr Justice Curran certainly had a case to answer.

The attorney general made sure that the defence did not know of the evidence of Mr and Mrs Steel by not disclosing that evidence to them. The contents of two reports by the officer in the case, County Inspector Kennedy, might not have been admissible in the law of evidence at that time, but the evidence about the telephone call from Mr Justice Curran to two members of the Steel family certainly was. That disclosure might have resulted in the acquittal of an innocent man.

Moreover, has there ever been a case where a senior judge, his barrister son, his solicitor and an officer of the court, with a police constable, together contaminated a crime scene in the way they did by removing Patricia Curran's body and placing it in the back seat of a car? Why did the police not get a search warrant to enter the Curran family home to look for clues relating to Patricia's presence, and perhaps her death, there? The answer well may be that calculated delay by at least two officers of the state, Judge Curran and the police constable, was the first step in an elaborate cover-up. Just who was being protected by the pretence that this was a 'stranger killing'? Did the officers of the state, the lawyers in the case and the trial judge, also cover up the truth and substitute an innocent man for the guilty one?

At the conclusion of the appeal court hearing judgment was reserved, to the intense distress of Iain Hay Gordon, who had waited so long for justice. Two months later, on 20 December 2000, the court quashed the conviction. An injustice had been put right.

The only surviving member of Patricia's immediate family was Desmond Curran. He gave up his practice at the bar and became a Catholic priest. His father, who died in 1975, resigned from the Orange Order, in anticipation of certain removal from it, in order to attend his son's ordination ceremony in Rome. Desmond Curran became a missionary priest in southern Africa. Did he know the truth about what happened to his sister? If he did, would he ever disclose it?

When interviewed in January 1995 for a BBC documentary programme about the case entitled *More Sinned against than Sinning*, Desmond Curran denied that any member of the family was involved in any way in Patricia's murder. He initially continued to insist that Iain Hay Gordon killed his sister but may have had a change of heart when he examined the detail of the court record that quashed Hay Gordon's conviction. On 4 September 2015 the *Irish News* reported the death of Rev. Desmond Curran in South Africa. An unknown source, said to be a parishioner, is quoted as saying 'he had "a past"' and 'he carried a burden'. Was that burden his knowledge of who the murderer was, or had he killed his sister?

This case reflects badly on the criminal justice system in Northern Ireland. The police made a number of conscious and wrong decisions at each stage of the investigation. First, an officer was involved in contaminating the crime scene by moving the body. Second, they failed to obtain a search warrant to enter the house and look for clues. Third, they deliberately concealed the relevant and admissible evidence of Mr and Mrs Steel. The judge nominated to try the case should not have had any knowledge of, or connection with, any of the prosecution witnesses in the case, especially his fellow judge, because of the perception of bias, if not actual bias, in favour of his judicial colleague. The trial judge also put intolerable pressure on the jury to reach a verdict without sufficient time to assess the evidence. The defence leading counsel totally failed in his duty to protect his client's interests. He should not have laid down conditions about his conduct of the defence case before accepting the brief. His failure to challenge before the jury the evidence given by the police relating to the confession and how it was obtained by Det. Supt Capstick even now seems inexplicable.

The truth in this case was consumed in lies, many of them told by those employed by the state. The agents of the state condemned an innocent man while the actual murderer went unpunished. Was this because it would be intolerable for the state to admit that a member of one of the most distinguished legal families in Northern Ireland was a murderer who would if convicted have faced the death penalty? No one could bring themselves to send an innocent man to his death by hanging, so the use of the convenient formula 'guilty but insane' ensured that Iain Hay Gordon would not die but the case would be closed and there would be no further investigation. That almost happened. In the absence of a full confession from the actual murderer, this case will remain unsolved. Unless or until that happens, Patricia Curran's killer will be unidentified and unpunished.

A medical doctor who was a member of the statutory board that used to advise whether a person convicted of capital murder was physically and mentally fit to be hanged wrote to the late Ludovic Kennedy, the writer and broadcaster and tireless campaigner for justice, about Iain's case in 1960. The doctor had examined Iain in Holywell psychiatric hospital at the request of his parents. He wrote:

> I think it only proper to add that in my experience of fifty or more murderers seen for the Director of Public Prosecutions I have never before experienced grave doubts about the prisoner's guilt. I have very serious doubts in this case and after serious consideration, my personal opinion is that the patient is not guilty. I can find no evidence that this patient is now suffering or has ever suffered from any mental disorder or disease.[1]

This medical opinion directly contradicts the evidence given at the trial in 1953. It is difficult to avoid the conclusion that the medical evidence given in court was false from beginning to end.

Ludovic Kennedy interviewed Iain at the BBC studios in London on 9 September 1970. The BBC indicated that the programme would be broadcast on 1 November, but it was withdrawn from the schedules and never shown. Ludovic Kennedy later found out that the prime minister of Northern Ireland, James Chichester-Clark, had brought pressure on the BBC to cancel the programme. Why did he do that? Was this the final cover-up of the truth in this dreadful miscarriage of justice? It might also be surprising to some that the prime minister of another jurisdiction can exert such pressure on Britain's national broadcaster.

According to the journalist Frank White, the evidence points to Lady Doris Curran, Patricia's mother, as being the murderer. He notes that Doris was first home on the night of the killing. If Patricia completed her journey home, they would have been alone there, with no independent eyewitnesses, long enough for the killing to take place somewhere in the house, probably in Patricia's bedroom. He also notes that Doris Curran was not happy with her daughter's lifestyle and her relationships with older men. He considers that it was all too convenient for Desmond Curran to find Patricia's body just as their family friends arrived to witness him doing so. He rejects the evidence that the 37 wounds were inflicted with a service knife and points out that there was no blood on the ground where Patricia's body was found. That points conclusively to Patricia having been killed elsewhere.

Frank White has told me that his research indicates that Doris was admitted to a psychiatric hospital in the Belfast area in either late 1952 or early 1953. She died on 29 May 1975 without ever having been released.

3 The Case of the Hooded Men

At 4 a.m. on Monday 9 August 1971, acting under the provisions of the Special Powers Act, Operation Demetrius was put into operation in Northern Ireland. The Stormont prime minister Brian Faulkner signed an order permitting detention and internment without trial. Thousands of British soldiers arrested 342 individuals. Many of them proved to be entirely the wrong people. They were not treated gently, but frequently beaten and criminally assaulted. Many had been blindfolded and absolutely terrified by being thrown out of a moving helicopter which they were told was high in the air; in fact it was only a few feet off the ground. Some were forced to walk barefoot over broken glass and barbed wire while they ran a gauntlet of soldiers wielding batons which were used to strike them around the body. The army acted on the contents of a list of names of 452 suspects drawn up by officers of the RUC. They were completely out of date and almost useless. One of those 'lifted' by the army was aged 77. He had been imprisoned in 1929 but was no longer involved in any IRA activity; another man was blind; yet another on the list had been dead for four years. It was dis-organised chaos, more especially when it was later discovered that the soldiers simply did not understand their power of arrest and the basis on which that power could be exercised.

Amongst those arrested were 12 men who were taken to a disused airfield in County Derry for a special purpose, namely to be interrogated in depth. Of those 12 men, 11 subsequently made allegations to a British government-appointed committee of physical ill treatment whilst being subjected to intensive questioning. A 12th man, Michael Montgomery, now deceased, did not complain to the committee. At a much later stage two other men filed similar complaints to the chairman of that committee.

It was obvious from the very outset that only Catholics, nationalists and republicans were interned, despite the fact that Protestant loyalist paramilitaries had been deeply involved in serious violence for years, leading to the banning of the UVF by Terence O'Neill in 1966.

The minority population saw this as proof, if proof were needed, that Brian Faulkner, who said 'we are at war with the terrorists', was interested only in debasing the Catholic 'disloyalists', as they were considered by the ruling party, and upholding the loyalist position of supremacy in a Protestant government for a Protestant people. As the noted politician and co-founder of the predominately nationalist SDLP, Austin Currie, wrote, arresting innocent Catholics while guilty Protestants remained at large, plus the brutality that accompanied the exercise, was a situation where no compromise was possible.

After 48 hours, 104 men were released, a clear admission that they were entirely innocent and should never have been lifted. Others, however, remained in custody, the legality of which was of considerable doubt.

Brian Faulkner claimed that 80 officers in the IRA had been arrested. The army said that 70 per cent of those in Crumlin Road prison were on its wanted list. Both statements were untrue. Many of those interned were the political opponents of the Stormont regime. (When direct rule was imposed on Northern Ireland a year later, in March 1972, no fewer than 110 men were released by the new secretary of state for Northern Ireland, William Whitelaw, with 14 days of his taking office. Were they dangerous terrorists?)

Within days of these unlawful arrests, allegations of brutal ill-treatment and torture began to circulate from those detained in Crumlin Road prison and the prison ship *Maidstone*. These were denied, first by the army and later by the government in London. Predictably, the Stormont government petulantly dismissed them as outrageous IRA propaganda. The international community began to take more notice of events in Northern Ireland and they were not impressed by what they saw.

Of those arrested, 12 individuals were moved to one or more unidentified centres for 'interrogation in depth'. That extended over several days. The order to do so was signed personally by Brian Faulkner. When the London newspapers, especially the *Sunday Times* Insight team, began to report how these men were treated, the London government realised that they may have made a serious error of judgement, especially in the light of the escalation of violence in which 22 people died and almost 7,000 were made homeless in the widespread rioting and house burning that followed the start of Operation Demetrius.

One of the 12 individuals selected for special treatment and interrogation was Patrick Joseph McClean, aged 39, a married man with eight children. He was a remedial teacher and a member of the local Northern Ireland Civil Rights Association (NICRA) in County Tyrone. When the media revealed how he was treated by his fellow countrymen, the home secretary, Reginald Maudling, appointed on 31 August 1971 a commission of inquiry, headed by Sir Edmund Compton, a long-standing civil servant. With him were appointed two commissioners, one of whom was Judge Edgar Fay QC, a circuit judge whose area of expertise was railway law. He had a great deal of experience in conducting public inquiries, but none in relation to the police and the army. The third commissioner was Dr Ronald Gibson, a former chairman of the Council of the British Medical Association. During the Second World War he had served in the British Army Medical Corps. Presumably, his medical knowledge and expertise would be of assistance in determining any disputed clinical issues.

The three men were tasked to enquire into allegations against the security forces of physical brutality in Northern Ireland arising from events on 9 August 1971. The committee began its work on the day of its appointment. It considered the complaints of 40 people, only one of whom appeared in person.

The committee's report, published on 3 November 1971, received an ambivalent reception.[1] On the one hand the unionist *Belfast Newsletter* claimed: 'Allegations of Brutality Rejected by Compton' and on the other, the nationalist *Irish News* reported: 'Compton Report backs Allegations of Ill-treatment'. Even a summary reading of the report indicates that both headlines are accurate. For some unknown reason the first Compton Report deals with only 11 men who were initially subjected to the 'five techniques', namely, (a) enforced posture facing a wall with legs spread apart and hands high above the head; (b) head being hooded in a bag at all times except during interrogation; (c) being subjected to continuous loud and deafening noise; (d) sleep deprivation for two or three days and (e) food deprivation for two or three days. In fact, following their arrest on 9 August there were 12 detainees subjected to these procedures. Army records include the twelfth, Michael Montgomery, whose existence is completely ignored in Compton's final report. He appears as 'Number 4' in the army list. That list shows that the total time he spent hooded and at the wall was 28 hours, and that he was interrogated for 13 hours ten minutes. He was 37 years old at the time of his arrest, married with five children, and a supporter of the civil rights movement in Derry. He never recovered from the treatment he received at RAF Ballykelly, after which he was interned for almost two years, until 1973.

(Eleven years later, in December 1984, he died following a heart attack at the age of 49.)

In the uproar that followed the publication of the Compton Report, one Tory government minister, Geoffrey Johnson Smith, a former television journalist, told the media that no one tried to be objective, but were trying to blacken the reputation of the British army. That is a popular tactic – 'Don't accuse our gallant soldiers, for if you do you not only help the enemy, you become one of the enemy.'

There were allegations, without any evidence, that some of those arrested were actually involved, directly or indirectly, in murder.

So much for the presumption of innocence. It is a matter of record that not one of the 14 detainees subjected to the five techniques was charged with any criminal offence following their detention in August 1971.

In the event, on 16 December 1971, the government of the Irish Republic lodged an application before the European Commission of Human Rights alleging breaches of Article 3 of the European Convention that no one should be subjected to torture or inhuman or degrading treatment or punishment.

Efforts were made to persuade the Irish government not to proceed with the case but to reach a friendly settlement. That would be in the interests of both governments, it was suggested, and would avoid any propaganda victory for those who opposed the policies that were aimed at achieving a just and equitable settlement agreeable to both sides. On the one hand, the Irish minister for foreign affairs, Garret FitzGerald, told the General Assembly of the UN that the UK and Irish governments had agreed on the formation of an executive, the reform of the RUC and the civil service, and the creation of a Council of Ireland. On the other hand, the attempt to persuade the Irish government to abandon its case at Strasbourg failed. On 22 August 1973, Edward Heath wrote in a memorandum, 'we shall have to fight them at Strasbourg by every means possible. The attorney general must throw himself wholeheartedly into the battle. Dublin will regret it.'

The British government's response was to try to delay any substantive hearings for many months and then to chide the Irish government for raking up the past. That did not work. The Irish attorney general, Declan Costello SC, disregarded every effort to persuade him not to proceed.

Two hundred separate allegations were made by the Irish government against the British government, which was prepared, after initial denials, to agree that some detainees were ill-treated, but claimed that these were regrettable lapses. It constantly stressed that there was no policy to torture anyone.

The tactics used by Declan Costello were highly effective. It was the Irish government's view that the use of the five techniques was authorised at the highest political level, and not the work of some imaginative NCO. It was not expected that anyone in the British establishment would admit responsibility for authorising conduct which on any objective view was clearly illegal.

Declan Costello astutely relied on the evidence of two witnesses from the 14 who had been subjected to the five techniques, Patrick Joseph McClean and Patrick Joseph Shivers. Costello could not have known at the time this evidence about McClean and Shivers was being gathered by the European Commission, that early in 1972, according to a document revealed in RTÉ's *Prime Time* television programme *The Torture Files*, there was in existence a highly relevant fact which must not be disclosed under any circumstances.[2] Part of the document reads, 'Ministers were told Shivers may have been interrogated in depth in error. If so, it seems equitable to settle out of court if we can do so without prejudice to our public position.' That surely means that any civil claim for damages by Shivers should be settled and not contested, if this would enable the British government to avoid telling the truth about the ill-treatment by the state of an completely innocent man. What would the European Commission have made of this evidence if the UK government had, instead of concealing the truth, properly disclosed that information to them?

Patrick Joseph Shivers was 40 years of age at the time of his arrest. A plasterer by trade, he lived in Toomebridge, County Armagh and was the father of five children, the youngest of whom was ten weeks old. He was an active member of NICRA. According to Lauretta Farrell (an American academic writing a book about the hooded men) local police officers told him on his release that they had no idea why he had been arrested. That might well be the basis of what was recorded in the state documents about settlement of the litigation he brought against the UK. Dr Farrell explains that Shivers was subjected to the five techniques. During interrogation he was asked questions about IRA arms dumps, about which he knew nothing. He was given his first drink of water after about four or five days. A document marked 'Secret' found in the National Archives shows that the total time he was hooded and at the wall was 49 hours 50 minutes and he was interrogated for 11 hours 10 minutes. These timings from the secret document are difficult to reconcile with paragraph 64 of the subsequent Committee of Inquiry's Report that Mr Shivers was standing at the wall for 23 hours. Does that mean that for the remaining 26 hours he was hooded?

However that may be, according to Dr Farrell he began to hallucinate: he thought he saw his son Finbar, who had died at the age of six months; he saw his own funeral, with his children circling his coffin as his dead son led him up to heaven.

His wife, Mary, eventually traced his whereabouts, after being given false and misleading information about him by the Stormont Ministry of Home Affairs. He had been moved from RAF Ballykelly to Crumlin Road prison. On his release soon after, his family saw him descend quickly into a state of paranoia. He died in 1985 at the age of 54.

Sean McKenna was arrested on 9 August together with his son, also Sean, from their home in the staunchly republican town of Newry, on the Armagh/ Down border. The older man, aged 42, was taken to Ballykinler Army base in County Down, and then to the RAF base at Ballykelly. He complained that he was beaten on the legs, hands and buttocks to force him to maintain the required posture on the wall. That complaint was denied. The Compton Report, however, does note the recording of what is described as 'mild heart trouble . . . Mr McKenna had raised the question of previous heart trouble.'[3] The medical officer had questioned him about it but was satisfied from McKenna's account of his history and treatment that there was no need to pursue the question further with his doctor. 'In the departure record a query mark is placed against the entry of heart trouble, Nothing abnormal was discovered on examination at Crumlin Jail by the prison medical officer on the 18th August, save a tingling in the fingers of both hands.'[4]

According to the Compton Report, McKenna was at the wall for a total of 30 hours.[5] The document marked 'Secret' in the National Archives shows the times he was hooded and at the wall was 25 hours 15 minutes. He was interrogated for 10 hours 15 minutes. This treatment seems unlikely to have been calculated to improve his heart condition

In his statement, cited by Farrell, he said he was forced to stand spread-eagled against a wall and was beaten in that position. 'He remembered being subjected to a deafening, continuous noise, similar to hissing from a steam pipe, and lost all sense of time. He remained hooded for the duration of his time at Ballykelly, and was given just a slice of bread and a mug of water daily . . . he was unable to answer any questions, could not remember his own name or that of his children . . . on his return to Crumlin Road Gaol a member of the Special Branch had to wash and shave him, and he remained unable to read or focus. He continued to have crying spells and anxiety attacks . . . he was continually weeping.' During his detention his hair turned white. He was moved first to Long Kesh, where he suffered hallucinations, thinking that secret messages were being sent to him via the television. He had severe headaches and seizures. In March 1972 he was sent to the prison hospital suffering from acute anxiety, severe headaches and bouts of weeping. On his release from custody in March 1973, he was admitted to a psychiatric hospital for treatment. This very sick man had been interned without charge or trial for two years.

In preparation for court proceedings, he was examined by two doctors, Professor Robert Daly and Dr Leigh of the Maudsley Hospital in London. Professor Daly reported that McKenna had a feeling of impending fatal illness such as a brain tumour or heart attack. Dr Leigh, who first examined him on 10 April 1974, found him tense, anxious and sobbing. He was contemplating suicide. Another examination disclosed that he was suffering from severe angina – chest pains.

On 3 June 1975 Dr Leigh wrote that in his view it had not been wise to proceed with the interrogation, and that it would be hard to show that the interrogation did not have the effect of worsening his angina. This seems to be part of his medical opinion prepared in respect of a civil claim for damages. Dr Leigh added that McKenna's psychiatric symptoms could be the result of the so-called 'deep interrogation' procedures and he noted that angina could lead to sudden death. Two days after Dr Leigh wrote that report, on 5 June 1975 Sean McKenna died suddenly after suffering a heart attack. He passed away without knowing the outcome of his case before the European Commission. He was 45 years of age.

On 2 September 1976 the European Commission ruled on a unanimous vote that in using the five sensory deprivation techniques the UK was guilty of breaching Article 3 in the form not only of inhuman and degrading treatment but also of torture.

The response in London was aggressive and the politicians recruited the pliant media to go on the offensive. The London *Times*, among others, accused the Irish government of providing propaganda for the IRA. Had that newspaper forgotten the report in its sister paper, the *Sunday Times*, about the men?

[A]ll were blindfolded by having a hood, two layers of thick fabric, placed over their heads. These hoods remained on their heads for up to six days. . . . During the period of their interrogation they were continuously hooded, barefoot, dressed only in a large boiler suit, and spread-eagled against a wall . . . the only sound that filled the room was a high-pitched throb . . . the noise literally drove them out of their minds.[6]

The case went to the full Court of Human Rights. This was the first time one state had taken proceedings against another member state of the European Commission. On 18 January 1978 the court held by 16 votes to one that the use of the five techniques constituted inhuman and degrading treatment, in breach of Article 3, but further held by 13 votes to four that such techniques did not constitute torture within the meaning of that Article. The court said, 'although the five techniques, as applied in combination, undoubtedly amounted to inhuman and degrading treatment, although their object was the extraction of confessions, the naming of others and/or information and although they were used systemically, they did not occasion suffering of the particular intensity and cruelty implied by the word "torture" as so understood.' The court further explained:

> The Court considers in fact that, while there exists on the one hand violence which is to be condemned both on moral grounds and also in most cases under the domestic law of the Contracting states but which does not fall within Article 3 of the Convention, it appears on the other hand that it was the intention of the Convention with its distinction between 'torture' and 'inhuman or degrading treatment' should by the first of these terms attach a special stigma to deliberate inhuman treatment causing very serious and cruel suffering. (paragraph 167)

One of the judges, Demitrios Evrigenis of Greece, delivered a dissenting opinion, that the techniques did amount to torture. He had been a professor of law as well as a legal practitioner and had suffered a term of imprisonment for his political beliefs. Perhaps he had a better insight into the meaning of torture than some of his judicial brethren.

The British media was both delighted and excited by the court's decision. So was the UK government. One official document claimed that the decision of the court was exceptionally favourable to the government and that the secretary of state was satisfied with the outcome.

The Tory *Daily Telegraph* posed a question on the use of the five techniques: 'can a State threatened by anarchy be properly and realistically expected NOT to employ such methods?'[7] Much earlier (in October 1973), the DPP, Sir Norman Skelhorn QC, had told a forum at Harvard Law

School, 'when dealing with Irish terrorists any methods were justified'. Supporters of brutal fascist regimes in Western Europe and South America would treasure that remark, which seemed totally out of character.

The attorney general of the UK government, Samuel Silkin QC, gave an undertaking to the court that his government would not permit or condone the use of those five techniques in the future, whether in Northern Ireland or elsewhere. The court accepted that a series of measures had been adopted from 1971 to ensure that prisoners would in the future be properly treated. These included medical examinations of people held for questioning by the police, strict instructions to the security forces, and rigorous procedures for investigating complaints. Edward Heath had given a similar undertaking in 1972. On 2 March of that year he announced in the House of Commons:

> [T]he government, having reviewed the whole matter with great care and with particular reference to any future operations, have decided that the techniques which the Committee examined will not be used in the future as an aid to interrogation. . . . I must make it plain that interrogation in depth will continue but these techniques will not be used. It is important that interrogation should continue. The statement I have made covers all future circumstances. If a government did decide – on whatever grounds I would not like to foresee – that additional techniques were required for interrogation, then I think that, on the advice which is given in both the majority and minority reports, and subject to any cases before the courts at the moment, they would probably have to come to the House and ask for powers to do it.

That statement is crystal clear. No more use of the five techniques; and if circumstances change, only the House of Commons can reverse the decision that they would not be used again.

Only one of the detainees appeared before the Compton Committee hearings to give oral evidence about the allegations against the security forces. He had no connection with any illegal organisation. (In fact he was a part-time member of the UDR.) All the others refused to do so. They objected to the hearings being held in private and that they were refused legal assistance at the outset. Later the home secretary changed his mind and said the detainees could be accompanied by a legal representative if they gave oral evidence to the committee, but such a legal representative would not be allowed to cross-examine witnesses or have access as of right to transcripts of evidence. That surely means that such legal assistance would be confined to being a hand-holding exercise that would achieve nothing, and certainly not justice. The detainees refused legal representation offered only on this basis. They also objected to the fact that the commission could not compel witnesses to appear or compel the production of documents. An examination of the records of their detention would have made interesting reading.

The politicians perhaps should have borne in mind the warning that Lord Justice Salmon gave in his Report of the Royal Commission on Tribunals of Enquiry in 1966 that it is only when the public is present that the public will have confidence that everything possible has been done for the purpose of arriving at the truth. In the absence of this and measures such as compelling witnesses and producing documents, the government would lay itself open to suspicion that it wished the truth to be hidden from the light of day.

In contrast, many of the army and police personnel complained against by the internees were legally represented by three senior members of the bar of Northern Ireland when the committee took evidence. Any hostile questioning, however unlikely from this committee, would be resisted and the privilege against self-incrimination would be invoked if the questions might lead to the embarrassing truth.

The chairman, Sir Edmund Compton, was a fully paid-up member of the establishment, having been educated at Rugby School and Oxford University. However, somewhat surprisingly, the prime minister, Edward Heath, described it as 'one of the most unbalanced, ill-judged reports I have ever read. They seemed to go to endless lengths to show that anyone who did not receive three star treatment has suffered hardship and ill-treatment.' Apparently Heath was complaining that the report did not exonerate the army (in which he had served during the Second World War). Be that as it may, the *Observer* newspaper called the report 'six grains of truth and a bucket of whitewash'.[8]

For some incomprehensible reason the three committee members invited ridicule for their report by their bizarre definition of 'brutality'. Instead of giving it its ordinary dictionary meaning they ventured, 'We consider that brutality is an inhuman or savage form of cruelty, and that cruelty implies a disposition to inflict suffering, coupled with indifference to, or pleasure in, the victim's pain.'[9] Does this mean that the intention and disposition of the interrogator determines the scope of his conduct, and that if he truly cares about the consequence of that conduct and takes no pleasure in inflicting pain, his actions are not brutal? Since by their terms of reference the committee were asked to investigate allegations of physical brutality, in accordance with their own bizarre definition they found none.

In its fight against terror, the British state developed five particular techniques to extract information from someone who might be unwilling, or even unable, to give it. Such information was required for intelligence purposes. The techniques were practised, according to the former Lord Chief Justice Parker (educated at Rugby School and Trinity College, Cambridge) in counter-insurgency operations in Palestine, Malaya, Kenya and Cyprus, and more recently in the British Cameroons (1960–61), Brunei (1963), British Guiana (1964), Borneo/Malaysia (1965–66), the Persian Gulf (1970–71) as well as in Northern Ireland in 1971.[10]

The British army in the main was against internment without trial. So was the chief constable of the RUC, Graham Shillington. General Sir Michael Carver, the chief of the general staff, told Edward Heath not to surrender to Brian Faulkner's threat to resign, which would be followed by the UK having to impose direct rule. Then, on 5 August 1971, General Harry Tuzo, the general officer commanding Northern Ireland, restated his objections to internment to the defence secretary, Lord Carrington, in London. Brian Faulkner, however, pressed for its introduction before the British Cabinet. They needed little persuading. In fact plans for it were well under way. A document marked 'Secret', dated 9 August 1971, disclosed in a search of the National Archives, shows that Brigadier J.H.H. Lewis wrote a minute for the London government that 'Ballykelly has been designed with the knowledge of the RUC under the professional guidance of the Joint Services Interrogation Wing, Ashford, in the light of the latest techniques evolved from recent operation. . . . It is the RUC who will conduct the interrogation in depth – NOT the Army. Not to use the centre and the techniques (within their safeguards) would be to lose one of the major advantages of internment.' The linked documents show that the following day Lord Carrington discussed it with Reginald Maudling, the home secretary. Neither expressed any dissatisfaction with the brigadier's minute.

It is now known that in April 1971, some four months before internment was introduced, officers and men of the English Intelligence Centre held a seminar to teach the five interrogation procedures to members of the RUC. It is believed that the MOD's Joint Services Interrogation Wing was basically responsible for the training. These techniques were never published or even written down anywhere. Was that because they were regarded as illegal in domestic and international law?

The authorities worked on the assumption that information can be obtained more rapidly if the captive is subjected to strict discipline and isolation, with a restricted diet. All 12 men chosen for special interrogation complained about their treatment. They complained about being hooded at all times except when they were being interrogated. They described the hood as a navy or black bag of tightly woven or hessian cloth. Compton described it as a black pillowslip. Wearing it while being moved from one place to another, said Compton, reduced to the minimum the possibility that the wearer would be identified by other detainees. So to that extent it provided security for the detainee.[11] One is bound to wonder whether the detainee involved realised that this treatment was for his benefit and safety. Compton does accept, however, that the hood might increase the person's sense of isolation; if so, that would be helpful to the interrogator thereafter.[12] So it was for his benefit as well. Everyone was a winner.

The group of 12 described being held in a room where there was continuous deafening noise; it was like the escaping of compressed air, the roar of steam, the whirring of helicopter blades or a drill. They said they were returned to this room, and subjected to this noise, between periods of interrogation. Was this not part of a softening-up process? Is not being forced to face a wall with arms outstretched above the head, hood around the head, surrounded by deafening noise, likely to loosen the tongue?

The staff supervising this technique did not deny that this happened. They admitted to Compton that while the detainees were held together awaiting interrogation, or between interrogations, they were subjected to a continuous hissing noise, or what they describe as 'electronic mush'. The noise was loud enough to mask extraneous sounds and it was neutral, i.e. there was no music or speech. Perhaps they regarded this as the important point, that the noise was loud enough to prevent effective oral communication between detainees. If the object of the noise was to prevent one detainee talking to another (and only Compton and the two other commissioners were likely to believe that), why not simply keep them apart?

The supervisor told Compton that some of the detainees kept their hoods on even at times when they could have removed them. Perhaps they came to like the feeling of isolation and unreality that such a technique brought about and didn't want it to end.

With regard to the enforced posture against the wall, the detainees complained that they were forced to maintain this posture, and failing to do so meant being struck with a baton. This went on for between two and four days. Compton admits that the detainees were indeed treated in this way. The length of time any detainee spent in this posture was between four and six hours. If the detainee needed to lower his arms to restore circulation, he was permitted to do so. But anyone who attempted to rest his head against the wall or to sleep in this posture was prevented from doing so. Anyone collapsing on the floor was picked up by the armpits (even Compton doesn't claim this was done gently and kindly) and made to resume the approved posture. Compton noted that the approved training was for the staff to part legs, not by kicking them, but by pushing them with the inner calf of their own leg. Staff denied using a baton to make the detainee stand against the wall.

According to the report, Patrick McClean was in the standing position at the wall for 29 hours.[13] But that figure could be misleading because Compton notes that McClean 'persisted in collapsing from the start and after a short time was not forcibly held up but allowed to lie on the floor'.[14] Was that an act of kindness on the part of some concerned interrogator? Or was it simply that a frightened and intimidated individual was unable to stand in the required position? Compton's use of the word 'persistent' in this context implies that this was the conduct of a rather spoiled individual who insisted on having his own way. In any event, Compton records that although the record shows that McClean was at the wall for 29 hours, he was hardly ever in the required posture. That being so, one wonders why he was there at all.

McClean made a statement, available to and read by Compton, that he was assaulted on a number of occasions in different ways. He was bounced on, rolled along the ground, punched with fingers in the stomach, kicked in the testicles, his arms were twisted and his head bumped on the floor. He said he was denied toilet facilities. Compton did not believe that latter claim any more than he believed the others. He said 'the lavator[ies] were there. It was Mr McClean's fault that he did not use them.'[15] So when he did wet himself, on three separate occasions, that was entirely his own fault.

Compton seems not to have linked this allegation with that made by James Auld, another of the group of 11 detainees. He was made to stand against the wall in the required posture. While he was there he asked to go to the toilet; he was refused, and his hooded head was banged against the wall for talking. When he arched his back, he alleged, a baton was rammed into it to straighten it. The police records show that he was standing against the wall for 43½ hours.

The supervising officers who were asked about this by Compton denied the allegations. He said, 'It was not clear to us how a man in the required posture, hooded and surrounded by a loud noise, was expected to indicate his need. We were told he would have to use gestures. Such gestures might initially be construed merely as an attempt to move from the required posture. If this was so, he would be put back in the posture in the manner described, at any rate to start with.'[16] Does this indicate that the detainee could not communicate with his interrogators, because of the noise and the posture he was forced to adopt? Clearly the hood over his head prevented him from speaking in a meaningful way.

Another detainee, Joseph Clarke, complained that his hands went numb when he was forced to stand against the wall. If he sought to restore the circulation by closing his fist, he said, his hands were beaten against the wall until he opened them and replaced them in the required posture. The total amount of time he was forced to assume the posture against the wall was 40 hours. If he rested his head against the wall it was banged and shaken. Following questioning he was beaten until he collapsed. He was revived and beaten again. He resisted this and fought back. He was then beaten again, even more severely than before. Again he resisted and so his wrists were handcuffed behind his back, causing an injury to his wrist.

In response to these allegations the supervising staff said that as a result of maintaining the required posture for a considerable period of time, the hands or arms would become numb. They therefore rubbed the hands or swung the arms to restore normal feeling. Compton does not indicate what degree of gentleness was used to rub the hands, but one wonders whether it was done in a sympathetic way. The committee thought it was probable that there could have been 'pins and needles' and numbness in the fingers and hands as a result of prolonged pressure against the wall. However, they felt assured that the supervising staff were aware of this and took steps to control it. The beatings were denied.

The injuries to the wrists were caused by a pair of handcuffs that were too small. They were eventually replaced by a larger pair. The staff wrote notes describing Joseph Clarke as 'a strong young man who resisted with considerable force attempts to make him adopt and maintain the required posture'.[17] He was described in the same paragraph as 'aggressive and resisted strongly'. Would that explain why he was forced to stand against the wall for 40 hours? Was there a determination on the part of his interrogators that whatever his body strength, they would break his spirit? He was recorded as having an injury to his right knee and a red mark on his arm. 'They [the staff] could not tell the Committee how these injuries were suffered.'

In its conclusions regarding the five techniques, the Committee decided that the posture on the wall, the hooding, the noise, the deprivation of sleep and the deprivation of food and water all constituted physical ill-treatment. Their bizarre definition of the word 'torture' precluded a finding that the 11 chosen men had been tortured.

Six men complained that they had been forced to run over broken glass and rough stones to a helicopter; that they had been menaced by police dogs; kicked into the helicopter and pushed or forced to jump out of it after 15 seconds. This was alleged to have happened at Girdwood Park Regional Holding Centre in Belfast on the day of internment, 9 August 1971.

Eleven witnesses denied these allegations. They conceded that there was a 'deception' – a deliberate deception – no less than five times, three involving detainees and two dummy runs with members of the security forces. It took this form. An RAF Wessex helicopter was flown into Girdwood barracks with the intent of deceiving onlookers into believing that the detainees were being taken away from the holding centre. The plan was to take them in groups to the helicopter, put them on board for a short space of time (an airman inside the helicopter closed and opened the doors), then remove them and surreptitiously return them to the main building. Compton gives three reasons for this being done: (1) Onlookers (whoever and wherever they might be) would believe an airlift was taking place. (2) This might help to reduce the attention being paid to Girdwood from outside and (3) obviate the danger of attack on its perimeter or the danger of sniping from outside. Some may not find these three reasons very compelling, or indeed very comprehensible.

The personnel involved in this deception were unanimous that no detainee was inside the helicopter when it left the ground. When one of the detainees attempted to break away while approaching the helicopter, he was, says Compton, 'manhandled without undue roughness'.

Somewhat strangely, Compton thought this deception exercise was meaningless and should not have been undertaken. The men involved had been taken to Girdwood for identification and interrogation to decide whether they should be detained or released. Equally strangely, when it came to deciding which side was truthful about the allegations of assault, being frightened by dogs (which were certainly there or nearby) and being taken off the ground in the helicopter, Compton decided that he should give special weight to the evidence of the RAF crewman inside the helicopter, whom he calls 'an independent eyewitness'. Was he not a serviceman, like the other individuals involved, albeit in a different service? Could he really be called 'independent' in circumstances such as these? In the event, not-withstanding his reservations about accepting their evidence, Compton decided, 'The physical experience they were forced to go through under these circumstances does constitute a measure of ill-treatment.'[18] But surely that was the entire object of the exercise, to intimidate the detainees and soften them up prior to interrogation. Since such conduct was illegal, why not say so?

The Compton committee does not say where these interrogations took place. The venue was an official secret. It was thought by some to have been Palace Barracks in Holywood, County Down. Two Catholic priests, Fr Denis Faul and Fr Raymond Murray, both civil rights campaigners, consistently maintained it was RAF Ballykelly, County Derry. They were in fact correct. A document marked 'Secret' found in the National Archives by a researcher acting for the Pat Finucane Centre in Derry reads in part: 'It is very important to keep secure the existence and location of the centre at Ballykelly where the 12 detainees in question had been interrogated.' If the European Court had known about the existence and location of RAF Ballykelly, might it have considered afresh the central question: If the premises were designed for the use of interrogation techniques, does it follow that whoever authorised its existence did so for an unlawful purpose, namely to subject detainees to unlawful assaults? And at a date much earlier than the government was ever prepared to admit?

Neither does Compton say in the report who carried out the interrogations and whether any of them gave evidence to the committee. He records that over 17 hearing days the inquiry heard from 95 army witnesses, 26 police officers, 11 prison officers, five regimental medical officers, two medical staff officers, two civilian officers and two specialists.[19] The report does not claim that any of them were officers of the Special Branch of the RUC. They, of course, could not be identified by the hooded detainees. While they carried out the interrogations, officers of the English Intelligence Centre were present in the control room, presumably to ensure that their oral instructions were being followed to the letter.

The Committee relied to a great extent on the evidence available from the medical doctors who examined those detained in the various holding centres. Compton did not disclose that many of these doctors were imported into Northern Ireland for about two weeks, for the purpose of being present and conducting examinations after internment was introduced on 9 August 1971. It was not disclosed, so far as is known, that many of them were medical officers in the British army.

In summary, the committee accepted that the fingertip posture on the wall provided security for the detainees and their guard against physical violence during the reception at the barracks and while awaiting interrogation. The hooding, by preventing identification, provided security for both detainees and guards; the continuous noise prevented them overhearing or being overheard and was thus an additional security measure. The bread-and-water diet may have formed part of the atmosphere of discipline. The committee seemed unable to think of any useful alternative purpose for the deprivation of sleep for days and night and so said nothing in support of such a practice.

The weakest part of the Compton Report must surely be in its approach first to the application of legal principles and second to the conflict of evidence between the security forces and those they detained. In the case of Felim O'Hagan, aged 16 years, who was arrested at Lurgan in County Armagh, presumably on 9 August, the report fails to give the date or the time of the incident. Felim complained that he was taken forcibly from his family home with his arm twisted up his back and struck with a baton across the shoulders.[20] Two soldiers were involved, one a private, the other an NCO. The private claimed that he had to force entry into the house by smashing a plate of glass because Felim O'Hagan's mother had refused to open the door. Once inside, the soldier saw a young man sitting in a chair in a downstairs room. The NCO ordered the soldier to arrest him. According to the private, he asked him to come along with the arresting party. The young man made no reply and made no move. The soldier then put Felim O'Hagan in an arm lock. Compton notes, 'the lock had been successful in making Mr O'Hagan leave the sitting position and accompany the arrest party. The young man had been plainly frightened by the proceedings.' He had not spoken to anyone, although his mother kept shouting that the soldiers had got the wrong man. Compton said that it was necessary to maintain the arm lock outside the house because it appeared even then O'Hagan was reluctant to accompany the soldiers. It was admitted that the soldiers had batons but they claimed they had not used them.

The NCO in charge of the arresting party told the committee that he had orders to arrest three men in Mr O'Hagan's house, and he had photographs of all three. None of them was in the house. He went outside to consult a superior officer, telling him that the only male in the house was O'Hagan. 'The officer ordered that the youth should nonetheless be taken along.' The NCO said he repeated the words of arrest to Mr O'Hagan, who made no response and continued to sit in the armchair. He had heard the soldier ask O'Hagan to accompany the troops, but Mrs O'Hagan had told the youth to remain where he was. The NCO claimed he was sure that if O'Hagan had gone when first asked to do so there would have been no trouble. He blamed the boy's mother for telling him to stay where he was. He further went on to say that when the soldier approached O'Hagan to take him into custody, he had shied away and the chair he was sitting in had fallen over. The soldier, then, in Compton's elegant phrase, 'assisted him to stand, simultaneously putting on the arm-lock . . . there had been no need to use excessive force as Mr O'Hagan was obviously frightened and the arm-lock largely a formality'.[21] The committee came to the conclusion on this evidence that the arm lock was a controlled use of force, and is only painful if resisted. It was not used with the object of hurting but it was required to make the arrested person comply.

Compton says nothing about whether the soldiers had grounds to justify the arrest of a 16-year-old boy in his own home. British soldiers did have the power to arrest under the 1922 Special Powers Act. Under Regulation 10 the arrester had to be of the opinion that the arrest should be realised for the preservation of peace and maintenance of order. Under Regulation 11 the arrester had to suspect the individual of having acted or being about to act in a manner prejudicial to the preservation of the peace or maintenance of order, or of having committed an offence against the Regulations. None of those existed here.

This arrest was clearly unlawful and the use of force to effect it was equally unlawful. If, however, the soldiers who had been ordered by a superior officer to arrest Felim O'Hagan had been called to account for unlawfully arresting him and detaining him, would they have resorted to the 'Nuremberg Defence' so dearly loved by the German High Command, namely 'I was only obeying orders'? Compton also appears to blame the 16-year-old for any hurt he endured – if he hadn't struggled, the arm lock would not have caused him any pain.

In the same way the committee dismissed claims by five other men that they were forced to carry out strenuous exercises of long duration after being taken to Ballykinler Camp. They said that anyone who refused or failed to carry out an exercise was kicked, punched or struck with a baton.

This was denied. The men were taken to an empty hut after being arrested. Some Special Branch officers of the RUC complained that they could be seen as they passed by the windows of that hut. Accordingly the men were required to sit on the floor. Because they got cold they were instructed to change their positions and do simple exercises. The committee took the view that the exercises were devised to counteract the cold and stiffness about which the five men complained. However, the committee considered that the exercises were thoughtlessly prolonged after they had served their purpose. This did not amount to cruelty or brutality but the complainants may have suffered 'hardship'. It is highly doubtful that the five men agreed with that conclusion.

In another case, the Association for Legal Justice sent a copy of a statement made by Joseph Hughes to the Home Office in London. He was arrested in Belfast on 9 August. He complained that he was pulled by the hair out of his house into the street. There he was struck with a baton and kicked. He was forced to run 400 yards in bare feet. He was compelled to lie face down in a lorry, where he was again kicked. A soldier inflicted a wound to his stomach with the barrel of his gun. Six members of the security forces gave evidence about this arrest. The sergeant in charge of the arrest party said that Hughes refused to leave his house so he was compelled to do so. The sergeant seized one arm and the hair on his head, took him downstairs and handed him over to a junior NCO. That soldier held him in exactly the same grip – by the arm and the hair –and forced him to run 400 yards, barefoot, to a waiting vehicle. It was denied that Hughes was kicked and struck with a baton. The NCO involved demonstrated the hold in the committee room. It was used regularly on such occasions and even had a name – the 'Kado'. The committee concluded that the use of the 'Kado' grip can be harsh, but it was a recognised method of controlled use of force and no more force was needed than was necessary to get Hughes into custody for his own safety from what might have been a gathering hostile crowd. But was it really necessary to run a man some 400 yards in his bare feet, in the early hours of the morning, grasping him by one arm, and grabbing the hair on his head with the other hand?

There was no finding on the infliction of the stomach wound. The committee expressed its regret that the Girdwood Park admission system had not provided them with medical records on the condition of arrested persons on their arrival. Why had they failed to do that? Who benefited from the absence of those records? Joseph Hughes was released from custody the next day, 10 August.[22] The army had mistreated, and alienated, a totally innocent man.

There was no presumption of innocence in his case, or in anyone else's, in the view of the political, military and legal establishment in the UK. The allegations of brutality and ill-treatment made against the security forces in Northern Ireland were vehemently denied. It was all, prior to the publication of the Compton Report, terrorist propaganda. In the event the British government paid out very substantial damages to those who were ill-treated in the custody of the state. The state at various levels knew of, and approved of, everything that was going on. The Prime Minster, Edward Heath, the home secretary, Reginald Maudling, and Lord Carrington were all told of the strategy but not the detail of the five techniques to be used on detainees. The individual who could have told them but failed to do was Sir Dick

White, the chief co-ordinator of intelligence in a special Cabinet committee in London. He was a former member of both MI5 and MI6.

A confidential memo marked 'For UK eyes only' that was sent to him and to Ian Gilmour, a Parliamentary under-secretary of state for the army and later defence secretary, set out the line the government should adopt to defend the use of the five techniques. The senior army officer, a lieutenant colonel in overall charge of the in-depth interrogation at Ballykelly, maintained that the detainees' allegations of torture were untrue. Their interrogators had told them to lie about the abuse in order to protect them from any retribution from the IRA after their release from custody. That was not the line advanced in explanation to the Compton committee where the state admitted the use of the five techniques. It is believed that same officer had been in charge of a five-man detachment sent to Aden in January 1964 to conduct sensory deprivation interrogation on detainees there. He seems to have been rather good at his job.

The work of the Compton committee was not quite complete. On 19 October 1971 the *Sunday Times* made reference to three men, Bernard McGeary, Tony Rosato (a student at Queen's University, Belfast) and William (Liam) Shannon.

William Shannon was arrested in the street by an army patrol at 11.30 p.m. on Saturday 9 October 1971. His father, uncle and two cousins had been interned on 9 August 1971. The family complained that they had been subjected to harassment by the security forces since that date. No one who knew him was told where he was or what had happened to him following his arrest. He had simply disappeared. To add to the mystery, another man called Liam David Rogers appears on the army list under the heading '2nd Operation' as prisoner no. 13, but nothing further seems to have been said about him apart from the fact that he was hooded and standing at the wall for nine hours and five minutes and interrogated for 38 hours and 39 minutes.

Tony Rosato was released after two days of questioning at Palace Barracks. There was no evidence of any sort against him. He complained that a gun had been discharged behind him, near the back of his head. He was terrified but he was aware enough to realise that William Shannon was also detained in the same place. On his release from custody Tony contacted the press. In a normal society an individual in his position would have contacted the police rather than the media, but he did not live in a normal society. He had even less confidence than before in the sectarian and bigoted members of the RUC and would not trust them to do anything.

After nine days it was admitted that William Shannon was in custody in

Crumlin Road jail. On his release he made a statement describing how he was taken to the military barracks at Holywood and held there from Saturday evening until Monday evening. He was interrogated by a member of the Special Branch, who spread-eagled him against the wall. His legs were kicked from under him and he was assaulted. His jacket was removed and he was threatened that he would be injected with a syringe, said to contain a truth drug, that the officer was holding. On the Sunday a shot was fired behind his head as he stood at the wall. Uniformed officers nearby were emptying and reloading their pistols. The next day, when against the wall, he was struck by a plastic hose. He was hooded and subjected to the hissing noise.

The allegations made by William Shannon and Tony Rosato were considered by Sir Edmund Compton alone. There was no new Command Paper. He alone dictated and signed an addendum to the report which was not published with it. Several hundred typed copies were distributed to MPs with the main report. Compton simply accepted that William Shannon had been 'ill-treated' in the same way as the other 11 cases he had considered. Tony Rosato's claim that a gun had been discharged behind his head could not have been true, Compton found, because the officers were required by the regulations to empty their pistols before entering the interrogation area. He seemed to believe that because the regulation existed, it must have been observed.

The Compton Committee, and others, seemed to have missed the importance of what happened to William Shannon in particular. The Special Branch officers and their tutors must have known that the Compton Committee was examining their use of the five techniques, at the very same time as they were interrogating Shannon (and Liam David Rogers) and by their conduct showed a calculated indifference to that inquiry because they knew they would not be called to account for anything they did to anyone in their custody. They were simply above the law.

They were above the law because they were acting on behalf of a state that paid lip service to the rule of law while they chose to disregard it. As was once said, 'when those who make the law break the law, there is no law'.

On 24 October 1971 the *Sunday Times* printed further allegations of ill-treatment of detainees, one of whom was described by a psychiatrist who treated him as 'almost frozen with fear'. Even as the disbelieving public began to read the Compton Report, the same newspaper published a report on 28 November of further allegations of ill-treatment made by ten men. Their doctors claimed that their injuries were consistent with their evidence of how they had been inflicted. The home secretary looked the other way.

Prime Minister Edward Heath was not impressed by the Compton Report. He appointed a three-person Committee of Privy Councillors to consider authorised procedures for interrogating persons suspected of terrorism. The three were the recently retired Lord Chief Justice, Lord Parker of Waddington; the Conservative and Unionist politician John Boyd-Carpenter (Stowe School and Balliol College, Oxford); and Gerald Gardiner, who had been Lord Chancellor in Harold Wilson's Labour government. The committee first met on 3 December 1971 and reported on 31 January 1972, the day after the Bloody Sunday shootings in Derry.[23]

As might be expected, the two establishment figures, Parker and Boyd-Carpenter, found that subject to safeguards and for the purpose of security, 'these techniques should only be used where it is considered vitally necessary to obtain information'.[24] That concept might have appealed to those members of Hitler's Gestapo who interrogated agents of the Special Operations Executive who parachuted into France during the Second World War in support of the French Resistance Movement. Getting information from those agents might have saved many German lives.

Parker and Boyd-Carpenter also recommended that 'Her Majesty's Forces should neither apply nor be party to the application of these techniques except under the . . . express authority of a UK Minister.'[25]

It is clear beyond any doubt that the home secretary, Reginald Maudling, was stating the UK position and understanding of the conduct of sensory deprivation procedures when he wrote in the introduction to the Compton Report:

[I]n the present circumstances in Northern Ireland . . . it is imperative to obtain all available intelligence in order to save the lives of civilians and members of the security forces; it is therefore essential to interrogate suspects who are believed to have important information. The principles applied in the interrogation of suspects in Northern Ireland since August this year, and the methods employed (which are necessary not only for reasons of security and control but also to protect the lives of those being interrogated against the risks of reprisals) are the same as those which have been employed in all emergencies of this kind which Britain has been involved in recent years.

He then refers to rules which were issued in 1965 and revised in 1967 in the light of the recommendations of Roderick Bowen QC in a report on the procedures for the arrest, interrogation and detention of suspects in Aden.

Maudling concluded his introduction by stating that the government did not regard the findings of the Compton Committee as in any way reflecting adversely on the responsibility and discipline with which the security forces in Northern Ireland were conducting their fight against a vicious and ruthless enemy. Is that another way of saying to the army, 'Carry on regardless'? As we shall see, that is exactly what they did.

Parker and Boyd-Carpenter say that '700 members of the IRA and their positions in the organisation were identified . . . details of possible IRA operation; arms caches; safe houses; communications and supply route, including those across the border and locations of wanted persons . . . the discovery of individual responsibility for about 85 incidents recorded on police files which had previously been unexplained'.[26] If this is true, the security forces had indeed struck a rich vein of information. Might the noble lord and the politician have wondered, however, how this information could be verified, and whether when it was provided to them the providers might have had a vested interest in their believing it?

The author of the Minority Report, Lord Gerald Austin Gardiner, was of the establishment, but not in it. Educated at Harrow and Magdalen College, Oxford, he served in the Brigade of Guards at the end of the First World War. In the Second World War, because he was too old for military service, he joined the Friends' Ambulance Unit in 1943. He said he was making a good deal of money prior to that from his practice as a barrister, and it didn't seem right while people were away at the war. In June 1944 he was in Europe following the D-Day landings and was one of the first on the Allies' side to see the horrors of the concentration camp at Belsen.

What is most striking, and indeed shocking, is his statement, 'Some of the 14 were only too anxious to give information and were "co-operative" from the start and in their case the procedures appear to have been unnecessary.'[27] Does that mean that some were subjected to sensory deprivation techniques in an effort to persuade them to give information that they were prepared to supply voluntarily? How many of the 14 were in this group? What information did they give? How did they acquire that information, if, as was later proved, there was no evidence against them amounting to the commission of a crime?

Lord Gardiner considered that the five techniques were both secret and illegal. He accepted that the government of Northern Ireland, when approving the procedures, had no idea that they were illegal. As for the RUC, they assumed that the army had satisfied themselves that the procedures they were training the police to employ were legal.[28] He chides the British government, however, for including in the Joint Directive on Military Interrogation in Internal Security Operations Overseas the wrong Geneva Convention (signed by the UK in 1949 and ratified in 1958), which deals with the treatment of prisoners of war. The directive should have referred to the Fourth Geneva Convention, also signed in 1949, that relates to the protection of civilian persons in time of war rather than prisoners of war. Was that inclusion an oversight or deliberate?

He also comments on the failure of the records relating to the wall standing, something which the Compton Committee and Parker and Boyd-Carpenter did not address, for, as Gardiner points out, the Compton Report does not indicate how long any detainee was standing continuously at the wall. There were only partial, not full, records? Why? Those partial records do disclose, however, that some detainees were standing continuously for up to 16 hours. Was that not torture? It is almost impossible to comprehend how any individual can be forced to stand spread-eagled at a wall continuously for hours on end without their physical and mental health being undermined.

Perhaps most damning of all is Gardiner's view that 'no Army Directive and no Minister could lawfully or validly have authorised the use of the procedures. Only Parliament can alter the law.'[29] He was clearly under the impression, almost certainly shared by the other members of both committees, that no minister had actually authorised using the five techniques in this case. He may have been totally wrong.

By the beginning of March 1977 counsel for Ireland before the European Court, Declan Costello, was pressing for the prosecution of or disciplinary proceedings against those who had carried out the in-depth interrogations. He could not have known of the existence of a letter written in that month, a copy of which was found in the National Archives in Kew, London, by RTÉ's Investigation Unit, and outlined on television by the journalist Rita O'Reilly, who fronted the RTÉ television programme *The Torture Files*. It was written by the then home secretary, Merlyn Rees, to the prime minister, James Callaghan, on 31 March 1977. It was headed: 'Meeting between the attorney general of the Republic of Ireland and the United Kingdom'. The text begins:

> I have read with interest the attorney general's minute to you of 25
> March about the meeting with the Irish attorney general on 23
> March when Mr Costello raised the proceedings brought by the

Irish government to the European Court of Human Rights, and in particular the possibility of either prosecuting or taking disciplinary action against those responsible in 1971/72 for acts found by the Commission to have been in breach of Article 3.

He then wrote the following and most damning and astonishing words:

> It is my view (confirmed by Brian Faulkner before his death) that the decision to use methods of torture in Northern Ireland in 1971/72 was taken by ministers – in particular Lord Carrington, then Secretary of State for Defence.
>
> If at any time methods of torture are used in Northern Ireland contrary to the view of the Government of the day I would agree that individual policemen or soldiers should be prosecuted or disciplined, but in the particular circumstances of 1971/72 a political decision was taken.
>
> I do not believe that the Irish Government understands the nature of the situation in 1971/72 – a situation which, to his credit, Mr Heath ended.

In the margin of that document the then chief of the general staff wrote, 'This could grow into something awkward if pursued.' It is being pursued. Telling the truth is of some importance.

On 15 October 1974 the British government was advised that in civil cases brought against the state, 'because of the possibility that conspiracy may be proved against those others involved, every effort must be made to continue to prevent the cases coming to court'. That clearly means that disclosure of the truth in civil proceedings could provide sufficient evidence to mount a criminal prosecution against identifiable individuals, something which the state was determined to avoid at all costs.

In response to the RTÉ television programme the MOD in London said in a statement:

> The UK government in no way seeks to defend the use of the interrogation techniques declared illegal by the European Court. However we haven't been provided with any evidence to substantiate the allegations made about the way the British case was presented to the European Commission of Human Rights so are unable to comment further.

Lord Carrington caused a letter to be sent on his behalf saying that he had nothing to add to that Ministry's statement.

As a matter of law it is difficult to see whether there is evidence that would be admissible at a criminal trial to show the involvement of anyone in the political establishment in the decision to subject detainees in Northern Ireland to the five techniques. If this did not happen, however, why did Merlyn Rees write to the prime minister in the way, and with the words, that he did?

Was it significant that Lord Carrington appeared not to deny what Merlyn Rees had written about giving authority to use the five techniques? Lord Carrington might have been fortunate in avoiding prosecution at the time; if he authorised the commission of an unlawful act, that might have made him a party to a conspiracy to cause serious injuries to others, contrary to common law. As Lord Gardiner noted in his Minority Report, no minister had the lawful authority to authorise such unlawful conduct.

One might have hoped and expected, in the light of the statement of the prime minister Edward Heath in 1972, that the five techniques would not be used again in Northern Ireland or elsewhere, and the solemn undertaking to the European Court in 1998 given by the UK attorney general meant that sensory deprivation techniques would never be used again by the British army. Events showed that to be a false hope.

The British army used some, if not all, of the five techniques again, this time in the war in Iraq.

The Case of Baha Mousa

Baha Mousa, a 26-year-old hotel receptionist living in Basra, Iraq, was mourning the recent death of his wife from cancer when he was arrested by soldiers from the 1st Battalion the Queen's Lancashire Regiment (1 QLR) on 14 September 2003. He did not know then that he only had two days to live. His father, Colonel Daoud Mousa, who had called at the hotel to collect his son after his night shift, watched events inside the hotel through a window. He saw four or five soldiers, including Private David Fearon, steal some money from a safe inside the telecommunications shop.[30] Colonel Mousa described what he had seen to Lieutenant Michael Crosbie, an intelligence officer. He was told by that officer that his son would be released in two hours. That did not happen.

Private Fearon, it seems alone, even though others were involved in stealing, was called to account. He was ordered, as a punishment, to fill 200 sandbags, which was, according to Sir William Gage, a former Lord Justice of Appeal, 'a lenient sentence'.[31] A more apt description might be 'insulting'.

Only a month before these events, on 14 August 2003 Captain Dai Jones, aged 29, attached to the QLR, had been killed in Basra, Southern Iraq, in a bomb attack on an ambulance in which he was travelling. Nine days after that, on 23 August, three members of the Royal Military Police (RMP) had been shot dead in Basra. Almost exactly two months before that, on 24 June, six RMP officers had been murdered at Majar al-Kabir near Basra. In the light of these ten terrible murders it might be safe to say that some British army soldiers were not well disposed towards the people of Iraq.

Nine other civilians were arrested with Baha Mousa. They were taken from the Ibn Al Haitham hotel in Basra to a temporary detention centre for interrogation. Firearms and bomb-making equipment were said to have been found on the hotel premises. All the detainees had hessian sandbags placed over their heads for long periods of time. Some of them had two sandbags, or even three, over their heads. They were forced to adopt stress positions and then interrogated. In the searing heat of Iraq, these men must have suffered greatly. At least two of the forbidden five techniques were used, in breach of Britain's undertaking not to use them again.

Baha Mousa died two days after his arrest. A post-mortem examination found that he had suffered postural asphyxiation and had at least 93 injures to his body. He had several fractured ribs and a broken nose. It was later established that he had been savagely beaten and that he had been hooded for nearly 24 of the 36 hours he spent in army custody. One soldier, Corporal Donald Payne, a member of the Provost Section of 1 QLR, was alleged to have violently assaulted Baha Mousa in the minutes before he expired, punching and possibly kicking him, and using a dangerous restraint method to pin him down. A later inquiry decided that while this conduct had been a contributory cause of his death, Baha Mousa had already been weakened by lack of food and water, heat exhaustion, fear, previous injuries and the hooding and stress positions imposed on him by British soldiers.

Seven soldiers from 1 QLR were court-martialled in September 2006 for various offences, including abusing detained civilians in Iraq. Corporal Payne denied the manslaughter of Baha Mousa and perverting the course of justice. He was found not guilty. In his case there was the legal difficulty of establishing that it was Payne's conduct that actually caused the death of the victim. He did admit, however, 'inhumane treatment of a man, namely Baha

Mousa, protected under the Fourth Geneva Convention'. He was sentenced to a year in prison and discharged from the army. Some might consider that a light sentence.

Baha Mousa's family sought a judicial inquiry into his death. The MOD refused that request. An application for judicial review of that refusal succeeded in the Divisional Court of the Queen's Bench Division. The Civil Division of the Court of Appeal upheld that ruling. The Judicial Committee of the House of Lords ruled in June 2007 that the Human Rights Act 1998 did apply to detainees in Iraq who were held in the custody of the British army at a British army place of detention.

Thereafter the London government set up a public inquiry under the Inquiries Act 2005, headed by Gage. At the hearings, which began in July 2009 and lasted for 115 days, 247 witnesses gave oral evidence and 101 witness statements were considered.

The Gage Report was published on 8 September 2009. It said that Baha Mousa died after suffering an appalling episode of gratuitous violence and that there had been a very serious breach of discipline by the soldiers. He totally condemned the conduct of Corporal Payne, whom he called 'a violent bully, who inflicted a dreadful catalogue of unjustified and brutal violence on the Iraqi detainees, while at the same time encouraging other junior soldiers to do the same'.

In Chapter 2 of the report William Gage referred to the Compton and Parker reports, the latter of which looked more broadly at the future use of the techniques considered in the Compton Inquiry, and to the five techniques. He found that Edward Heath's undertaking not to use those techniques again anywhere had become largely forgotten. Knowledge of this ban had 'largely been lost' by the time of the Iraq war and there was no proper, generally available MOD doctrine on interrogation of prisoners of war. Although compliance with the Geneva Convention was taught at all levels, there was, he found, little reference in any of the policy and training manuals to the prohibition of the five techniques. There was no reference in the tactical questioning manuals to the ban on the use of the five techniques. He blamed 'corporate failure' at the MOD for the use of banned interrogation methods in Iraq.

Perhaps most damning of all, he found that the use of hooding and stress positions of suspected Iraqi insurgents had become standard operating procedure among the soldiers of 1 QLR. He said that a large number of soldiers assaulted Baha Mousa and the other detainees arrested with him, and that many others, including several officers, must have known what was happening and did nothing. He condemned those who stayed silent for the lack of moral courage to report abuse.

At the time he published his report Gage may not have known of the evidence that the former Lieutenant Nicholas Mercer, commander, legal, in the British forces in Iraq in 2003, gave to RTÉ's *The Torture Files* about seeing 40 prisoners, hooded, some of them in stress positions, with generators running outside an interrogation tent; so three of the prohibited five techniques were being used simultaneously. 'I knew instinctively what was going on,' he said. He took it up with the interrogation team, who said, 'We don't answer to you, we answer to London.' That brazen approach says much about the willingness and readiness to act as if the law was inapplicable to them.

In December 2012, Derek Keilloh, a former medical officer with the rank of Captain in 1 QLR, was found guilty of misconduct and struck off as being unfit to practise as a doctor.

The Medical Practitioners Tribunal Service, part of the General Medical Council, heard that he attempted to resuscitate Baha Mousa in the detention centre in Basra but failed to do so. He saw none of the 93 injuries on the victim's body, but noticed dried blood around his nose. He also returned two other detainees to the room where they had been repeatedly assaulted, and where further assaults were committed on them throughout the night. Even allowing for the highly charged, chaotic, tense and stressful atmosphere that prevailed at the time, Keilloh must have seen the numerous injuries on the body of the dead man; and he had a duty as a doctor to protect the two other detainees.

The panel ruled that Keilloh had lied about the injuries to the military police investigating the case; thereafter he gave false evidence to the subsequent court martial and to the Gage Inquiry, even when he was given the opportunity to disclose the truth; that he lied continuously and repeatedly; that he could not, and should not, practise as a doctor ever again.

In 2005 General Jackson, then the head of the British army, invited Brigadier Robert Aitken, director of army personnel strategy, to conduct a review of events in Iraq, focusing on the treatment of detainees. His report, some 36 pages long, was published in 2008.

The report pointed to inadequate training of British troops, saying that there had been scant mention of the detention of civilians. It said that most of the troops seemed to be unaware of a ban on the five techniques and that everyone in the army needed to be told that none of the techniques should ever be used, anywhere. The ban imposed by Edward Heath in 1972 was not included in the MOD guidelines on the treatment of prisoners, issued in 2001. The revised 2006 guidelines said that the five techniques must never be used as an aid to tactical questioning or interrogation.

The Aitken Report, which did not really explain fully the failings that led to the death of Baha Mousa, was condemned as a whitewash by lawyers acting for the Iraqi civilians, who said it was just another case of the army investigating the army. They rejected the suggestion that while a tiny number of soldiers behaved badly, the vast majority showed courage, loyalty and integrity. One lawyer said that there was the clearest evidence disclosed during a court martial that systematic abuse by UK soldiers in Iraq was rife.

Media reports say that the former chief of the general staff, General Sir Richard (now Lord) Dannatt, commenting on the Aitken Report, has suggested that many members of the armed forces lacked moral values when they joined up. There are many people in Northern Ireland who will totally agree with that proposition. The general said:

> I think you've got to look at the proportion of people who come into the armed forces from chaotic backgrounds. . . . Respect for others was almost the most important of all the values soldiers were taught. Without it, that's when you're into bullying or abusing Iraqi citizens.

He added, according to a report in *The Guardian*, 'soldiers are fiercely loyal – to their comrades, not necessarily to Queen and Country or to the truth'.[32]

The Army, the Truth and Northern Ireland

To the nationalist people of Northern Ireland, Lord Dannatt's words reflect much of what they have been maintaining for more than 30 years, namely that the truth is concealed by and on behalf of the state in Northern Ireland. Many found that the soldiers they encountered in the streets and in their homes throughout the province were poorly educated almost to the point of illiteracy; they were mostly from areas of high unemployment and unable to get any other job; they had no respect for anyone; and they were brutal and coarse to everyone they encountered. They had no regard for the truth and would systematically lie if they thought that lie would be believed. They seemed not to know the difference between right and wrong, had no moral standards, and some, especially in the Scottish regiments, would during house searches enthusiastically damage or destroy religious objects like holy pictures and statues.

Some might recall a man called Massie McAleer who gave a first-hand account to the journalist Anne Cadwallader about an incident involving British soldiers. He was the undertaker who arranged the funerals of Marion Teresa Bowen and her two brothers, Seamus and Michael McKenna, who died of multiple injuries following the explosion of a 70 lb bomb, probably placed next to the hot water cylinder inside the house they were renovating in Killyliss, near Dungannon in County Tyrone. A loyalist terrorist group calling itself the Protestant Action Force, a cover name for the UVF, planted the bomb. That was on or about 17 April 1975. Marion was expecting her first baby on 7 May 1975.

Following the post-mortem the pathologist asked the police to look for the unborn baby. She had been blown clear from her mother and her body was found among the rubble and the ruins of what had been a bedroom. It must have been a most shocking sight.

Massie McAleer told Anne Cadwallader that, later that day, when he was loading the baby's coffin into the hearse, British soldiers were standing around laughing. Some even kicked at the wheels of the hearse. He gave further evidence of that incident in 2011 to the Historical Enquiries Team (HET) of the Police Service of Northern Ireland (PSNI). They reported that his evidence 'makes uncomfortable reading'. Is the English language not rich enough to find words to describe more accurately that shocking and outrageous conduct on the part of uniformed soldiers tasked to keep the peace?

The HET report continues: 'What happened to the family whilst trying to come to terms with the loss of their loved ones cannot be excused.' It can, however, be explained. Those soldiers had no respect for the living or the dead, no concept of right or wrong, and no understanding of why they were in Northern Ireland any more than they understood what they were doing in Iraq. This was not an isolated incident. There were many others.

Postscript

In February 2015 a researcher from the Pat Finucane Centre uncovered some useful and perhaps shocking information in the National Archives in London regarding the interrogation of the 14 hooded men. Sara Duddy, on behalf of the Centre, informed the Irish attorney general Máire Whelan that there was documentary evidence showing that the interrogation sessions of the hooded men in Ballykelly had been monitored and taped. It was claimed that some 400 hours of tapes were made and then sent to the Joint Services

School of Intelligence (known officially as SSI) based at Templer Barracks in Ashford, Kent.

Two things are not known. First, was the Irish government aware of the existence of these tapes at the time the case went before the European Commission on Human Rights in 1976? It seems unlikely, because these tapes would constitute very strong and material evidence of the use of the five techniques and their effect on each individual. Second, are the tapes still in existence, or will they be briefly available, then, like some of the firearms used by members of the Parachute Regiment on Bloody Sunday in January 1972, either get lost or go unaccountably missing?

As Sara Duddy told Máire Whelan, not only would the tapes indicate the scope and extent of the torture of each individual, they would also help to identify the military personnel involved. For that reason my view is that the tapes will never see the light of day. These men were acting on orders. But whose? Are they likely to stay silent if placed in the dock in a criminal court and protect others on whose instructions they deprived suspects of food and water, subjected them to white noise, hooded them, deprived them of sleep, forced them to stand against a wall and assaulted them if they did not?

4 The Window Cleaners

HUGH RICHARD HANNA, known as Richard, aged 16 years and six months, was the only Protestant member of his local youth club in Belfast – everyone else was Catholic. When he told his father that he had been taunted by a group of Protestants about his club attendance, his parents kept him at home every night from Tuesday 14 September 1976 until the following Sunday, 19 September 1976.

The evening of the next day, Monday, he was allowed to go to the youth club only on condition that his friends from the club walked part of the way home with him. When he left the club premises he was followed and set upon by a group of youths. There were no taunts on this occasion, just extreme and vicious violence, in the course of which he suffered substantial head injuries that ultimately resulted in permanent loss of hearing; the retina of his left eye was totally and permanently detached; his nose was broken. He was unconscious when he was admitted to the Mater Infirmorum hospital.

Richard was kept in hospital for three weeks. About two weeks after his release from hospital he was arrested at about 10 a.m. on the morning of 29 October 1976. RUC officers took him to the North Queen Street police station in the city, where he was detained and questioned. He had been implicated in the sectarian murder of a 28-year-old Catholic accountant, Peter Gerard Johnson by Robert James Hindes, a schoolboy aged 14 years and 11 months. (There is now reason to believe that in fact Hindes meant to implicate Robert Hanna, who lived near Richard, and with whom Hindes was on friendly terms. The police simply arrested the wrong person.)

An informer had told the RUC that Hindes had been boasting at school that he had shot someone in Cooldarragh Park, an area just off the Upper Cavehill Road near the Cliftonville Golf Club in north Belfast. A search of

Hindes' home revealed property stolen from the house of the informer who had provided the police, perhaps maliciously, with his name.

A member of Peter Johnson's family told the police that Johnson's house had been broken into in March 1975 and jewellery and £500 in cash had been stolen. There had been another burglary in August 1976 when cigars were stolen and floorboards removed.

On 28 October 1976 RUC officers sought out Robert Hindes and invited him to accompany them to the Fortwilliam police station to assist in their enquiries. He was not under arrest and could have left the police station at any time, but it is not now possible to say whether he knew that. He was interviewed by a woman detective constable and he admitted to her that he had broken into the informer's home and stolen some property. Not only that; he also admitted breaking into Peter Johnson's house in late March or early April 1976 and stealing property.

Later that morning, Hindes was interviewed for about 40 minutes, during which time he admitted that he had an airgun, which he kept under his bed. He also admitted that he had broken into a house on Ballysillan Road, which adjoins Cooldarragh Park.

Later in the afternoon, at 2.35 p.m., Hindes was arrested by two police officers in connection with the murder of Peter Johnson on 17 September 1976. He was no longer helping the police with their enquiries; he was now in custody and no longer free to leave the premises.

Immediately after his arrest, Hindes was interviewed again, this time under caution. This meant that his replies to questions, and any statement he might make, could be used against him at any subsequent criminal trial in relation to that killing. He said he knew nothing about the murder and denied that he knew Cooldarragh Park, where the deceased's body had been found.

The officers told him they believed that he was in the house at number 45 Cooldarragh Park when Peter Johnson was murdered and that he had been in the house previously when a sum of money was stolen. (That was something he had earlier admitted to the woman police officer.) He then claimed that he had only acted as lookout. When he was asked who was with him, he said that he was not sure, but one was called 'Pee Wee' Hanna, and the other was about 19 years old and six feet tall.

Questioned about the shooting of Peter Johnson, he said he had gone to the house with 'Pee Wee' Hanna and another man later referred to as 'C'. He claimed that 'Pee Wee' Hanna was carrying a small revolver which he used to fire two shots at Peter Johnson after a bedroom door had been kicked in. Hindes claimed that he then ran out of the house by the front door.

The officers did not believe this account and told Robert that the deceased had not been shot with a small revolver. They showed him a weapon and urged him to tell the truth. That approach, some may regard, is inconsistent with the right to stay silent. (That right is not universally admired: according to Sir Peter Imbert, later commissioner of the London Metropolitan Police, 'the right to silence might have been designed by criminals for their special benefit and that of their professional advisers. It has done more to obscure the truth and facilitate crime than anything else this century'.[1])

Then Robert volunteered a different version of events. He now claimed that Richard Hanna had given him a .45 pistol which he kept in his bedroom overnight before going to Johnson's home. Three of them were involved: Richard was carrying a pistol; Robert carried the .45; 'C' was unarmed. The house was in darkness when they entered. Two went upstairs. Richard opened a door and fired a total of three shots at someone or something on the bed in the room. 'C' said 'Let's go' and they ran from the house. Robert claimed he handed the .45 back to Richard Hanna.

That interview was followed by another at 7.30 in the evening. On this occasion Robert Hindes was accompanied by his father. Robert made a voluntary statement under caution in the presence of his father, and both father and son signed the statement when it was completed, having been written down by a detective sergeant. In the statement Robert said he had gone to the house to steal and did not intend to kill anyone.

The next day the woman police officer interviewed Robert again. His father was not present. Robert had not been charged, even though there was sufficient evidence to charge him on the basis of his confession to the police. He told the officer that when he had broken into the house in Cooldarragh Park the householder was not at home. His role was to keep watch. 'Pee Wee' Hanna and 'C' were with him.

When he was charged with the murder of Peter Gerard Johnson he replied 'No'. This was at 1.02 p.m. on 31 October 1976. By this time the 14-year-old schoolboy had been in police custody for 75 hours. He had been interviewed no fewer than six times without access to legal advice or in the presence of an appropriate adult. This was a deliberate and cynical breach of the rules governing the treatment of a young person in police custody.

The two other individuals, one named, the other described – 16-year-old Hugh Richard Hanna and 'C', who was aged 20 at the time – were taken to North Queen Street station in Belfast on 29 October. As far as the RUC were concerned, Robert Hindes had implicated both of them in the brutal murder. Apart from what Robert had said, there was no evidence of any kind against either of them. Robert Hindes was a self-confessed thief who had given a number of conflicting explanations of his conduct and it might be thought that his credibility as a witness would be dubious. There was no independent supporting evidence confirming Hindes' account, no eye-witness evidence, and no forensic evidence linking them to the crime scene. The only hope of making progress against them was for the police to obtain an oral or written confession of murder.

I cannot ascertain whether the two were arrested or were assisting the police with their inquiries, but in any event Richard Hanna's first interview at noon on 29 October was under caution. He had been reminded of his right to stay silent, but he did not.

At first he denied that he was involved in the Johnson murder, but then he went on to say that he had met Robert Hindes with two friends. They agreed to break into some property that night and met at 7 p.m. in order to do so. Then they separated. When Robert Hindes and 'C' met up with him again Robert was carrying two guns in his pocket. The three of them went to a large semi-detached house in Cooldarragh Park. It was in darkness. Robert Hindes used a crowbar to force the front door open. He went upstairs. The other two followed. They went into a bedroom, where Robert took out a gun and handed it to Richard. They went to another bedroom, where a man was lying on the bed. Robert fired one shot at him. Richard said he could not do it, so 'C' took his gun from him and fired one shot before all three ran from the house.

A second, 40-minute interview followed at 2.35 p.m. and Richard repeated his confession. He also described 'C', who had been at the same school as him, but in a class above him. In fact, he was about three years younger than 'C' and would be more than a year below him at school. Should that have placed the police on notice that Richard's confession might not be accurate or truthful?

There was a third interview that day, at 8.50 p.m. It lasted for one hour and 25 minutes. The police wanted to know what had happened to the two guns after the murder. Richard Hanna said that 'C' took them, put them in a plastic bag and threw them away among some nettles in Kilcoole Park. When the police searched the park the next day, with Richard pointing out the nettles, they found nothing. Taken to Cooldarragh Park, however, Richard did point out number 45, the house where Johnson had been shot.

Back at North Queen Street station the police arranged for Hanna and Hindes to be interviewed together. They did not deny that they knew each other; they went further. Asked if they were members of the Ulster Defence Association (UDA) and if they were acting under orders to shoot Peter Gerard Johnson, Robert Hindes said they were members and it was a UDA job. Richard Hanna said this was correct and that 'C' had provided the guns used, and taken them away afterwards.

(The UDA is a loyalist paramilitary group claiming 40,000–50,000 members in late 1971, many of whom were unapologetically dedicated to sectarian murder. About 200 of them have been convicted of murder in Northern Ireland over the past 40 years. When involved in such crimes they used the cover name of the Ulster Freedom Fighters (UFF) to avoid embarrassing those members of the security forces who had in the past openly admitted membership of the UDA. It was perfectly legal for them to join that organisation, for it was not until 10 August 1992 that Sir Patrick Mayhew QC issued an order proscribing the UDA and declaring it an illegal organisation.)

At the joint interview Robert Hindes and Richard Hanna each admitted firing one shot at Johnson, thereby rather neatly tying up the case against each of them.

There had been a deliberate and cynical breach of the rules governing the interrogation of children and young persons in the case of Robert Hindes. Now it was Richard Hanna's turn. No appropriate adult was present during any of those early interviews at the police station, as required by the Administrative Directions appended to the Judges' Rules 1964. He had no access to legal advice. When he fainted, he did not receive any medical attention. He was not permitted to take the medication prescribed for him at the hospital following his injuries on 20 September. (His father subsequently told the CCRC that his wife, Richard's mother, went to the police station on the evening of 29 October 1976 and told the police that their son needed his medication. A police officer said he could not take it from them.)

No medical examination was carried out on him (or on Robert Hindes) while he was in custody, despite a requirement in RUC Standing Orders that this should be done. If it had been, there might have been reason to doubt whether Richard was fit to be detained and subjected to long interviews. It is clear that the wording of RUC Force Order 87/96 of 22 June 1976 is mandatory, and that those arrested under terrorist legislation, as Richard Hanna was, must be examined on arrival at, and departure from, a police station. No explanation for this failure was ever given.

James Hanna had followed his son to the police station following his arrest on the morning of 29 October 1976. He was not allowed to see him until late in the evening of 31 October. About 11.30 that evening he was allowed to be present while Richard dictated a short confession statement to a police officer, setting out some (but not all) of the details he had earlier admitted, in his father's absence, relating to the shooting dead of Peter Johnson. James Hanna might have been forgiven for wondering why his son had admitted to being out on the Thursday evening when his parents had kept him at home. Had they simply forgotten this? The Hannas knew full well that on the Thursday night of the murder their son was with them at home and could not therefore have been involved in the killing to which he had just confessed.

Following his statement, Richard was charged with Johnson's murder. It is an extraordinary fact that nowhere in that confession statement (later to be Exhibit 6 in the bundle of prosecution documents) is the day or the date of the murder of Peter Johnson ever mentioned. If that information had been readily apparent, would not James Hanna have appreciated its significance and realised that his son could not have committed the murder?

That left one outstanding member of the alleged group, namely 'C'. He was arrested on 2 November 1976. At the time, he was 20 years of age and thus the oldest of the gang of three. He was interviewed over three days. (I can find no evidence of any interview when he previously attended the police station, apparently not under arrest.) At first, he denied all knowledge of the murder of Peter Johnson. He tried to account for his movements on the night of the killing. He admitted that he knew both Richard and Robert, for they had all attended the same school.

At the eighth interview on the second day of his detention, sometime between 3 p.m. and 5.20 p.m., he began to crack. He said that two men ordered him to do a job because of the trouble he and his family had caused the UDA. He was told to pick up two guns and take them to a club, where he would be given further instructions. Later, he met the two boys and walked with them to a house in Cooldarragh Park. They entered the house by forcing the front door and went upstairs. There they shot Johnson, who was in bed.

He could not, however, describe the house in Cooldarragh Park or give any information about it. The police asked him if he was telling the truth and he replied that he was not; he had only said all this to get out of the police station. During all further interviews he continued to maintain his innocence, and on the third day he was released without charge.

On 27 April 1977 Richard and Robert were sent for trial. Richard's solicitor served notice of an alibi, as he was legally bound to do. It simply said, 'He was in the house at the time.' On any view this is ambiguous – which house was he claiming he was in?

I cannot see from the evidence whether his parents were named in the alibi notice as being able to confirm his alibi. They should have been so named, assuming they were willing to give evidence on behalf of his defence, as they certainly would have been prepared to do.

On 22 June 1977 Richard Hanna and Robert Hindes appeared before the Belfast City Commission. Both entered pleas of guilty to murder and the possession of firearms and ammunition with intent to endanger life. Because of their ages they were each sentenced to be detained at the secretary of state's pleasure on the first charge and seven years' detention on the second. There was no appeal either against conviction or sentence by Richard, by then aged 17, or by Robert, 15. Both had been represented by senior and junior counsel who must have considered that their confessions were sufficient to prove their guilt. They were apparently advised by counsel that there was little point in one accused pleading guilty and the other pleading not guilty.

Peter Johnson, the murder victim, probably did not have a single enemy in the world. He was, however, a Catholic living in north Belfast, which, to a group of sadistic UDA killers, was enough reason to kill him.

Peter had spent the evening of Thursday 16 September 1976 socialising with his friend Bernard Joseph Cole in Belfast city centre. The pair had separated on the Cavehill Road, near Peter's home, just after midnight. Apart from the killers, Bernard was the last person to see Peter alive.

The body was discovered by Peter's girlfriend, Mary Margaret O'Sullivan, at about 7.15 p.m. the next day. She had heard and seen nothing of him at any time throughout that Friday and, fearing the worst, went to his house. She noticed that the front door was open, went upstairs and, to her horror, saw Peter lying dead in the bedroom. He had been badly beaten and shot twice, once in the face and once in the head. A doctor called to the scene, Dr John McClure, considered that Peter had been dead for at least 12 hours.

According to James Hanna, Richard's mother, who was a Catholic, simply lost the will to live when her son in whose innocence she passionately believed was sent into custody. She died while he was serving his sentence. After nine years inside, Richard Hanna and Robert Hindes were released on licence in November 1983.

While he was in prison, members of the UDA frequently told Richard that they knew he was innocent because they knew the identity of the man who had fired the fatal shots. He was one of their own. That encouraged Richard and his father to begin a campaign to prove that he should not have been convicted of a crime in which he had no hand or part.

Twelve years later, in April 1997, Richard submitted an application to the CCRC, which had been set up by the Criminal Appeal Act 1995 to investigate and process allegations of miscarriages of justice. He sought an inquiry into his case and asked that it be referred to the Court of Appeal in Northern Ireland.

The test that the commission must apply in deciding whether to refer a case is set out in Section 13 of the 1995 Act. It must not refer a case unless it considers that there is a real possibility that a verdict would not be upheld if the reference to the appeal court were to be made. In the case of a conviction, verdict or finding, the real possibility must be judged, save in exceptional circumstances, on the strength of an argument or evidence not raised at trial or on appeal or application for leave to appeal.

Seven months later, in October 1997, since there had been a plea of guilty in this case, and no appeal or application for leave to appeal, and no exceptional circumstances, the commission declined to entertain Richard Hanna's application. Richard was devastated by this decision. His father, however, would not give up. He was convinced, as his deceased wife had been, that his son was innocent. He persuaded the Northern Ireland Office to ask the RUC to carry out a fresh investigation into the murder of Peter Johnson.

The officer appointed to do so was Samuel Kincaid, later to become assistant chief constable, crime. He was a brilliant investigating officer and his far-reaching inquiry was thorough, impartial and detailed enough to persuade the CCRC to refer the case to the Court of Appeal in Belfast. However, on the very day that the case was listed for mention in that Court, in March 2004, Richard Hanna was found dead by his partner at their home in Northamptonshire.

On Friday 23 April 2004 the Lord Chief Justice of Northern Ireland, Lord Kerr, announced that his appeal (together with that of Robert Hindes) could proceed in the name of his next of kin, his father, James Hanna.

In October 2004 counsel for the DPP in Belfast informed the appeal court that the Crown would not seek to uphold the convictions. On Wednesday 19 January 2004, Lord Justice Campbell, sitting with Lord Justice Sheil and Mr Justice Coglin, said that the Court, after considering the papers and hearing the submissions of counsel, would allow the appeal and would give its reasons at a later date.

A report for the appeal court from an educational psychologist, based on an examination carried out on Robert Hindes on 5 January 2005, placed him intellectually in the 'low average' category with a verbal IQ of 83. That placed him at the top of the bottom 13 per cent of the population.

A consultant psychologist who had examined Richard Hanna on 25 May 2002 had concluded that he was abnormally suggestible and likely to change his answers to questions when placed under pressure to do so. This made him potentially vulnerable, especially in the light of his injuries and recent discharge from hospital, as well as his age at the time he was interviewed and confessed to murder. Why did his defence team not obtain such evidence prior to his appearance in court in June 1977, especially in the light of his fragile state of health, and the fact that he had been in police custody for some 51 hours before he confessed?

The appeal court was told that, although both Robert and Richard claimed while in custody to be members of the UDA, police inquiries showed that this was not so. After they were both charged, information was given to the RUC to suggest they were not involved in the UDA in any way. This information was not disclosed to the defence before the date fixed for their trial. Nor were the defence told that soldiers in an army observation post at Dunmore Park, some 880 yards southwest of Cooldarragh Park, had recorded hearing two gunshots from that direction at 3.02 a.m. on Friday 17 September 1976. This was much later than the times the two appellants claimed to have entered Peter Johnson's house.

Most significant of all, in the view of Assistant Chief Constable Kincaid, the pathological evidence showed that Johnson had been beaten about the face with a blunt instrument, causing severe injuries. There were two lacerations to the right forehead with fractures causing flattening of the underlying skull, which the doctor thought indicated that considerable force was used. The medical examination showed that his blood-congested lungs continued to function for about 30 minutes until he was fatally shot. Neither Robert nor Richard ever admitted being in the house for that length of time and mentioned not a single word about the assault. Samuel Kincaid stressed in his scrutiny of the evidence that the pathologist's report was compiled after the confessions to murder. The RUC officers who obtained that confession evidence would therefore not have known at the time they interviewed Hanna and Hines that Johnson had continued to breathe for half an hour before he was shot.

The court allowed the appeals and quashed the convictions. Lord Justice Campbell ruled that the test to be applied was whether the court considered the conviction unsafe. It was accepted that the only evidence against Richard and Robert was their admissions to the police. Quoting a previous case as authority, he said that if, in a case where the only evidence against a defendant was his oral confession which he later retracted, it appeared that such confession was obtained in breach of the rules prevailing at the time, and in circumstances which denied the defendant important safeguards later thought necessary to avoid the risk of a miscarriage of justice, there would be at least prima facie grounds for doubting the safety of the conviction – a very different thing from concluding that a defendant was necessarily innocent.

Lord Justice Campbell also noted that, in addition to Richard Hanna's complaints about not being allowed access to a lawyer or adult, the refusal of medication and not being given access to a doctor when he fainted during interrogation, he also alleged that he was abused both physically and psychologically during questioning. In addition, he claimed that he had been wrongly identified to the police; that his legal representation was inadequate; and that he was pressurised into pleading guilty. When the police inquiry checked his claim that Robert Hindes was referring to another person with whom he associated, they found that there was such a person living close to Richard who may have kept company with Robert Hindes. When he was approached about the appeal, Hindes admitted he had been lying when he implicated Richard Hanna. Robert then alleged that his confession was extracted from him after he was physically and psychologically ill-treated, that he was slapped, and that the words of his confession statement were those of the police and not his own.

There was no word of regret or apology from anyone for the failings in the criminal justice system that blighted the lives of two young men. Richard Hanna never knew that his conviction had been quashed. The Cambridge coroner recorded that his death had been accidental. His father, James, left Northern Ireland and began a new life in Canada.

The RUC always knew that Peter Johnson was murdered by members of the UDA. I suspect that they also knew that his death was part of an ongoing murder campaign against innocent Catholics living in a small area of north Belfast and that they now know the identity of the killer. Of course, knowledge is one thing; evidence and proof beyond reasonable doubt are quite another.

Three other murders committed in the same area at around this time seem to have a common origin and may be the work of the same killer or group of killers.

The first murder in this obscene campaign was committed on 22 January 1976. The victim was Niall O'Neill, a 26-year-old off-licence manager, who lived in Thirlmere Gardens, an area adjacent to a primary school and just across the Cavehill Road from 45 Cooldarragh Park, where Peter Johnson was shot dead. The killer climbed through a window some 15 feet above the ground at about 4 a.m., entered a bedroom and shot O'Neill six times at point-blank range. His body was discovered by his brother, a Catholic priest, who was asleep in the house at the time of the murder and who had heard nothing.

A week later, there was another killing. This time the victim was Joseph McAlinden, a married man aged 40, with four children. He managed a city-centre pub owned by his father. The victim and his young family lived on the Upper Cavehill Road, a short distance from the scene of the first killing on 22 January. A gunman used a ladder to climb in through a bedroom window. Hearing a noise, Joseph McAlinden got out of bed to investigate. He was shot three times at point-blank range. His wife actually saw the gun being fired at her husband. She comforted him as he lay dying on the floor.

The third murder took place on 27 May 1976 at about 3 a.m. The victim was Gerard Masterson, aged 34, who was married with one child. The family lived at Allworthy Avenue, near Belfast Royal Academy, very near the junction of the Cavehill Road and the Antrim Road, just a few hundred yards from the other murder scenes. On this occasion the killer forced an entry through the front door, ran upstairs and fired several times at the victim. Gerard Masterson died shortly afterwards.

The fourth killing was the murder of Peter Johnson on the night of 16–17 September. If the shots heard by the army were those that killed him, that murder took place at 3.02 a.m. Entry into the house was, as in the previous case, through the front door.

As well as the timing of these events, their geographical closeness and the religious persuasion of the victims, in all four cases the telephone lines to the house had been severed, making a call for help impossible. These were planned sectarian assassinations of carefully chosen victims in an area where the killer seemed able to access premises without fear of meeting either the army or the police.

Three weeks after Peter Johnson's murder came the final killing, perhaps the most horrific of all. There were two victims, Catherine O'Connor, a widow aged 68, and her son-in-law, Francis Thomas Nolan, aged 34. They were chosen, like the others, simply because they were Catholics. In any normal society, where policing is for the public good, officers would be patrolling these killing fields with a view to preventing another atrocity. Not so in Belfast, or any other area of Northern Ireland, for this was no ordinary society.

Just before 2 a.m. on Wednesday 6 October 1976, two men broke into the family home of Catherine O'Connor and her family in Victoria Gardens, just off the Cavehill Road. It runs almost parallel with Thirlmere Gardens, a short walking distance away, where Niall O'Neill died.

Mrs O'Connor was apparently woken by the sound of someone entering the house through a kitchen window. She screamed, and the intruder stabbed her at least 38 times. She was found by her daughter (whose children, aged four and two, were also in the house at the time), clutching her rosary beads in her bloodstained hands. Francis Nolan attempted to defend his mother-in-law, but was shot three times at point blank range. He died almost immediately.

One of the men believed to be involved in all these killings is a former burglar known as 'the window cleaner' because he and his accomplices frequently used ladders stolen from tradesmen in Belfast to gain entry into premises through a window in the early hours of the morning. In total this man and his fellow murderers are believed to be responsible for 25 sectarian murders of innocent Catholics in the city of Belfast. They have never been brought to justice.

A BBC Northern Ireland *Spotlight* programme, *A Legacy of Murder*, broadcast in October 2005, named the person the programme makers believed to be directly linked to the murder of Peter Johnson. He is Thomas Alfred McCreery, born on 1 February 1945. He was thought to have been at the relevant time a commander in the UDA.

The RUC considered that the killing was the work of a ruthless loyalist gang who they suspected were operating as the Window Cleaners in the same area of north Belfast. Two days after Johnson's murder they arrested two men, described in a secret RUC report as 'C' (who was in the UDA) and McCreery. He was named in the television programme as the leader of the Window Cleaners, but he was never questioned about the murder of Peter Johnson. Why was this? He was arrested many times, but never convicted of any terrorist offence. Did he enjoy some kind of special protection or immunity from prosecution? If so, who provided that protection or immunity? Was it the state?

A fellow loyalist, whose identity was disguised, told the programme that McCreery was 'a bit of a maverick'. He openly boasted about his activities in clubs in the Ballysillen and Ardoyne areas of the city. The anonymous loyalist confirmed that McCreery was the leader of the Window Cleaners gang and that everybody in the area knew it. Another loyalist, George Adams, who served time in prison with Richard Hanna, told Richard that he and many others knew that Richard did not murder Johnson, and wondered why he was in prison for a crime he did not commit.

The Truth about Thomas McCreery?

As time went on in the killing fields of north Belfast, Thomas McCreery graduated into another area which was more lucrative but equally dangerous; drug running, both sourcing and supplying. He was also not averse to racketeering and running protection rackets. Other loyalists began to regard him with suspicion. On 17 January 1991 he was shot and seriously wounded as he sat in a car outside the Heather Street Social Club, off the Shankill Road. A woman who was in the car with him, a Mrs McEvoy, was also shot and injured. He had gone to the club to talk to the senior ranks of the UDA to see if they could come to an arrangement on drug dealing in that area of North Belfast. It was apparently thought there might be an understanding about payment of some of the proceeds and profits being paid over to the UDA.

The gunman who shot him was a fellow loyalist, Ken Barrett, one of the UDA's most prolific killers. He pleaded guilty in September 2004 to no fewer than 12 terrorist charges, including the murder of the Belfast solicitor Pat Finucane, wounding his wife with intent to do her grievous bodily harm, wounding Mrs McEvoy and attempting to murder Thomas McCreery. On 21 October 2005 Thomas McCreery issued a statement through a Belfast solicitor, Barra McGrory (now the director of the Public Prosecution Service in Northern Ireland):

> I wish it to be known that I had no act or part in the murder of Peter Johnson as alleged by the BBC in their *Spotlight* programme on October 18. Furthermore, the allegation that I was involved with a murder squad known as the 'window cleaners' is based on nothing more than a patchwork of lies, speculation, rumour and innuendo and I absolutely refute that.

The BBC stood by the programme. They seemed very confident in the truth of their allegations. They had invited Mr McCreery to take part in the programme but he had declined to do so. Some may find that unsurprising.

Thomas McCreery, according to the journalist David McKittrick's report in the *Independent*, was a drug dealer and middle man who recruited Protestant hitmen. He had been well known in the Belfast loyalist underworld since the early 1970s.[2]

It is known that he left Belfast hurriedly shortly after being shot in 1991, no doubt fearing another attempt on his life. He headed for Margate in Kent. In spite of his injuries he clearly had no intention of reforming or retiring. He had a long history of service in the UDA, and rather than closing the book he opened a new chapter of it.

After the shooting in 1991 the UDA issued a statement that 'we wish to make it clear that no matter what happens, he is still under sentence of death'. As far as is known McCreery has not returned to any part of Northern Ireland since January 1991.

The BBC programme contained another startling revelation about Thomas McCreery. It claimed that court documents show that he was paid £35,000 to kill a top Metropolitan Police informer and that he arranged for two hitmen from Northern Ireland to carry out the killing.

The drug-dealing informer, who was shot dead outside his home in Belvedere, Kent, on Sunday 26 April 1991 was David Norris, a married man aged 49. As he got out of his car two men on a motorcycle approached him. The pillion passenger was carrying a gun. It was a type of hit typical during the Troubles. Norris ran, but fell, seriously wounded and pleading for his life. The gunman fired several more shots from a .25 semi-automatic pistol from point-blank range, killing him.

Four men were charged with conspiracy to kill David Norris. They were John Green, Terence McCrory, Patrick Doherty and George McMahon. According to prosecuting counsel at the Old Bailey in April 1993 police enquiries disclosed that during 1990 a number of south London dealers were supplying drugs, mainly cannabis, to Protestant dealers in Northern Ireland. Stuart Warne, the main link between the two groups, used the Red Star parcel delivery service to send the drugs to Belfast.

When Thomas McCreery left Belfast in 1991, it was alleged that he had moved to Kent with a man called Steven Pollock. They were later joined by a third man from Northern Ireland, Renwick Dennison, aged 26. The three would set up drug deals through Stuart Warne. He was supplied with the drugs, so he claimed, by two men from south London, Patrick Doherty, aged 35, and George McMahon, aged 46.

Police investigations into the drug running led to the arrest of Warne and Dennison. They admitted their involvement in supplying drugs to dealers in Northern Ireland, but they had more sensational allegations to make, which led to them being sent to prison for life for conspiracy to murder and drugs offences, offences to which they had pleaded guilty.

Prosecuting counsel told the court that one of the men in the dock, Patrick Doherty, told Stuart Warne he was prepared to pay £35,000 to have Norris killed because he had 'grassed up a number of firms', including telling the police about a warehouse containing drugs in Greenwich, south London. The same man said he would pay £20,000 in cash for the killing of another man, John Dale, who ran a drinking club in East London, and who apparently was in the habit of ripping people off in drug deals.

Counsel alleged that two men, Terence McCrory, aged 30, from Belfast, and John Green, aged 32, from Falkirk in Scotland, were the hitmen who shot Norris, a claim they both denied. Their efforts to kill John Dale failed and they both travelled to Belfast. In their absence Renwick Dennison traced John Dale, acquired a sawn-off single-barrelled shotgun and shot him in the head outside his home. By some miracle, he survived.

According to the prosecution it was Thomas McCreery and Steven Pollock who had organised the murder squad. They were not in court, said counsel; they were on the run. Prosecuting counsel told the jury, 'McCreery struck Warne as being professional. He indicated that the men could not use their own equipment [for the killings] because it would look like it was an Irish job.' Their additional reward for arranging the contract to kill was the promise of access to large quantities of cheap cannabis, which they would send to Belfast by Red Star.

On 24 May 1993 Judge Lawrence Verney, the Recorder of London, stopped the trial at the close of the case for the prosecution. He ruled that the evidence of Stuart Warne and Renwick Dennison could not be relied upon and he directed the jury to acquit the four men in the dock. This is not surprising given that the prosecution case rested on the credibility of two men imprisoned for life for drug offences and conspiracy to murder. Since they were accomplices of those in the dock, their evidence would require additional corroboration; they could not corroborate each other. What is surprising is that the prosecution considered that there was a realistic prospect of conviction in a case relying on such flawed witnesses.

It is assumed that when Terence McCrory and John Green left the dock, they returned to Belfast.

The most astonishing fact about the entire case is to be found in the book by two brilliant investigative journalists, Michael Gillard and Laurie Flynn, published in 2004 and republished in 2012. Its title is *Untouchables: Dirty Cops, Bent Justice and Racism in Scotland Yard.* They write:

The police never managed to arrest McCreery and Pollock. Intriguingly, Detective Sergeant Alec Leighton remembers being told officially that after surviving the punishment shooting, UDA insider McCreery had been 'relocated' to Kent by the British authorities. If this is correct then McCreery was collaborating with one of the key state agencies running the dirty war in Northern Ireland, which may explain why he was never caught. 'You don't relocate criminals unless they are witnesses (which McCreery wasn't) or informants' Leighton explained.

Was this yet another case of a prolific killer at large in Belfast, bringing terror and mayhem to innocent Catholic residents in mixed areas, who was allowed immunity from prosecution by the security forces because of his usefulness as an informant?

It is known that in May 1997 Thomas McCreery was arrested in Alicante in Spain in connection with a £20 million drug-dealing operation. His good luck continued; at his trial he was acquitted. He remained in his luxury villa in southern Spain and in spite of the extradition arrangements that exist between Spain and the UK, he has not been returned to either Northern Ireland or England, even though, as the BBC programme notes, there is a fresh murder inquiry into the death of Peter Johnson, and he must still be one of the suspects.

It is my view that Thomas McCreery will never stand trial for that or any other criminal offence committed in Northern Ireland or in England. He knows too much and might embarrass those who seek to bring him to justice if ever he has to speak up in his own defence. The price of his silence is the obstruction of justice.

5   The Troubles and the Truth

BETWEEN 1922 AND 1968 the British politicians who were ultimately responsible for the governance of Northern Ireland knew little and cared less about the province. The two main Westminster parties, Labour and Tory, hoped that the problems that escalated on the streets of Belfast and Derry in 1968, and which they could barely identify, let alone solve, would quickly disappear and the province could be left to fend for itself. There is anecdotal evidence that one government minister in London said that as long as there were fewer deaths from political violence in the province than from road traffic accidents, these would be acceptable to the government of the day.

For 25 years, from 1973 to 1997, the Provisional IRA carried out a bombing campaign in England in furtherance of what it termed 'the armed struggle', in which it killed 115 people and grievously injured almost 2,500. The Provisional IRA's self-proclaimed purpose was threefold: first, to end what it described as Britain's unlawful occupation of six countries of the province of Ulster; second, to end the one-party unionist state there; and third, and perhaps most fundamental, to reunify the island of Ireland. The IRA's political wing Sinn Féin described that purpose not as an aspiration but as 'a constitutional imperative'. That organisation at that time had neither the sympathy nor the support of the majority of the people on the island of Ireland.

Northern Ireland has always been a sectarian state. Its architect, Sir Basil Brooke, designed it as a one-party entity that discriminated against the minority nationalist, mainly Catholic, community. The majority unionist community used its political power to suppress nationalist aspirations and human rights. In the words of Lord Trimble, former First Minister of Northern Ireland and former leader of the Ulster Unionist Party, who jointly won the

91

Nobel Peace Prize with his political opponent John Hume, the leader of the SDLP, Northern Ireland was a 'cold house for Catholics'.

There was an opportunity to settle the fundamental disputes between the two communities – the Protestant, loyalist majority and the Catholic, republican minority – at Sunningdale in 1973, but Britain showed that it did not understand the source of the conflict by inducing the constitutional loyalist party, the Ulster Unionists, led by Brian Faulkner, to form a power-sharing assembly with the constitutional nationalist party, the SDLP, led by Gerry Fitt. That assembly was brought down by the Ulster Workers' Council, which called a general work stoppage on 15 May 1974 that brought the province to a standstill. There were power cuts and factory closures. The stoppage was highly effective. It was a political strike, not an industrial one. If only the Catholic section of the workforce had been called out on strike, the action would have been completely ineffective: the giant shipbuilders Harland and Wolffe, based in Belfast, around this time employed about 9,000 loyalists and 400 nationalists – most of the latter in menial jobs.

It took years for the politicians to discover that they should have been dealing with Ian Paisley and his Democratic Unionist Party (DUP) on the one hand, and Gerry Adams, the IRA and its political wing Sinn Féin, on the other. They were the power brokers, without whose support there was no prospect of peace. As evidence of British politicians' abysmal ignorance about Northern Ireland, one need look no further than one Conservative and Unionist politician in Margaret Thatcher's government who has now returned to the political obscurity from which he should never have emerged. He said that people who used violence against Catholics were playing into the hands of the terrorists. In other words, the loyalists who killed Catholics were not terrorists; only republican/nationalist killers could be properly so described. I think that view was shared by others in his party.

The main victims of loyalist killings were ordinary members of the Catholic community. It is thought that 121 Catholics died as a result of sectarian assassination in 1975 alone; an average of more than two murders every week.

To members of the majority community, patriotism and duty to the Crown were paramount. The obligation to defend the Crown against the minority community, which was in essence not loyalist and therefore must be disloyal, was equally paramount. The manifestation of their patriotism was their pride in the British army and their police service, the RUC, together with the part-time reservist police, the B Specials.

The RUC was formed in 1922 to replace the Royal Irish Constabulary, the RIC in the North. Their establishment strength of officers was fixed at 3,000. By the time of the 1963 Constabulary Act that number was unchanged, even though the workload of each officer had increased substantially. The RUC was always a paramilitary-style force, and its uniformed officers were always armed. The concept of 'policing by consent' was unknown in Northern Ireland. The RUC was never accepted by the Catholic/nationalist/ republican element of the divided community.

The Criminal Investigation Department of the RUC was underfunded and overstretched during the Troubles, and it seemed incapable of even the simplest investigation into 'ordinary' crime. Even when one of the RUC's own officers, PC Trevor Buchanan, was murdered in Coleraine, County Derry in May 1991, the crime was recorded as suicide. It was not until the murderer, a dentist called Colin Howell, confessed in January 2009 to murdering Buchanan, whose wife Hazel was Howell's mistress, and Lesley Howell, his own wife, that the terrible truth came to light.

Colin Howell and Hazel Buchanan, a Sunday school teacher, conspired together to murder his wife and her husband by carbon monoxide poisoning. Both victims were overcome by gas fumes in their own homes. When they became at least disabled, and very probably dead, Colin Howell put the bodies in the boot of his car. He then drove four miles to a row of cottages at Castlerock and parked the car in a garage of one of the cottages that had belonged to his wife's deceased father. He left Lesley's body in the boot of the vehicle, put Trevor's body in the driver's seat, attached a tube to the exhaust pipe and turned on the engine.

When the bodies were found, should not alarm bells have rung when Lesley Howell's body was found in the boot? Surely a couple involved in a suicide pact would want to die side by side?

Even the most basic police inquiry would have tested the soles of Lesley's trainers to see if there were traces of material from the garage floor, which would establish whether she got into the boot of the car in the garage where her body was found. Every scene-of-crime officer knows that every contact leaves a trace. Since she was disabled or possibly dead at the time the vehicle reached the garage, she never stood on that garage floor, so there could have been no forensic link between the soles of her trainers and the floor. That would have spoken volumes to a competent and conscientious police officer. If Lesley Howell did not get into the boot of the car in the garage, where did she do so?

As a result of this chronic failure by the RUC, Colin Howell and Hazel Buchanan (who married David Stewart, a former RUC senior officer, after she broke up with Howell) might have got away with a double murder. After Howell confessed to the killings, he entered a plea of guilty and was sent to prison for life. Buchanan denied agreeing to kill her husband and her lover's wife. Colin Howell gave evidence for the prosecution against her, but she exercised her right to stay silent. The jury convicted her and the judge imposed the only sentence allowed by law: life imprisonment. He recommended that she should not be considered eligible for parole for 18 years. Her husband and children have stood by her.

The legal system in Northern Ireland was not detached and impartial, but directly reflected the sectarian politics of a very confused society. The law was indifferent (as were some of the lawyers) to blatant discrimination in housing, employment and education. The right to vote was not universal. Local government boundaries, especially in places like the city of Derry, were manipulated so that in areas were loyalists were in a minority, they could ensure the election of their candidates in local and central government elections.

The Protestant government for a Protestant people in Stormont, so cheerfully boasted about by the prime minister, Sir James Craig, in April 1934, could be relied on to pass repressive legislation to silence the nationalist minority who refused to accept the undemocratic partition of the island of Ireland.

The Northern Ireland Civil Authorities (Special Powers) Act 1922 was greatly admired by the sectarian government of the Republic of South Africa that was deeply devoted to the practice of apartheid. The Act allowed internment without charge or trial and arbitrary arrest without warrant; prisoners could be flogged or subjected to the death penalty for certain firearms or explosive offences; coroners' inquests could be dispensed with; and public meetings could be forbidden by ministerial order. The 'catch-all' provision in section 2 (4) said: 'If any person does any act of such a nature as to be calculated to be prejudicial to the preservation of the peace or the maintenance of order in Northern Ireland and not specifically provided for in the regulations, he shall be deemed to be guilty of an offence against the regulations.' That clearly gave the government of the day the power to arrest and charge anyone they wanted to, for any reason, in the interests of maintaining law and their order. When John Vorster, the South African minister for justice, introduced a new Coercion Bill, he said he would be willing to exchange all the legislation of that sort for one clause of the Northern Ireland Special Powers Act. That Act was renewed in Stormont every year until 1933, when it was made permanent.

The attitude of the UK parliament in London was one of total indifference. The Saville Report on the Bloody Sunday shootings notes that after the partition of Ireland in 1922 the new state of Northern Ireland continued to send MPs to London – all, without exception, unionists who supported the Conservative and Unionist government when they were in power – as well as electing their own MPs to the parliament in Stormont.[1] 'However a Parliamentary convention developed at Westminster preventing discussion there of issues considered by the Speaker to be within the proper authority of the Stormont Parliament and government. The convention, which evolved from a series of rulings by successive Speakers, lasted until the late 1960s.' The journalist Peter Taylor wrote that as a result, between 1922 and 1968 'the time spent on Northern Ireland matters at Westminster averaged less than two hours a year'.[2]

Little wonder, then, that British governments of all political hues failed to comprehend that there were two concurrent campaigns of violence in Northern Ireland: on one side the republican (IRA and Irish National Liberation Army (INLA)) forces against the British state and British army; on the other the loyalist paramilitaries (and those in MI5, MI6 and the British army who aided and abetted them) against the Catholic population of the six counties that make up Northern Ireland.

Following the failure of the IRA campaign between 1956 and 1962, which the nationalist people of the North did not support or approve of, it appeared that some progress towards reconciliation between the two communities could be made, especially when Terence O'Neill became prime minister in 1963. He said that Ulster was at the crossroads and urged the politics of peace to avoid violence and the bloodshed of innocent men women and children on both sides of the sectarian divide. When he and Seán Lemass, the driving force behind the economic revival in the Irish Republic, met at Stormont on 14 January 1965, there was great hope of forgetting the past and reshaping the future. One man stood in their way: Ian Paisley, the self-styled Moderator of the Free Presbyterian Church. He had founded that Church after disagreement with the mainstream Presbyterian Church in Belfast, who apparently found his views extreme and dangerous. With others of like mind he formed the Protestant Unionist Party (PUP), preaching the politics of hate and division and claiming the supremacy of the loyalists of Northern Ireland over everyone else, but mostly over the Catholic minority. He was greatly helped by a pliant media that could be relied upon not to let the truth get in the way of a good story. His church in the Ravenhill Road attracted great publicity in the newspapers when, according to the press, 'a member of the IRA' fired shots at it. No one was injured, but it was a frightening experience. A subsequent police inquiry discovered the identity of the gunman: he turned out to be one of Paisley's closest associates who had nothing to do with the IRA.

Senior British politicians got their first insight into the mindset of Ian Paisley after a member of the RUC, Constable Gordon Harron, was shot dead on 21 October 1972. He and a colleague from the road traffic department had stopped a car containing four men. The killer, a member of the UDA, was the last to emerge from the vehicle. He fired 13 shots at Harron, who died four days later. At that time the death penalty was in force in Northern Ireland for the capital murder of soldiers and police officers. The then secretary of state for Northern Ireland, William Whitelaw, records in his memoirs that the Royal Prerogative of Mercy was exercised in the province not by the Queen, as it is in the remainder of the UK, but by the secretary of state. 'Immediately Ian Paisley, the militant Protestant, demanded a reprieve for this "good Protestant" and threatened dire consequences if I did not oblige.' A reprieve was granted.[3] Would Ian Paisley have made the same representation in the same threatening manner if the killer of a servant of the Crown had been a Catholic? Was Paisley so powerful that he could confront the state and win? William Whitelaw tried to justify his decision to grant a reprieve: 'Fortunately, as it turned out in the violent turbulence of the time, there was a strong case for a reprieve, which I duly gave.' I find this explanation devoid of any meaning. Only 17 years previously, in July 1955, the British home secretary, Gwylim Lloyd George, had refused to grant a reprieve to Ruth Ellis, the mother of two young children, who had been convicted of the murder of her lover David Blakely. Lloyd George, a son of former prime minister David Lloyd George, told the barrister and writer Fenton Bresler, 'we cannot have people shooting off firearms in the street; this was a public thoroughfare where Ruth Ellis stalked and shot her quarry. And remember that she did not only kill David Blakely; she injured a passer-by. As long as I was Home Secretary I was determined to ensure that people could use the streets without fear of bullet.'[4] The passer-by was Gladys Yule, who was shot in the hand when the last bullet fired by Ruth Ellis ricocheted off the pavement near the body of the victim.

Does it not seem extraordinary that a woman should hang in London because she killed one person and slightly injured another, while in another part of the UK, the killer of a police officer escaped execution, not on merit, but through political interference?

One RUC officer was murdered in 1969, two in 1971, 11 in 1971 and

16 (including Constable Harron) in 1972. A Freedom of Information request to the RUC in 2012 indicates that no fewer than 300 officers were murdered during the Troubles. Would all the 225 police officers who followed Constable Harron to an early grave have been brutally murdered if his killer had gone to the gallows?

Ian Paisley threatened not only William Whitelaw but the whole political edifice in Northern Ireland. Merlyn Rees, the Northern Ireland secretary in Harold Wilson's Labour government, accused him of meeting representatives of organisations that sought to bring down the system of government. He was further accused of being a democrat in London and a demagogue in Belfast, associating with people who were backed by armed paramilitary groups.

Paisley specialised in slogans, which he either invented or adopted: 'No surrender'; 'O'Neill must go' (O'Neill did go, forced out of office on 1 May 1969 by those who feared any sign of political advance for the nationalists); 'No Pope here'. One wonders how someone who claimed to be a follower of the founder of Christianity could have been responsible for the increase of bigotry, loathing, violence and hatred that consumed Northern Ireland for so many years.

The Northern Ireland Civil Rights Association (NICRA) was formed in 1967. Its founders were greatly influenced by the civil rights movement, led by Martin Luther King, in the USA. NICRA's demands were simple: an end to the rigged electoral system; an end to discrimination against two fifths of the population; the reform of the sectarian RUC; and the abolition of the B Special Constabulary.

In August 1968 the first civil rights marches took place. They were declared illegal. Counter-demonstrations, often organised by Ian Paisley, were gently policed by the RUC. When faced with the civil rights marchers the loyalists were delicately shepherded away, leaving the RUC to wade into the marchers with wooden batons, which they used with undisguised glee and unmitigated violence. Some of this was witnessed and recorded by the media on 5 October 1968. Even the politicians in Westminster could scarcely believe what they were seeing on the television news.

The response of the Stormont government was instant and dispropor-tionate. The civil rights movement was regarded as a direct threat to the legitimacy and very existence of the state of Northern Ireland. The government failed to see that refusing even to contemplate reform was a foreseeable but unintended act of encouragement to resort to the use of violence to achieve the civil rights movement's objectives of parity of treatment and esteem. The use of force to break up marches, while not protecting the marchers from loyalist sectarian violence, was the road to disaster. The unionists convinced themselves, without undue difficulty, that the civil rights movement was a cover for the activities of the Provisional IRA, when it was nothing of the sort.

On 1 January 1969 some civil rights supporters, headed by the newly formed People's Democracy group, which was mainly made up of fewer than 50 students from Queen's University Belfast, organised a four-day march from Belfast to Derry. During the walk they were harassed by small groups of men armed with sticks and stones. When they reached Burntollet, not far from the city of Derry, on the fourth day of the march they were stopped by the RUC. Their numbers had by now increased to about 200. They were confronted by several hundred men wearing identifying armbands who were believed to be members of the hated B Special Constabulary. As about 80 members of the RUC stood and watched, that group laid into the marchers with cudgels, stones, crowbars and planks of wood. Many were injured but continued in the direction of the city, where they were ambushed again. There were more injuries. The marchers were bloodied but unbowed. There is no record of any of their attackers being arrested, charged or convicted of any offence of violence during those four days, even though many of the incidents were witnessed by the 80 police officers whose responsibility it was to uphold law and order that day. Some were later seen chatting to some of those who had been involved in inflicting injuries on the defenceless marchers. Eighty-seven of the marchers received treatment in Altnagelvin hospital in Derry.

The violence continued on the Bogside. The barricades went up. Men and women were knocked to the ground, assaulted and insulted. The report of a commission set up by the governor of Northern Ireland, Lord Grey of Naunton, and headed by the Scottish judge Lord Cameron, said:

> We have to record with regret that our investigations have led us to the unhesitating conclusion that on the night of 4/5th January a number of policemen were guilty of misconduct which involved assault and battery, malicious damage to property in streets in the predominately Catholic Bogside area giving reasonable cause for apprehension of personal injury among other innocent inhabitants, and the use of provocative sectarian and political slogans.[5]

What could the learned judge have meant by the use of the word 'misconduct?' Was he not describing blatant criminal offences? In any event, the pretence that the RUC was a police service faithfully and impartially serving the whole of the population of Northern Ireland was gone for ever.

On 21 April 1969 the pliant press described an attempt to disrupt and damage the water supply to the city of Belfast at the Silent Valley reservoir as the work of the IRA. Subsequent arrests proved that it was in fact the work of the paramilitary group the UVF, whose aim was to destabilise the government of Terence O'Neill. He resigned as prime minister on 28 April and went to the House of Lords, where no doubt he found the atmosphere a little more agreeable than the bully-boy tactics of Ian Paisley that had driven him out of office.

On 12 July there was serious rioting throughout Northern Ireland. On 12 August there was the 'Battle of the Bogside' in Derry when a thousand RUC officers, using CS gas, invaded the area, ostensibly to contain a riot there. In Belfast thousands of people, mostly Catholics, were burned out of their homes, leaving them homeless. A nine-year-old schoolboy, Patrick Rooney, was shot dead in a flat in the Divis Tower as he lay in bed at about 1 a.m. on 14 August 1969. According to the inquiry chaired by Lord Scarman, no fewer than 13 flats in that building were fired on by a high-velocity weapon, a Browning submachine gun, of the type used by the RUC that night. Lord Scarman concluded that there was no justification for the RUC shooting into the flats in the way they did. Nor was there any justification for the loyalist mobs who trailed behind the police vehicles, looting the burning houses they had overrun in the presence of the police, whose responsibility it was, in theory at least, to protect life, limb and property.[6]

No one was charged with the unlawful killing of Patrick Rooney; and no one was charged with the unlawful killing of Samuel Devenney, who died on 16 July 1969. He was a 42-year-old undertaker, married with 11 children. He was struck by an officer of the RUC who caused him multiple injures, including a fracture of the skull. The attack took place in his own home, when rioting that was taking place some distance away spilled over to William Street in Derry, where he lived. I question whether there was a full and independent investigation into his death.

On 24 March 1970, the prime minister, Harold Wilson, agreed to see Bernadette Devlin[7] in London. She wanted a full investigation into Samuel Devenney's murder. She was never likely to get that. There was a limited inquiry conducted by a British police officer, Sir Arthur Young. It got nowhere. He said there was a conspiracy of silence among the police officers in the city that night: they did nothing, they saw nothing and they said nothing.

As the rioting continued the RUC buckled under the weight of their attempts to contain it. Ten people died and 154 were wounded by gunfire as chaos swept the province. Drastic measures were called for.

In Downing Street the government decided to send the British army into Northern Ireland, under the command of Lieutenant-General Sir Ian Freeland, in support of the civil power. According to Austin Currie, one of the founder members of the SDLP, the British government should have taken the extra step at that time and suspended the Stormont government. That would have allowed for a fresh start. Their decision not to do so allowed the Provisional IRA to portray the British army as the 'stooge' of the political failures in government in Belfast.

On 19 August 1969 there was a meeting between the two governments in London. They issued a policy statement later known as the Downing Street Declaration. The British government said, 'nothing which has happened in recent weeks in Northern Ireland derogates from the clear pledges made by successive United Kingdom governments that Northern Ireland should not cease to be a part of the United Kingdom without the consent of the majority of the people of Northern Ireland'. The politicians simply failed to appreciate that the British government now firmly and openly aligned itself alongside the loyalist people of Northern Ireland. It has always operated on two colonial principles: first, to purchase one part of the host population, in this case those who supported the Union with Britain, and intimidate the other part, namely the nationalists; second, that the enemy of my enemy is my friend. Britain would never undertake opposition to loyalism because that would involve fighting on two fronts – against the republicans on one side and the unionists, who they saw as their natural allies, on the other.

In the following year, 1970, 28 people died violent deaths. According to David McKittrick in his book *Lost Lives*, 19 of the deceased were civilians, two were members of the RUC and six were members of the IRA. He claims in the book, 'republican activity was responsible for twenty deaths, while army action caused six deaths'. From 19 June 1970, local politicians in Belfast pressed their natural allies in the newly elected Conservative and Unionist government, led by Edward Heath, for extra troops, stronger security measures and more arrests of nationalists and republicans. They met with little success. In a province accustomed to rain between showers, there were more riots than rain, and the security situation looked difficult, if not impossible, without a fresh political initiative. In London, Edward Heath was busy with Britain's application for admission into the Common Market and he preferred to leave the question of Northern Ireland to the home secretary, Reginald Maudling. That was an unfortunate choice. Maudling was always regarded as lazy, even by his friends and supporters: he is now known to have been corrupt.

In the following two years, 1971 and 1972, there occurred two events that were so traumatic and dramatic that they almost plunged the province into civil war. Their consequences continue to ripple through the province of Ulster to this very day. The first was the introduction of internment without trial in August 1971. The second was the shooting dead of 14 innocent civilians in Derry on Sunday 30 January 1972.

Some of the most senior officers in the British army were against internment without trial, which they regarded as a blunt instrument. They told Edward Heath their view. The loyalist politicians, headed by Brian Faulkner, who had succeeded Terence O'Neill as prime minister in the province, were all for it, provided it was restricted to one section of the population – those who were, in his view, disloyal to the state. According to the distinguished American academic J. Bowyer Bell:

> The bottom line was practical internment would depend on the RUC lists, and such lists made no more exclusive by recent experience, were haphazard and specifically sectarian – not a single Protestant was thought subversive by the police. Maudling in London had suggested to Faulkner that a few Protestants might be taken as token, but nothing was done. Stormont wanted the disloyal intimidated, not an exercise in community relations. So the police and the army were primed to cause the maximum damage to those relations; the RUC as willing creatures of bigotry and the army as advocates of torture. . . . The politicians at least should have known the risks.[8]

The British government told the European Court of Human Rights, after the Dublin government took the case there, that there were three principal reasons for the decision to exercise extrajudicial powers against the campaign of violence carried out by the IRA. First, the normal procedures of investigation and criminal prosecution had become inadequate. Second, there was widespread intimidation of the population, making it impossible to obtain sufficient evidence to secure convictions, unless there was an admissible confession or police or army testimony. In addition, the terrorists could operate in areas where the RUC could not, and thus proper police enquiries could not be carried out. Third, the ease of escape across the border into the Irish Republic presented difficulties of control.

As for the decision not to intern any loyalists, the court was assured that the possibility was discussed: the security forces were aware of some loyalist terrorist activity in 1971, and there were also certain Protestant extremists, described as 'rabble rousers' (could they have had in mind a certain individual in a clerical collar?) whom they suspected of acts of violence or intimidation but which did not amount to terrorism. Although it is fashionable to claim that no Protestant was arrested, detained and interned in August 1971, in fact there were two. This is the view of Michael Farrell, a founder member of People's Democracy, who was among those arrested on the first day of internment without trial. He later became a successful solicitor in Dublin. He doesn't name either man, but one is known to have been the writer John McGuffin, who wrote two compelling books about internment without trial.

The British government always had a golden rule in its role of bringing centuries of 'civilisation' to the outposts of the Empire, namely that the English common law's principles of due process, fair trial and the rule of law would prevail wherever the Union flag was unfurled. Justice for all and equality before the law was of fundamental importance. Readers of this book may judge for themselves whether this principle was adhered to in Northern Ireland.

It is now known, following the discovery in the National Archives in Kew by researchers from the Pat Finucane Centre in Ireland, of a number of formerly secret and/or confidential papers, that the British army in Northern Ireland was seeking, and received, preferential treatment from three attorneys general between 1971 and 1979. They were Basil Kelly QC, the last attorney general in Northern Ireland before direct rule from London was imposed in 1972; Sir Peter Rawlinson QC, who held that office in Edward Heath's Conservative and Unionist government from 1972 to 1974; and Samuel Silkin QC, who was attorney general in the Labour government from 1974 to 1979. All three of them received, and acted upon, requests for immunity from prosecution where the RUC sought to bring British army soldiers before the courts on serious criminal charges.

The army had a number of requests. They asked first that the ordinary civil law court process system should not apply to soldiers charged with serious criminal offences; instead they should appear before a court martial, thus allowing the army to select the personnel involved in those proceedings. Second, they wished to be allowed to make representations on the merits of any particular case, and further to be consulted on whether the prosecution was in the public interest. All these matters really must be decided by the attorney general alone, without outside considerations or pressure from anyone, and certainly they were not the concern of the British army, which had no *locus standi* in the decision-making process.

One such case was that of William McGreanery, a 41-year-old single man with no connections to any terrorist organisation, who was shot dead shortly after midnight on Wednesday 15 September 1971 near Eastway Road, at a junction where the Creggan meets the Bogside in the city of Derry. The soldier (later referred to as Soldier A) who killed him was a member of the 1st Battalion Grenadier Guards. The most senior police officer in Derry at the time was Chief Superintendent Frank Lagan. On 8 November 1971 he submitted a report to the chief constable of the RUC recommending that Soldier A should be charged with murder.

According to a confidential record found by researchers from the Pat Finucane Centre, this case was discussed at a meeting held on Wednesday 1 December 1971 between the attorney general for Northern Ireland, Basil Kelly, and J.M. Parkin, an assistant secretary and head of C2, a central department of the army, at the British army headquarters, Northern Ireland. Kelly told Parkin that the RUC had recently recommended that he should charge Soldier A with murder, the offence having been committed while he was on duty. Kelly said that his 'junior' (meaning counsel at the independent bar or a barrister in the attorney general's department at Stormont) had advised him that a charge of manslaughter at most should be preferred against Soldier A. Further on, the note reads, 'the attorney general promised to tell HQNI if he decided upon reflection to institute proceedings in either case.' Was that as an act of courtesy, or was Kelly giving the army the opportunity of making representations to him as to why no prosecution should be commenced? Should he have been doing that?

The police report found that the army were installed in a protected sentry post in an elevated position near a factory wall in the Lower Creggan. There had been trouble around that sentry post the previous day, when one soldier, Sergeant Martin Carroll of 45 Regiment of the Royal Artillery, was shot dead and another, Sergeant James Black, also of the Royal Artillery, was injured by gunfire. These incidents occurred some five weeks after the introduction of internment without trial, when the atmosphere throughout the province was highly flammable.

According to a police statement submitted to the chief constable under the imprimatur of Superintendent Frank Lagan, Soldier A, who fired the fatal shot, claimed he saw three men get out of a car at Stones Corner, near a traffic island. One separated from the others. (He was apparently about a hundred yards from the sentry post when he did so.) Soldier A claimed that the man had a rifle in his hand and came to the aim position towards the protected sentry post. Soldier A moved from his position. He told another soldier, Soldier B, who was in the sentry post, what he was looking at, and simultaneously fired one round of 7.62mm ammunition from his self-loading rifle (SLR) at the man, whom he could see clearly. The man fell, mortally wounded. He was pulled away by another man, while a third took possession of the rifle, which Soldier A could see was of .303 calibre. Soldier B apparently did not see that action or that individual. If he had done so, might he have been asked why he did not open fire on the armed man?

Soldier A told the police that he was not using any visual aids to enable him to identify his target. The police report rather drily comments that 'Soldier B cannot help further in any material detail.' Does that mean that he heard the words spoken as the rifle was fired, but he did not see the man who was said to have an unwieldy .303 rifle, in the open, without trying to take cover or conceal his position, on a public road with the street lighting on, in the early hours of that Wednesday morning? And that man was aiming at a protected sentry post which was some 100 yards away from where he was standing. Did the soldiers inside the sentry post present themselves as an easy target, or were they in a concealed position?

The RUC began inquiries. In accordance with the agreement, which I consider was certainly unethical if not unlawful, between the chief constable and the general officer commanding the British army in Northern Ireland, the Special Branch of the RMP had primary responsibility for interviewing soldiers involved in fatal shootings, and any civilian witnesses were interviewed by the RUC's CID. This was an inept, ineffective and unsatis-factory approach to the investigation of a serious crime. The arrangement was put on a formal footing by an RUC Force Order that applied between September 1970 and September 1973. It was later described in a leading criminal case in May 1974 by Lord Chief Justice Lord Lowry as 'an unorthodox procedure'. He added, 'we deprecate this curtailment of the functions of the police and hope that the practice will not be revived'.[9] There is much suspicion that it was in fact revived.

A number of witness statements were taken on 15 September from the men who were with McGreanery when he was shot. They told the police that he was unarmed at the time of his death. Those statements were not shown to the RMP.

Soldier A was interviewed at 1.45 p.m. the next day, 16 September, some 36 hours after the fatal shots were fired. Some may find the delay inexcusable and inexplicable. In any case, the RMP did not interview Soldier A properly and effectively and put to him the purported evidence of the civilian eyewitnesses, so that he could challenge or deny the content of those statements. Since those witnesses denied that McGreanery had any weapon in his possession at the time he was shot dead, Soldier A should have been apprised of that. For reasons I don't understand, the statement taken from Soldier B was not timed or dated. It should have been.

A post-mortem was conducted on the body of the deceased man by Dr Derek Carson, the assistant state pathologist in Northern Ireland. He prepared a report that was sent to the chief Crown solicitor in Belfast. He outlined the direction of the fatal bullet and surmised the position William McGreanery must have been in in relation to the line of fire. He noted the wounds to the left forearm and detailed its position, which he regarded as being in an unusual position in a man who was walking at the time he was shot. This was most helpful to Soldier A, who claimed that the deceased was standing still when he opened fire. Dr Carson said that the bullet must have come from the front of the deceased, somewhat to his left and slightly above him, at a time when his left forearm was held in front of him. The bullet could not have come from the right side.

The chief Crown solicitor seized on that statement to claim that 'this evidence [which might be more accurately described as an opinion] destroys most of the civilian evidence which to be true would require the deceased to be shot on the right hand side and certainly not at the time the forearm must have been flexed at the elbow and held up in front of the chest, either vertically or horizontally or in some intermediate position'. However, he did admit that 'Dr Carson's evidence does not of course prove that the deceased had a rifle but it is strongly suggestive of the fact that he was holding his arms in the position of aiming a rifle.'

That professional opinion, which some may regard as speculative and presumptive rather than factual, was sufficient to persuade the attorney general Basil Kelly that it supported Soldier A's version of the incident and therefore there would be no prosecution against Soldier A for either murder or manslaughter. This was in spite of the fact that an experienced police officer, Superintendent Frank Lagan, disagreed with Dr Carson's analysis of the evidence of the wounds. He noted that he could not 'assimilate the probable positions of the deceased's left arm with that of holding a rifle or with his left arm extended to give that impression'.

There the matter rested until an investigation into the case was carried out by the Historical Enquiries Team (HET), set up by the PSNI in 2005 to re-examine all deaths attributable to the security situation between 1968 and 1998, and composed of former police officers, many of them English.

The team reported in 2010 that:

[T]wo of the most contentious issues in the case revolve around whether Mr McGreanery was armed and whether he posed a threat to the soldier(s). On the one hand Soldier A is adamant that he genuinely thought a rifle was being aimed in his direction and was therefore (he says) fully justified in shooting at the 'gunman'. Soldier B, whilst not seeing a weapon, says he heard Soldier A comment about seeing a rifle immediately prior to the fatal shot being discharged.

There is an abundance of evidence from the civilian witnesses to say that Mr McGreanery was not armed and therefore posed no threat whatsoever to the soldier(s). Soldier A is prepared to concede, on the basis of what the civilian witnesses say, that he was mistaken about the rifle . . .

Had Mr McGreanery been armed with a rifle and been intent on shooting a soldier, it would have been an extremely foolhardy thing to do from the location at which he himself was ultimately shot . . .

The most unlikely location from where to mount an attack with a rifle would have been where Mr McGreanery had been standing when he was shot. There was no cover behind which he could have concealed himself, and he would have known that he was in full view of the soldier(s) throughout the entire period. Several ideal vantage points would have been available to him nearby had he wished to engage the soldiers with a rifle . . .

Inferences were drawn by the pathologist during the investigation in 1971 that the gunshot wounds to Mr McGreanery's left forearm were indicative of him having been in the 'aim' position with a rifle at the time he was shot. That itself is feasible, but the HET are not convinced it is the only explanation available. He could have been 'mimicking' the aiming of a rifle, although that would have been an extremely reckless thing to do, or he could simply have raised his forearm for some other reason at that crucial moment, such as placing a cigarette in his mouth, or fixing his hair, for example.

The report concludes:

> [I]t is the view of the HET that [McGreanery] was not pointing a rifle at the soldier at the time. He was not involved with any paramilitary organisation, he was not carrying a firearm of any description, and he posed no threat to the soldiers at the observation post.

On any view, this is a total vindication of William McGreanery's reputation, and establishes beyond doubt that he died a completely innocent man.

The assistant state pathologist, Derek Carson, was back at the centre of controversial events when he carried out post-mortems on six of those who lost their lives in Derry on Bloody Sunday on 30 January 1972. Still later, in May 2002, he gave evidence to the inquiry conducted by Lord Saville into those deaths. He was subjected to the following cross-examination by Richard Harvey, counsel for the family of Jim Wray, aged 22, who was shot dead by a paratrooper in Glenfada Park. (According to Lord Saville, he was shot twice, the second time probably as he lay mortally wounded on the ground.[10] If Lord Saville's conclusion is correct, does it not mean that the paratrooper who administered the *coup de grâce* on a defenceless dying man got away with cold-blooded murder?)

Mr Harvey of Counsel asked:

Q. Did you have any military experience that would have included the firing of weapons?

A. I perhaps did, but I do not think that would have influenced me in any way.

Q. What was your military experience?

A. I was a member of the Territorial Army on the medical side.

Q. What rank did you hold?

A. At that stage I was probably holding the rank of captain.

Q. You left the Territorial Army with what rank?

A. Colonel.

Dr Carson denied being influenced in any way or by any person or organisation. He was, he said, completely independent. There is not a shred of evidence to prove otherwise.

In the case of William McGreanery, should Dr Carson really have become involved in a murder investigation where any appearance of bias and partiality had to be avoided at all costs? No one suggests he was biased or partial, but might he have appeared to be, to the detached and objective observer, when he volunteered his contentious professional opinion that William McGreanery was holding a rifle at the time a soldier shot him dead? Did those responsible for his appointment as assistant state pathologist in Northern Ireland consider that his position as an independent and impartial expert whose main responsibility in conducting a post-mortem was to establish the cause of death might be compromised by the fact that he was a captain in the army, 'albeit in the Territorial Army, a volunteer reserve force', that was acting in Northern Ireland in support of the civil power, and would become involved in investigating contentious killings?

In 2010 the Pat Finucane Centre showed Dr Carson's post-mortem findings to a highly respected doctor in Derry, Raymond McClean. In his view the original findings in no way supported the view that McGreanery was aiming a rifle. 'The findings were so general as to be meaningless' was Dr McClean's conclusion.

It cannot be denied in this case that a senior member of the RUC, Superintendent Frank Lagan, considered that there was sufficient evidence to charge Soldier A with murder. He had written to the chief Crown solicitor, 'taking all the circumstances into consideration I cannot find that Soldier A's action was justifiable and I therefore recommend that he be charged with the murder of William F McGreanery'.

A lawyer advising the attorney general took the view that there was sufficient evidence to support a prosecution, but that the appropriate charge would be manslaughter. Does it not seem extraordinary in the face of those two separate views of the evidence justifying a charge involving unlawful killing, that Soldier A was not charged with any offence at all? The main reason may be that there was no competent independent investigation of the fatal incident by the police, involving interviewing both soldiers and putting to them the content of the witness statements of those at the crime scene, but there may be another reason.

On 23 December 1971, following consultations with Basil Kelly, the attorney general, the chief Crown solicitor wrote to the chief constable: 'If Soldier A was guilty of any crime in this case, it would be manslaughter and not murder. Soldier A, whether he acted wrongly or not, was at all times acting in the course of his duty and I cannot see how the malice, express or implied, necessary to constitute murder could be applied to his conduct.'

I find this difficult to understand. It may be a truncated version of the law stated in Archbold's *Criminal Pleading, Evidence and Practice*, the standard textbook for criminal lawyers. Under the subheading 'Killing by officers and others' – which would include the police and prison officers as well as soldiers acting in support of the civil power – it states, 'where an officer of justice, in endeavouring to execute his duty, kills a man, this is justifiable homicide, or manslaughter, or murder, according to circumstances'. This clearly means that the fact that the officer of justice is actually on duty when he kills will not protect him from being called to account for that killing. If the chief Crown solicitor took the view that simply killing while on duty was a defence to murder, I think he was wrong.

The *mens rea* of murder – the mental element of the charge of murder that must be proved to accompany the conduct that causes the death of the victim – was described in 1971 as 'malice aforethought'. 'Aforethought' does not necessarily mean premeditation, but it implies foresight that death would or might be caused. 'Express malice' meant either an intention to cause death or grievous bodily harm to the victim or knowledge that the act that causes death will probably cause the death of, or grievous bodily harm, to some person. 'Implied malice' arises in cases where no malice is expressed or openly indicated, and the law will imply it from a deliberate cruel act committed by one person against another.

When Soldier A shot William McGreanery he should have been asked, and he clearly wasn't, by the special investigation branch of the military police, 'When you aimed and discharged your firearm at him, what did you intend to do?' If he replied (and he answered truthfully), 'I intended to kill him or cause him serious injury'(i.e. grievous bodily harm), that would be the sufficient mental element, the *mens rea*, the express malice, for the offence of murder.

(When Ruth Ellis was on trial at the Old Bailey, she was asked just one question in cross-examination by counsel for the prosecution, Christmas Humphreys: 'Mrs Ellis, when you fired that revolver at close range into the body of David Blakely, what did you intend to do?' Ellis replied: 'It is obvious that when I shot him I intended to kill him.')

Is it not correct that when Soldier A fired the aimed shot – and he insisted that it was aimed – his purpose, his object, his intention was to kill or cause serious injury to the person at whom he discharged his SLR? That being so, I find the statement of the chief Crown solicitor on 23 December 1971 quoted above to be devoid of any legal meaning. Once Soldier A admitted that he was shooting to kill the victim, the only question then to be decided was simply: was Soldier A justified and acting lawfully when he was shooting to kill? Only a criminal court could have answered that question, and no criminal court ever did.

The greatest tragedy arising from this case was the death of an innocent, unarmed man. But another great tragedy lay ahead. If the attorney general for Northern Ireland had decided to put Soldier A on trial, to make it clear that the British army was accountable for shootings in disputed circumstances and was not at liberty to open fire when it was not lawful and justifiable to do so, would the 1st Battalion of the Parachute Regiment have opened fire so readily on unarmed civilians 38 days later on Bloody Sunday?

On 14 July 2011 General Sir Peter Wall, the chief of the general staff, wrote a letter of apology to William McGreanery's niece and nephew, who had sought an official apology for their uncle's death. The general wrote:

> [I]t is evident that the soldier who shot him was mistaken in his belief that he had a weapon, and this error, tragically, resulted in the death of an innocent man . . . . I would like to express my sorrow and regret for his death which, in the years since it occurred, had deprived you of an uncle's support and affection. I do not believe that anything I can say will ease the sorrow you feel for what has happened, but I hope that this apology, and the findings of the Historical Enquiry team will be of some comfort to you.

The truth has been neglected for almost 40 years. At least it surfaced in the end, but there are many, too many, other cases where this did not occur.

6 Can You be Irish and Innocent ?

IN THE CASE of the six men from Northern Ireland wrongly convicted in 1975 of the Birmingham pub bombings in which 21 died and 182 were seriously injured, one judge, the late Lord Denning, the retired Master of the Rolls and at one time the most senior civil judge in the UK, said of the men involved, 'we shouldn't have had all these campaigns to get the Birmingham Six released if they had been hanged. They'd have been forgotten and the whole community would have been satisfied.' Is that really so?

There can be little doubt that if the death penalty had been in force in 1975 these six innocents would have hanged. Would they have been forgotten? Most certainly not by the 27 children who would have lost their fathers, the eldest of whom was then only 16 years of age. The lives of those children, and the men's wives, in the years after the wrongful conviction of their fathers and husbands, is perhaps best described as 'hell on earth'. The house of one of them, Gerard Hunter, was ransacked; his wife and three young children fled from the premises in fear. Others left the Birmingham area as soon as they possibly could.

Some argue that the case against the Six was flimsy, and subsequent evidence shows that to be so. At the time any fair-minded judge would have questioned the unchallenged evidence in their case that someone gave instructions to the police station where they were held that no detained persons register should be properly opened and recorded, and asked, 'Why'? No one ever did. That register notes the movement of the detained person around the police station, and matters such as when refreshments were provided and toilet facilities granted, as well as identifying anyone who had access to the person in police custody. That document, as will be seen in an equally controversial case set out in the next chapter, that of the Guildford Four (where it was described as the detention sheet), was of considerable relevance.

For reasons never explained, no record was ever properly made of police interviews with the Six; when, where, for how long and by whom the interviews were conducted. Was this in preparation for an entirely false scenario, calculated to deceive any subsequent trial court?

The six men wrongly and jointly convicted of the Birmingham bombing were Gerard Hunter, Richard McIlkenny, William Power, John Walker, Hugh Callaghan and Paddy Joe Hill. Five of the six (not including Hugh Callaghan) were planning to travel to Belfast to attend the funeral of James McDade, who had been killed when a bomb he was planting in the telephone exchange in Coventry exploded prematurely on 14 November 1974. After the bombing in the city centre, ten West Midlands Police officers began an investigation, initially in Heysham, where the five Belfast travellers were first detained by the police. Nine of the ten officers were members of the Serious Crime Squad of the West Midlands Police.

The Serious Crime Squad, or 'the Serious' as they liked to be known, was first formed in February 1952 in the City of Birmingham police as an experimental unit to assist the work of the regular CID. Its initial name was the Special Crime Squad. After a number of changes and reorganisations, in April 1974 the Squad was given the name it bore until its disbandment on 14 August 1989.

Members of the Squad regarded themselves as an elite police unit, dealing with ruthless and dangerous criminals committing serious crime, mainly armed robberies against soft targets, and their speciality seemed to be obtaining evidence, especially confession evidence in cases where, but for that confession, there would be no convictions. They worked in groups of three, known as a crew, with a detective sergeant, detective constable and a uniformed constable acting as driver. The total number of officers in the Squad is difficult to establish; it seemed to be about 30 at any one time. There were few applications to join the Squad from members of ethnic minorities or female officers, perhaps on the assumption that they were not likely to be successful. The Squad operated a closed shop, working very long hours, maintaining its own sources of information and contacts in the criminal fraternity. As a sign of its exclusiveness and solidarity, it even had its own distinctive brand of clothing, a necktie with the emblem of a swooping eagle.

Four of the six innocent men were alleged at their trial to have confessed to the police during interrogation to the mass murder in Birmingham by placing a bomb in the Tavern in the Town and the Mulberry Bush public houses in the city centre in the evening of 21 November 1974. Both pubs were within walking distance of New Street station, the departure point for trains to the Belfast ferry. The four later alleged at their trial that the confessions were false, fabricated and obtained by ill-treatment. The police denied this. The jury believed the police, not the four accused men.

On 25 January 1989, under the protection of parliamentary privilege, Clare Short, the Labour MP for Birmingham Ladywood, raised in the House of Commons the case of her constituent Paul Dandy. She described his treatment at the hands of some members of the Serious Crime Squad. She told the House that while she was investigating his case of allegations of falsification and fabrication of confession evidence, further serious allegations had been put to her by a number of solicitors and retired policemen in Birmingham. They alleged that the West Midlands Serious Crime Squad had for many years been engaged in serious and widespread malpractice. That situation continued as she spoke. She said, 'my constituent Paul Dandy was arrested in February 1987 and held as a Category A prisoner at Winson Green for ten months during which time he attempted to commit suicide.' (He had slashed his wrists.)

Ms Short continued:

In November 1987 all charges against him were dropped because his solicitor had obtained forensic evidence which showed his confession – the charge against him was based on his confession – had been forged by the police. The prosecution consulted its forensic expert, who confirmed the finding and the charge was dropped. . . . The test showed that the critical page containing Mr Dandy's admission had been rewritten and the confession inserted. It had not been there when the statement was taken. Not surprisingly Mr Dandy made a very serious complaint against the police. . . . It amounts to a conspiracy to pervert the course of justice – forgery by the police in an attempt to frame an individual on a very serious charge . . . the case was investigated by the Birmingham police force . . . there was a long delay while inquiries were made . . . after that long delay the eventual finding was that the police concerned were not to be charged with a criminal offence or even disciplined for having fabricated evidence. They were merely reprimanded for disposing of the original page of the statement.[1]

Ms Short did not ask why that was done: the reason is obvious. The police were falsifying the evidence and concealing the truth.

She went on to quote further examples, saying that a solicitor she had known as a friend for many years had told her, 'Dandy is the tip of the iceberg.'

> No solicitor in Birmingham would say anything other than that the Serious Crime Squad is fundamentally dishonest. The men in the Squad decide who are guilty and frame them. The malpractice goes back to at least the mid-1970s. I remind the House that the serious crime of the Birmingham bombers goes back to that time. Many people are convinced that the wrong men were convicted of that terrible crime. So we are talking about something widespread, deep and serious. This solicitor was angry that in a few cases where there had been evidence that might have led to things being cleared up, there was a cover up and in the individual cases nothing was done. A retired policeman who had served honourably in the Birmingham police force says that the problem is that the Serious Crime Squad is an elitist squad in which there is enormous pressure and competition to get results and convictions. Many men who have served in it for a long time have fallen into malpractice and protect each other constantly. They cut corners. Everyone knows it. The policeman said that other policemen look the other way and that a good many policemen in Birmingham refuse promotion so as not to have to serve in that squalid way. Ambitious policemen go into the Squad and they have to go along with the malpractice.[2]

It was probably the invention of the electrostatic detection apparatus (ESDA) by two staff members of the London College of Printing that led to the downfall of the Serious Crime Squad. It certainly helped establish some of the truth in the Birmingham Six case. The test established that some of the police officers' statements of interviews were not contemporaneous, as they had claimed at the original trial in August 1975. They had been written up at different times on different pads using different pens. Some parts had been added to or altered afterwards. Such misconduct begs the question: if the Six were guilty, as some members of the establishment continue to maintain, why was it necessary to falsify the truth?

The ESDA test works by an electrostatic process, in much the same way as a photocopier. What ESDA does is actually very simple. If you write on a piece of paper that is resting on another piece of paper, it is likely that, as you write, the pressure of the pen or pencil point will create indentations on the sheet beneath. If there was carbon paper between the two sheets one could read these indentations as blue or black images; without the carbon paper the indentations are at best difficult to read and usually more or less invisible. ESDA reveals the indentations almost as effectively as carbon paper. If one applies the ESDA process to the apparently blank under-sheet, the machine produces a legible image of those indentations, even if there have been one, two or even three other pages between the top sheet and the page being examined.[3] To carry out the test the sheet to be analysed is placed on a brass surface, which is covered with clingfilm and an electronic charge passed through it. Carbon-coated granules are then spread across it. They stick only to the indentations made from the writing on the sheet of paper above, disclosing the contents of the top sheet of paper.

Tom Davis, a staff member at the University of Birmingham, had had 13 years' experience as a forensic document analyst when in 1987 he was asked to apply the ESDA machine to allegedly contemporaneous notes of three interviews with Paul Christopher Dandy following his arrest in February of that year and where it was claimed by the police that he had confessed to an armed robbery. Although he was only 21 years of age he did have a criminal record. He worked as a market trader and the Serious Crime Squad claimed that he was involved in a robbery at a Birmingham shop owned by the Midlands Electricity Board (MEB), where a security guard had been shot in the leg and £20,000 had been stolen.

During a number of interviews at the police station, Dandy denied any involvement in the crime, claiming an alibi. He said that during an interview with a detective sergeant and Detective Constable (DC) Laurence Shaw, he saw one of the officers writing down a reply different from the one he had just given and in anger grabbed the paper and tore it up. He refused to answer any further questions.

In a third interview, the detective sergeant claimed that he said to Dandy, 'The anorak we recovered from your house today has been positively identified by the security guard who was shot.' According to that officer, Mr Dandy replied, 'I wish I'd shot the fucker in the head then he wouldn't have identified fuck all. I wish to conclude the interview. Return me to my cell.'

When his defence solicitors received the papers from the prosecution they observed that it was recorded that at this third interview he was asked by the police, 'Will you sign an authority for us to look at your bank account?', to which the reply was 'No.' The next words were, 'I take it from your earlier reply that you are admitting being involved in the robbery at the MEB,' to which it was noted he replied, 'Youse are good, Thursday, Friday,

Saturday, Sunday and you've caught me now you've got to prove it.' Mr Dandy denied making any such admission.

Tom Davis was approached by Dandy's solicitor, Ewan Smith, who asked him to examine the interview notes and subject them to the ESDA test. He discovered that two pages of the alleged interview had been rewritten and the crucial sentence 'and you've caught me now you've got to prove it' did not appear in the ESDA image on the page beneath. The inference was that this sentence must have been added at a later stage. Tom Davis considered that there were indentations on one of the sheets from the second interview which match word for word the text of the last page of the third interview. His professional opinion therefore was that 'the obvious inference is that the police wrote out an early version . . . which didn't have the incriminating bit; and they then decided they were going to fit Mr Dandy up, and so rewrote the interview and inserted the damaging admission.'

Paul Dandy's trial began at Birmingham Crown Court in November 1987. He had been in custody for about ten months on remand, most of it spent in solitary confinement in the most desperate conditions. The case only lasted for two days when the prosecution, whose own forensic witness supported the evidence of Tom Davis, decided to offer no further evidence against him. The jury was directed to find him not guilty and he walked free. His was the first case in which ESDA evidence was given. It was not the last.

Both the detective sergeant and DC Shaw were reprimanded by the chief constable for falsifying notes and losing a page of an interview record. (Another more senior officer, Detective Superintendent Brown, who had supervised the investigation into Paul Dandy but was not among the officers who interrogated him, was also disciplined for the neglect of duty.)

The fact that there were disciplinary proceedings in relation to Dandy's case was confirmed by a letter dated 16 November 1993 from the Crown Prosecution Service (CPS) to lawyers acting for Dennis Fitzgerald Clarke and Anthony Michael Jones. The CPS said:

> Both officers appeared before the Chief Constable on 12 October 1988 charged with neglect of duty in respect of a record of interview where parts of it were destroyed and rewritten, they failed to retain the destroyed notes, omitted to include the fact in their statements and failed to inform the Crown Prosecution Service in the relevant prosecution.

The explanation that the two officers put forward was that the original record had been torn and bloodstained. One suspects that whoever's blood it was, it probably was not that of the police officers.

When the prosecution case against him collapsed, Paul Dandy sued for wrongful arrest and malicious prosecution. Among the police officers asked to make a witness statement to defend that civil action for damages was the detective superintendent. He claimed that two or three days after Dandy confessed, the interviewing officers told him that Dandy had somehow managed to destroy some of the contemporaneous notes being made by the police, while the interview was still in progress. These pages had therefore been rewritten. Superintendent Brown said that even if the defence had not come up with the ESDA test results he had always intended to raise this matter with prosecuting counsel at the original trial before the police officers gave evidence to the jury. He omitted to say why he had waited ten months for the trial to take place, during which time he mentioned not a single word about the lost documents to the CPS. There may also be some difficulty in reconciling his version of events about the notes being torn up and destroyed because of the bloodstains. It is not likely to be resolved at any immediate time in the future.

The Squad was disbanded in August 1989 when even the chief constable could no longer stomach its activities. On 21 August the Police Complaints Authority (PCA) issued a press notice stating that on 14 August Geoffrey Dear, chief constable of the West Midlands Police, announced that he was disbanding the Serious Crime Squad and was moving several officers to non-operational administrative duties. He asked the PCA to supervise an investigation with the following terms of reference:

> To investigate individual complaints against members of the West Midlands Police Serious Crime Squad and additionally to investigate the work practices and associated matters. Initially, the investigation will relate to matters occurring in 1986, 1987, 1988 and 1989 . . . There were 754 arrests by the Serious Crime Squad between January 1986 and 14 August 1989. These arrests produced 669 files of which 663 have been recovered. The search for six files continues. There are also important documents missing from files that have been recovered. Seven pockets books relating to the investigation have not yet been recovered. The search continues . . . A total of 85 individuals, of whom 37 were still in prison, have made formal complaints.

Among those who did not complain, however, were the six men wrongly convicted of the Birmingham pub bombing, since the inquiry did not examine any case before 1986, and for good reason. At that time no one in a position of authority wanted to look at the case of the Six again. They were not released from prison until 14 March 1991. The subsequent report into 'the Serious' drafted by Donald Shaw, the chief constable of West Yorkshire Police, was never made public. It must be interesting reading.

It is self-evident that no one had seen the storm clouds gathering over Birmingham, for it seems that someone failed to heed the warning set out in a report submitted in 1985 by Commander Hay of the London Metropolitan Police after a series of complaints against the Squad. The report criticised the Squad's interviewing techniques and its failure to complete pocket book entries, and commented on the inordinate length of time that officers continued to serve with the Squad. Two of them had been in the Squad for some 15 years. Another, who had served only three years, is of some interest because he is believed to have been involved in at least five separate prosecutions in which there were allegations of fabricated confessions, planted evidence, inconsistent timings, flawed identification evidence, missing documents and incomplete information supplied to defence lawyers.

Gamekeeper Turned Poacher? The Case of Laurence Shaw

Former DC Laurence Shaw served with the Serious Crime Squad of the West Midlands Police from 1986 to 1989. He was one of the officers in a case against four accused men who alleged that their confessions had been fabricated, and the timing of interviews was inconsistent. The four accused were acquitted by the jury on 25 June 1987. Then, on 11 July 1987, another four men were acquitted. Shaw was one of no fewer than 12 officers of 'the Serious' against whom allegations of fabricated confessions, planted evidence, inconsistent timings of interviews, missing documentary evidence and flawed identification evidence were apparently made. They denied all these allegations. According to the distinguished writer and researcher Tim Kaye, at the time an academic at the University of Birmingham, DC Shaw was described as an unreliable witness in a case of two men acquitted by a jury in 1988. On 16 January 1991 the appeal court set aside a conviction where there were allegations against five officers of the Serious, including DC Shaw, of fabrication of confession evidence, inconsistent timings of interviews and a failure to provide the defence with complete disclosure of the evidence.[4]

DC Shaw is perhaps best remembered because he carved out a special place for himself in the crime scene of the West Midlands by changing sides and committing armed robberies, for which he received substantial terms of imprisonment.

According to the journalist Kim Sengupta, Shaw 'was known for socialising with criminals while a serving officer'.[5] He served in the police for 24 years, during which time he received a commendation for bravery from the Squad for saving a life. When the Serious Crime Squad was disbanded, he was suspended from duty while the PCA carried out an investigation into nine separate complaints against him. He was not prosecuted for any crime arising out of that inquiry, but he was reprimanded for his part in the case of Paul Dandy, who in 1995 was awarded £70,000 in damages against the police relating to allegations that they had fabricated his alleged confession to armed robbery.[6]

After his suspension was lifted, Shaw returned to work. He left the police service in May 1998, claiming that he suffered from depression and had panic attacks if he even went near a police station. According to his barrister, David Mason, he then invested a lump sum from his pension into a business venture in licensed premises in Shropshire, but that failed. He moved from the Midlands to Chapel Ground, West Looe in Cornwall with his girlfriend Tracey Graham and in order to supplement his annual pension of some £10,495 he turned to crime.

On 22 December 1999, some 15 months after leaving the police, he returned to the village post office on Widney Road at Bentley Heath in the West Midlands, a location he knew well, for he had been based nearby in Solihull. He would have remembered that the post office had no surveillance equipment installed at that time. He was wearing a full-face balaclava and carrying an imitation firearm when he entered the premises and told the terrified manager, Pauline Wilkes, and her assistant, Anita Howard, 'This is not a game, this is for real.' He ordered the two women to empty the contents of the safe into a blue holdall he had with him and when told there was a time delay on the safe calmly replied that that he would wait. He escaped with £18,559 in cash.[7]

On 26 July 2000 he returned to the same post office, this time wearing a baseball cap and a scarf concealing his face. He was armed with the same imitation weapon. Told once again by the terrified Pauline Wilkes, 'You know there is a time delay,' he again waited patiently, standing by the door, until the sum of £29,132 was eventually handed over. He told the staff 'Sorry for all the trouble' as he made his brazen exit from the premises.

On Friday 26 January 2001 he borrowed a Range Rover from a publican in West Looe and travelled to Knowle in the West Midlands. He stayed overnight in the Heron's Nest public house. The next day, armed police officers intercepted his vehicle and arrested him. Inside the Range Rover they found a double-barrelled sawn-off shotgun, two handguns, shotgun barrels and eight rounds of ammunition. Shaw admitted that he was preparing to carry out a robbery at Barclays bank in Knowle by breaking in over the weekend and awaiting the arrival of the staff on Monday morning. There would be no customers around to complicate things, he told the *Sunday Mercury* newspaper: 'we planned to wear overalls so that when we walked out carrying tools, it would not arouse suspicion. Nobody sees workmen – they are just part of the scenery. I reckon we would have got away with about £125,000 from the bank. If I hadn't been shopped, I would have done one more robbery and then retired to the Algarve.'[8] He admitted that he knew the bank's layout and routine because he had visited the premises as part of his detective duties.

When he appeared at Warwick Crown Court on 23 April 2001 he admitted responsibility for the two post office robberies. One wonders whether media reports that he was wearing his Serious Crime Squad tie as he stood in the dock are actually true.

He had told detectives interviewing him that he carried out the raids in the late afternoon on days when the weather was bad: 'That way passers-by would have their heads down and would be scurrying home as quickly as they could. If robberies are carried out quietly and calmly, bystanders don't notice anything because there is nothing to notice. Even if they respond to police appeals for witnesses, I know from bitter experience in the job that they are absolutely no help to police inquiries.'[9]

Judge Richard Cole accepted that Shaw, who was then 49 years of age, had been a conscientious police officer for much of his career, but said he had no option but to impose a long custodial sentence for such grave crimes. He sent the disgraced former officer to prison for 12 years. Shaw claims he knows the identity of the person who informed on him, but he has never publicly disclosed who that person was.

Shaw later told a journalist working for the *Sunday Mercury* newspaper that he had been approached by the Anti-corruption Unit of the West Midlands Police. He was, so he said, offered a recommendation for a lighter prison sentence if he co-operated with the unit. He declined to do so because there wasn't much information to give and in any event he said he was proud to have served with the Serious Crime Squad, whose officers were the finest in the country. That was his view of them. Another former police officer who had worked undercover told the same newspaper that he knew of Shaw's reputation during his time with the West Midlands force. He said:

> Larry Shaw was nothing more than a crook with a police badge. He became seduced by the glamour of the underworld and became far too friendly with criminals he was supposed to be taking down. During his time in the force there were multiple investigations into his actions, but they could never quite get anything to stick. For example when he was in the West Midlands Serious Crime Squad he was accused of taking off a suspect's socks, wiping them on the carpet of a vehicle involved in an armed robbery, and then charging the suspect with the crime, based on that forensic evidence. The suspect was found not guilty and Shaw was investigated but he manage to slip off the hook – like he always did.[10]

Clearly this rather unique method of evidence gathering failed on that occasion, but it showed imagination, cunning and fierce determination to try to get a conviction at any cost.

Even after his release from prison early in 2007, after serving about half of his sentence, Shaw was not a reformed character. In August 2010 he entered Lostwithiel post office in Cornwall, wearing a balaclava and carrying an imitation single-barrelled shotgun, which he pointed at the head of the postmaster inside the office and demanded money. He got none, but he did get caught, ending up in the dock charged with attempted robbery and unlawfully possessing an imitation firearm. A Crown Court judge sent him to prison for 13 years in December 2010. He apologised for the embarrassment his conduct had caused his former police colleagues, but he told the *Sunday Mercury* that he was not ashamed of his crimes, and he said that 'he was welcomed to the reunion of the Serious Crime Squad after his release from his first robbery sentence'.[11] His present whereabouts are not known.

One of the Birmingham Six: Paddy Joe Hill

Paddy Joe Hill will never forget his first meeting with an officer of the Serious Crime Squad. As noted above, he was one of the five men who travelled from Birmingham New Street bound for Belfast on the evening of 21 November 1974 to attend the funeral of James McDade. Paddy Joe's primary purpose was to see an elderly aunt who was seriously ill, but he intended to go to the funeral as well. He had known James McDade since they attended the same school in Belfast.

Paddy Joe had left Belfast at the age of 15 and had not returned there for 14 years. He was married a local girl from Birmingham; they had five young daughters and a baby son aged 23 months. He was unemployed, because of illness, and had very little money, so he had borrowed the cost of the rail and ferry fare to Belfast from a Catholic nun at a local convent run by the Little Sisters of the Assumption. He arrived at New Street railway station at 7.45 p.m. The boat train, the Ulster Express, departed on time, ten minutes later. According to the distinguished lawyer Sir Louis Blom-Cooper QC, a friend and admirer of the former chief justice, Lord Lane, 'the bombs had been placed in the two public houses at around 5.30 p.m. or shortly thereafter'.[12] He does not cite the source of this information. I do not think he made it up. If it is true, and I find no reason to disbelieve it, Paddy Joe Hill could not have been one of the bombers on that fatal November day. In addition, the evidence is that all the men arrived at New Street well after 5.30 p.m. Did someone in authority see them arrive and say nothing, even about them not leaving the railway station once they had arrived? Were not the police on high alert in public places such as railway stations at that time, bearing in mind that an IRA bombing campaign had been waged in the Birmingham area for many, many months? A schedule dated 12 August 1975 prepared by the West Midlands Police indicates that in the previous year the IRA had bombed business premises twice in Solihull and three times in Birmingham city centre, including three incendiary devices placed in shops in the New Street area, on 8 August, and twice on 30 August 1973. All three shops were within walking distance of the two public houses that were bombed on 21 November 1974.

In the first six days of September 1973, explosive devices were placed outside business premises in Sherlock Street, Calthorpe Road and Holdford Road in Birmingham and in Highfield Road, Edgbaston, a suburb of the city. Extensive damage was caused on each occasion. On Sunday 9 September a bomb exploded at a motor accessory business in Sutton Coldfield. Extensive damage was caused to the premises and an 18-year-old man was seriously injured as he tried to escape from the building. At 9.40 a.m. on Monday 17 September 1973 a device planted at Bilton House, Highfield Road, Edgbaston killed Captain Ronald Wilkinson, an army bomb disposal expert, when it exploded prematurely as he tried to dismantle it. Following that tragedy, the IRA did not bomb Birmingham for another four months.

Between January and April and in July and August 1974 there was a concerted bombing campaign in Birmingham and neighbouring towns: 37 bombs and incendiary devices were planted, of which 23 exploded, causing extensive damage to property. Some of the bombs that failed to detonate provided valuable forensic information about their makers.

There was a lull during September 1974, and when the bombing campaign was renewed, the nature of the targets changed. On 24 October an explosive device placed under the car of a magistrate in Edgbaston failed to activate. Four days later, in the same location, a similar device placed under the car of another Birmingham magistrate, a retired army officer, failed to detonate.

On that same day, 28 October, a car driven by the wife of Labour government minister Denis Howell was damaged when a bomb underneath the vehicle exploded, but fortunately only minor damage was caused to the car.

If the police were not waiting and watching for bombers in the city centre of Birmingham and its surrounds, they certainly should have been.

Of the four men Paddy Joe Hill had arranged to meet at the railway station, John Walker, originally from Derry, had arrived in England in 1952; Richard McIlkenny had come to England in 1956; Gerard Hunter and William Power in 1963. Both Hunter and Power were from Belfast and they also knew James McDade. The sixth man, who also went to the railway station but did not intend to travel, was Hugh Callaghan. He was from the Ardoyne in Belfast and had arrived in Birmingham at the age of 17 in November 1947.

Did no one ever ask why these six family men, with their settled lives in England, would enter into a conspiracy to plant two bombs in city centre pubs, blowing the occupants to smithereens, knowing what would happen to them and their families if they were caught? For what cause would they abandon their loved ones and murder and maim their fellow human beings?

One of the barristers who appeared for the prosecution at their trial in Lancaster in August of the following year told me he thought they expected a heroes' welcome when they landed in Belfast. Nothing could be further from the truth. The plain people of Ireland, North and South, have never supported the campaign of the Provisional IRA and their armed struggle to reunify the island of Ireland; nor do they endorse the violent means the IRA employs to achieve that objective. The reaction was one of deep sorrow and immense shame that anyone could be so heartless and callous as to kill and maim so many for a political aspiration that should have been achieved by democratic means. I told him my view, which had been formed even before the trial of the Six. I believed in their innocence, based not so much on their characters, their lifestyle and their family commitments, but on the fact that no active service unit of the Provisional IRA would ever travel on a bombing mission, with or without an explosive device, on a public bus. They would arrange safe transport to, and, just as important, away from the scene. All of the men travelling to Belfast on 21 November 1974 went to New Street Station on the bus. I simply refuse to believe members of the IRA would have done that.

Paddy Joe Hill had been separated from his travelling companions when they all arrived at Heysham in Lancashire to board the ferry to Belfast. He went through the security check and boarded the boat. When his four companions were stopped at security and asked by the police to explain why they were travelling to Belfast, one of the four asked, 'What about our mate?', at which Paddy Joe was taken off the boat and brought to Morecambe police station.

As he records in his autobiography, the introduction was short, brutal and totally unexpected. In the early hours of Friday 22 November 1974, Paddy Joe Hill sat reading a book in the police station when a man approached him, staring at him with hate-filled eyes. 'Soon, you little Irish bastard, you dirty little murdering pig,' he said. When asked what he was talking about, he said, 'You'll find out soon, you little Irish bastard.' He then spat in Paddy Joe's face and walked away.[13] This was Hill's first, but sadly not his last, encounter with an officer of the Serious Crime Squad of the West Midlands Police.

In the summer of 1975 the trial drama was played out in Lancaster Castle. The guilty verdicts recorded against the Six were inevitable and expected. Who was going to believe the evidence of six Irishmen – and the trial judge Mr Justice Nigel Cyprian Bridge made it clear he did not – against the police, especially officers of the West Midlands Serious Crime Squad?

For years after the convictions of the Birmingham Six the Squad basked in its reputation of having brought them to justice. On 14 March 1991 the Six were released from custody when their convictions were finally quashed. They had spent over 16 years in prison for murders they had not committed. No police officer has ever been convicted of any criminal offence arising out of that case.

The ESDA test played an important part in discovering the truth, most especially in relation to two interviews between the police and Richard McIlkenny. McIlkenny said that there was one short interview early on 22

November 1974; the police said there were two interviews, the first commencing at 12.30 p.m. and finishing at 1.30 p.m., later than McIlkenny claimed. For some unknown reason, the most senior officer at that interview recorded the date as being 'November 20, 1974', which was in fact a day before the pub bombings actually took place and therefore could not be correct.

The ESDA test was carried out by Dr David Baxendale of the Home Office Forensic Science Laboratory, Birmingham. He found that the first interview was recorded on ten pages of notes, the second on nine pages. Dr Baxendale found that pages 1–6 and page 11 all came from the same notepad. Pages 7–10 were from a different notepad. Pages 1–11 were written with a black ballpoint pen, but on pages 7–11 the ink was more heavily deposited, and that led him to the conclusion that a different pen was used on these pages. He also concluded that neither of the notepads used for pages 1–11 was of the same paper as the standard notepads issued to the Lancashire police in 1974. The test also indicated that the notes of the interview originally ended at the top of page 7. The original page 7 was then torn up, with a new page 7 substituted, and pages 8–10 added.

The appeal court judges in 1991 could not understand why the police had done all this, because they did not claim that McIlkenny confessed to murder during this first interview. But, said the court, 'nobody has been able to think of an honest explanation for the result of the ESDA test . . . At best the officers were lying when they told the [trial] court that one officer was noting the interview continuously from 12.30 to 1.30. At worst they must have put their heads together to fabricate that part of the interview at which the Superintendent was said to have been present, or perhaps even the whole interview'.[14]

The second police interview was alleged to have taken place the following day, 23 November, from 10.10 a.m. to 11.20 a.m. Then followed a written confession statement that finished at 12.05 p.m. The interview was recorded on pages 12–19. Dr Baxendale found that pages 12–16 were from the same notepad as pages 1–6 and 11. Page 17 was from a different notepad, and so was page 18. So four different notepads in total were used for the two interviews. The ink on page 17 was different, and he noted that it was at the end of page 17 that McIlkenny was alleged to have confessed. If the interview was being recorded continuously one would have expected page 17 to bear the imprint of page 16, but it did not. It bore the imprint of a different page 16. Since the existing page 16 bears the imprint of page 15, it looked as though the officer started on a different rewrite of page 16 and then for some reason tore it up. Similarly, one would expect page 18 to bear the imprint of page 17, but it did not. It bore the imprint of an earlier version of page 18, which had since been torn up.[15]

The irresistible inference from the foregoing is that the police officers concerned had not told the truth. One again has to ask, if there was a true confession obtained from Richard McIlkenny in this case, why falsify the documents recording it?

Three officers involved in this case, and in particular connected to this interview, appeared at the Central Criminal Court. The trial judge directed an acquittal on the basis that they would not receive a fair trial. A hard-hitting editorial in the *Independent* newspaper said:

> Mr Justice Garland has made a terrible error by abandoning the case against three police officers charged with conspiring against the Birmingham Six. He said that publicity prejudicial to the trial prompted his decision. As an explanation, that is deeply disillusioning – a final insult to people who spent 16 years in jail for crimes they did not commit. . . . Nearly 20 years after 21 people died in the Birmingham pub bombings, the perpetrators are still free. And the authorities have yet to identify those who framed the wrong men.[16]

That is the inevitable consequence of convicting the innocent – the guilty escape justice.

On 14 August 1989 the West Midlands Serious Crime Squad was disbanded by its chief constable. He said it was the blackest day of his career. The allegations of misconduct during investigations and suspect confession evidence were too numerous to resist. The list of cases where the appeal court quashed convictions obtained by officers of the Squad is still incomplete.

The Mysterious Death of Police Constable Tony Salt

It should not be thought – contrary to what politicians may claim – that the safeguards for suspects after arrest, during detention and interrogation introduced by the Police and Criminal Evidence Act 1984 (PACE) meant a complete end to the abuse of police powers and the fitting-up of suspects in custody, as the following case shows.

On the evening of Saturday 16 April 1989 two officers of the West Midlands Police, Constable Tony Salt and Constable Mark Berry were on duty but not in uniform, keeping observation on an illegal drinking club in the Small Heath area of Birmingham. Their task was to log the arrival of people and cars at the unlicensed premises.

Several times during that evening they left the observation post to drink alcohol at a nearby public house. By 2 a.m. it was admitted by PC Berry that they had consumed seven or eight pints of beer and a measure of spirits and half a can of lager. Eyewitnesses said they both appeared to have difficulties standing, using a pool table as a means of support. They argued and almost came to blows at one stage, before they left the public house.

They separated, but shortly after that PC Berry saw PC Salt collapse on the ground in an alleyway near the illegal club. PC Berry radioed for assistance. His colleague was taken to hospital but was found to be dead on arrival.

The next day the assistant chief constable of the West Midlands Police told a press conference that Constable Tony Salt had broken cover to check a suspect car. Someone with martial arts skills had assaulted him, dragged him to an alley and there beaten him to death.

Three men, all of West Indian origin, were eventually arrested in connection with the death of PC Salt. One of them was taken to Queen's Road police station in Birmingham. It was there that some members of the Birmingham Six alleged at their trial that they had been assaulted and beaten. One of the Six, Paddy Joe Hill, wrongly convicted with the other totally innocent five men, wrote in his autobiography that as he sat on a bench in a cell, 'suddenly the flap on the cell door opened, a shotgun was poked through it and a voice screamed, "who the fuck told you to sit down, you murdering little bastard?"' He was told that if he was sitting down when the officer returned, he would be shot. The gun was withdrawn and the flap was closed.[17] That conduct was later denied by the police. Those denials were believed by the jury that convicted the Six.

The first man arrested in connection with the death of Constable Salt eventually admitted that he had stolen the officer's wallet containing money and also a martial arts weapon the police believed the officer had with him when he died.

Following the arrest of a second man, he too admitted the theft of money and the weapon. A third man, the doorman at the illegal club, claimed that the police intimidated and slapped him, then made threats against his family, saying that drugs would be found in his house leading to the arrest of his girlfriend and that his children would be taken into care. He then confessed, admitting that he prevented PC Salt from entering through the door of the club by putting his arm up to the officer's neck. He was charged with murder, as were the other two men.

The case began to fall apart when the pathology report concluded that the most likely cause of death was that, in his drunken state, PC Salt had fallen and hit his head on the bucket of a JCB digger parked near the club. His head injury would have prevented him from walking the distance from the door of the club to the place where he fell. The doorman's confession to using violence against PC Salt had been obtained by the police before they received that pathology report.

Worse was to follow. A defence lawyer saw that there was a gap in the numbering of pages in a bundle of documents and asked to see the missing pages. They were handed over. One was a statement from the bereaved Mrs Salt stating that her husband always carried his martial arts weapon with him and it was not at their home. PC Berry made a statement that PC Salt had shown him the martial arts weapon shortly before he died. Then a second statement, dated 1 May 1989, from Mrs Salt was handed to the defence. She now said that she had found the martial arts weapon on the floor of the family car. It had not been stolen at all. She handed it to the police. It subsequently disappeared, as important exhibits tend to do in criminal cases involving the innocent.

For good measure Mrs Salt then went on to disclose that when her husband left the house on the night he died he had borrowed money from her, about £5 in small change. That was far less than the notes said to be in the stolen wallet. The case against the three men collapsed. They were released from prison custody. They received substantial compensation from the state for their wrongful arrest and detention.

On 11 November 1991, Chris Mullin, the campaigning journalist, author and later a minister in a Labour government and who fought so courageously and untiringly on behalf of the Birmingham Six, asked a Home Office minister in the House of Commons if he would call for a report from the chief constable of the West Midlands Police, explaining why PC Mark Berry had been permitted to retire from the police service on medical grounds before disciplinary action could be taken against him following the false statements he had made about the circumstances of the death of his colleague, PC Salt. Mullin was told that was a matter for the chief constable and his request that the minister should set up a public inquiry into the death of PC Salt met with a short answer. 'No'.[18]

One might have expected, in the light of nationwide publicity given to the activities of the West Midland Police by the media that led up to the disbandment of the Serious Crime Squad in 1989 and the quashing of more than 30 convictions in the appeal court on the grounds that some members of the Squad were alleged to have fabricated evidence, tortured suspects and written false confessions, that the activities of PC Salt and PC Berry would receive substantial publicity. After all, their case was in the public arena only a matter of weeks after the release from prison of the Birmingham Six on 14 March 1991. A number of officers from the West Midlands were involved in that investigation and trial. Apart from one television documentary programme made by the Granada Television *World in Action* team, there was virtually no publicity given either to the Salt case itself or the relevant matters raised by Chris Mullin in the House of Commons.

On 12 December 1991, during a motion to adjourn the House, Chris Mullin tried again. He made a detailed statement about the Salt case which he said should be of particular interest to members of the Royal Commission who were considering under what circumstances confession evidence should be admitted at a criminal trial. He then launched a devastating broadside against parts of the legal establishment:

> The case demonstrates that, despite the safeguards provided by PACE (The Police and Criminal Evidence Act 1984), West Midlands police officers are still able to persuade people to confess to crimes they did not commit and even tape-recorded those false confessions. It demonstrates that all the bland assurances – we may hear more of them later – that everything has been fine since PACE are nonsense. The case also shows that, even when West Midlands police officers have been caught fabricating confessions and attempting to pervert the course of justice, they can rely on their superiors, up to the Chief Constable himself, to make sure that the truth is covered up. They can rely on the Crown Prosecution Service to connive in the disappearance of inconvenient evidence. They can rely on the silence of the police authority to whom the Chief Constable is supposed to account. Finally, they can rely on the Home Office to block any inquiries from inquisitive Members of Parliament.[19]

PC Tony Salt was only 30 years of age when he died. The inquest into his death was closed without a full hearing of the evidence. I can find no explanation anywhere why this occurred. PC Mark Berry retired on full pension from the West Midlands Police on medical grounds. No criminal or disciplinary charges were brought against him.

7 Defending the Innocent: the Guilford Four

Chronology of Events

1974

5 October: Start of Phase One of IRA bombing campaign in the UK. A Provisional IRA active service unit places time bombs in the Horse and Groom and Seven Stars pubs in Guildford, Surrey. Five people die, more than 40 are injured when they explode.

7 November: Members of the same active service unit throw a bomb into the King's Arms pub in Woolwich, south London. Two people die, more than 20 are injured.

21 November: Another active service unit of the Provisional IRA places time bombs in the Mulberry Bush and Tavern in the Town pubs in Birmingham city centre. Twenty-one people die, 182 are injured.

Five men are arrested at Heysham in Lancashire in connection with the Birmingham bombings.

22 November: A sixth man is arrested in Birmingham in connection. All six men, the Birmingham Six, are later charged with 21 counts of murder.

27 November: The House of Commons debates the Prevention of Terrorism (Temporary Provisions) Bill.

28 November : Paul Michael Hill (aged 21) is arrested in Southampton and taken to Guildford police station.

29 November: The Prevention of Terrorism (Temporary Provisions) Bill is rushed through both Houses of Parliament and becomes law.

30 November: Gerard Conlon (aged 21) is arrested in Belfast, taken to Springfield Road police station and then to Guildford. Many others are arrested on this date, including Hugh (Gerard Conlon's uncle) and Kitty Maguire in London.

1 December: Giuseppe (Patrick Joseph) Conlon tells police at Springfield Road police station that he intends to travel to London to get legal aid for his son.

2 December: A firm of Belfast solicitors sends a telegram to Paddy Maguire telling him of the arrest of his nephew Gerard Conlon.

Giuseppe Conlon travels on the overnight ferry to England, arriving at the Maguire home in northwest London about midday the next day.

3 December: Police raid the Maguire home at 43 Third Avenue, searching for explosives. Paddy Maguire, aged 43, Anne Maguire (40), Vincent Maguire (16), Patrick Maguire (13), Sean Smyth (38), Giuseppe Conlon (52) and Patrick O'Neill (35) (the Maguire Seven) are all removed from the house and tested for the presence of nitroglycerine (NG).

Carole Richardson, aged 17, and her boyfriend, Patrick Armstrong, are detained by the police. (These two, with Paul Michael Hill and Gerard Conlon, became known as the Guildford Four.)

4 December: Gerard Conlon is charged with murder.

7 December: Anne Maguire, Patrick Armstrong, Carole Richardson and others are charged with murder.

1975

27 January: A Provisional IRA active service unit places seven time bombs in London at various sites. Sixteen people are injured. This marks the end of Phase One of its campaign.

8 February: The Provisional IRA announces a ceasefire.

18 February: The attorney general signs fiats consenting to the prosecution of the Maguire Seven.

24–25 February: The five counts of murder against Anne Maguire are with-drawn at court. Her two sons, Vincent and Patrick, are then charged, with her, with the unlawful possession of NG in suspicious circumstances.

15 April: Paul Hill is charged with the murder of Brian Shaw in Belfast.

23 June: Paul Hill is convicted of the murder of Brian Shaw.

9 July: Brendan Dowd is arrested with others in Liverpool.

27 August: A time bomb is placed in the Caterham Arms public house in Surrey. This marks the start of Phase Two of the IRA bombing campaign.

16 September: The trial of the Guildford Four begins.

22 October: The Guildford Four are convicted.

6–13 December: Joseph O'Connell, Harry Duggan, Edward Butler and Hugh Doherty are arrested at a flat in Balcombe Street, northwest London, after a six-day siege.

1976

27 January: The trial of the Maguire Seven begins.

4 March: The Maguire Seven are convicted of unlawful possession of NG in suspicious circumstances.

11 May: Brendan Dowd and other IRA members are convicted at Manchester Crown Court of attempted murder and conspiracy to cause explosions.

1977

24 January: The trial of the four men captured at Balcombe Street begins.

7 February: All four men are convicted of murder and causing explosions.

20 July: The Maguire Seven's application for leave to appeal against conviction begins.

29 July: Their application for leave to appeal is refused by Lord Justice Roskill.

10 October: The Guildford Four's application for leave to appeal against conviction begins.

28 October: Their application for leave to appeal is refused by Lord Justice Roskill.

1980

23 January: Giuseppe Conlon dies in prison, aged 56.

1989

16 January: The home secretary tells the House of Commons that he has decided to refer the case of the Guildford Four back to the Court of Appeal.

26 July: The Lord Chief Justice fixes the date of their second appeal court hearing for 15 January 1990.

17 October: The Crown Prosecution issues a press release stating that they will not oppose the appeal.

19 October: The Guildford Four's convictions are quashed. They are released from prison.

20 October: The home secretary sets up an inquiry under Sir John May, a retired Lord Justice of Appeal, into the case of the Guildford Four, then adds the case of the Maguire Seven to the ambit of that inquiry.

1990

12 July: The May Inquiry publishes an interim report into the Maguire Seven case. The home secretary refers their case back to the appeal court on the same day.

12 November: The DPP issues summonses against three Surrey police officers who interviewed Patrick Armstrong.

1991

14 March: The convictions of the Birmingham Six are quashed by the appeal court. The home secretary sets up a royal commission on criminal justice.

26 June: The convictions of the Maguire Seven are quashed by the appeal court.

11 July: A stipendiary magistrate declines to send the three Surrey police officers for trial.

1992

24 January: The High Court reverses the decision of the stipendiary magistrate.

27 March: Three retired Surrey police officers, Vernon Weir Attwell, a former detective constable, John Sutherland Donaldson, a former detective sergeant, and Thomas Lionel Style, a former chief superintendent, are sent for trial.

3 December: The May Inquiry publishes its second report on the case of the Maguire Seven.

1993

20 April: The three former Surrey police officers appear at the Old Bailey charged with conspiracy to pervert the course of justice.

19 May: All three accused men are found not guilty by the jury and discharged.

1994

22 April: Paul Hill's conviction for the murder of Brian Shaw is quashed by the appeal court in Belfast.

30 June: The May Inquiry publishes its final report on the case of the Guildford Four.

Note: The Guildford bombings were carried out by Brendan Dowd, Joseph O'Connell, another man and two young women whom they refused to identify. They confessed to the killing of the deceased on oath in the Criminal Division of the Court of Appeal during the Guildford Four's failed appeal against conviction between 10 October 1977 and 28 October 1977. Both men also admitted their involvement in the throw-bomb incident at Woolwich in which two people were killed. Harry Duggan and Edward Butler also confessed on oath at that appeal court hearing that they were jointly responsible for the Woolwich bombing. In spite of these voluntary confessions, not one of the four men was ever charged with any offence arising out of the two separate bombing incidents. The Four were convicted in February 1977 of various other offences that included causing explosions. They were released from prison in April 1999.

The Guildford Four, Paul Hill, then aged 21, Patrick Armstrong (25), the late Gerard Conlon (21), all natives of Belfast, and the late Carole Richardson (18), who was English, were convicted in October 1975 of five counts of murder and conspiracy to cause explosions. The three men were sentenced to life imprisonment for placing a bomb in two pubs in Guildford, Surrey, where five people died. The first two, Paul Hill and Patrick Armstrong, were also convicted of the throw-bombing of a pub in Woolwich, killing two people. Paul Hill had been convicted in Belfast Crown Court in June 1975 of the murder of a former British soldier. Carole Richardson was only 17 at the relevant time, so was ordered to be detained until the queen's pleasure be known for bombing both public houses. The judge, Sir John Donaldson, recommended that Gerard Conlon should serve not less than 30 years in prison. The recommendation in Patrick Armstrong's case was that he serve not less than 35 years in prison. As for Paul Hill, the judge indicated that he should never be released except on the grounds of age or infirmity. It was intended that he be buried alive in the prison system.

Those actually responsible for the Guildford and Woolwich bombings, and who freely admitted carrying them out on oath in open court, were members of the Provisional IRA: Joseph O'Connell, Harry Duggan and Edward Butler. They were captured with another man at Balcombe Street in London on 12 December 1975. A fourth man, Brendan Dowd, who had been arrested in Liverpool earlier that year, on 12 July, also admitted his part in those incidents. When arrested, so it was claimed, he was repeatedly punched and kicked in the head, rendering him unconscious for four days and leaving him with many injuries, including a broken jaw. He was tried by Mr Justice Joseph Cantley at the Assize Court sitting in Manchester and sent to prison for life. The judge was regarded by many as an upholder of the establishment and its principles, rather snobbish but respected by his professional colleagues. He was very partisan in his views, even during the conduct of a criminal trial. He had been appointed Leader of the Northern Circuit, a measure of his popularity among fellow barristers. He was sent to the Old Bailey in London to try the four men captured at Balcombe Street, and when asked to stand down on the ground of the appearance of bias declined to do so. That apparent bias arose from the fact that his name had been found on a list of IRA targets for assassination.

His best-known criminal case was another high-profile one also tried at the Old Bailey, in 1979. In May of that year four men appeared before him charged with conspiracy to murder. One of them was the Liberal Party politician Jeremy Thorpe, a barrister who had been educated at Eton and Oxford. There is some suspicion that Mr Justice Cantley was assigned the case to ensure that Thorpe would not be convicted. The trial judge virtually anointed Thorpe a saint in the course of summing up the case to the jury. In reality Thorpe was a fraudster and a rampant, violent and dangerous predator. Mr Justice Cantley went about destroying the reputation of the witnesses for the prosecution, especially Norman Scott, whom he described as a hysterical, warped personality, a whiner, a parasite, and an accomplished sponger who was skilled in exciting and exploiting sympathy. When a former Liberal politician, a former colleague of Thorpe's in the House of Commons who had also been a Methodist lay preacher, admitted while giving evidence for the prosecution that he had had a number of affairs with several women, that led Mr Justice Cantley to brand him an odious person and a humbug. Is it really part of the responsibility of a trial judge to make such derogatory observations about witnesses? Counsel in the case had certainly not praised the integrity of these witnesses, but should not the judge rise above that and concentrate on the law and the facts? After such a demolition job it was hardly surprising that Thorpe and his co-accused were acquitted by unanimous verdict of the jury. This case was not regarded as a triumph for British justice.

When the four Irishmen appeared before Mr Justice Cantley in January 1977 they faced numerous charges. He was not one of their admirers, as he had been of Jeremy Thorpe. He made little attempt to disguise from the jury his open hostility towards them. After their conviction Mr Justice Cantley told them they were 'criminals who called themselves soldiers', an observation more telling about him than about them.

The judge later wrote to the home secretary, as was customary at the time, to explain his reasons for a particular or specific recommendation attached to a sentence of life imprisonment. It was also established practice that the home secretary would consult the trial judge, if he was still alive (and the current lord chief justice if he was not), to determine issues such as the date of release from a life sentence. In his letter dated April 1977 Mr Justice Cantley told Merlyn Rees that he had doubts whether the accused men would ever be fit to live in a civilised community. He clearly intended that the men should never be released from prison. (They were in fact released as part of the arrangements made under the Good Friday agreement in 1998.)

The sworn evidence at the Guildford Four appeal in October 1977 that Joseph O'Connell, Harry Duggan and Brendan Dowd were responsible for the Woolwich throw-bomb incident, and that Joseph O'Connell and Brendan Dowd had, together with three others (whom they refused to name), bombed the two pubs in Guildford was simply not believed at the time. It seems extraordinary that those who freely confessed in this way were not believed, and those who denied the truth of their coerced confessions in police custody were not believed either.

The Guildford Four continued to languish in prison for another 12 years, despairing that they would ever see the outside world again.

The truth could not be suppressed for ever. To the dismay of some establishment figures, and the vicious opposition and fury of others, all the convictions were quashed in October 1989 and the Guildford Four were released from prison. There was some compelling evidence, so it was alleged, that the police had fabricated and falsified the confession evidence on which all four had been convicted. They had been in custody since November and December 1974. As will be seen later in this book, there was evidence at the very outset of their trial that tended to undermine the reliability and credibility of the prosecution witnesses. Unfortunately for the Guildford Four their barristers did not ask to see the detained person's register at any stage of the trial. If they had, justice might have prevailed and the Four might have walked free.

Among those in the legal establishment who expressed their views on the merits of the case of the Guildford Four was Sir James Miskin, the Old Bailey's most senior judge, known as 'Whispering Jim'. He spoke of his career on the day of his retirement on 26 July 1990 in an interview with the BBC's Newsroom South East. Asked if he still supported capital punishment in the light of the Guildford Four case, he said 'That was a mad decision, was it not? They did not give any thought to the fact that three years after it had happened that there was a full appeal and that was no suggestion from any source that police documentation showed the confessions had been cooked up.' It should have been recognised, he said, 'that there was a live risk the IRA could have bribed a young, hard-up police officer to cook up some documents to help free the Four'. According to the London *Times*, he added, 'I am not saying it did happen . . . but there should have been a full inquiry.' If Sir James had read a report of the Crown's case in the Court of Appeal he had not understood it. Counsel for the Crown made it clear to the court that relevant documents had been identified by the three officers concerned and they could offer no satisfactory explanation for those documents. He also failed to consider the evidence that a true interview with Paul Hill had been suppressed and false evidence given by the police in its place.

Lord Denning also intervened in the case and foolishly went even further, telling A.N. Wilson in August 1990 that if the Guildford Four had been hanged they probably would have hanged the right men. 'Just not proved against them, that's all.' Within two weeks the *Spectator* magazine, which had published the defamatory material, apologised. This was, especially for Denning, then in his declining years, a most humiliating climb-down. That did not prevent the Lord Chancellor, Lord Hailsham, from intervening, for he told the television programme *World in Action* that the quashing of a conviction does not necessarily establish innocence of the crime. As a statement of the law, this may be right, but the inference was clear. To Lord Hailsham and some others in the legal and political establishment these four accused persons were not innocent but factually guilty.

Returning to the case of the Guildford Four, in July 1990 a journalist wrote in *The Guardian*, 'Behind closed doors senior members of the legal establishment are alleging that the Guildford Four, or some of them, may have been involved in the bombings after all. Even as Lord Lane (the Lord Chief Justice) quashed their convictions he still believed they were guilty. From conversations I have had with members of the judiciary, I can say he would not be the only judge to think so.'

That was the position adopted by those establishment members (including Lord Hailsham) who maintained the guilt of the Guildford Four and regretted that a number of police officers may have lied in order to secure a conviction. Nothing will ever induce them to change their minds.

The legal correspondent of *The Times*, Marcel Berlins, told the BBC *Panorama* programme that no fewer than three judges had suggested to him that the Guildford Four were not necessarily innocent. One of them put it more crudely: 'they are as guilty as hell'.[1] That totally false claim still exists today despite the fact that on 9 February 2005 the then prime minister Tony Blair issued a public apology to the Guildford Four (and the Maguire Seven), saying, 'I am very sorry that they were subject to such an ordeal and injustice. They deserve to be completely and publicly exonerated.' Those words fell on some deaf ears in the legal and political establishment.

The details of the case are simple. At about 8.50 p.m. on Saturday 5 October 1974 a bomb exploded in the Horse and Groom pub in Guildford, Surrey. It had been placed under a seat in an alcove in the public bar. It had been carefully concealed there by young man and a young woman, posing as a courting couple. No warning was given. Five people died. One was a 21-year-old civilian; the other four, two men aged only 17 and two women aged 19 and 18, were service personnel. More than 50 other people were injured. Some of their injuries were beyond description. Later, the prosecution were to claim that the 'courting couple' were Patrick Armstrong and Carole Richardson. A second bomb placed in the nearby Seven Stars pub exploded at about 9.30 that evening. Eleven people were injured in that explosion as they began to re-enter the pub, a search of which had found nothing. The bomb had been carefully concealed under a seat in the most crowded part of the premises.

The reaction of the public and the media was one of outrage at the senseless slaughter of the innocent victims. Unsurprisingly, members of the Conservative and Unionist Party in the Home Counties called for the restoration of the death penalty for acts of terrorism. Among them was a barrister and MP, Sir Michael Havers QC, who later appeared as leading counsel for the prosecution at the trial of the Guildford Four. The Provisional IRA later attempted to murder him in November 1981 by bombing his house in Wimbledon. No one was injured in the explosion, which caused extensive damage to the property. He and his family were away from home at the time.

Paul Michael Hill was born in Belfast in August 1954. Like hundreds of others of his age and background he had been lifted more than once by the British army in his native city, interrogated but not charged with any offence. His photograph was, however, taken by the army on 18 May 1974; at that time he had shoulder-length fair hair. It is claimed by some that on 9 October 1974 an army intelligence officer based in Belfast saw a photo fit of two women in the *Sun* newspaper. That was four days after the bombings. He telephoned the Surrey Police at Guildford saying that Paul Hill could easily be mistaken for a woman and that he suspected him of being one of the Guildford bombers. In fact the photo fit was not of one of the bombers at all, but of one of the two women who had died in the Horse and Groom. Not everyone believes that account of how Paul Hill became a suspect in the case; other anecdotal evidence seems to point to an informer who had been a friend of his and who was apparently paid some £350 for providing information, which in the event turned out to be false.

Although army intelligence records dated August and September 1974 claimed that Paul Hill had gone to England in August 1974 as part of an IRA bombing team, it is a matter of record that from the time of his arrival in the UK he claimed unemployment benefit using his own name and providing an address to which he could be linked. He had in fact travelled to England from Belfast on 23 August 1974 with his sister, his girlfriend and another man. When the four left the ferry at Heysham in Lancashire, both men were interviewed by a Special Branch officer. Paul Hill gave his true name and date of birth. When he was found asleep and drunk on a bus on 19 September 1974 in Bitterne near Southampton he gave a police officer his true name, date of birth and current address. He was clearly not trying to conceal his presence or identity from the police in England at any stage, despite a former commander of the Bomb Squad's description of him in a book published in 1977 as 'a Provisional IRA explosives expert'.[2]

Sometime in late September 1974 he met his friend from Belfast, Gerard Conlon, in Southampton. They decided to travel to London together on 20 September 1974. There they stayed one night with Gerard Conlon's uncle and aunt, Hugh and Kathleen Maguire, at their home in Paddington. That contact between them was to have devastating consequences for the lives of Mr and Mrs Maguire; Paul Hill named Hugh in his second statement, dated 29 November 1974, saying that he had stayed in Hugh's home for two days because he was ordered to do so. The police drew the inference from that, quite wrongly, that it was a 'safe house' for members of the IRA, so they raided it and detained the occupants. Hugh and Kathleen Maguire were held in custody for a week before being released without charge.

Gerard Conlon was born in Belfast on 1 March 1954. He went to the same school as Paul Hill. On 3 August 1974 he returned to the UK from Belfast, with a girlfriend, to stay with relations in Southampton. While there he applied for a National Insurance number, providing his full name, address, date and place of birth. All this has to be read in conjunction with the version of events described by ex-Commander Bob Huntley. He relates, 'Conlon, twenty one, had been sent over by the IRA high command to await orders on bombing raids. Hill, a fellow IRA lieutenant, was slipped into England to stay in Southampton as a "sleeper".'[3] As set out above, that was quite incorrect. Paul Hill had not 'slipped' into England at all; he had arrived at Heysham, where he had given his particulars to a Special Branch officer, and later obtained social security benefits in his own name. Gerard Conlon had also disclosed his details to the authorities when he returned to the UK. Would they have done that if they had been on a terrorist mission to bomb England?

On 21 September 1974 Paul Hill and Gerard Conlon left Paddington and moved into a hostel, Hope House, at 20 Quex Road, Kilburn, which was run by the Oblate Fathers, an order of Catholic priests. Fr Paddy Carolan was in charge of the premises when they arrived and he recalls them being wet and miserable when they got there. He did not want to take them in for he knew nothing about them and they had no introductory letter from their parish priest in Ireland, as would be the norm, but he took pity on them. After they filled in cards giving their personal details, they were allocated to a four-bed room, the St Louis, with two other men, Patrick Carey and Charles Burke, both of whom were Irish. Charles Burke was a slightly eccentric individual who dressed almost entirely in green; he was known to others in the hostel as Paul the Greengrocer, for that was his occupation. He later became an important witness whose existence – and evidence – was not disclosed to the defence at trial.

Fr Carolan was at the time the Irish representative on the Camden Race Relations Board. Another member of the board was a senior police officer from the Hampstead area, and Fr Carolan asked him to send uniformed police officers to the hostel from time to time because he had been asked by his religious superiors to be very vigilant for any attempt by the IRA to use the hostel as a cover for their operations. The police did regularly visit the premises and the senior officer from Hampstead told Fr Carolan that the police were getting all the information they needed. (It is probable that they had an informant, perhaps even a police officer who was Irish, living on the premises at that time.)

On Saturday 5 October 1975 Fr Carolan left London to visit his mother in Ireland. The pub bombings took place in the evening of that day. After Paul Hill's arrest he named Fr Carolan in his second statement of 29 November 1974: 'Paul came to the house and told both to go to Quix [*sic*] Road and tell the priest that we had just come over from Ireland. We went there and saw Father Carlyn [*sic*] who put us up.' Clearly someone decided that that incriminated the priest enough to justify bringing him in for questioning. Immediately after his return from Ireland, Fr Carolan was taken to Guildford police station for interrogation. It is not clear whether he was under arrest. During the questioning one of the officers, Inspector Timothy Blake, now deceased, was very rude and rough with him, so much so that Fr Carolan complained to another officer that he was the greatest bastard he had ever met. The response was that that particular officer, Blake, was the only Catholic at that police station. Fr Carolan was never charged with any criminal offence, for there was no shred of evidence against him.

Between 23 September 1974 and 11 October 1974 both Paul Hill and Gerard Conlon were employed as labourers by a construction company in London, so both were in full-time employment at the time they were supposed to have bombed Guildford. On 11 October they went with others to the Carousel ballroom in Kentish Town to see the well-known Irish group the Wolfe Tones. There they met and chatted to, among others, Gerard Conlon's aunt, Anne Maguire. She, her husband (and all their children) have cause to regret that she ever met Paul Hill and her nephew Gerard Conlon that evening.

On 19 October 1974 Gerard Conlon left Hope House to return to Ireland and took the train for Holyhead. There he was questioned by the police, to whom he gave his full particulars, including his address as the Quex Road hostel. Would the Guildford bomber have done that? He then took the night ferry to Dún Laoghaire, County Dublin. From there he returned to his home in Belfast.

Paul Hill left Hope House on 20 October to stay with relations in the Archway area of London. But not for long. He terminated his employment with the construction company on 22 November and the following day he travelled to Southampton with his pregnant girlfriend Gina Clark, a former neighbour in Belfast. There they stayed with Gina's brother. At about 10.40 a.m. on Thursday 28 November, police officers descended on the house and arrested Paul Hill on suspicion of causing explosions. It is unclear whether Gina was arrested at the same time, and what reasonable grounds of suspicion of which particular offence would give rise to the power of arrest in her case. She was certainly held at the police station, because Paul Hill recollects hearing her voice, high and distraught. According to him, in his auto-biography written with Ronan Bennett, Gina had been strip-searched and was told she was being booked for murder. He further claimed that a woman police officer called her 'a fucking IRA bastard and an IRA bitch'. In the event Gina was released from police custody without charge.

Paul Hill claims that he was assaulted and abused by the police while in custody. He claims that one officer threatened him with a gun poked through the flap of his cell door. The court that tried him rejected his claims as untrue. Would they have done so if they had known that at some date in the future a retired police officer would tell the appeal court in Belfast that he had seen a fellow officer dry fire a gun into a cell at Guildford police station at the relevant time, and that another retired officer told the same court that he had heard the officer boasting about what he had done?

Hill was also interviewed by RUC officers about the murder of Brian Shaw, a former British soldier, in Belfast. That interrogation led to Hill being charged with, and, at Belfast Crown Court in June 1975, convicted of involvement in that murder. It therefore followed that by the time he came to trial for murder with other members of the Four in London in September 1975 the trial judge, and of course all the lawyers on both sides, knew of that conviction. Hill's conviction for that alleged offence was later set aside on appeal.

Paul Hill began to name names to the interrogating police officers. As a result, Gerard Conlon was arrested at 5.30 a.m. on Saturday 30 November at his parents' home in Cyprus Street, Belfast, taken eventually to the Springfield Road police station and detained there. After being interviewed he was flown to London and detained at a Surrey police station. He too began to name others. According to ex-Commander Huntley, 38 people were arrested as a result of what the police were told. There is a dispute between Hill and Conlon about who first named Conlon's aunt, Anne Maguire, as being involved in the Guildford bombings, but certainly the police arranged a confrontation between them, when Conlon looked at his aunt and said, 'I wasn't the first to mention your name.' In an agonised voice Anne Maguire cried out to him, 'Gerry, I've got four children.' Asked by a police officer where he had last seen her, he replied that he had already told him this in his statement. He then left the room. Anne Maguire was charged with murder. Apart from the false allegations made against her by Conlon and Hill there was no admissible evidence against her. Someone at some stage realised that the rules of evidence meant that the allegations, unsworn and uncorroborated by an independent witness, were worthless. The charge of murder was dropped. It was not, however, the end of an agonising journey for Anne, her husband and their four children.

Also included in the list of suspects compiled by the police from information supplied by Hill and Conlon were Patrick Armstrong and his girlfriend Carole Richardson. There is no doubt about who first actually named Carole. It was Paul Hill.

Patrick Armstrong was born in Belfast in September 1950. He went to the same school as Paul Hill and Gerard Conlon but was some four years ahead of them. He first arrived in the UK after doing casual work on building sites in Belfast and was happy to be away from the stifling and dangerous atmosphere that was building up in that city. He also did not miss the constant stop-and-search policies being operated against young men of his age group by British soldiers no older than he was.

Armstrong drifted from job to job and place to place, ending up living in a squat in the Kilburn area of London with other young Irishmen and, frequently, local girls. Among them was Carole Margaret Richardson, who was born in London on 19 June 1957, making her 17 years old when she went to the police station on Tuesday 3 December 1974. She was a very troubled and lonely soul, in many ways little more than a child, and she had been taking drugs on that day. Her father had deserted her mother before she was born, so she never knew him. She had left school, where she had long history of truancy, at the age of 15 without a single academic qualification. She was put before the Willesden Juvenile Court for alleged dishonesty and made the subject of a supervision order, eventually being taken into the care of the local authority.

Carole was asked by Surrey police officers to assist them in their enquiries at about 6.40 p.m. on 3 December, at her mother's home in Kilburn. I can find no evidence anywhere that she was ever placed under arrest. She is now deceased. A copy of the Detention Sheet RBI/27/3, provided to me by the CPS, shows that when the police took her to the police station she had only 45 pence in her possession. One sheet, which is supposed to be an accurate record of the treatment of a suspect in a police station, records that she arrived at a police station at 1 p.m. and was later interviewed by the Bomb Squad at 3.50 p.m.; another sheet records that she was placed in another cell elsewhere at 1.35 a.m. on 4 December 1974. On Detention Sheet RB1/27/3 is written the following: 'Prisoner to be under constant supervision in cell block and is not allowed out of the cells under any circumstances.' Does that indicate her mental state, or is it an indication that she was under the influence of a prohibited substance?

While she was serving her sentence after conviction, a medical report was prepared on her on 30 April 1986 by the distinguished consultant forensic psychiatrist, the late and greatly lamented Dr James MacKeith, a graduate of Trinity College, Dublin. Apparently the doctor at Styal prison in Cheshire, where Carole was being held at the time, contacted her solicitors in March 1984, some nine years into her prison sentence, indicating his belief that she was innocent and that something must be done about it. It is not often that a member of the Prison Medical Service forms such a view and takes such steps. The Home Office decided that Carole should be examined by a psychiatrist, which is how Dr MacKeith became involved in the case.

In his report, which was eventually given to Carole's solicitors with the permission of the Home Office, Dr MacKeith noted that Carole had had at least 14 short-term jobs between August 1972 and December 1974. She was almost continually in employment, working as a clerk, a cashier and a sales assistant in London. However, by the age of 13 years she had become involved in petty theft and sometimes stole money from home. She was arrested for shoplifting. At the age of 15 she was placed on probation for two years after being found guilty of burglary. From the age of 13 she drank alcohol and began abusing drugs. She smoked cannabis on a regular basis, and was for some years prescribed amphetamines by her doctor. She took LSD, sometimes by injection, and also took cocaine on two occasions. For some months before December 1974 she was taking barbiturates, as many as 20 capsules a day. She had begun to live in a squat following her mother's partner's decision to ban her from her own family home because of her behaviour – not returning home on several successive nights, without any explanation. It was in a squat that she began her relationship with Patrick Armstrong around August 1974. She named him to the police and provided them with the address where he was living, resulting in his arrest at 9.25 p.m. on Tuesday 3 December 1974. Without that information it seems very unlikely that the police would ever have found where Patrick Armstrong was living at that time. When he was taken into custody it was found that he was covered in scabies. His cell had to be fumigated constantly. His appearance and demeanour gave every indication of his lifestyle as a drifter of no fixed abode. It was later claimed that Carole Richardson had been trained by the Provisional IRA in counter-interrogation techniques. Apparently that training did not include a prohibition on naming another person who would otherwise not have been found and arrested by the police.

At the trial of the Guilford Four, virtually the entire basis of the prosecution case against them was confession evidence that they disputed and forcefully denied.

Paul Hill made a total of six confession statements, four of which were written by him. Gerard Conlon made two such statements. He wrote them both in his own handwriting. Patrick Armstrong made three statements. He wrote none of them. Carole Richardson made four statements, three of which were written by her. At their trial the Four claimed that they had been subjected to police brutality, threats, intimidation and inducements, and that some of the evidence against them had been concocted. The jury did not believe them. We know a great deal more about confessions in police custody now than we ever did in 1974. Patrick Armstrong undoubtedly confessed to the murders. He claimed at his trial that the confession evidence was extracted from him by threatening and violent conduct, and was fabricated and falsified by the police. The jury rejected this explanation. The following statements from former police officers about confession evidence may throw some light, even though it may not been seen in that way by the wilfully blind, on whether Patrick Armstrong and two of his three co-accused were telling the entire truth in their evidence on oath in the witness box.

I Confess – to You, Officer

In 1960 John Symonds became a trainee detective in the London Metropolitan Police, an aide to CID. He told the London *Times* on 31 March 1994 that he found himself sucked into a system that 'corrupted my soul'.

> Then I found a type of corruption, completely new to me, where, in order to become a detective, you have to prove beyond doubt that you are prepared to perjure yourself, and where there's no chance of ever being selected as a detective unless you're prepared to get together, make up evidence, go to court and carry it off. I must say that within the next few years I spent as a detective, I lied practically every day, and so did everybody else. The net result was that a lot of innocent people were sent to prison.

Another more senior officer put it rather differently. On 3 November 1973 Sir Robert Mark, who had been appointed as Commissioner of the London Metropolitan Police in 1972, gave the prestigious Dimbleby Memorial Lecture on BBC Television. He told his audience:

> Most detectives have a strong sense of commitment. It would be unnatural if they did not feel personally involved in some of the cases and it would be untrue to suggest that they are not sometimes outraged by the results. All are under occasional temptation to bend the rules to convict those whom they believe to be guilty, if only

because convention has always inhibited them from saying how badly they think those rules work.

Just how many gave in to that temptation to bend the rules can only be guessed at. Certainly the numbers cannot have been in single figures, for as Sir Robert himself admitted in his autobiography he told officers of the CID, that 'they represented what had long been the most routinely corrupt organisation in London, and that nothing or no one would prevent me from putting an end to it and that if necessary I would put the whole of the CID back into uniform and make a fresh start'.[4]

Another London Metropolitan Police commissioner, Sir Paul Condon, also used the BBC News in December 1998 to get his message across. He admitted that some officers 'bent the rules' and lied. All for a good reason, of course; to ensure a conviction when they had convinced themselves that a person was guilty but there might be insufficient evidence to prove it. He said, 'I think there was a time when a minority of officers were prepared to bend the rules, massage the evidence, not for personal gain, or even in their own terms, to tell lies about people. But I think elaborating on things that were said in a way to make sure the case had the strongest chance of going through to a conviction.' Would that not require the officer concerned to decide that the accused person he was 'fitting up' was in fact guilty?

In September 1992, Sir John Woodcock, the chief inspector of constabulary, coined a memorable phrase, 'noble cause corruption', the idea held by some officers that it was permissible to fabricate evidence or commit perjury in order to convict 'factually guilty' suspects who would otherwise be acquitted'.[5]

A more junior officer, but one who worked on the front line, was Chief Inspector Euan Read, who joined the police service in 1978. He served with the Thames Valley force. On 8 February 1995 he told the journalist David Rose, 'my main aim was to get confessions . . . There were no contemporaneous notes; notebooks could be compiled days later. You assume any ability to be dishonest and the mind boggles. Documents could be changed and, sure, I saw people who'd been beaten up, threatened, told "you fucking write this or else".'[6] Does that have the ring of truth? Why say it if it is untrue?

Was Patrick Armstrong speaking the truth when he described his treatment in police custody? Would the jury who rejected his evidence have paused for thought if they had read these quotations from senior and, I believe, truthful police officers who have nothing to gain by being open and honest about the past?

In their book *The Flying Squad* about the unit based at Scotland Yard in London (and known to me and some of my contemporaries as 'The Lying Squad'), Neil Darbyshire and Brian Hilliard described the antics of that rather elite group, who had a high opinion of themselves, as follows: 'the squad detectives, and doubtless many other CID men were not above giving fabricated evidence and "gilding the lily" to convict those they believed to be guilty, and . . . the courts, although they must have had some inkling of what was going on, were generally prepared to turn a blind eye to such corner-cutting, trusting that the detectives were putting the right men in the dock.' If this it true, why not abolish trial by jury, let the police decide who is guilty and who is not, and let the judiciary sentence in accordance with what the police consider meets the merits of the case?

It is self-evident that a confession in a criminal case that is involuntary and untrue is as good as a true confession if a jury can be persuaded to believe it. The quotations from the retired police officers cited above do not stand alone. Two others, both of whom reached the very top of their chosen profession, have described the tactics used to obtain vital confession evidence, so often essential when there was no other evidence against a suspect the officers 'knew' to be guilty.

Peter Neyroud, a former chief constable of Thames Valley Police, said in the BBC television programme *Re-trial by TV* broadcast on 3 April 2011: 'I joined in 1980. Very early on, as a temporary detective, we were very, very strongly told "confinement brings confessions". We prepared confessions. We wrote them out before we sat down with the people and we got them to sign them. They weren't their words.' Is that not exactly what happened to the Guildford Four – held in unlawful confinement and then signing a prepared confession, in some instances written for them by a police officer?

Neyroud went on to allege that the courts knew this was happening and did nothing about it. However that may be, can there be any doubt that the reprehensible, corrupt and unlawful practices he described did not begin in 1980 but had been going on since at least the early 1960s?

The second senior police officer who told the indiscreet truth was Keith Hellawell. He joined the police service in the West Riding of Yorkshire in 1962, becoming a detective two years later. He attained the rank of chief constable, first of Cleveland and then of West Yorkshire. He has no reason to lie about the past. In his autobiography *The Outsider*, published in 2002, he wrote that previously the service was 'brutal, authoritarian and corrupt' but that it had changed. The blurb on the book jacket says, 'He lifts the lid on police brutality, corruption and abuse of power.' He certainly does that in relation to police interviews. He shockingly claims, 'we used to make up the names of people we had "interviewed" in connection with our inquiries and wrote down a list of relevant places we had "visited". In reality, except for the more serious crimes, we did nothing but interview at length all the people who were arrested for other offences, many of whom were quite amenable to admitting crimes they had not committed, just to keep in our good books.' It did not end there. According to him there was further scope for perjury and deception on the part of indolent police officers immersed in a culture of habitual lying.

Hellawell continues: 'People arrested for street disorder would be physically assaulted on arrival at a police station if they spoke out of turn, and their injuries would be attributed to "falling". If they complained, no action would be taken. Those arrested for crime would, if necessary, be beaten into confessing; they had no right of access to a solicitor, and would be detained until they signed a confession. . . . I am not suggesting that every prisoner was assaulted or had confessions beaten out of him; merely that this was an accepted course of action if it seemed necessary.'

Those in the legal and political establishment who maintain the guilt of the Guildford Four may have to consider their position in the light of these startling statements from two senior police officers.

The Guildford Four Once More

Because the treatment of Carole Richardson by the police in custody is, I believe, central to the understanding of the case, it is necessary to examine in detail just how she came to confess to crimes she had not committed.

Her first recorded interview at Guildford police station took place between 1.15 and 6.20 p.m. on Wednesday 4 December 1974. During that time she wrote a statement under caution. She mentioned Patrick Armstrong, who had invited her to go for a drive at a time when she was under the influence of drugs. She was, she wrote, 'completely smashed on downers'. The statement started at 4.25 p.m. and concluded at 4.49 p.m. Three police officers, one a woman, were present during the writing of that statement, in which Carole did not admit any bombing offence. Carole had no legal adviser present, and there is no record that she was told of her right of access to legal advice.

By the evening of that Wednesday Carole was becoming hysterical and extremely distressed, which is hardly surprising since the police told her that others were accusing her of involvement in bombing offences. She later accused the police of assaulting her during the interview. The police surgeon, Dr Kasimir Makos, was sent for. At 8.50 p.m. he examined her in the presence of a woman police officer. He concluded Carole was fit for further detention but because she was then in a highly hysterical state, hyperventilating and trembling, he gave her a 200 mg capsule of Tuinal, a sedative. That seemed to calm her down.

Carole was interviewed again the next day, Thursday 5 December. I can find no time of the interview, but a statement made by Dr Makos was read to her, the contents of which she denied. She made a second statement under caution, which is recorded as having been written in room 322 at Guildford police station by a woman detective constable between 4.15 and 5.15 p.m., continued from 6.00 p.m. to 7.30 p.m. and then completed between 8.00 and 9.40 p.m. Two male officers were also present at the time. In that statement she admitted being in the Horse and Groom with Patrick Armstrong when he pushed a parcel under their seat and they kissed. Some lawyers might have expected that she would be charged with an offence relating to this, since there was clearly sufficient evidence with which to charge her. That would be in accordance with the Judges' Rules 1964, which govern the interrogation and treatment of suspects in custody. But that was not done. No reason for not doing so has ever been publicly stated anywhere.

The next day, Friday 6 December 1974, Carole was interviewed from 11.35 a.m. to 1.45 p.m. A second interview started at 3 p.m., when she admitted that she had been present at a house when three bombs were being made. She wrote a third statement under caution in room 19 in Godalming police station between 6.43 p.m. and 8.30 p.m. In it she described how the bombs were made. The same three police officers were present. In the afternoon of the next day she was charged with murdering one of the young women who had died in the Horse and Groom. On the following Monday morning Carole was taken before the Guildford Magistrates' Court and remanded in custody. She was not, however, finished with the interviewing police officers. Up to this time she had been questioned by the police for about five hours on 4 December; no times were given for interview(s) on 5 December but she made a statement over one hour and 15 minutes; on 6 December she was questioned and made a statement for some seven hours and 40 minutes. According to the police, on her return to Godalming police station in the late morning of that Monday she said she wanted to see Patrick Armstrong because there was something not right about what she had previously said. She was interviewed in the afternoon at 2.40 p.m. but no detailed notes of that interview were ever produced. She wrote another statement under caution, her fourth, between 5.50 p.m. and 8 p.m. A typescript note of the interview accompanying it showed that it ended at 6.30 p.m., but this had been changed in manuscript to 8 p.m. and it was further written that there had been a break in the interview for 45 minutes between 6.30 p.m. and 7.15 p.m. Even more significantly, according to the detention sheet, two senior officers, a detective superintendent and a detective chief inspector, saw Carole in the police cell from 9.10 p.m. to 10.15 p.m. No record of what was said during that time was ever disclosed, as it should have been. The next day, Tuesday 10 December 1974, the same detective chief inspector saw Carole in her cell for ten minutes between 11.50 a.m. and noon. Again, whatever was said was not disclosed, though it is unlikely that on either occasion there was a social chat about the weather.

The content of this fourth statement was to be a source of some embarrassment to the prosecution at the subsequent trial because in it Carole Richardson confessed to entering the second pub in Guildford, the Seven Stars, when even the prosecution accepted that she had not done so. She wrote:

> After we left the café what I said about boming [sic] the Horse and Groom is right after we got in the car we drove for a while, I would say about five minutes the road in which we stopped was badly lit and I didn't notice any cars pass us or going in the other direction the road was about 12–14 feet wide. The driver turned around and said 'go in and have a drink' so I got out of the car from behind the passenger [sic] seat and crossed behind the car and walked about 10 yards we entered the pub which was or looked like old brick with I think a flat front, as we went in Paddy said 'get me a short' and then he said 'I'll be back in a minute' and walked away, so I went to the bar and got him a Pernod and I had a rum and black. I was at the bar for about 4 minutes. Then I walked away from the bar, and Paddy came over to me we stood about 4ft from the bar, inside the pub it wasn't so bright and the people seemed younger and I could hear music, the bar was curved round into a corner. The inside wasn't as nice as the Horse and Groom I think there was a ciggarette [sic] machine on one wall. There was a man standing at the bar he was plump and he stood on my toe. While we were standing drinking Paddy said 'thanks don't worry it'll be alright'. We finished our drinks left the pub and went back to the car, the driver started the car and we reversed out of the road. And drove up the road and back to London. As far as I know Paddy did not carry anything into

the pub and if he did I didn't see him . . . I didn't know that there was going to be a bomb planted in the second pub but I guessed there might be when I saw the four of them talking together.

The prosecution case against Carole Richardson claimed that she had left the Horse and Groom at 6.53 p.m. on Saturday 5 October together with Patrick Armstrong, the other half of the courting couple, and that they had placed the bomb under the bench on which they were sitting prior to their departure. They relied on the evidence of two soldiers to prove the time. Carole could not remember when or at what times she had been in the various pubs where she had been taken on that particular Friday. Her diary, which she kept rather carefully, would have helped, but it could not be found. In fact, it had been destroyed by someone at the squat. But she had two friends who could remember: Lisa Astin, aged 16, who lived in the same squat as Carole; and 'Geordie Frank', whose real name was Frank Johnson. He lived in a squat in the Brixton area. He had friends in a band called Jack The Lad. They were scheduled to play in a concert at South Bank Polytechnic on that Saturday evening, 5 October 1974. Frank telephoned them to ask whether he and two friends could be added to the guest list. They agreed. There is no doubt that Frank, Lisa and Carole did attend that concert on that Saturday evening, because a photograph of Carole was taken with one of the musicians in the band, proving beyond any doubt that she was there. There was evidence that Carole and her two friends were at the polytechnic at times put between 7.40 p.m. and 8 p.m. Members of the band and staff at the polytechnic whose integrity and honesty was not challenged proved those times, on which there was no total agreement. The accommodation officer thought the trio arrived at 8 p.m. One of the band members agreed with that. Others put the time between 7.40 p.m. and 7.50 p.m.

Two questions arise from this. First, how could Carole have been leaving the Horse and Groom some seven minutes before seven o'clock and yet be in the Elephant and Castle area some 52 to 67 minutes later? Second, how did she have time to enter the second pub, the Seven Stars, and still get to the polytechnic within those times?

To answer the first question, the police arranged for a police car, observing the speed limits in force in 1974, to make the journey. It took 52 minutes. A second journey, ignoring the speed limits, took 48 minutes. It is not clear whether the vehicle used was a marked police car or not. A solicitor's clerk made the same journey, in, of course, an unmarked car. He did it on Saturday 4 October 1975, leaving the Horse and Groom at 6.58 p.m. It took him 64 minutes to travel from Guildford to the polytechnic. On any view these timings were very tight for the journey said to have been undertaken by Carole Richardson: among other considerations, whoever did that journey would have to find where the car was parked in Guildford (where there were many restrictions), then find a parking space near the polytechnic and then walk from there to the premises. I would have hoped that the defence team would have required proof that the two runs made by the police took place on a Saturday evening at times similar to those under scrutiny. I cannot find any evidence that they did.

To answer the second question, the prosecution at the trial did something which, if it were not so serious, would have been amusing. Carole had written a fourth statement describing her visit to the second pub, with the flat front, in great detail, from the length of time she spent there to a plump man standing on her toe. Sir Michael Havers QC told the court that this version of events was not true. Carole Richardson had not bombed the Seven Stars. That statement had been put forward as part of an IRA counter-interrogation technique designed to cause confusion. Why the IRA should choose Carole Richardson, only 17 and a very troubled young woman, the only non-Irish member of the group of four, to be trained in such a technique is mystifying. When and where that training took place was never mentioned by anyone. Surely a better technique would have advocated answering no questions and making no statements at all to the police. It also begs the question, why were the prosecution so determined to abandon the content of that fourth statement while at the same time claiming that her confessions were voluntary and true? The answer is simple: when the statement was obtained the police did not realise that if it was true, Carole could not have made the journey to South Bank Polytechnic in the time available. Because of the time they claimed she left the first pub and the time they had to accept she was back in London, the fourth statement, with all its detail, had to be disregarded and treated as untrue. As indeed it was.

Carole's explanation for her four statements was short and simple. The police had assaulted her; she had confessed partly out of panic and partly to stop the police getting to her. The statements set out in her own handwriting were virtually dictated to her. She was forced to do what she did; she was terrified of what might be done to her if she continued to deny involvement in the bombings.

It is clear, moreover, that no one realised the significance of the times the courting couple left the pub. The exact or even approximate time seemed not to matter – until Carole realised that she could prove conclusively that she was at the polytechnic that Saturday evening. It should be remembered that the prosecution case against her was that early on that evening she had taken part in a cruel and callous bombing in which five young people were killed, and then, seemingly without a care in the world, gone to a pop concert with two friends.

It was not Carole, however, who first remembered her whereabouts on the night of the Guildford bombings. Her friend, fellow occupant and drug user at the squat, Lisa Astin, aged 16, had been arrested in December but released on police bail. (Anne Maguire recalled Lisa allegedly starting a small fire in the police station where they were being held.) On or about Saturday 13 December 1974 Lisa met up with Frank Johnson. They naturally discussed Carole's and Lisa's arrests. Three days after that Carole wrote to Lisa from Brixton prison asking her to find out the date when the Jack The Lad band had played at South Bank Polytechnic. By this date Frank had returned to Newcastle but he now recalled meeting Carole and Lisa on that first Saturday in October at the Charlie Chaplin pub some distance from the polytechnic. The two young women were wearing long dresses and were in bare feet, something that no doubt would have attracted attention of other people in the pub. No one came forward to say they had seen them. I question whether the police made any effort to find any witnesses who might have seen them in the Charlie Chaplin. If, however, it was true that they were in the pub before going to the concert, no matter at what time, Carole Richardson could not, on the timings available, have bombed Guildford.

Frank Johnson wanted to help Carole. He went to the local magistrates' court. They passed him on to some local solicitors. They simply did not want to know. He went to the police in his native Newcastle, who sent for the Surrey Police. The three officers who had interviewed Carole Richardson arrived. Subsequently Frank Johnson was arrested, not once but twice, on the basis that if he was with Carole on the evening of 5 October 1974, then he was one of the Guildford bombers; or he was trying to protect her by lying for her and thereby perverting the course of justice. In the circumstances, after two and a half days in custody at Guildford police station, to which he had been taken, he did what most young men of his age and disposition would do; he changed his story and told the police exactly what they wanted to hear. He made a statement saying he had lied to protect Carole. Since this was a clear confession to, at the very least, an attempt to obstruct or pervert justice, one would have expected him to be charged with an offence. He was not. He was simply released from police custody. But of course if he ever went back to his original story, as indeed he did at Carole's trial, the prosecution would find it easy to discredit him by producing the statement in which he had admitted lying on her behalf. A later judicial inquiry conducted by a High Court judge, Sir John May, concluded that the first arrest could not be justified and the second arrest was not a proper exercise by the police of their powers.[7] So that wasn't justified in law either. For reasons I do not pretend to understand, Lord Justice Roskill in the appeal court made reference to 'This alibi evidence, as we have said, bears all the marks of concoction . . . the jury must have asked themselves why this alibi had been concocted and reached the conclusion there was only one explanation for its concoction.'[8] Surely the only important issue was the time at which Carole Richardson and her two friends arrived at the pop concert, because even the prosecution accepted that she and they were at South Bank Polytechnic on that Saturday evening. They had not given a false account of going to the polytechnic; that had actually happened. But to Lord Justice Roskill what counted was the fact that in Carole Richardson's fourth statement in which she confessed to bombing both pubs, she made no reference at all to her attendance at the concert. For that reason, then, the learned lord justice surmised, she and they must have concocted a false alibi. But is that right? Can many people remember on 9 December in any one year, on calm reflection, not in the oppressive atmosphere of a police station, where they were on the evening of 5 October in that same year?

It should be noted for the record that the jury convicted Carole Richardson of involvement in bombing the Seven Stars in addition to all the other charges relating to the Horse and Groom, perhaps on the grounds that she had been a party to the common design to carry out bombings in public houses in Guildford, and had never retreated or withdrawn from that common design.

As for Frank Johnson, he later brought an action against the police claiming false arrest and wrongful imprisonment. He lost, not on the merits of his case, but on the basis that he had brought the proceedings too late in the day, and statute barred him from succeeding in his claim for damages. Because he had initially approached the police with the intention of helping Carole Richardson establish the truth, they knew long before she and her legal team did of the existence of the witnesses in the pop band and how they could help her case. Any attempt to get these material witnesses, about whom the defence at first knew nothing, to change their evidence to allow Carole ample time to travel from Guildford after placing the bomb simply failed. Although they did not agree with each other on the times, it is clear that the band members gave Carole an alibi for that evening – the only dispute was the exact time she and Lisa arrived at the concert venue. None of them put it later than 8 p.m. that Saturday evening. The police did not tell her solicitors what their enquiries had disclosed, leading to an accusation by Carole's leading counsel that this was behaviour straight out of the book of dirty tricks. The detective chief inspector to whom this allegation was put denied it.

The trial of the Guildford Four opened on 16 September 1975 at the Old Bailey in London. Security around the court building was extremely tight; armed police officers with automatic weapons were perched on rooftops overlooking the court. The atmosphere in and around the building was extremely tense.

The case began with disturbing conduct by leading counsel for the prosecution, Sir Michael Havers QC: he showed exhibits in the case to the press for the purpose only of prejudice and to ensure a hostile attitude by the press to the four young people in the dock. Havers was a rising star in the law and in politics and a dangerous opponent to cross, in or out of the courtroom. When he told the jury at the Guildford Four trial that their confession statements (in which there were numerous conflicts of fact, such as who drove the cars to Guildford, how many cars there were, and who actually placed the bombs) 'fitted together like a jigsaw', I think he was playing the role of a politician who can find a problem for every solution, rather than a barrister.

According to Paul Reynolds, the world affairs correspondent of the BBC, Havers distributed copies of photographs of some of the dead victims of the two pub bombings to the press on that first day. Reynolds recalls two of the photographs vividly. One was of a young Scots Guardsman lying on a mortuary slab with his lower limbs blown off. Another, from the Woolwich bomb, showed a soldier with the whole of one leg missing. 'Presumably', Mr Reynolds told the BBC World Service, 'Havers thought this would put the press in the right frame of mind to cover such an important trial.' On any view this was conduct of the most reprehensible kind. The press were not at that time entitled to see these photographs, which were court exhibits.

There is another serious allegation against Sir Michael Havers. According to the experienced ITV journalist Norman Rees, he told the jury on the opening day of the trial that Patrick Armstrong and Carole Richardson would be identified by two soldiers as the courting couple who placed the explosive device in one of the Guildford pubs. Speaking to camera on the ITV evening news, Rees said 'two soldiers had seen the couple kissing and cuddling in the corner of the bar on the night of the explosion. At the time they were in the process of planting a time bomb under their seat. Sir Michael said the couple would be identified by the soldiers as Patrick Armstrong, aged 24, and Carole Richardson, aged 17.' That was totally misleading and wrong. They were never identified by anyone. On Friday 13 December 1974 Carole Richardson stood in no fewer than eight identification parades, all held at Guildford police station. No one picked her out as the bomber. Patrick Armstrong was never put on a parade at any stage. Two soldiers, both paratroopers, Paul Lynskey and John Cook, had given detailed descriptions of the courting couple they saw in the pub. It was on these two witnesses that the prosecution relied to establish the time the couple left the Horse and Groom. John Cook described the young woman as having 'natural blonde hair'. The photograph of Carole Richardson taken on the night of 5 October at South Bank Polytechnic shows that she was not blonde but brunette. He further described the man involved as having wavy, dark hair. Patrick Armstrong had straight, long fair hair. No effort was ever made by the prosecution to explain these differences.

Norman Rees's report was supported by *The Times*,[9] which said that Patrick Armstrong and Carole Richardson were the bombers, without stating whose evidence would prove that. Clearly, however, if that was alleged by the prosecution, they would have to prove it in evidence. The report goes on, 'The Crown says that the couple were Mr Armstrong and Miss Richardson . . . and they were hiding the bomb under the seat, setting the device in position as they kissed and cuddled.' That statement was based on their confessions. It was not true.

In dramatically claiming to the jury that Carole Richardson and Patrick Armstrong would be identified as the Guildford bombers, I suggest Sir Michael Havers might have been breaching the guidelines laid down for prosecuting counsel by the General Council of the Bar, as set out in the booklet *Conduct and Etiquette at the Bar*, which at the time was given to every newly qualified barrister. Under the heading 'Duty of Counsel for the Prosecution' it states:

> Crown Counsel is a representative of the State, a 'Minister of Justice'; his function is to assist the jury in arriving at the truth. . . . It is not his duty to obtain a conviction by all means, but simply to lay before the jury the whole of the facts which compose his case . . . it cannot be too often made plain that the business of counsel for

the Crown is fairly and impartially to exhibit all the facts to the jury
. . . *in opening a case, counsel must not open any fact as a fact in the
case which he is not in a position to prove.* [emphasis added]

Was Sir Michael acting fairly and impartially when he misled the jury about
the alleged visual identification of two accused when he must have known
that the soldiers had never identified either Carole Richardson or Patrick
Armstrong? Did he introduce a 'fact' that he was not in a position to prove?
Or did he perhaps hope against hope that in the course of their evidence the
soldiers would point them out in the dock? (At that time, identification in
court was still allowed.)

As for the two other accused, neither Paul Hill nor Gerard Conlon,
against whom there was no evidence of any kind except their own repeated
confessions in police custody, were never invited to stand on an identification parade – for one very obvious reason: no witness would ever say that
either man was seen in or near either of the two bombed pubs or anywhere
else in Guildford.

There are also allegations that Sir Michael was involved in the non-
disclosure of a witness statement taken by a police officer in January 1975,
which, if true, totally exonerated Gerard Conlon of the Guildford
bombings. That statement claimed that on the night of the Guildford
bombings Conlon was in bed in a hostel in northwest London and he could
not therefore have been one of the bombers. If he was not, how could he
incriminate others, and they in turn incriminate him?

Although it is sometimes claimed that there was no other witness who
gave evidence against the Four and that the case against them was exclusively
set out in their confession statements, in fact there was one witness whose
evidence, if true, implicated Patrick Armstrong. That witness was Brian
McLoughlin. He was aged 17 and lived with others, including Carole
Richardson and Patrick Armstrong, in the squat in Linstead Street.
McLoughlin was a useful member of the squat because he was a prolific
shoplifter, and gloried in his ability to steal food, which was always
welcomed by the residents of the squat.

Prosecuting counsel Sir Michael Havers told the jury in opening the case
that McLoughlin's evidence was 'very powerful supporting evidence'. When
he gave evidence before the jury he was ushered into the witness box by one
of the two prison officers who had brought him to court from a Borstal
institution where he had been sent for training – in theory to wean him off
his dishonest ways. These were many, for he had several convictions for

offences of dishonesty. He swore in evidence that Patrick Armstrong had invited him to blow up a pub. Apparently McLoughlin declined to do so. He also claimed that on one occasion while alone in the squat he had opened a parcel bound in brown paper and string, thinking it contained non-prescription drugs, of which he was a user. In the parcel, according to him, were two guns. Whether he was shocked or surprised is not now readily apparent. He had to admit, however, that although he was living in the Linstead Street squat in October 1974 with Carole Richardson and Patrick Armstrong he knew nothing and heard nothing about the Guildford bombings until January 1975. He had further to admit that his friendship with Patrick Armstrong was such that on one occasion he gave him a brand-new suit. When McLoughlin next appeared before a criminal court, one of the offences he admitted was the theft of that suit, so perhaps he was not as generous and kind-hearted as he might have first appeared.

He was such an appallingly poor witness that even the trial judge, Mr Justice Donaldson, shrank from accepting he was as reliable and credible and invited the jury to disregard his evidence. No one can now say whether they did, for no one knows the basis on which a jury comes to a decision. No one ever asked why the prosecuting authorities saw fit to put McLoughlin forward as a witness. Neither was it ever explained why Sir Michael put a witness with a criminal record of dishonesty in the witness box when he obviously had a purpose of his own to serve; to ingratiate himself with the police and seek a reduction in his custodial sentence. Was it an attempt to bolster a weak case?

Even after the Four confessed, the police continued their enquiries to try to obtain more evidence as proof of their involvement. On 18 January 1975, DC Standen of the Surrey Police obtained a statement from Charles Edward Burke at an address in Kilburn, northwest London. As mentioned above, he was known to Gerard Conlon as Paul the Greengrocer and was one of the four sharing the St Louis room in Hope House on Quex Road. It should be stressed that the police officer traced him; he did not approach the police in order to make a witness statement that, if true, would have destroyed the prosecution case against Gerard Conlon.

Charles Burke said of Gerard Conlon and Paul Hill:

They never discussed work but I knew they worked on the buildings. I was in work all the time, seven days a week at B & M Fruiterers, 308 Neasden Lane. Paul was the quiet one but Gerry was mouthy . . . On the Friday before I left Quex Road, the 4th October

1974 I remember Paul said he was going to Southampton for the weekend to see some friends. *When I left work on Saturday 5th October 1974, I had found a new place to live, this address, as I was fed up sharing a room. I got back to Quex Road about 7.00 p.m. because we take stock on a Saturday night. I packed my gear, and Gerry was in his bed. He was the only other person in the St Louis room. He said he was broke and asked to borrow a quid, but I never let him have it. About 7.30 p.m. I caught a taxi and left Quex Road for the last time.* [emphasis added]

It is not difficult to imagine the consternation this statement must have caused to all those involved in the prosecution of the Guildford Four. Here was an independent witness providing evidence that Gerard Conlon was not bombing Guildford on the night of Saturday 5 October 1974 – he was in bed in a hostel in Quex Road at the very time, around 7 p.m., that the police claimed, and he had confessed, he was involved in placing the two bombs in the pubs.

My view is that DC Standen realised the vital importance of this evidence because he followed it up by going to Hope House four days later, on 22 January 1975. There he took a witness statement from Sister Mary Power, a nun on the staff at the hostel. She was responsible for keeping an accurate record of the residents at the hostel. Her statement reads: 'my records show that they, Hill and Conlon, were still there the week ending the 4th October with the same room mates. The same arrangement appears to have been maintained except my records show that Charles Burke left the hostel on the 5th October, and his bed was left vacant until the end of the week, the 11th of October.' This is very compelling evidence supporting Charles Burke's claim that he had left the hostel on Saturday 5 October 1974, which is one reason why he would remember that evening. Just as important, Sister Power's statement contained Burke's new address in Kilburn, so anyone wishing to interview him knew exactly where to find him. For reasons unknown, that address seemed to fade into the background and become irrecoverable. Just as lawyers don't ask questions to which they do not know the answer, the police don't ask questions to which they don't want to know the answer.

DC Standen's work was not yet concluded. He took a witness statement from Peter Vine, a self-confessed thief, who was the manager of B & M Fruit Stores, where Charles Burke was assistant manager. Their statements clash. According to Vine, he remembered going for a drink on 5 October 1974 at a working men's club in the Paddington area with Charles Burke. Burke was, Vine claimed, very keen about his new lodgings in Kilburn, where he had been living for the previous five or six days. Vine thinks it was 'from the previous Monday night, which would be the 1st October'. (Vine was wrong about the date; that Monday was 30 September). Vine's statement goes on: 'The reason I remember Saturday 5th was because one week later, on the 12th October, I was nicked for having the takings away and wheeled into Willesden.'

If this statement is true, Charles Burke's statement must be false. There really is no other option. In attempting to decide between the two – the self-confessed thief and the person of good character – how much weight should one give to Sister Power's statement, which drew on her records? These records show that Charles Burke left Hope House on Saturday 5 October 1974. Most impartial observers might favour Burke's account. In the event the jury never heard it and were not given a choice as to who to believe.

I have never been able to discover whether Vine was successfully prosecuted for the theft of the takings from the shop or whether, in gratitude for his potential undermining of a vital defence witness, he was rewarded by the prosecuting authorities by having the case against him dropped. Neither can I discover how much he actually stole, and when he stole it – for it seems from his statement quoted above that 12 October 1974 was the date of his arrest, not necessarily the date of the theft.

On 24 March 1975 the solicitors then acting for Gerard Conlon served a notice of alibi on the prosecution in accordance with Section 11 of the Criminal Justice Act 1967. That notice said, 'our client will say that at the time of the explosions he was in London in an Irish hostel at Quex Road, London NW6 where he was then living.' The name and address of a witness then living in Belfast was provided in the notice. The names of two other witnesses, a man and a woman, were given, but no address for either was given. No witness statement had been asked for, or provided to, the defence solicitors on that date in March, so they were relying on what Gerard Conlon told them about these potential witnesses and their evidence. In the event, none of the three gave evidence for the defence at Conlon's trial.

It will be noted that no reference was made in the notice to the existence of Charles Burke. Even when he came to give evidence in his own defence at the Guilford Four trial, Gerard Conlon did not mention anything about Charles Burke being in the room on the night of the bombings. But it is a matter of record that Gerard's solicitors did know of the existence of Charles Burke. It may be that they obtained his name from the records kept at Hope

House. In any event they wrote to Charles Burke on 4 April 1975, asking for an opportunity to interview him, but for reasons unknown their letter was addressed to him not at his new address in Kilburn, which Sister Mary Power had recorded, but to his family home in Newcastlewest in County Limerick. His family there had not had sight or sound of him for years.

To compound the difficulty, when the home secretary many years later asked the Avon and Somerset police to carry out an inquiry into the case, they interviewed Charles Burke and took a statement from him dated 9 June 1988. In that statement he confirmed that what he had stated in January 1975 was true, but by this date, some 13 years later, he could only remember the name of Paul Hill as being one of his roommates in Hope House. The legal team acting for Gerard Conlon in 1988 were not told about this statement.

The duties of the prosecution in relation to the presenting evidence and calling witnesses, which were laid down by the Court of Criminal Appeal in 1946, are known as 'the rule in the case of Bryant and Dickson'. This states simply that where the prosecution have taken a statement from a person whom they know can give material evidence but decide not to call him as a witness, they are under a duty to make that person available as a witness for the defence but they are not under any further duty to supply the defence with a copy of the statement they have taken.

According to Archbold on *Criminal Pleading*, which was in effect at the relevant time:

> Certain prosecuting authorities and prosecutors not infrequently use this authority as a justification for never supplying the defence with the statement in such circumstances. It should be borne in mind however, that an inflexible approach to these circumstances can work an injustice. For example the witness's memory might have faded when the defence eventually seek to interview him, or he may refuse to make any further statement. *It is submitted that the better practice is to allow the defence to see such statements unless there is a good reason not to do so.*[10] [emphasis added]

On my reading of the case I consider that the barrister on the prosecuting team responsible for disclosure was (Eliot) Michael Hill QC, a very experienced criminal practitioner who had been one of the eight Treasury Counsel team prosecuting day after day at the Old Bailey in London. I think it was his decision not to disclose Charles Burke's statement, or that of Sister

Mary Power, and I further consider he was wrong not to do so. He later tried to justify his decision by claiming that the defence knew about Charles Burke, but he was unable to explain how or when they knew. Certainly no member of the Four's defence team ever admitted that they did know of this witness's existence. That would of course have required an explanation why they had not called him into the witness box, but in fact they simply did not know of his evidence and its importance. Surely nothing would have been simpler for Michael Hill than to disclose at the very least the name and address of that witness, but he chose not do so. The name of Sister Mary Power was not disclosed either. Perhaps he should have gone even further, for Lord Denning had said in a case in 1965, 'The duty of prosecuting counsel or solicitor, as I have always understood it, is this: if he knows of a credible witness who can speak to material facts which tend to show the prisoner to be innocent, he must either call that witness himself or make his statement available to the defence'.[11] For reasons I have never understood, Michael Hill disregarded this approach as well. What he did was this. Because there were some 2,000 statements from witnesses whom the prosecution did not propose to call, Michael Hill advised the DPP to serve not merely the names and addresses of those witnesses but also their statements. That advice did not include the disclosure of the existence of Charles Burke, Sister Mary Power or even Peter Vine. Michael Hill seems not to have asked himself the simple question: if the defence knew about Charles Burke, why was his name not included in the alibi notice served under the provisions of the Criminal Justice Act 1967? Perhaps he did, and in doing so provided the answer to his own question. It was noted on the papers that Burke's evidence was 'destroyed' by Vine's evidence. That was the entirely wrong approach. It is not for counsel in a case to assess the merits of the conflicting witnesses. In addition, such evidence would only be destroyed if Vine was a reliable and truthful witness. But was he? How splendid it would have been if Michael Hill had chosen to follow the view of Mr Justice Avory, who stated in one case that 'counsel for the prosecution throughout the case ought not to struggle for a verdict against the prisoner, but they ought to bear themselves rather in the character of ministers of justice, assisting in the administration of justice'.

The end of this part of the case is to be found in the closing speech of Sir Michael Havers to the jury in the Guildford Four case. He told them that Gerard Conlon did not have an alibi. That statement was incorrect: he did have an alibi and he gave evidence on oath from the witness box in support of that alibi, and was there subjected to cross-examination in an attempt to damage or destroy his standing and credibility as a witness. But he called no witnesses in support of that alibi. The trial judge, Mr Justice Donaldson, told the jury, 'He [Havers] said he had not got an alibi. That is not true. Conlon has got an alibi. What he has not got is independent witnesses to support him.' Donaldson did not know, though certainly Michael Hill did, that there was at least one material witness, Charles Burke, who could have supported him, but was simply not able to do so. He may not even have known that his evidence was so vital in the case. Was Michael Hill acting as a minister for justice when he failed to disclose that material evidence?

In his judicial inquiry into the case, Sir John May came to the conclusion that Crown counsel behaved at all times in the honest, if mistaken, belief that Conlon's team had traced Burke, knew what he could say and might yet call him. Sir John decided, however, that if Burke's statement had been disclosed it might have led to a different verdict in respect of Conlon. I do not share that view. The climate at that time, together with the confession evidence, would have resulted in the conviction and imprisonment of four innocent young people, whatever evidence favourable to the defence was put before the jury.

The trial judge at the original Guildford Four trial (and the related case of the Maguire Seven that followed soon afterwards) was Sir John Donaldson, described in a not unfriendly newspaper article by the *Observer* journalist Alan Watkins as Margaret Thatcher's favourite judge. I have no doubt that he was. Sir John was a man of brilliant intellect but he had no experience of trying criminal cases. He had never tried cases at the Old Bailey prior to 1975. He was hated by the Labour Party and the trade unions because he chaired the Industrial Relations Court, which was intended by the Conservative and Unionist government that created it to reduce or, ideally, destroy the powers of the trade unions. In October 1973 he had made an order exercising the power of sequestration against the assets held in the so-called political fund of the Amalgamated Union of Engineering Workers, which had failed to obey an order of the court.

He tried the Guildford Four in 1975 and the Maguire Seven in 1976. Between those trials he tried the case of a London gangster called Freddie Foreman, who was charged with murdering another gangster, Thomas 'Ginger' Marks. Because of the state of the prosecution evidence Sir John invited the jury to stop the case and acquit Foreman, which they did.

In 2007 Foreman published a book called *Freddie Foreman: The Godfather of British Crime*, in which he describes how he murdered Thomas 'Ginger' Marks. He admitted that he had got away with murder. Sir John, in accordance with tradition, made no public comment on the outcome of the case or the confession in the book. He never uttered one public word of regret or apology either to the Guildford Four or to those involved in the Maguire Seven case, where he may have overstepped the boundaries of what a trial judge can be expected to do, resulting in the wrongful conviction of those seven people. It is questionable whether he had sufficient experience in criminal law to try these difficult cases at all. When he died in 2005 his obituary writer in *The Guardian* commented that 'he may have been all at sea in the criminal law but he calmed the waters of the Court of Appeal after the waves generated by Denning'.

When, however, the Guildford Four and the Maguire Seven cases went to appeal, their counsel forcefully complained about his conduct of both trials. The presiding judge in the Criminal Division of the Court of Appeal was Lord Justice Roskill. He and Sir John Donaldson were very close friends. When eventually Sir John Donaldson was sent to the House of Lords, who should be the noble lord introducing him into the House but the self-same Lord Roskill? He would not hear one word of criticism against Lord Donaldson but went out of his way to praise his fair and impartial conduct of both trials. There can hardly be any doubt that Lord Donaldson had descended into the political arena when he told Paul Hill, Gerard Conlon and Patrick Armstrong, 'you three men are sentenced to life for murder and I want you to understand what that means, and I want your fellow members of the IRA to understand, and I want the people who sent you to this country to understand.' He went on to say, 'your crime was not directed at those you killed, it was directed at the community as a whole, every man, woman and child living in this country. You obviously expected to strike terror into their hearts and thereby achieve your objectives. If you had known our countrymen better, you would have realised it was a vain expectation.' Was he referring to the political objective of the IRA, and does the statement 'our countrymen' mean he was not dealing with a citizen of the UK, which all the people of Northern Ireland are, as all four accused people in the dock were, but a foreign national who was not British but Irish?

8 Defending the Innocent: the Maguire Seven

THE TRIAL OF the Guildford Four concluded on 22 October 1975. Through-out their trial one name was mentioned over and over again – Mrs Anne Maguire. In his statement under caution made on 3 December 1974 Paul Hill had told the police that she was the woman he had first claimed he did not know but then went on to say she 'is a woman called Annie who I first met in a Maida Vale club and another time at the Carousel ballroom in Camden Town and on both times she was with Hugh Maguire and his wife Kitty. She told me she was from Belfast and was from Abysinia [*sic*] Street.' Mrs Maguire did see Paul Hill at the club in Camden Town, and she is from Abyssinia Street in Belfast. Paul Hill's statement made the following day claimed that Paddy Armstrong told him that 'Gerry and Annie were going to do the Horse & Groom and Paul and Carole the Seven Stars'. He went on to describe how Annie and Gerry (not Armstrong, therefore, but Conlon) went into the Horse and Groom. They carried a plain brown bag, like a carrier bag – which presumably was supposed to contain the bomb. It must have been difficult for the prosecution to tailor this version to the case they put before the jury. They did not claim that Anne Maguire was in Guildford or that she carried any bomb into the Horse and Groom. They claimed that the two bombers of that pub were Patrick Armstrong and Carole Richardson.

Gerard Conlon also implicated Anne Maguire. In his statement under caution written by him on 3 December 1974, he claimed, 'My aunt Annie showed six of us how to make bombs. Annie is the woman in the flat I have spoke about in my first statement.' The situation in December 1974 was that if Paul Hill or Gerard Conlon mentioned your name to the police, you were in – arrested and detained at a police station on suspicion of being a terrorist simply on the basis of their word alone.

Anne Maguire, *née* Smyth, was born in the Falls Road area of Belfast on 14 November 1935, the second of eight children. She left school at the age of 14 and went into employment in the area. She married Paddy Maguire, the only boyfriend she ever had, on 26 September 1957. They left Belfast for London immediately after the wedding. They had four children: Vincent (born in 1958), John (1959) and Patrick (1961). Patrick was the only child of the family born in Belfast, where Anne had returned while Paddy sought more spacious accommodation for the growing family than the one-bedroomed flat they had lived in since they married. The youngest child, Anne Marie, was born in 1966. They were a very happy family, proud of their Irish background, devoted to their Catholic faith, but determined to integrate into the host population in a country where they intended to live for the rest of their lives. No one in the family had any interest in politics. As a result of being taken into detention by the police, who chose to believe Paul Hill and Gerard Conlon's outrageous lies about her, Anne Maguire spent seven years of a 14-year sentence as a Category A prisoner, and served a total of ten years. She wept as she was sentenced, and when her husband Paddy was sentenced to 14 years' imprisonment, the maximum sentence available, and her sons Vincent and Patrick went into custody for five and four years respectively. It almost broke her heart to be parted from them and her daughter, but she stayed resolute and strong because she knew that she was innocent of any charge laid against her.

Of all the cases of wrongful conviction, I regard the Maguire case as the most saddening of all. But is it not a fact that the wrongful imprisonment of the innocent is a form of state terrorism where legislation such as the Prevention of Terrorism (Temporary Provisions) Act 1974, which was rushed through Parliament after the Birmingham pub bombings, gave the police greater powers to detain suspects and obtain confessions that turned out to be entirely untrue and then convict and imprison the innocent? No one denies that the Act was aimed at Irish terrorism. The danger always existed that being Irish meant, in the minds of some, being a terrorist.

Paul Hill was the first person to be arrested under the provisions of that Act. He broke down very easily under the weight of questioning and the treatment he received in police custody. No one believed the claim that he made in Belfast Crown Court, but did not repeat at the Old Bailey, that a gun had been pointed through the flap of the cell door where he was being held in Guildford. (The reason for not making the allegation at the Old Bailey may have been that had he done so the prosecution would claim that by reason of Section 1(f)(ii) of the Criminal Evidence Act 1898, he was making an allegation against a witness for the prosecution, which meant that the trial judge would have the discretion to allow the prosecution to put Paul Hill's character and previous convictions to him. Thus the jury who tried him at the Old Bailey might have been told that he had a conviction for murder – of a former British soldier. In the event they were never told that, but Sir John Donaldson knew of that conviction, and in my view this was yet another reason why he was so hostile to Paul Hill and the other three in the dock.)

One of the foremost intellectuals in the British army stationed in Northern Ireland in the early 1970s was Brigadier Frank Kitson, now General Sir Frank Kitson. He upset his political masters in 1971 when he said that internment without trial had been done in the wrong way, at the wrong time and for the wrong reasons. The politicians in Stormont under Brian Faulkner of the UUP certainly did not want to hear that. Brigadier Kitson had served in Kenya, Cyprus, Malaysia and Oman, where the local population had difficulties with the presence of the British army that sometimes resulted in violence and murder. In 1971 Kitson wrote a book, *Low Intensity Operations*, in which he suggested that the successful prosecution of a counter-insurgency conflict necessitated the moulding of the criminal justice system as an instrument of state policy. Added to that was the failure to understand that while the conduct of the IRA might have been unlawful, their objective was political, namely the end of the British presence in Northern Ireland. All the accused in the Guildford Four and the Maguire Seven cases were seen by the police and legal establishment (in the form of Mr Justice Donaldson and Michael Havers QC) as members of a group opposed to the legitimacy of continued British rule in the province of Ulster and were treated accordingly. The passing of the Prevention of Terrorism Act in 1974, which was openly aimed specifically at Irish republicanism, enabled the police to obtain confessions and convictions, thereby reducing pressure on the politicians and allowing them to claim that the battle against the terrorists was not only being fought, but was actually being won. Claims by those convicted that they had been repressed and ill-treated in police custody were simply not believed, either by the judiciary or the public at large.

The trial of the Guildford Four started on 16 September 1975 and ended on 22 October 1975. The trial of the Maguire Seven began three months later, on 14 January 1976, and ended on 4 March 1976. All the prejudicial observations, comments and so-called evidence about 'Auntie Annie's bomb kitchen' extensively reported in the media during the

Guildford Four trial might have, and in my view must have, been known to any potential juror sworn to try the Maguire Seven. Who could have forgotten the evidence that in the course of his trial, the police gave evidence that Gerard Conlon had said 'he had visited his auntie Annie (Mrs Maguire) with other young Provisional IRA terrorists at a house in North London, where she gave them lessons in making time bombs. "Watch carefully, you may have to do this yourselves one day" she told the assembled class.'[1] How that evidence, denied at the trial by Gerard Conlon, who admitted that he said it, but said it was untrue, must have damaged her character and reputation. Furthermore, no attempt was made by her defence counsel to seek to stay the proceedings on the ground that the pre-trial publicity had been so prejudicial and damaging to her case that she would not get a fair trial. I do not, however, consider for one moment that Mr Justice Donaldson would have agreed with the argument and stopped the case against her.

The Maguire Seven were: Anne Maguire; her husband Paddy; her two sons, Vincent (aged 16 at the time of his arrest) and Patrick (aged 13); her brother-in-law, Giuseppe Conlon; Sean Smyth, Anne's brother; and Patrick O'Neill, a long-standing family friend, who had from time to time lodged with the Maguire family. The allegation against them was that they had 'between 1st and 4th days of December 1974 knowingly had in their possession or under their control an explosive substance, namely nitro-glycerine (NG), under such circumstances as to give rise to a reasonable suspicion that they did not have it in their possession or under their control for a lawful object'.

In fact, documents held in the National Archives show that the original charge put the date of the offence as being 3 December 1974, and this was amended by leave of the court on 14 January 1976 to between 1 and 4 December. I cannot see any logical or legal reason for that amendment, because the prosecution case against the Seven was essentially that on the afternoon of Tuesday 3 December, the only time they were all together at the Maguire family home, they handled NG.

The same prosecuting team in the Guildford Four case were nominated by the attorney general to prosecute the Maguire Seven. I consider that they shared the view of the judge chosen again to try their case, Sir John Donaldson, that this was a true Bill of Indictment and that the Maguire Seven, like the Guildford Four, were guilty as charged.

The sequence of events in this case is of the utmost importance. As noted above, Paul Hill was arrested on 28 November 1974. Gerard Conlon was arrested on 30 November 1974. His father, Giuseppe Conlon, went to

Springfield Road police station to see him but was told he had left there and was being taken to England. He made contact with a Belfast firm of solicitors, Messrs Nurse & Jones. On Monday 2 December Giuseppe was told that Mr Jones would travel over to England that evening to provide legal advice and assistance to Gerard Conlon. The solicitors sent a telegram to Paddy Maguire saying, 'Re your nephew Gerard Conlon arrested and held in Guildford police station. Father has instructed as solicitors Nurse & Jones . . . Please telephone . . . Bernard Simon, Solicitor, 40 Bedford Street, London . . . will be in contact tonight or tomorrow. Please reply. Nurse & Jones.' Anyone who thinks, as someone apparently did, that a member of the Provisional IRA would use a firm of highly respectable solicitors to send information by telegram to London for a sinister and unlawful purpose would be greatly mistaken.

Paddy Maguire, who had served for three years in the Royal Inniskilling Fusiliers regiment in the British army and had no truck with any illegal organisation, put that telegram in his pocket, then in the bin, and told no one in the house about it. He had no intention of helping Gerard Conlon in any way. He rang the solicitors in London and told them he wanted nothing to do with Gerard Conlon. He cared very little for him: he was a worthless layabout; when he stayed at the Maguire home he had stolen the children's pocket money, and he would never be welcomed back there again. In the meantime, the solicitor Mr Jones decided not to travel to London when he was told that under the provisions of the new antiterrorist legislation, he would not be allowed access to his proposed client for seven days. In the light of that, Giuseppe Conlon decided to travel to England himself. His doctor, Joe Hendron, later an outstanding politician in the SDLP, advised him not to travel on the grounds that he was too sick to do so. He was 52 years of age at that time and his health was extremely poor; he suffered from fibrosis, extensive tuberculosis in both lungs, and emphysema. His condition had been stabilised by a rigorous course of anti-TB drugs, but he was barely able to walk. He had no connection with the republican movement in Northern Ireland, nor any interest in politics at all. He had served in the Royal Marines during the Second World War, from 1941 to 1946, and after working for about a year in England after the war he returned to Belfast and married his wife, Sarah, in 1947. Together they set up home and started their family in the city of Belfast. He had been unable to work for the previous 11 years.

Disregarding his doctor's advice, he decided to travel on 2 December by the night ferry to Heysham in Lancashire. There he joined a line of people being subjected to a security check. The official who questioned him was DC Christopher Quinn of the Port Unit, Heysham Harbour, who made a witness statement dated 19 December 1974, two weeks and two days after he had seen Giuseppe Conlon. During that time it is presumed he was continually working and questioning incoming travellers from Northern Ireland to England. According to his statement he asked Giuseppe where he had come from and was told, 'I've come from my home in Cyprus Street.' When asked where he was travelling to, he replied 'I'm going down to Surrey to pick up a vehicle.' According to the officer he had no documents to verify his name and address, except a club card which had his name and address on it. Presumably that was some kind of social-club card. The officer then examined what he described as 'a small blue airline type bag with a shoulder strap'. Giuseppe was asked to empty his pockets. DC Quinn noted that he found nothing of interest. Giuseppe was then allowed to proceed to the nearby train for London. The police officer watched him board the train. If the officer had asked him to produce a driving licence as evidence of his name and address, Giuseppe would not have been able to produce one. He had never held one. He was unable to drive a motor vehicle of any kind.

Giuseppe Conlon always maintained that the officer made a mistake in claiming that he said he was going down to Surrey to pick up a vehicle; that was actually said by either the person ahead of him or behind him in the security line. What is most relevant, however, is the fact that there is in the National Archives a photograph of Giuseppe's case taken by the police when they searched the Maguire house. It is not a small 'airline-type' bag, it is a small, weekend, hard-sided attaché case. *It has no shoulder strap.* Because the photograph is in black and white it is not possible to determine the colour, but in my view it is not blue.

The RTÉ television programme *Today Tonight* shows that suitcase lying on the floor inside the Maguire house, adding the comment that it had not been searched but it was lying with the lid open. They identify it as Giuseppe's suitcase. I have examined the list of exhibits in this case, 60 in all. The photograph taken by the police is not one of those exhibits. However, exhibit 50 is the actual attaché case belonging to Giuseppe Conlon. It was produced at the trial but seemed to play no significant part in the evidence. It should have done because it contradicted the evidence of an important witness for the prosecution, DC Quinn. Why was this overlooked, if it was, by Giuseppe Conlon's defence counsel?

Was it this witness, DC Quinn, upon whom Michael Hill QC relied when he confidently told the attorney general in the statement of facts that it could be 'proved' that Giuseppe Conlon had lied about his reason for travelling to England?

When the judge summed up the case he seems not to have attached to the incident the same importance that Michael Hill did in his document sent to the attorney general. He did tell the jury to consider whether the police officer was 'surprisingly accurate' in a lot of the evidence that was agreed about the Heysham incident. But he went on to suggest that Giuseppe Conlon was concealing the fact that he was coming over because his son had been arrested and he would not want to tell anyone that. 'That might be a perfectly innocent explanation,' said the judge, 'in which case there is really no significance in the Heysham incident. On the other hand you may take a different view. It is a matter for you. Perhaps on any view it is rather a fringe matter but it is obviously a matter which you ought to consider if you want to.'[2] I beg to differ. The judge was assuming that the officer's recollection of events more than two weeks later was correct and the defence version was wrong. It would not have been a fringe matter at all if the RUC had disclosed at the time, rather than years later, that they had been told Giuseppe Conlon's reason for going to the UK, and they knew at the time that reason was true.

There is another consideration. In cases involving prosecutions under the Explosive Substances Act 1883, the fiat, or consent, of the attorney general is required. In normal circumstances the office of the DPP would prepare a short summary of the case and put it before the attorney general for his personal signature. But this case was an exception and the document seeking the fiat was drafted by Michael Hill. The attorney general at the time was Sam Silkin QC. He was not regarded by lawyers as having one of the best legal minds, but there was no doubt of his personal and professional integrity and intellectual honesty. He refused to grant his fiat for a conspiracy charge of causing explosions against the Maguire Seven, but told his legal secretary in a note dated 17 February 1975 that there was some evidence to support a charge of unlawful possession of explosives – but only just. The *Independent on Sunday* reported that he thought the case against the Maguire family was flimsy.[3] Yet he still signed the fiat the next day. The two young Maguire children, Vincent and Patrick, were not charged with the offence until 25 February 1975, but were they in the fiat? If they were not, the case against them was defective from the start. Under Section 7 of the Explosive Substances Act there can be no prosecution except by leave of the attorney general. In the case of *R. v. Bates*, the court ruled that the absence of such consent invalidates the proceedings.[4] This raises the question: did the prosecution tell the attorney general that Vincent and Patrick had not been charged, and was an explanation given why they had not been? The delay in charging them from December to February does call for a detailed and reasoned explanation.

In addition, the prosecuting authorities would have to consider whether it was in the public interest to prosecute a 16-year-old and a 13-year-old when, if they had been involved at all, it could only have been at the behest of an adult in their own home. When the Dublin-born Conservative MP Jonathan Aitken induced his 16-year-old daughter to make a false witness statement in the course of a libel action against *The Guardian* in 1995, the prosecution did not continue proceedings against her when her father pleaded guilty to a charge of perjury, for which he was sent to prison for 18 months. She would not have been involved but for him. In the same way, *if* Paddy and Anne Maguire were disposing of NG at 43 Third Avenue (and, I stress, they were not), their two sons could only have been involved in order to help their parents. Did someone consider that factor before deciding to prosecute Vincent and Patrick? I suspect not.

In order to gather knowledge and material for drafting the application to grant the fiat, on 7 February 1975 Michael Hill and the other counsel on the prosecution team, together with Surrey police officers and professional officers from the office of the DPP visited the Royal Armament Research Development Establishment (RARDE) based at Woolwich. There they saw a demonstration of the procedures of testing for the presence of NG, namely the thin-layer chromatography (TLC) test.

After that visit Michael Hill drafted a statement of facts for the attorney general's attention. I take great exception to the following paragraph: 'Whilst Anne Maguire had been implicated by Hill, Conlon, Richardson and Armstrong in the preparations for and the execution of the Guildford bombings, she and her family had no reason to suppose that they had been implicated in the bombing campaign since nothing that had been published about the police investigations seemed to point to them.'

It might have been worthwhile for Michael Hill to remind himself of a basic rule of the law of evidence; that what one person says to the police about a person, in the absence of that other person, is not admissible evidence against them. It is hearsay. It is not said in their presence, so they are unable to challenge or deny it. Perhaps he should also have reminded himself that none of the Guildford Four made any allegation against any member of the Maguire family, except Anne Maguire herself. So why should her family have 'no reason to suppose' that they had been implicated in the bombing campaign? The answer may well be that from the very outset Michael Hill formed the conclusion that the Guildford Four and the Maguire Seven were guilty. And this included the two children. For them there was no question of the presumption of innocence.

The note continued: 'However, the Talbot bombing took place on 30 November and, since one bomb did not explode, they will have feared that examination of that bomb might lead to them.' I find this outrageous because it presupposes that the Maguire family were terrorists; the assumption that they actually knew about the bombing was false, for they did not, and the claim '*they will have feared that examination of the bomb might lead to them*' (emphasis added) is entirely wrong – they would have to have been involved in acts of terrorism, which was not proved, in order to experience that fear. If they were not involved they would have nothing to fear from that bombing incident; only if they were would they be fearful. Michael Hill was arriving at conclusions that were fundamentally false, and it is not for an advocate in a criminal case to start constructing the edifice upon which the police inquiry was based. Where is the evidence that 'since one bomb did not explode, they will have feared that examination of that bomb might lead to them'? Who is the witness who could have proved that allegation? The answer to both questions is simple. There was no evidence and there was no witness.

The Talbot Arms is a public house in Little Chester Street in Belgravia, London. At about 10 p.m. on Saturday 30 November, two short-fuse 6 lb bombs were thrown through a window into the pub. One exploded, the other did not. Five customers inside the premises were injured. The fingerprints of Brendan Dowd and Joseph O'Connell were found on the bomb that failed to explode. They were never charged with the offence of bombing the Talbot Arms and with injuring those inside it. Some might be interested in finding out why they were not. The defence of the Maguire Seven were never told of this forensic finding. Brendan Dowd and Joseph O'Connell had no knowledge of, and no connection with, any of the Maguire Seven.

Michael Hill further wrote: 'in the early hours of 3 December 1974, Patrick Joseph Conlon [Giuseppe Conlon] crossed from Belfast to Heysham, told the security services that he had crossed to collect a heavy goods vehicle from Tunbridge Wells, and travelled directly to the Maguire home at 43 Third Avenue, Harlesden.' I find that statement incomprehensible. I have noted above the statement of DC Quinn in which he said that the man in Heysham port to whom he spoke and identified as Giuseppe

Conlon said he was going down to collect a vehicle in Surrey. Tunbridge Wells is not in Surrey; it is in Kent. Nothing was said about a heavy goods vehicle. The officer also stated that the man had no identification on him save the club card. Giuseppe Conlon was seriously ill; he could barely walk, and when he did he was very short of breath. (He died in prison in January 1980 at the age of 56.) Would any police officer looking at him think him capable of driving a heavy goods vehicle? Would he not have expected such a driver to carry his HGV licence with him, if only to prove to anyone from whom he collected the vehicle that he was authorised to drive it? And if he didn't have that licence with him, wouldn't a police officer ask him why?

Michael Hill went on as he began: 'Patrick Conlon's explanation to the security services at Heysham was a lie and can be proved to be such.' My objection to this is two-fold. How can anyone explain DC Quinn's evidence when set side by side with what Michael Hill claims about the heavy goods vehicle and Tunbridge Wells? Are we expected to disregard it? Second, and more important, it is not for counsel in a case to decide on the reliability and credibility of a witness. That is a matter for a jury to decide, whether they believe one witness or another. Michael Hill, still treating the elderly Irishman not just as a member of the suspect community, but as guilty, presumes that the police officer was accurate, truthful and not mistaken about what was said to him more than two weeks previously, and that Giuseppe Conlon was lying. Hill was apparently never told, although he should have been, that the RUC in Springfield Road police station confirmed that Giuseppe Conlon told them he was intending to travel to London to help his son, who had been arrested there. It seems the jury were never told that either, as they should have been, and it was the responsibility of his defence solicitors to obtain that information and put it in evidence before them. Much later, in the course of the campaign to free the Guildford Four and the Maguire Seven, on 30 March 1981 Divisional Commander James Crutchley wrote to Fr McKinlay at St Peter's Church, Albert Street, Belfast, as follows:

Detective Inspector Ivan Morrison noted that on 30 November 1974 Gerard Conlon was detained by police at Springfield Road police station in connection with the Guildford bombings. Whilst there awaiting the arrival of police escort his father called to enquire about his son. He was told that Gerard was being taken to Guildford for questioning there. He stated that he would have to go there to make sure he was treated right. Detective Inspector

Morrison believes that in fact Patrick Joseph Giuseppe Conlon went to England to see about his son on either the first or 2 December 1974.

Since this is clear beyond doubt, why should he lie to the police at Heysham when he told the police in Belfast the truth about his purpose in going to England?

On 20 December 1983 the Conservative and Unionist MP David Mellor, then a minister, wrote to Christopher Price MP, 'the fact that Mr Conlon may have travelled to England with an innocent mind does not mean when he got here he did not take part in the offence'. That was not the case against him at his trial – it was alleged that he had travelled to England to warn others about the arrest of his son and to help them to dispose of explosives in a London house which was a bomb factory.

The most damaging evidence that harms, if not destroys, the prosecution case against Giuseppe and the remaining accused is to be found in two places. First, former Commander Bob Huntley, the head of Scotland Yard's Bomb Squad, wrote in his autobiography *Bomb Squad*, 'Three days after Gerard Conlon's arrest, his fifty-three year old father came to England to see solicitors about Gerard's defence. *Police tailed him from the night ferry at Heysham, Lancashire, to the Harlesden home of Anne Maguire, the "aunt Annie" who – it was alleged – taught bomb making to the Guildford team'* [emphasis added].[5] It gets better; Huntley continues, 'Alarm bells rang when he turned up. Anne Maguire, her husband, two sons, brother and a family friend living with them, got rid of the explosives stored in the house.'[6]

Not a word about this was mentioned at the Maguire Seven trial. It was covered up. Did the police stay watching the house all day, or did they neglect their duty, do nothing and simply go away? My belief is that, with the enormous resources available to the London Metropolitan Police and the Bomb Squad, which had its own surveillance team, they watched the house all day and saw nothing incriminating and, rather than tell the truth, hid this information and evidence from the jury at the trial.

If anyone believes that Huntley was wrong in his recollection of these events, one has only to look at the article in *The Times* that said, 'Mr Conlon's movements were followed by the police the moment he got off the ferry at Heysham. He was followed to Willesden, where seven hours later he was arrested with the members of the Maguire family.'[7] Is this not complete corroboration of what Huntley wrote? Since the prosecution always claimed that the surveillance on the Maguire home did not start until about 7 p.m.

on 3 December 1974 it must have been of considerable importance to conceal the fact that Giuseppe Conlon was followed all the way from Lancashire to London. It would have been a grave dereliction of duty to simply watch him enter the house and walk or drive away without doing anything. He was supposed to be on his way for an unlawful purpose; to visit a bomb factory. Surely this episode must have been recorded in writing by the police? Where are those records now? Why were they not made available to the defence at the trial? Is it a fact that the house was under police observation all day, and the prosecuting authorities knew it?

The movements of those living or visiting the Maguire house, 43 Third Avenue, on that day, Tuesday 3 December 1974, are important. It should be borne in mind that the police were claiming that this address was a bomb factory, and that people there were engaged in disposing of explosives on that day. Sean Smyth, Anne's brother, left the house at about 6.45 a.m. to his work refuelling vehicles for Fitzpatricks at Wembley stadium. Sean had lived at the Maguire home since July 1974. He had left his wife and four children in Belfast to work in London, sending money home each Friday like thousands of other Irishmen in a similar position. He had left school at the age of 14, was unable to read, and able only to write his own name and address. (When his son, also called Sean, died from cancer at only 20 years of age while Sean Smyth was serving his sentence, he was refused compassionate leave to attend the funeral.) He was a law-abiding, hardworking man trying to meet his responsibilities as a husband and a father. Sadly his marriage did not survive his term of imprisonment.

Sean Smyth returned to the house in the evening, at around 6.30 p.m., just before Paddy Maguire arrived back from Harrow Road police station (a ten-minute walk from his home) where he had gone to inquire about his brother Hugh, whom he had been unable to contact all day. (Hugh and his wife, Kitty, had been arrested earlier, having been named by Gerard Conlon, and were in police custody.) Sean Smyth washed, changed his clothes and was told of Gerard's arrest before sitting down for his evening meal. The others in the house had eaten earlier.

Anne Maguire left home at around 7.15 a.m. on 3 December to go to her cleaning job at a firm of accountants. She then returned home and at about 8.50 a.m. she took her daughter, eight-year-old Anne Marie, to school. Returning home about 15 minutes later, she made some tea for Paddy. At around 9.40 a.m. she went to her two other cleaning jobs, at a betting shop and a greengrocer. On the way home she did some shopping at a bakery, then at a greengrocer. She then called in on a local jumble sale. She arrived home between 1.30 p.m. and 2 p.m. and had lunch with her two sons, Vincent and John. John had arrived home from school at about 1.30 p.m. with his friend Hugh McHugh, known to everyone as 'Ginger'. Later in the afternoon, at about 4 p.m., John's girlfriend, Maxine Ryan, visited the house, staying for about half an hour. Soon after 4 p.m. Anne Marie arrived home with a schoolfriend called Marie Baker. Anne made them tea and sandwiches in the kitchen. Between 4.15 and 4.30 a neighbour called Mrs Roach came to collect a parcel from Mrs Maguire. They chatted for about five minutes, then Mrs Roach left. At around 4.30 p.m. John Maguire and Ginger McHugh left the house. Mrs Roach came back again at about 5.30 p.m. to ask Anne whether she could let her have some Bisto. Anne had none but gave her an Oxo cube. Mrs Roach left the house and as she was leaving commented on how good the stew smelled. Patrick Maguire left home at about 8.45 a.m. to go to school. He was back home at about 5.30 p.m. He had his tea and just before 6.30 p.m. he went to a local youth club, not getting home until around 9 p.m.

In January 1976 at the Old Bailey in London, the cream of the legal profession in England was vehemently and vociferously proclaiming before Margaret Thatcher's favourite judge and a jury that on that Tuesday afternoon, a large quantity of explosives was being removed from the bomb factory at 43 Third Avenue. For reasons never explained by anyone, those involved removed them so successfully that they were never discovered, and not even the slightest trace of explosives was found anywhere in the family home or even nearby. Yet four people – Ginger McHugh, Maxine Ryan, little Marie Baker and Mrs Roach – all unconnected to the Maguire family, had free access to the premises. The police did admit that the curtains were open and it was possible on that December evening, with the house lights on, to see the movement of everyone inside the house. It is readily apparent now why the police would have wanted to hide the fact that the house might have been, as it should have been, under close observation during that day from the time of Giuseppe Conlon's arrival until the police took away the family members from 43 Third Avenue on that Tuesday evening.

John Maguire arrived home sometime between 5.15 p.m. and 5.30 p.m., his brother Patrick not long after. The eldest brother, Vincent, an assistant gas fitter with the North Thames Gas Board, had evening classes at Paddington Technical College between 6 p.m. and 8 p.m. He left the house at about 5.40 p.m. to start the first class. Giuseppe Conlon had arrived at about 1.30 p.m. He had intended to stay with Hugh and Kitty Maguire – they had enough room to put him up – but he could not get in touch with them. We now know why he could not: they were both in police custody, simply because they had been named by Gerard Conlon. Is that a reasonable ground for suspecting them to be guilty of an arrestable offence?

Giuseppe and Paddy decided to go to the local pub. Paddy was probably surprised to see him because the telegram from Belfast the previous evening had said nothing about Giuseppe travelling to London. They returned to the house from the pub, arriving home at about 3.30 p.m. Anne Maguire was home by this time and she was genuinely surprised to see Giuseppe, particularly because she knew about his poor state of health. She was then told the reason for his arrival and about Gerard Conlon's arrest.

Paddy Maguire was at home all that Tuesday morning; he was unemployed at the time. At about 8 a.m. he decided to telephone Sean Tully, a close friend of Hugh Maguire's, to ask if he knew of Hugh's whereabouts. He spoke instead to Mrs Tully, who was unable to provide any helpful information. As noted above, he was at the pub with Giuseppe for two hours in the afternoon, returning home at about 3.30 p.m. He left the house again to go to Harrow Road police station to ask about his brother. He told no one he was going to the police station because he had had a few drinks and they might worry that he might be troublesome at Harrow Road. He explained his anxiety about his brother to a young policewoman at that station. She told him that another person (was it perhaps Sean Tully?) had also been making inquiries about Hugh Maguire. Paddy suggested to the policewoman that a police officer might accompany him to Hugh's home in Westbourne Terrace; he was afraid he might be ill or something worse, and perhaps the officer would break down the door if there was no response to knocking. He was told, 'there's no need for that'. Paddy then returned home, no wiser than when he left. Did the police know more than they were prepared to say? I criticise Paddy's defence team for not tracing that policewoman and compelling her to attend as a witness to give evidence of exactly the time this incident happened. It would have been useful also to know just how much information the police at Harrow Road had about 43 Third Avenue. Had the officer(s) who had followed Giuseppe Conlon, if they did, call at that station to make a report of exactly what they were doing and why they were doing it? Was it seriously suggested that Paddy Maguire had spent the early afternoon, after the arrival of Giuseppe Conlon, removing NG from his home, the bomb factory, and then gone to the local police station to make inquiries about his brother? The issue of timing is of most relevance to the case of Sean Smyth, who had been working at Wembley stadium on that Tuesday, and that of Patrick O'Neill. It is thought that Sean arrived at the house at about 6.30 p.m. The time he left work should have been proved by evidence called by his defence team, by the production of his time sheet or card if that was available. Added to that would be the time of his journey back to 43 Third Avenue. Does it look as though when Paddy Maguire left the house to go to the police station he left some NG there for Sean Smyth to help remove when he got home?

Perhaps the saddest of all the sad and devastated individuals in this very sad case is Patrick O'Neill, who was a long-standing friend of the family. His wife, Helen, was in hospital at the time, following complications in her pregnancy. It was hoped she would be released from hospital on Tuesday 3 December 1974, but that arrangement was cancelled. Patrick O'Neill rang Anne Maguire and asked her to help look after his daughters, Jacqui, aged eight years, Sharon, aged six, and Jean, aged four. The normal childcare arrangements had to be changed because Helen's sister, who had been looking after them, had to return home on learning of the illness (and subsequent death) of her father. That left the children's father in great difficulty. He turned to Anne Maguire; she would not refuse to help. The small family group arrived at 43 Third Avenue between 6.40 p.m. and 7 p.m. and Anne Maguire made arrangements to feed the children. Maxine Ryan called at about 7 p.m. and told John she would meet him at the local youth club. John Maguire left the house at about 7.20 p.m.

At about 6.40 p.m. Sean Tully arrived at the house for his second visit of the day. Giuseppe Conlon made a phone call to the London solicitors who would undertake his son's case. The police now claim that two officers, Det. Sgt Charles Hunter from Shooters Hill police station and Det. Sgt Elbourne, using a private, unmarked car, began to keep 43 Third Avenue under observation. They put the time as being 7 p.m. They saw a man drive away from the premises in a dark-coloured Ford Escort. That was almost certainly Sean Tully. Patrick O'Neill set off with the other men to the local pub, including of course Paddy Maguire, back from his visit to Harrow Road police station.

The police say the men's departure from the house to the local pub, the Royal Lancer, was timed at 7.45 p.m. That was denied by them. Patrick O'Neill claims he had arranged to speak to his wife over the phone and did so at 8 p.m. It wasn't until after that phone call that the men left the house, at about 8.15 p.m. That disputed time became known at the subsequent trial as 'the missing half hour', during which time, as both Mr Justice Donaldson and Lord Justice Roskill (in the course of the appeal) hinted, the four men disposed of the NG on their way to the pub. Lord Justice Roskill said, 'Certainly so far as the four male applicants were concerned, and this includes Smyth and O'Neill, there would have been an opportunity extending over half an hour to have handled explosives knowing perfectly well what they were doing, between the time when, on the police evidence, they left the house and the time when the police entered the public house'.[8]

Sean Tully returned to 43 Third Avenue for a further visit. He had discovered that Hugh Maguire had been arrested and told the family so. That return visit was put at after 7 p.m., prior to the men leaving the house. John Maguire returned from the youth club at around 8.45 p.m. Police officers arrived at the house at that time and asked where Paddy Maguire was. Did they not know where he was? Moreover, I cannot explain why they asked about Paddy because the person named by Gerard Conlon and Paul Hill as one of the Guildford bombers and bomb maker was Anne Maguire, not her husband. Nothing at all was alleged against him or against anyone else at 43 Third Avenue. Anne Maguire, or perhaps her little girl, Anne Marie, opened the door to those officers and let them into the house, accompanied by a number of dogs.

The police took John to the pub for him to point out his father. It was very shortly after 8.45 p.m. The police took the four men from the pub and took John Maguire home. Patrick was walking home from his youth club when to his surprise he saw his father and his brother John pass him in a police car. He had gone to school that morning before 9 a.m. and did not return home until about 5.30 p.m. He had had his tea and gone to his youth club at about 6.30 p.m. On those timings he had only about one hour to take part in concealing or removing explosives from the house. Vincent Maguire returned from his evening class at about 9 p.m. He saw two police vans and a police car parked at his home. A man was standing in the hallway of the house; others were standing inside. They had a police dog with them. The man at the door saw Vincent and told him in a brusque voice to move on. 'What do you mean?' Vincent asked, 'I live here.' The man called out to the others, 'Here's another of them' and Vincent was forcibly taken into his own home.

The police used sniffer dogs to search the house for traces of explosives. They found none. There was nothing to find. Significantly, the police returned the next day for a further search. This time they were equipped with an explosives vapour detector – a 'sniffer'. Again there was no trace of NG or any other explosive substance. They removed clothing and other articles and took them away for further examination. I maintain that when they did that they were acting unlawfully; they had no search warrant. In 1982 the Divisional Court of the Queen's Bench Division of the High

Court decided in the case of *McLorie v. Oxford* that 'once an arrest was completed, a police officer had no right at Common Law subsequently to enter the premises without a warrant in order to search for or seize an instrument of the crime known to be on the premises'.[9] That may have been some six years after the Maguire Seven case, but it was stating the law, not making the law. Ironically the judge who read the judgment of the court was Sir John Donaldson. The point about the unlawful search and seizure was not taken at the trial. It should have been. Most important of all, however, when the sniffer device was placed over a kitchen drawer that had been taken from the kitchen the previous day for the purpose of testing the 39 lightweight plastic gloves kept there (of which 22 appeared to have been used), the result of the test was negative. Just as it was for every item, including clothing, throughout the house.

The long day was not over for the Maguire family, their friends and relations. Giuseppe Conlon, Paddy Maguire, Sean Smyth and Patrick O'Neill were taken to Harrow Road police station, where their hands were swabbed, to test for the presence of explosives, by Det. Sgt Lawrence Vickery. Anne Maguire and her three sons, Vincent, John and Patrick, were taken to Paddington Green Station, and there tested by Det. Sgt Kenneth Day. Both officers had received one day's training, at RARDE in July 1974, on how to take the swabs. According to Sir John May's inquiry into the case, Det. Sgt Day had very little experience up to that time in December. Both officers were sure that they read and followed the instructions on the box before swabbing, but Det. Sgt Vickery was not entirely sure that he had washed his hands between swabbing different suspects, whereas Det. Sgt Day did remember doing that. Washing hands between swabbing different people was laid down in the rules to avoid possible contamination. The swabs were then sent to RARDE for forensic analysis using the TLC test. This was done the next day, Wednesday 4 December 1974.

The results were immediately passed to the police. The swabs taken from Sean Smyth, who had arrived home from work on 3 December *after* Paddy Maguire had left for the police station to inquire about his brother Hugh, were all positive. So he was the most heavily contaminated. Does it appear from this that Paddy intentionally or otherwise left some quantity of explosive material available for Sean Smyth to handle? So the house wasn't entirely swept clean prior to Paddy's departure? Does anyone really believe that? Giuseppe Conlon's swabs were all positive, except for the first swab applied to his dry left hand. Patrick O'Neill, who had arrived at 43 Third Avenue about the time of Paddy's return to the house, provided positive tests from beneath the fingernails of both hands. So for reasons that also defy comprehension in his case, if the prosecution was right, there was a bulk of NG available for him to handle as well. That also applied to Paddy Maguire, the odd note being that the dry swab in his case was positive, but the follow-up swab, not dry but soaked in ether, was negative. That should have set off some alarm bells, because this is scientifically inexplicable. Vincent Maguire's and his brother Patrick's swabs on the right-hand nails were positive. Much to the dismay, no doubt, of every operational police officer taking part in the case, no positive result was recorded on any swab taken from Anne Maguire. Her hands and fingernails were entirely clean. That was also the result of the swabs taken from her son John, who seems to have spent more time at home than anyone else on that day.

One of the scientists at RARDE, Walter Elliott, in a statement dated 5 December 1974, said, 'in my opinion . . . traces of NG found on the swabs and nail scrapers indicate that an explosive substance has been handled recently'.[10] That was the sole basis of the prosecution case against six of the Maguire Seven.

After the tests were completed in the early hours of 4 December, the Maguire boys were allowed to go home. Patrick O'Neill was also released on bail to await the results of the forensic tests. The police had the power to hold him for seven days without charge under the terms of the Prevention of Terrorism (Temporary Provisions) Act 1974 but chose not to do so. Was that because the police officers watching the house saw his arrival with the three children, and that left him little time to become involved in any wrongdoing at the Maguire home? He made no attempt to abscond, was still available to the police for questioning, and he went back to work the next day. On the following Saturday morning he was told the results of the forensic tests, and was arrested. Why did it take so long to do that?

As noted above, the 39 plastic gloves used by Anne Maguire were left in the drawer on the living room table on the Tuesday evening. At 5 p.m. the next afternoon Det. Sgt Vickery, using a pair of rubber gloves, put them in a single plastic bag and took them to a locked cupboard in the Bomb Squad Exhibits Room at New Scotland Yard. They were left there for five days. No one has explained why. On Monday 9 December Vickery took them from the locked cupboard and handed them to another officer, a detective sergeant. He took them to RARDE, where they were tested by a young and inexperienced junior member of staff, David Wyndham. He had been employed at RARDE for nine weeks. His academic qualifications seemed to be limited to Ordinary Level, but did include physics. He recorded a positive test for the presence of NG on one of the gloves, using the TLC test. It was not possible to say whether the trace was on the inside or the outside of any particular glove, for they had all been tested together. *The Guardian* described young Wyndham as 'an 18 year old trainee with two months experience'.[11] Why was this task entrusted to such a junior member of staff if the prosecuting authorities and the police really believed that Anne Maguire was a dedicated terrorist, a member of the Provisional IRA, a vital cog in the IRA, who was running a bomb factory from her own home?

Even more disquieting than that is the fact that one of the scientific officers at RARDE, Walter Elliott, made a statement dated 18 December 1974 that he himself had carried out the tests on the gloves, when he had not. Was that an error or a lie? Sir John May, in the course of his inquiry, looked at the 18-year-old trainee's notebook and stated, 'it was quite clear that it was not a contemporaneous record of the results of the tests which he had carried out; it was merely a listed fair copy of some other notes somewhere else'.[12] Why was this allowed to happen, and why was there no contemporaneous note, i.e. made either at the time or immediately after the test, made by young trainee? Did he know how to make one?

It is a matter of record that a second test was carried out on all the Maguire samples using a different TLC test. All were negative. The defence at the Maguire Seven trial were never told this. In fact they, and the jury, were entirely misled by the RARDE scientists who told them that 'second tests (on the hand swabs and gloves) were not necessary or practicable'. In the interests of justice and truth, they were both. When it came to the May Inquiry, two of the scientists denied knowledge of these second tests until they examined the RARDE papers, shortly before Sir John began his public hearings. Even then, when they both first gave evidence before him, they did not tell him of the existence of the second tests. These two scientists, based at Woolwich, where the throw bomb in the pub had taken two lives, were heavily criticised by Sir John May in his interim report on the Maguire case. He said: 'It had become clear to Mr Elliott and Mr Higgs following the consultation in July 1975, if not before, that the Crown's case rested on the specificity of the TLC test using toluene to identify NG. They knew the test was not specific for NG when advising the prosecution team and when giving evidence, but they failed to say so. They knew that a second system was available to resolve the two substances, but they did not mention it.'[13]

In claiming that the TLC test here was specific, they meant it was unique. There was no other substance that would produce the reaction it did in this case. Sir John May acquitted the scientists of being part of a conspiracy to deny justice to the defendants, but he added, 'they imperfectly understood their duties as forensic scientists and as witnesses'.[14] He noted, perhaps more in sorrow than in anger, that Elliott had given evidence that he had carried out the tests on Anne Maguire's gloves when he had not. Wyndham had tested the gloves. For what reason had Walter Elliott given this misleading evidence? Was it just sloppy practice at RARDE?

As for Det. Sgt Vickery, he told the May Inquiry that he was unable to recall whether he was wearing gloves when he removed the plastic gloves from the Maguires' home. Evidence then emerged that he had attended   the scene of the throw bombing at the Talbot Arms pub in Chelsea on 30 November (committed, as we now know, by Brendan Dowd and Joe O'Connell and nothing whatever to do with the Maguire Seven). It was Det. Sgt Vickery who had taken charge of the device that did not explode. If traces of NG can linger for about ten days on a plastic glove, could not this officer have been the innocent source of the contamination of some of the Maguire Seven samples? More particularly, he was the one who had taken the gloves from 43 Third Avenue. A report in the *Independent* newspaper notes:

> The Bomb Squad officer who carried out swab tests that showed positive traces of explosives on the hands of four of the Maguire Seven had been in contact with explosives two days earlier, it emerged yesterday. Three days before the tests, Det. Sgt Lawrence Vickery had sifted through the rubble of the Talbot Arms public house in Chelsea, blown up by the IRA on 30 November 1974. The next day he took some of the debris and an unexploded bomb, later made safe, to the MOD laboratories for tests. This was not disclosed during the Maguires' trial in 1976.[15]

Clearly it should have been, and if the Maguire Seven had received a fair trial, it would have been.

Just as significant are some of the notes made by young Mr Wyndham at RARDE relating to Anne Maguire's gloves. These notes were marked 'Tite Street' at the top and then those words are crossed out. Tite Street, Chelsea is the site of the Talbot Arms public house. Was it just an unhappy coincidence that the property named in the notebook should appear on the same page as Anne Maguire's name and test results? It will not be forgotten that Michael Hill linked the throw-bombing incident there to the Maguire family in his statement of facts submitted to the attorney general.

No credible explanation has ever been advanced as to why the gloves taken from Anne Maguire's house languished for five days at Scotland Yard. As we've seen, her hands were not contaminated, yet she was the one person in whom the police had a considerable interest. None of the others was named or otherwise identified as being involved in terrorist offences. We've also seen that when the sniffer device was passed over the gloves at the family home there was no positive response. Now that had changed. It is my view, if this was not a case of innocent contamination, the glove involved (and it seems there was only one) was deliberately and maliciously contaminated by someone, probably a police officer, because the thought of putting Anne Maguire's two children on trial without her being in the dock as well was anathema to the police. So someone decided, on the basis that 'we know she did it' or 'noble cause corruption', to fix the evidence against her. That was never part of the defence case at the trial, but should it have been? Anne Maguire, a person of excellent character who had never been in court for anything, let alone the crime of murder, would have had nothing to fear by making that allegation against the police, but would the jury of Londoners have believed the word of a woman from Belfast, especially in 1975? As for the trial judge, he made clear his view to the jury: if there was contamination of the samples by anyone else, it was innocent and not done for any sinister purpose.

Reference has already been made to the wish of Sir Robert Mark, the London Metropolitan Police commissioner, to catch more criminals than they employed. How was that progressing?

On 24 March 2014 the *Daily Mail* reported that Mark Ellison QC, in the course of his review of the evidence in the case of the murdered black teenager Stephen Lawrence, had found a memo written by Det. Supt David Hurley regarding corrupt police officers in the London Metropolitan Police. That officer alleged that corrupt officers 'stole and trafficked illegal drugs; shared reward pay outs with informants; sold confidential police intelligence to criminals; fabricated applications for more rewards and accepted bribes to destroy and fabricate evidence'. The fabrication of evidence is exactly the allegation I make in the case of Anne Maguire's gloves.

It couldn't get much worse than that, one might think. But it did. The *Independent*, under the headline 'Something rotten in the Metropolitan Police', described the appearance of the commissioner, Sir Bernard Hogan-Howe, before the House of Commons Home Affairs Select Committee. The commissioner 'has admitted that rogue and corrupt officers may evade justice because of the "mass shredding" of sensitive corruption files held by Scotland Yard'. The report continued, 'MPs described the current situation as "terrible", "shocking" and "an out and out disgrace" as they ridiculed reports, purportedly emanating from Scotland Yard sources, that suggested the "mass shredding" of some of the Met's most sensitive files was due to the force's attempt to comply with data protection law'.[16] This is derisory, but it's a not unusual approach. When in doubt about where the truth lies, simply decline to disclose information on the grounds that the disclosure will breach someone's right to privacy. With the establishment that seldom fails.

On 6 May 2014 the *Belfast Telegraph* reported that a Press Association investigation had found no fewer than 300 data protection breaches at the Metropolitan Police premises. These involved assisting criminals and selling confidential information held by the police for cash. One officer is alleged to have used data from police indices to assist in criminality, while another leaked confidential information at a significant level to a prominent criminal with links to firearms. Yet another officer was caught leaking confidential information regarding drugs. Some officers misused the Internet to search dating sites, while others searched for pornography. That is hardly in accordance with the concept of keeping London safe. But did someone think that London would be safer if Anne Maguire was placed in the dock along with her husband and two children, and that the evidence had to be planted in order to achieve that?

I have never discovered the reasons why Vincent and Patrick Maguire were not charged at the same time as the other members of the Maguire Seven. I have long taken the view that the police hoped that Anne Maguire would confess to the Guildford bombings, and the murder of the deceased in the Horse and Groom. If she had, the prosecution would have abandoned the charge of possessing NG against her and all the other family members and their friend. Such a confession would have put her in the dock with the Guildford Four. The explanation from the state could then have been that young Mr Wyndham had made an error during the test on the gloves, and the tests on the others were not sufficient either, because there was the risk of innocent contamination in the process of obtaining the swabs. If she admitted being a bomber, of which there was no admissible evidence, her two sons would not be charged and they would walk free. If that happened it would have placed Anne Maguire (a devout Christian who was later, in May 2005, given a Papal Medal by Pope John Paul II for her charity to, and forgiveness of, others) in a most dreadful dilemma. Should she confess to something she had not done in order to open the gate to freedom for those nearest and dearest to her? Failure or refusal to do so would have terrible consequences for them. If faced with such a choice, Anne would never have contemplated telling a lie to deceive anyone, for doing so would be to deny her complete innocence of the charges against her.

On 25 February 1975 the prosecution abandoned the five Guildford murder charges against Anne Maguire. They had no choice because they had no evidence. On the same day they charged Vincent and Patrick Maguire with the unlawful possession of NG. Can anyone deny that these two events were connected?

9 The Judiciary on Trial

THE MAGUIRE SEVEN never had the semblance of a fair trial from the moment Sir Michael Havers QC got to his feet at the Old Bailey in London to make the opening speech for the prosecution. He outlined to the jury the evidence on which the prosecution proposed to rely in order to prove the guilt of the accused. Havers was at his extravagant and theatrical best. Those before the court were in a closely knit group, 'alarm bells had started ringing – it was a case of all hands to the pump'. According to RTÉ's *Today Tonight* documentary, Havers said that 'there was a hastily convened council of war'. It may sound dramatically attractive, but was it true?

Later he was to tell the jury that 'there had been a gathering of the clans', an emotive phrase which must have carried some weight with the jury since those in the dock were linked not just by their family relationship, but also, apart from the two Maguire children, by their strong Belfast accents.[1] When the jury retired to consider their verdict in March 1976, having listened to these dramatic phrases, more appropriate to a West End drama than a criminal court, did they remember that the 'gathering of the clans' did not start early in the morning of Tuesday 3 December? Instead of attending 'the hastily convened council of war', Sean Smyth went to Wembley stadium to work, Anne Maguire went to her cleaning jobs and young Patrick Maguire went to school. Patrick O'Neill took his time turning up for the 'council of war' – he didn't even get to the house until about seven o'clock in the evening, and that was after Paddy Maguire had gone to Harrow Road police station. Had the council of war been adjourned while Paddy left the house, and while waiting for Sean Smyth to return home?

In the course of cross-examination during the trial, Havers used an unforgettable phrase, directed at Patrick O'Neill, who had taken his daughters to the Maguire home. Patrick O'Neill was, he said, 'another homing pigeon going down to Paddy Maguire's'. That evocative and emotive language was very damaging to O'Neill's case and it hardly represented the truth. Would members of a terrorist organisation summon the help of a man of perfectly good character, not a member of their organisation, with no interest in politics, who had not been in Belfast for 17 years? Would they ring him up and tell him, 'When you come to the hastily convened council of war, while you're winging your way over to Paddy Maguire's, don't forget to bring the kids to the bomb factory'?

Sir Michael told the jury that the scientists would say that the TLC test would identify the substance as NG and incriminate each accused with the same certainty as fingerprints. In the course of time the scientists denied that they would say that, because it was not true. Havers further told the jury that the TLC test, using toluene as the solvent, was a specific test for the presence of NG. In other words, there is no other substance that would mimic NG in this way: it was unique. That was also untrue, and the scientists knew it even if Havers did not. The information provided to him caused him again to mislead the jury when he told them that the traces of NG under the fingernails established that the suspect had been manipulating or kneading explosives. In fact this too was wrong.

A study carried out in 1977 and published in 1982, 'Transfer of NG to hands during contact with commercial explosives', of which one of the authors was Douglas Higgs of RARDE, found that NG can migrate under the fingernails without the explosive being kneaded.[2] All of the Maguire Seven were serving their sentences at the date of the study in 1977, and would have appreciated it if Higgs had told someone in a position of authority in either the police service or the prosecuting authorities that his very important evidence in 1976 against them on this very important point had in fact been wrong. He did nothing of the sort.

Nor did Higgs fare much better when he gave evidence before the Criminal Division of the Court of Appeal in 1991, when the Maguire Seven had their convictions set aside. He admitted that he knew about a set of negative tests for explosives carried out on the Maguire Seven, but he must have 'forgotten' about them when he gave evidence for the prosecution at the original trial. That seems a rather convenient loss of memory at a very important time. He also told the appeal court judges that he did not know about the experiment during the trial which was aimed at discovering how NG traces can be transferred from one hand to another. If he had, he said, he would certainly have told the prosecuting counsel, Sir Michael Havers QC, about it. However, he later admitted, when he was presented with RARDE documents showing his initials, that he must have authorised the test. Patrick O'Connor, defence counsel, pointed out to him, 'that is diametrically opposed to your denial this morning to their lordships'.[3] Higgs's credibility and reliability as a witness for the Crown, at the appeal court, was now under great scrutiny. He had not been subjected to such compelling cross-examination at the trial in 1976, for he had told the original jury, 'I seek to establish that the TLC test is infallible and I believe it to be. I think we have now reached the point at which we have tested enough by TLC to exclude other substances. In a purely scientific sense the chances of a rogue elephant turning up are 1 in 10,000. In the real world they are millions to one.'[4] Even as he gave his sworn evidence in front of the jury they did not know that there was another substance that could mimic NG in the TLC test using toluene as the eluent, so his claim that it was unique – in that other substances could be excluded – was quite untrue.

The scientist who developed the TLC test was Dr John Yallop, recently retired from RARDE. He courageously gave evidence for the defence, telling the jury on 9 February 1976 that he had served in the government service for 32 years and at the Home Office Explosives Department at RARDE.[5] He said he would never contemplate the TLC test as being the sole test for the presence of an explosive; another confirmatory test was necessary. In this case there was no such confirmation. He was uneasy with the evidence that while the dry swab of Paddy Maguire's right hand was positive, the swab soaked in ether was negative. He said this was not how NG behaves. He was also uneasy with the fact that six people had been moving around a house in which no trace of an explosives had been found, so they had cleaned the house but not their hands. He added that he thought it 'seemed very strange that if you had got seven people, six of whom had got hands with explosives on and the seventh had taken the precaution of wearing gloves, it seems to me to be decidedly odd if one person of the team thought of that precaution, why didn't the others?' It again seemed inconsistent behaviour. The trial judge, Sir John Donaldson, did not care much for that evidence and said so, claiming that it had nothing to do with the scientific evidence and was a comment that ought to be made by counsel rather than the witness.[6]

One has to wonder why, since it is well known that handling NG causes the handler to suffer a blinding headache, Anne Maguire would allow her children to handle the explosive with their bare hands while she took the precaution of wearing gloves. Not one of the six said to be contaminated ever complained to anyone about a headache on or after 3 December 1974.

The views of Douglas Higgs can be contrasted with those of John Yallop, who told the jury, 'no competent scientist could do other than conclude that the hypothesis is incorrect . . . to do otherwise would be unscientific, illogical and pig-headed'.[7] Whatever the jury may have made of the conflict of evidence between these two scientists, Mr Justice Donaldson made no real effort to conceal his preference for the witness for the prosecution.

During the course of the summing-up there was a slight change of tack by the judge. He very fairly summarised for the jury the total of John Yallop's observations about the alleged crime scene at 43 Third Avenue:

First there was the issue of the positive dry swab but a negative ether swab. But what Mr Yallop says is that NG is absorbed into the skin very rapidly and in those circumstances you would expect the ether swab to show positive if the dry swab showed positive. In fact I think he has gone further logically, that you can have it wearing off the surface of the hand first so that you get a negative on the dry swab and still get a positive on the ether swab. The next point which struck him was that the sniffer which was used to detect NG in the house failed to react at all. The third he said that he found it very strange that people who were alleged to be handling NG should have been sufficiently careful with the material, not letting bits fall on the floor and so on, so that there would be no reaction from the sniffer but sufficiently careless with the material to allow it to get on their hands and leave traces that could be detected by a TLC test. The fourth point that he took was that where you have a store of explosives in this sort of context they are really quite useless unless you have got detonators. You see, he thought it very significant that nobody could find any detonators. He said the same about timing devices and he would have included in that alternatively fuses, something at any rate to make it go off. And lastly he said that he found it very odd, to say the least – I am not using his words of course, but trying to summarise his evidence, that you should have seven accused people six of whom had positive results on the tests of their hands and that there should be a seventh person who was 'clean' but a pair of gloves which reacted positively. The point that he was making was that if a group of people know sufficient about NG to know that it produces headaches and the like and is stuff which really should not be handled with bare hands, you would expect them all to use gloves or none to use gloves.[8]

This was a strong point in favour of the defence which the jury had to consider. But did they? Were they confused by the scientific evidence? Was it so detailed and so intricate that they concentrated on other evidence in the case, such as the 'gathering of the clans' and the 'hastily convened council of war'?

In the course of the trial, defence counsel Quentin Edwards QC put it to John Yallop that a sniffer device that had been used in the house, and in particular in relation to the drawer that the gloves were in, had not given a positive result, and asked him, 'how did that strike you?' Dr Yallop replied, 'I was a little surprised because it seemed to me to be favourable conditions for getting a positive result if in fact explosive vapour had been present'.[9] For my part I rely on that answer from the distinguished retired scientist as concrete proof that there was no trace of an explosive on any glove in the kitchen drawer on either 3 or 4 December 1974. However, Mr Justice Donaldson, who had recited the evidence of John Yallop to the jury from his own notes, went on to make a point which I regard as unfortunate when dealing with the failure of the sniffer to detect the NG on the gloves in the drawer at the Maguire house. He said 'You have been told that the effectiveness of the sniffer depends on the quantity of gas which is available.'[10] Why did he not identify the witness who gave that important piece of evidence? Try as I might I cannot find it anywhere in all the material available. And what does that sentence actually mean? Does it mean that the sniffer device was not working effectively, because he added, 'I don't think anybody has put a plain, exact quantity at which the sniffer works but its primary use, we are told, is for sniffing out and detecting large quantities of NG'?[11] Are we to understand that the police officer who wheeled the portable device into the house and then passed the hand-held sniffer over the kitchen drawer containing the gloves was simply wasting his time, because unless the NG was there in a large quantities the sniffer would not have detected anything? If that device was not efficient enough, why not seek out another method of detecting NG? Would it not have been fair also to the seven accused for the judge to remind the jury that at least one police dog was with the officers when they arrived at 43 Third Avenue, the supposed bomb factory? Surely the police brought with them a dog trained to sniff out explosives. In fact there were several police dogs at the house on that first Tuesday evening in December 1975. Not one of them detected any trace of NG or any other explosive substance on any item such as clothing or on the gloves.

Did the jury ask themselves: how did anyone handling a bulk of NG, and there must have been a considerable amount if it required seven pairs of hands to dispose of it, manage to avoid any contact with any part of their clothing? Or if there was contact, how did they clean their clothing but not their hands?

Perhaps most disturbing of all is the reference in Sir John May's second report to a note written by Roger Maitland, a legal assistant in the attorney general's department.[12] I knew him in London in the mid-1960s. He was an unconventional lawyer who challenged the status quo; he accepted very little at face value and was not overawed by rank, position or reputation. He was the only lawyer on the prosecution side who had serious doubts about the TLC test used at Woolwich. In his note dated 4 March 1975 referring to a meeting with the attorney general that took place on 18 February 1975, Maitland wrote that the two leading prosecution counsel, Havers and Hill,

> emphatically assured the A.G. that the Woolwich method of analysis provides conclusive proof of the presence of nitro glycerine. They said it was comparable to fingerprint evidence . . . With reference to the traces on the palms, Havers and Hill advanced two novel theories of their own: (c) That the defendants had been hurriedly breaking up a 25 lb roll of gelignite because they feared a police raid. (R.M. has not seen any case involving gelignite in a 25 lb roll.)
> (d) Alternatively, that the defendants had been hurriedly dismantling bombs, as they knew it would be unsafe to remove them without doing so.

In my view these two barristers' enthusiasm was no substitute for evidence. They jumped to the conclusion that there were bombs at 43 Third Avenue, that they were first dismantled and then removed. They seemed to care little for the fact that no explosive material was found anywhere. Both conveniently believed the false evidence of Paul Hill and Gerard Conlon that they had seen Anne Maguire make bombs in the kitchen of her own home. Nothing was going to be allowed to contradict that.

The note continues: '(e) That the absence of traces of nitro glycerine in the house (except on the rubber gloves) may be explained by the possibility that the defendants worked on polythene sheets.' In the list of exhibits there is no mention of polythene sheets found anywhere at 43 Third Avenue. Had the Maguire Seven successfully disposed of them as well? So well, indeed, that they were never found? It should be emphasised that the two barristers were only canvassing the existence of these sheets as a possibility, not as a fact. Should counsel in a criminal case be doing that?

What follows next in the note is devastating for the truth in the case. '*The A.G. was informed that Mrs Maguire's 18 pairs of rubber gloves were found in a pile and that, due to a blunder by the police, cross contamination was probable. The gloves had been tested as a batch and traces of nitroglycerine were found*' [emphasis added].

In the light of these notes, which one can assume are a correct record of what was said, it is difficult to see why the prosecution against Anne Maguire was sanctioned by the attorney general. Did he really consider there was a realistic prospect of conviction if and when the jury were told that the police had blundered and the evidence relating to the gloves had been contaminated? In fact the jury were never told about this. Nor were the defence. It seems superfluous to state that they should have been. They would have been if the Maguire Seven had received a fair trial.

It should be noted that at the May Inquiry hearings Michael Hill QC strongly disagreed with the accuracy of the paragraph of Mr Maitland's note regarding the roll of gelignite. Sir John May said, 'I accept that counsel did not advance any theory involving a 25 lb roll of gelignite. Nevertheless I am quite satisfied that the remainder of the note is a sufficiently accurate summary of what happened at that meeting.'[13] Michael Hill seems to have accepted that too, for he did not further challenge the note.

On any view it seems an odd thing to get wrong on Roger Maitland's part, if he did, but more important, counsel never challenged or denied the claim that polythene sheets might possibly have been used, or that the police blundered and that the samples taken from the gloves might have been contaminated. Such a probability rules out a verdict of guilty if proof beyond reasonable doubt is canvassed before the trial jury.

Returning to the summing-up of Mr Justice Donaldson: 'When I say large quantities I mean not what would be left on a glove, lumps of explosives, that is what it is intended for, and you will have to consider whether it is certain that the sniffer would have detected NG on the gloves in the drawer if there had been NG or whether it is possible that the quantity on the gloves was sufficient for two TLC tests – because there was a second swabbing – but insufficient for the sniffer to detect. That is a matter for you to decide.'[14] In this way the judge tried to reduce or even eradicate the evidence of the independent witness John Yallop, who favoured no particular side but simply sought to tell the truth. In doing this I consider Mr Justice Donaldson was not acting in an unbiased and objective manner. For example, he told the jury that Mr Yallop had misgivings over the absence of any detonators being found in 43 Third Avenue, because he knew that NG on its own is no use to a bomber. It requires a detonator to cause an explosion. Mr Yallop was also uneasy about the absence of any timing devices. The judge told the jury, 'if somebody was concealing explosives it would be a bit silly to leave the detonators behind, so was not Mr Yallop perhaps sounding around rather desperately if that really was a point that bothered him?' He added, 'So you may think that these last points don't amount to very much.'[15] That was his way of telling the jury, 'I don't think much of this point, so why should you?' In reality the importance was that it was not just the NG that had to be moved from the house (which I consider was under observation most of that Tuesday) but also the detonators and perhaps timing devices, and taken and hidden so successfully that they have never been found. The more objects there were, the more difficult it would be to conceal them.

It was common ground between both sides in the case that it was not sufficient for the prosecution to prove their case simply by adducing evidence of the forensic results. They had to prove that each of the accused in the dock actually handled a bulk of NG, and in that way the prosecution relied on the forensic results to prove the fact of handling.

In opening the case, the point has already been made that Sir Michael Havers QC misled the jury in a number of respects. He did it again when, after telling them that swabs showed that the accused had been handling NG, although no explosives were found when the police raided the premises (which was correct), he said that the explosives were packed up either at the house in Third Avenue or in one of the derelict houses situated behind. There was not a single witness who ever claimed that he or she saw that. It simply did not happen. That seemed not to deter leading counsel for the prosecution. 'Evidence would be given', said Sir Michael in confident tones, 'that all had not only handled the explosives but had kneaded and manipulated it to pack it into small bags to get rid of the evidence.'[16] Since no bulk of explosive was ever found, despite the detailed search of 43 Third Avenue, the derelict houses nearby and the canal that ran near the house, the suggestion that small bags were involved in packing up and removing a bulk of NG is pure invention on the part of leading counsel or someone who briefed him with this false information.

Who, if anyone, was to blame when justice miscarried and four of the Maguire family, with three others, lost their liberty for many years? I consider that the trial judge failed to give a full direction on the law relating to the character of the accused on trial before him. 'Character' in the law of evidence means reputation, disposition and convictions, or lack of them. A person at trial with no convictions recorded against them is entitled to ask the jury to consider their evidence as more likely to be truthful than if they had criminal convictions. Of course, being of good character does not amount to a defence – if it did, no one would be convicted for the first time. In addition, an accused person is entitled to rely on evidence that a person of his or her disposition is not the kind of person who would commit the offence with which they are charged. This can be seen in the case of the three former Surrey police officers; the trial judge gave them a good character direction not once but twice. The unfortunate Anne Maguire and her children, with the others, did not get such a direction once, let alone twice. Were the two prosecuting lawyers really acting as 'ministers of justice' in the way they conducted the trial and put the case before the jury?

As for the trial judge, my view is that he could not even contemplate that the four individuals in the first trial and the seven in the second could possibly be anything but guilty as charged. There was in that Old Bailey courtroom in the first three months of 1976 a determination that those in the dock would be convicted and punished for what they had done. The personification of that determination is to be found in Mr Justice Donaldson. As an example, it is obvious he went along with the approach adopted by Sir Michael Havers QC (without using Havers' extravagant language) when he told the jury:

> Now the Crown case on this is quite simple. They say that Mr Maguire senior, Vincent, Patrick, Giuseppe Conlon, Mr Smyth and Mr O'Neill all had traces of nitro glycerine on their hands; they say that Mrs Maguire's gloves had traces of nitro glycerine on them; they say that they are all members of a group who were together on the 3rd December. The Crown say that the Guildford arrests would create panic amongst those people, that they were in possession of explosives, and they say there is some evidence of panic, or at least grave concern, in relation to the arrest of Gerry Conlon and the disappearance and subsequent emerging on the arrest of Hughie Maguire.[17]

Let's just pause to dissect those statements. We know now, and the jury ought to have known then, that Paul Hill had been arrested on the morning of 28 November 1975. Gerard Conlon had been arrested at 5.30 a.m. on 30 November. If there was a panic in the Maguire household because of the

Guildford arrests, when did it start? I have found no evidence that any of the Maguire Seven knew anything about the arrest of Hugh Maguire until late in the evening of 3 December 1974 – up to that time all they knew was that they could not contact him. If Anne Maguire was an IRA bomb maker, as Paul Hill and Gerard Conlon were to claim, why did someone from that organisation not tip her off that they had been lifted by the police, one on each side of the Irish Sea?

In addition, a fair-minded judge (and I am certainly not going to accuse Sir John Donaldson of being that) would have pointed out that Paddy Maguire had gone to Harrow Road police station on that Tuesday evening to inquire about his brother Hugh Maguire. He wanted to know where Hugh was and what had happened to him and his wife. In fact, the only thing Mr Justice Donaldson said about the police station visit was, when describing the end of Paddy Maguire's examination in chief during the trial, 'I put my coat on. I went down to Harrow Road police station.'[18] Would not the interests of fairness have required the judge to give the time of that visit from the evidence available? By the time Paddy Maguire left 43 Third Avenue, neither Sean Smyth nor Patrick O'Neill had arrived at that house. Had Paddy Maguire really gone to the police station leaving behind a bulk of NG for the other two to handle and then mysteriously dispose of? If Paddy Maguire had left literally explosive evidence behind, what would he have done if the police had decided to leave the police station and go back to the house with him?

It is also difficult to understand what the judge meant by the Guildford arrests being the cause of the first panic, because he dealt separately with the arrest of Gerard Conlon but did not mention Paul Hill by name. Gerard Conlon had been arrested at 5.30 a.m. on 30 November 1974. The time of his detention (as opposed to arrest) is shown on his detention sheet RBI/12/492 as being 9.35 a.m. The judge could not have said that 'the Guildford arrests' of either Patrick Armstrong or Carole Richardson were a cause of panic, because neither was lifted by the police until that Tuesday evening, well after the 'hastily convened council of war' was said to have taken place. I don't consider that this inexperienced judge in criminal cases fully realised that. To spell it out, did it really take from 5.30 on the morning of Saturday 30 November to the following Tuesday for the panic to start?

The summing-up went on. Now Mr Justice Donaldson was determined to cover all bases to ensure there were no gaps in the evidence through which any of the accused might slip.

The Crown do not say that all those people necessarily handled the nitro glycerine simultaneously, they do not express any view about that at all; they simply say it was handled somehow or other; they do not even say where it was handled. You may think that the probabilities are that if it was handled at all it was handled at or near 43 Third Avenue. You may also think it is probable that it was handled during the afternoon of 3rd December but the Crown do not have to prove that and they do not allege any particular time of handling it or, as I say, that they all handled it together.[19]

When Mr Justice Donaldson summed up the evidence to the jury he deliberately descended into the arena in order to ensure the return of a guilty verdict. He seemed anxious to involve Vincent Maguire by describing him as being 'in an odd position, a special position, if you accept his evidence of having told the police that he had been handling something which looked suspiciously like nitro glycerine if it was not chalk. That is another matter you will have to consider. He had been handling that at about 3 o'clock in the afternoon. So if you come to the conclusion that Vincent was the odd man out on timing perhaps you may think that the answer was that Vincent had been handling nitro glycerine at an earlier stage, but there it is, you have to decide it, but you may wonder just how accurate are these times.'[20] Does anyone follow exactly what that means?

It will be remembered that Vincent was only 16 in December 1974; Patrick was only 13. In law Patrick was a child; Vincent was a young person. The Administrative Directions on Interrogation and the Taking of Statements[21] Rule 4, headed 'Interrogation of children and young persons', state, 'As far as practicable children (whether suspected of crime or not) should only be interviewed in the presence of a parent or guardian, or, in their absence, some person who is not a police officer and is of the same sex as the child.' No independent person was present during any interview Vincent or Patrick had with the investigating police officers. The defence seemed not to have argued about the admissibility of these interviews on the ground of a breach of Rule 4, probably on the ground that it is a matter of judicial discretion whether or not to admit the evidence of the interviews. There was not the slightest chance that Mr Justice Donaldson would have excluded that evidence, even though, as well as the child, the rule protects the police against allegations of misconduct during an interview.

And Vincent did make allegations of assault and ill-treatment against the police. So did Patrick and his mother. Anne Maguire said that in a moment of weakness she collapsed on the floor at the police station. She said an officer kicked her in the back and called her 'an Irish bastard'. The jury did not accept that these allegations were true. Vincent told them: 'I was hit and threatened. I heard Patrick screaming. I was threatened in the car going to the police station. I was beaten in the police station . . . Harvey ran at me with his forearm against my throat up against the wall. He twisted my head. He hit me in the stomach. It hurt and I cried . . . I decided to tell the story about the candle when I heard Patrick scream.'[22] Vincent made it clear during the trial that the object he was talking about was chalk and the word 'candle' was used first by a police officer, not him. In fact, he not only used the word 'chalk' to describe the object, he showed the police exactly what it was, and where it was in the house. A piece of chalk was exhibited at the trial. It appears on the list of exhibits as number 54. I find no reference to that exhibit in the summing-up of Mr Justice Donaldson.

The judge told the jury, 'Now let me leave those on one side and turn now to the evidence which affects the individual accused and only the individual accused. Vincent and the candle.' He went on to relate how two officers had interviewed Vincent on 7 December. One of them told him that traces of explosives had been found under his fingernails. He showed him the report from the scientists who said this was so. He told Vincent that his brother Patrick, his father Paddy, William Smyth and Patrick O'Neill also had traces of the stuff on their hands. Vincent denied touching or handling anything out of the ordinary. 'Not explosives. We have nothing to do with that sort of thing.' Asked what he meant, he mentioned the Troubles and the shooting dead of two of his uncles in Ireland 'by the Protestants'. It is a fact that two of his relations, his mother's uncles, had been murdered in Belfast. Anne Maguire's uncle Bobby was shot in 1973 and her uncle Vincent in 1974; both were regarded as 'reprisal killings'. (Those killings did not conclude the grief of the family. In 1983, while Paddy Maguire was still serving his prison sentence, his eight-year-old nephew was struck and killed by an army armoured car in Belfast.[23])

When the jury heard the evidence about the killings in Northern Ireland, and they heard it twice because Sean Smyth also gave evidence about one of the killings, did any of them conclude that perhaps the Maguire family were involved in some way in paramilitary activity? It would have been entirely wrong to reach any such conclusion, but did that prejudicial evidence have any effect on their final verdict?

They could have been left in no doubt when Mr Justice Donaldson told them the following: 'The detective constable said, "Let's get back to the explosives shall we?" . . . Vincent said "the only thing I can remember is a candle thing which I found under Sean's bed" . . . The constable said, "who is Sean?" Vincent said, "he is my uncle. His name is William Smyth and he is living with us." The constable said, "go on, tell me about it". Vincent said, "it was like a candle, about eight inches long and smooth like a sort of wax. I could get my fingers right round it. I don't know what it was."[24] Vincent added that bits broke off one end and 'it was like a big candle really'. Asked what he was doing looking under the bed he replied that he was looking for cards. He had held it in his right hand and did not show this object to anyone, then he put it back. Asked when this incident happened, he said, 'it must have been about 2 o'clock on that Tuesday. That is 3rd December.'[25]

Mr Justice Donaldson then referred back to the evidence given by Douglas Higgs. 'Mr Higgs was asked what comment he had to make on this candle thing that Vincent was said to have been talking about and he said, "it does not suggest a candle. I have seen things which fit this description better. There are sticks of gelignite with white wax wrappers eight inches long and one inch in diameter. They are covered at the end and if this comes undone it might break off. The consistency is akin to medium-soft marzipan."'

The judge then reminded the jury that in reply to his own counsel Vincent had said he knew perfectly well that what he had been touching was chalk and he meant of course, not the thin sticks of blackboard chalk but the thick sticks, one inch or so. He said he knew perfectly well it was chalk. When cross-examined by the prosecution he recited how he had been assaulted by the police. He could not remember whether he described it as a candle, he didn't think so. Vincent agreed with the prosecutor that he had heard Mr Higgs say it was a good description of a stick of gelignite. The judge then mentioned that although it was not in his note he had a distinct recollection that another officer who was questioning Patrick at the same time told Patrick that Vincent had said something about a stick and asked him what it was. Patrick said it was chalk. The judge then invited the jury to choose between the Maguire brothers on one side and the police on the other. Was Vincent beaten up, and were the police officers lying when they denied it? Vincent had never complained to anyone about the violence, which implied that he would have done so if he really was assaulted. Judges in their judicial capacity seldom if ever go into police stations, and if they do the treatment they receive is quite different from that meted out to suspected persons there under arrest. And who was Vincent to complain to? Should he have complained to one police officer about the violent conduct of another? This conflict could have been avoided if an appropriate adult had been present at the interviews involving Vincent and Patrick. If, in addition, they had been allowed access to legal advice there might be grounds for complaint if they had not told him or her what they said happened to them.

Mr Justice Donaldson then put this before the jury:

> Was it true that Vincent handled something which Mr Higgs says is a good description of a stick of gelignite? It was young Patrick who was asked about the stick of white material and he said, 'it is chalk. I got it from school. The gym master gave it to me'. And young Patrick, you know, he also alleged that he was beaten up. Again you may want to consider why young Patrick never complained at any time, why he had no marks or bruises so far as is known, and if it is untrue, why is he lying? Why is Vincent lying? Is young Patrick simply supporting Vincent in a lie? And what about Vincent? *Is he lying because he regrets now having told the truth about this stick of gelignite?* [26] [emphasis added]

In fact Vincent never said at any time to anyone that it was a stick of gelignite. Following those wholly misleading words, I believe, the Maguire Seven were bound to be convicted. They were facing certain imprisonment, but would they have been if the jury knew, as the investigative journalist Bob Woffinden disclosed, that 'Vincent remembered seeing some pieces [of chalk] under Sean Smyth's bed. He showed the police where, and the chalk was there, exactly as he had said.'[27]

Bob Woffinden further commented, 'In his summing up, the judge referred to . . . "a stick of gelignite". In doing so, he was quoting from the testimony of one of the prosecution witnesses. . . . What the judge failed to mention was that this same witness added that of course it could not have been gelignite, otherwise the mechanical sniffer would have detected its presence.'[28] Did the jury recollect that evidence, or were they persuaded by the judge's comment that this was an account of an explosive hidden in the Maguire house?

The judge returned to that evidence, purportedly dealing with innocent contamination:

> Well now, Vincent, he did, of course, describe what Mr Higgs said was a good description of a stick of gelignite so clearly, as far as he is concerned, there is a real issue as to whether he may not have

picked up a stick of gelignite. If he did, was that innocent handling or did he know perfectly well what it was or was he handling it for some particular purpose? You will have to make up your minds about that and of course, in that context you may find that the attack on the police is revealing; you may think it is not.[29]

Was that not an open invitation to the jury to consider that the reason Vincent alleged the police assaulted him was because he regretted he had admitted to them that he was handling NG? If the jury did not believe him on the assault point, did they then conclude it was NG, not a piece of chalk, that he handled in Sean Smyth's bedroom?

In dealing with the prosecution evidence against Patrick Maguire, the judge told the jury that there was one other matter the prosecution must prove, 'and this applies to young Patrick Maguire alone'. This was because in December 1974 Patrick was only 13 years old and was at that time in law protected by the legal doctrine of *doli incapax* – the rebuttable presumption that he was by reason of his age incapable of committing a crime. There was no evidence before the jury that Patrick had 'mischievous discretion', i.e. that he knew it was wrong to handle NG. The police had never asked him about that. If his counsel, Edward Terrell QC, had submitted at the close of the case for the prosecution that Patrick lacked 'mischievous discretion' it is difficult to see how the judge could have refused to allow that submission. That meant that Patrick would have been acquitted. But he failed to make such a submission. My view is that he had such a heavy workload – he was representing not just Patrick but also Vincent and their father, Paddy – that he simply overlooked the fact during the trial. The prosecution realised the position and asked Patrick, when he was in the witness box, if he realised that it was seriously wrong to handle an explosive substance, and he, being an honest and truthful person, agreed that he did. That being so, it seems totally unnecessary for the trial judge to deal with a point that by then had no force or validity. It has become an irrelevance.

The judge made it quite clear to the jury that his view was that while the four men, Paddy Maguire, Sean Smyth, Patrick O'Neill and Giuseppe Conlon, maintained that they left 43 Third Avenue for the pub about 8.15 p.m., he did not accept that timing. Patrick O'Neill maintained it must have been after eight o'clock because he had arranged to speak to his wife in hospital at that time. The police evidence, which Mr Justice Donaldson always favoured when it conflicted with the defence evidence, was that the men left the house at 7.45 p.m. This became known as the 'missing half hour'. The judge said, 'And if in fact the four accused are not telling you the truth about the time they were in the public house why aren't they telling you the truth?', the implication being that they were busy getting rid of the NG. But where? And under the eyes of the police officers trailing behind them?

On 29 January, the eighth day of the trial, the prosecution called a surprise witness whose evidence had not been mentioned by Sir Michael Havers QC when he opened the case to the jury. This evidence was so trivial and insignificant that it would have been regarded by some as a bit of light relief but for the fact that the case was so serious. The witness was Kenneth John Gordon Hackney, the senior housing assistant of Westminster City Council, whose office was about a hundred yards from 43 Third Avenue. His evidence covers seven pages of the transcript of the trial.

He told the jury that on the afternoon of Monday 28 October 1975 (some three weeks after the Guildford bombing and about five weeks before Tuesday 3 December) he interviewed Paddy Maguire, who had called at the council offices. Paddy had been drinking, giving Mr Hackney the impression that he was drunk. The council official had made a note that was produced in evidence and exhibited before the jury. It read: 'Mr M called and wanted to know if he could terminate his interest in his tenancy of 43 Third Avenue, but still reside there. I said no. Asked why, he said he didn't want to be responsible for the wellbeing of the premises. "It could be blown up." I rang the police at Harrow Road even though he was drunk.'

The prosecution were putting forward this evidence to invite the jury to convict Paddy Maguire of a terrorism-related offence. Would a terrorist, even a supporter or sympathiser, go to a public official and say that his own home might be bombed, even though he wanted to continue living there? What had probably happened was that Paddy had been drinking, had a row with his wife, perhaps when he told her he had resigned from his employment, and went to the council while he was in no satisfactory state to negotiate with anyone. Needless to say, the police at Harrow Road police station, in response to Mr Hackney's call, did nothing. This prosecution evidence proved nothing but the fact that when Paddy had been drinking he said things he would later regret.

After the evidence was concluded and counsel in the case had made their closing speeches to the jury, there was an important development. Dr John Yallop had always challenged the prosecution claim that the TLC test in toluene was unique for NG. He believed there was another substance which in identical tests and conditions would mimic NG. It will be remembered that Sir Michael Havers had claimed that not only was the TLC test unique and particular, he actually went further and claimed that the scientists would testify that the tests were like fingerprints.[30] It was then that John Yallop made a surprising discovery. He found a paper sent to him by one of the RARDE scientists, Walter Elliott, in the summer of 1974, which said that another explosive, pentaerythritol tetranitrate (PETN), gave, on the TLC test with toluene, an identical result to NG in colour, rate of climb along a plate, and final position on that plate. Only the rate of development of that colour (pink) was slightly different, which was not considered a major factor. That led Sir John May's inquiry to conclude, 'The Crown cannot now be taken to have proved that the traces on the defendants' hands and upon the gloves were of NG. The TLC/toluene test upon which the Crown relied as being specific for NG has been shown not to be so.'[31] The finding of PETN undermined the whole edifice on which the prosecution based their case.

Back at the trial courtroom, once that was known to the trial judge and counsel in the case, there was the problem of how to get this evidence before the jury. Dr Yallop had had a torrid time during Sir Michael's cross-examination. He had accused the scientist of giving misleading and selective evidence and put his professional integrity in doubt. At one stage defence counsel Quentin Edwards had to intervene to protect the witness (something which the trial judge should really have done) by saying, 'I wish my learned friend would not be so enthusiastic to start on the next question before the answer has been given to the last one.' There was no response to that intervention from Sir Michael. He continued to hector the witness, accusing him of backtracking on scientific views he had held for a long time.

Neither John Yallop nor the defence lawyers were keen that Dr Yallop should return to the witness box.

The new evidence was therefore agreed between the two sides and put in a form identified as Exhibit 60. Mr Justice Donaldson seemed mystified by this new development. The seven in the dock were charged with possessing an explosive substance, which was identified by the prosecution as NG. A scientific experiment showed that a substance identified as NG could in fact have been PETN. With his civil law experience that was no problem to Mr Justice Donaldson. The indictment claimed the Maguire Seven possessed one explosive; this evidence suggested that it was not necessarily NG but could have been another explosive. One simply applies the 'red pencil' approach: cross out one explosive substance (NG) and substitute another explosive substance (PETN). At one stage it seemed to have been suggested that the indictment should be amended to charging the Seven with possessing an explosive, either NG or PETN.

The 'red pencil' approach does not work in a criminal court, especially in this case. The new evidence completely undermined the prosecution contention that the TLC test in toluene was specific and unique. If there was another substance that could mimic it, it did not matter that that other substance was an explosive. Mr Justice Donaldson simply did not understand that point. He dismissed it as irrelevant because no one had suggested during the course of the trial that the substance found on the hands and the gloves was PETN. He was wrong.

On Monday 1 March 1976 Mr Justice Donaldson began to sum up the evidence to the jury.

As a long-time advocate for reform of the criminal justice system I have urged that counsel on both sides should play a part, with the trial judge, in drafting the direction to the jury on the law, so that it is agreed and cannot therefore be the subject of any appeal. I have also advocated that the judge should not sum up the facts of the case himself, nor make any comment on those facts or express any view on them. He is supposed to be an impartial umpire, holding the balance between the prosecution and the defence to ensure that the accused receives a fair trial. Most important of all, the criminal justice system must resist the pressure of the politicians, one of whom, the then prime minister Tony Blair, said in June 2002 that the biggest miscarriage of justice in today's system is when the guilty walk free. This approach undermines the basic principles of the presumption of innocence and due process – the right to fair treatment in custody and the right to a fair trial. Protecting innocent people from wrongful conviction is a primary duty of the state. At the time we are concerned with, 1974, the treatment of suspects in custody was governed by the Judges' Rules. These were first formulated in 1912 by members of the judiciary. As Professor Adrian Zuckerman wrote in 1991:

> These required the police, amongst other things, to inform suspects of their right to keep silent and to consult a solicitor, and keep a contemporaneous record of the interrogation. However, in practice the caution was administered in a perfunctory fashion calculated to ensure that it made no impact. The right to consult a solicitor was habitually denied to suspects yet the courts did nothing about it. As a result, the rule affording access to legal advice became a dead letter.[32]

Professor Zuckerman could well have had the cases of the Guildford Four and the Maguire Seven in mind as examples of how the Judges' Rules were so constantly and consistently ignored by those supposed to follow them, and those responsible for enforcing them.

At the conclusion of the summing-up and as the jury were sent to their room to consider their verdict, there was an intervention from Patrick O'Neill's defence counsel, Michael Self QC. Mr Justice Donaldson, in summarising the evidence, had told the jury: 'Mr O'Neill collected his children from school at about 3.45, one child and the other about 4 o'clock. He said he went out and got cakes in the Stockwell Road for the children at about 4 o'clock. He left for the Maguires at 10 to 6. He arrived, he says, at the Maguire's house at 7 o'clock and he received the telephone call from his wife at 8 o'clock and then about 8.15 or 8.20 he went to the pub.'³³ That was all. The judge was under a duty to put his case fully before the jury. In the foregoing, he had hardly done that.

Patrick O'Neill's evidence before the jury took up 40 pages of the trial transcript. He had given that evidence on Tuesday 17 February – just over two weeks earlier. How much of the detail of his evidence could the jury be expected to remember? What they did not know was that, in their absence, at the time the defence made a submission of no case to answer, Sir Michael Havers QC had said, 'it was no part of the case for the prosecution that O'Neill intended to be in possession of explosives when he went to the house in Third Avenue' and 'he may have gone with innocent intentions and been made use of'.

Patrick O'Neill began his evidence by disclosing that he had two convictions for motoring offences in 1961 and 1962. Apart from those, which were minor, and would now be regarded as spent convictions that could not be referred to without leave of the court, he was of good character with no convictions for crime or anything else. His counsel, Michael Self, reminded him (and the judge and jury) that DCI Grundy had told the court that Patrick O'Neill had no political affiliations whatsoever with Ireland. The only club he belonged to, he said, that could be considered a political club was the Paddington Conservative Club. He had four children by this date, the youngest member of the family, a girl, being just over a year old. He was born in Belfast (on 26 July 1940) and had left there to work and live in England when he was 17 or 18 years old. He worked as a pipe-fitter/welder with the same company for 14 years, and then for another employer for the previous three years. He had not returned to Belfast since 1969 and had no plans to return. (In the event, on his release from prison he was served with an exclusion order which sent him from England back to Northern Ireland, resulting in the final breakdown of his marriage.)

He had married his wife, Helen, in 1965. They and their daughters were extremely friendly with the Maguire family. His wife had entered Lewisham hospital on 25 November when she was expecting their fourth child. There were complications, and the doctors planned to give a blood transfusion, in three stages, to the unborn baby. The three young O'Neill sisters were sent to Helen's sister and her husband, Mr and Mrs Lynch, who lived with their own three children in Luton. It was hoped that Helen O'Neill would be released from hospital on Monday 2 December, but the doctors told her that she would have to remain in hospital for another week. That was a major problem for Patrick O'Neill, the second in just a few days.

Towards the end of the last week in November Mrs Lynch had told Patrick O'Neill that her father was gravely ill in County Wexford and she had to return home, so she could no longer look after the O'Neill children. Patrick collected them on Saturday 30 November and brought them back to their council flat in Stockwell Road, London. He had previously arranged with his employers to take the following Monday and Tuesday off work to help his wife settle back at home after her hospital stay. Now he needed someone to look after the children from Wednesday 4 December until Helen was released from hospital. He knew Anne Maguire would help. That is why he brought his three young children to 43 Third Avenue at about 7 p.m. on that Tuesday evening. It is my view that the police, who claimed they started to watch the premises only at about 7 p.m. (a claim that I do not believe), saw him arrive with the children. Did they honestly believe he was taking them to a bomb factory?

Patrick O'Neill had told the jury that on that Tuesday evening Anne Maguire took two of the girls to the local chip shop. That left a third girl, Sharon, who cried because she had been left in the house. Paddy Maguire sat her on his lap and read her a story from a book. She soon stopped crying. On any view that was a picture of simple domestic happiness. What the prosecution were alleging was nothing like that. According to them, all the family, including Paddy Maguire and Patrick O'Neill, were busy breaking up and disposing of NG, leaving them little or no time for consoling crying children and reading stories.

In his evidence Patrick O'Neill described how he was taken from the pub and had his hands swabbed by Det. Sgt Vickery. He was asked to make a statement, but it was not under caution, so he could not have been suspected of crime at that time. He was a witness more than a suspect at that point, but the police detained him overnight at the station. He was not under arrest and should have been told he was free to leave if he chose to do so. He did not know that and the police did not tell him. Unlike the others, he made no allegations of assault and ill treatment at the police station. The police took him to his flat the next morning and searched it. They found nothing, for there was nothing to find. They then took him back to 43 Third Avenue to collect his children and released him without charge or on bail pending further inquiries. He said that Det. Sgt Vickery (who had swabbed his hands) 'wanted to give me a lift to the station in the car because that day my youngest daughter Jean [who was four years old] gave him a kiss in the street. I said no, I will go by bus.'[34]

At 8.15 a.m. on the following Saturday the police came to his flat and arrested him. The scientists had said that the tests showed that he had been handling NG. He was about to lose everything in life that he held most precious: his wife, his children, his good character, his job, his reputation and his freedom. When he was asked in cross-examination by Sir Michael Havers why he had not left his children with his neighbours in Stockwell Road, he replied that he would not leave them with just anyone, only those he knew, trusted and had children of their own. Havers asked him if he was worried that his good friend Hughie Maguire was missing. When one considers that his wife was in hospital undergoing a painful and serious procedure that might result in the loss of their unborn baby, that he was compelled to make arrangements for his three little girls, which was difficult – if he was off work he was not paid (in fact he went back to work after his return home on Wednesday 4 December) – the whereabouts of Hugh Maguire would be the very least of his worries. It will be remembered that the prosecution were claiming that it was the arrest of Hugh Maguire that might have been one of the causes of panic at 43 Third Avenue. (In fact none of them ever knew of that arrest until Sean Tully told them sometime on the afternoon of Tuesday 3 December.)

One would have expected that in the light of this evidence, even in the short summary set out above, that Mr Justice Donaldson would have summed up his case adequately. He did not. Michael Self told him, 'I think your Lordship will agree with me that in the case of Mr O'Neill your Lordship has not put the basic details of his defence or any of the evidence of his witnesses. My Lord, I feel that it is something I should raise in a case that has gone on so long.'[35]

The judge agreed, realising that he had been saved from making the major blunder of failing to put Patrick O'Neill's case to the jury. He said, 'I think you are right, absolutely right. Let me try to deal with that, I won't say "off the cuff" but from recollection, and if I have omitted anything . . .'[36]

Before he could continue another defence counsel intervened, referring to some evidence given by Douglas Higgs. That may have distracted the judge.

He got off to a poor start, did not improve, and did not try do even his incompetent best to put before the jury Patrick O'Neill's case in answer to the allegations made against him by the prosecution. It will be remembered that his own evidence in chief and cross-examination covers 40 pages of the typewritten transcript. The judge summed up that evidence in 37 lines, less than one full page. This is what he told the jury.

> Mr O'Neill is not a completely casual visitor because, as you will remember, he is a friend of Hughie Maguire and of his family and so on but it is right to take account of the fact that he alone of the accused did not live at this particular house. His case is essentially this: that his wife was in hospital; owing to complications of pregnancy her stay in hospital was unexpectedly prolonged and he was therefore in the position that he had three small children on his hands and nowhere to park them. He turned to Mrs Maguire as somebody who could assist him in this dilemma and he took the three children to the house for that purpose and there was no other reason for him going to that house. He fixes the time. We know there is independent evidence of his picking the children up from school; there is a good deal of evidence which you will remember that he did make arrangements, almost at the last minute, to take the children to the Maguire household. He says that when he got there he deposited the children, he went for a drink with the others. He fixes the time for going to the pub by reference to the time his wife phoned him which he says and she says was 8 o'clock – that has to be looked at in the light of the evidence given by the other observers – and he says that all he ever did that night was to take his children to the Maguire household and leave them there. But for the intervention of the police he would have gone home. That is his case in a nutshell. The problem you have to consider, of course, is what did he do when he got there? Accepting fully his evidence, what did he do when he got there? What is the explanation for the state of his hands? You have his evidence. He does not have to prove anything anymore than the others; it is for the Crown to satisfy you so that you are sure that he was knowingly handling nitro glycerine or assisting others who were handling it. Mr Self, is there any other point in his evidence that you wish me to draw attention to?

He added, 'I have made, I hope, the position of Mr O'Neill clear. He says that he had a perfectly good reason for going into the house that night which has nothing to do with explosives; he wanted to park his children there. "I was there for that purpose and that is all I went there for."'[37]

Analysing that part of the summing-up, I consider that the reference to being 'a friend of Hughie Maguire' was highly prejudicial and irrelevant. Patrick and Helen O'Neill were old friends of Anne and Paddy Maguire; they socialised together; they were fond of each other's children. It was natural that one couple should ask for the help of the other. It was a prejudicial reference to Hughie Maguire because all the jury knew was that he was 'missing'. They did not know why. In the climate of the time, did they suspect it was in connection with acts of terrorism? I found no evidence, which would have been available from the police, that the jury knew that Hugh and Kitty Maguire had been released without charge after a week in custody. Why were the jury not told that the arrest led to nothing, if Mr Justice Donaldson thought it important to link Patrick O'Neill with Hugh Maguire rather than stress his friendship with Anne and Paddy Maguire? Patrick O'Neill would not have taken his three children to stay with Hugh and Kitty; they had no children of their own and they would not have relished the thought of minding three small children for a week.

Moreover, it simply was not right to tell the jury that Patrick O'Neill was the only one of the accused not living in this particular house. Giuseppe Conlon didn't live there either.

Patrick O'Neill was a person of good character, with no connection with any political organisation. He had lived in the UK for 17 years and had a splendid work record. He lived with his wife and three young children in local authority accommodation. His background and credit rating would thus have been checked to ensure he was a suitable tenant for council housing. He had lived as much, if not more, of his life in England than in Northern Ireland and had not visited his native city of Belfast since 1969. That was because everything he valued in his life was in England. He had no reason to be involved in any act of terrorism, for to do would risk everything he had, and for what purpose?

Would it not have been fair for Mr Justice Donaldson to remind the jury that Patrick O'Neill claimed to fix the time of his arrival at 7 p.m.? He said in his sworn evidence that his daughters wanted to watch a programme on television from 5 p.m. to 6 p.m. and the remainder of the time was taken up with the tube journey from southeast to northwest London. The timing of that could easily be checked. If he arrived at the time he claimed, that matched the time the police say they began to watch the house at 43 Third Avenue. Did they see him enter the premises? He would have had only a limited amount of time in which to handle and then dispose of any object in the house, whatever that may have been, and it was at about the time of his arrival that Paddy Maguire returned to the house after his visit to Harrow Road police station. As noted previously, it was not sufficient for the prosecution to prove traces of an explosive on the hands or gloves; they had to prove actual handling of a bulk of an explosive substance, namely NG. When, where and how had Patrick O'Neill disposed of any substance during the very short time available to him, and the presence nearby of the police? Should Mr Justice Donaldson have canvassed some of these points before the jury, in the interests of justice? Or was he just interested in obtaining a conviction?

The trial judge neared the end of his summing-up of the evidence with these words:

> I started off by telling you that each of the accused must be considered separately. Let me say that again. Before that I told you that you had to consider the whole of the evidence and on the whole of that evidence you had to decide whether you are sure that this offence has been committed. If you are not sure – I don't mean if you have a fanciful doubt but if you have a real doubt on any of the accused then each is entitled to be acquitted, but if, members of the jury, having considered all these matters *then it is your duty, your duty in accordance with the oath you have taken, to bring in a verdict of guilty.* [emphasis added]

It is not possible to recreate from the transcript the tone of voice in which the words 'your duty, your duty' were said, but did Mr Justice Donaldson make it crystal clear to the jury the verdict he expected them to bring in? One of guilty?

All the jury panel were drawn from the London area. None of them could fail but to be aware of the bombing campaign in London for which the Provisional IRA were responsible. They must have known of the eight people killed and 136 injured in a number of explosions and a shooting in London[38] in the four months leading up to the start of the trial in January 1976.

All this activity, with its massive coverage in the media, cannot have been too far from the minds of the jury when they listened to the evidence and came to a verdict in this case. And who could have forgotten the graphic pictures in the media of the dreadful scenes of the Birmingham pub bombing? That was just over some 13 months before the start of the Maguire Seven trial. Some of the young people in the two pubs in Birmingham were so mutilated, blinded by shards of glass, that they cried out for death. One retired police officer who attended the scene told me that he cannot ever forget the sight of the dead and the sounds of the dying as he entered the premises shortly after the two bombs exploded. The entire nation was not likely to forget that terrible, senseless event.

The jury reached unanimous verdicts of guilty against six of the seven accused, after deliberating for two days. Patrick Maguire was convicted on a majority verdict of 11 to one. Someone on that jury held out and was not prepared to convict him. That was illogical, for the evidence against him was exactly the same as it was against the other six.

The press coverage after the convictions was unrestrained. A headline in *The Times* read, 'Mother taught IRA recruits to make bombs'. That was followed by 'Members of Scotland Yard's anti-terrorist squad and Surrey Constabulary are convinced that Mrs Maguire was a vitally important cog in the Provisional IRA network operating in London.' As a measure of the truth and accuracy of that newspaper report one should read what follows next: 'A telegram from a Belfast firm of solicitors to the Maguires gave a warning that Mr Conlon senior was arriving that day after his son had been arrested in Ulster in connection with the public house bombings.'[39] As noted above, there was no mention in that telegram of Giuseppe Conlon senior arriving in London that day. That was a simple fabrication. One might wonder, if it was true that Anne Maguire was a vital cog in the IRA machine, why the telegram was not sent to her rather than to her husband. And in any event, do terrorists exchange and impart information by telegram?

In the event leave to appeal against conviction was refused by the full court of appeal. The submissions of virtually all leading counsel for the defence were littered with complaints about Mr Justice Donaldson's conduct of the trial, but most especially his summing-up to the jury at the end of the case. He had virtually dismissed the suggestion that the sniffer device that had been used in 43 Third Avenue to test the drawer containing Anne Maguire's gloves established that there was no NG on them while they were in the kitchen drawer. That should have been left to the jury to decide.

There was of course no mention in the appeal court of the police error that might have resulted in innocent contamination of the samples, probably because that was not generally known until Sir John May's inquiry.

The presiding judge at the application, Sir Eustace Roskill, a lord justice of appeal and a close friend of Sir John Donaldson, the trial judge, went out of his way over and over again to praise Sir John's conduct of a long and difficult trial.

Perhaps the strongest criticism of Sir John Donaldson came from Michael Self QC, who had fought magnificently before the jury for his client. He complained particularly about the failure to link evidence that Patrick O'Neill gave about washing his hands after using the toilet at 43 Third Avenue, and the possibility of innocent contamination from the towel. That was mentioned by the defence, who established that the portable sniffer device would have found a positive reaction to the presence of NG on that towel – the point being if it did that there was no reason why the same device should not have found NG on the gloves – if it was there. The judge 'nowhere referred to the possibility of innocent contamination from the towel which we have already mentioned'.[40]

Lord Justice Roskill went on to make the same error as the trial judge when he said that, although 'the use of the word "group" may be criticised, the Judge in different places made the position regarding O'Neill's time of arrival absolutely plain, so the jury cannot have thought he was in the same position as the others who resided in the house. At page 89G the Judge has emphasised at the beginning of the passage complained of that O'Neill "alone of the accused" did not live in the house.'[41] That was wrong. The status of Giuseppe Conlon as a visitor to 43 Third Avenue had been mistakenly overlooked once again.

Michael Self forcefully complained that nowhere in the summing-up did the judge refer to the defence witnesses Helen O'Neill and her brother. Her evidence was important to fix the time of the phone call from the hospital that she put at 8 p.m., the time when the police said Patrick O'Neill had left the house. That failure was of some significance. Defence counsel also complained that the judge made no reference to Patrick O'Neill's untarnished work and general record. That seemed not to matter to Mr Justice Donaldson, or to the appeal court judges. It should have done. Since he had, because it was necessary, mentioned his two motoring convictions, it was essential that the judge direct the jury on the meaning of character, and how Patrick O'Neill was a man of perfectly good character, apart from those minor transgressions, and how that should stand him in good stead when considering whether he was telling the truth.

Lord Justice Roskill described the summing-up as 'Long and otherwise admirable'.[42] I respectfully disagree. The weight that a jury attach to the trial judge's summing-up cannot be independently calculated because they are forbidden to discuss publicly their discussions in the jury room, but I consider the weight to be very substantial – all the more reason why it should be comprehensible, impartial, unbiased and totally fair.

There was one moment in the appeal court hearing that might have caused some slight embarrassment to Sir Michael Havers QC. It has already been noted that he had conceded that Patrick O'Neill may have gone to 43 Third Avenue 'with innocent intentions and been made use of.' Lord Justice Roskill said:

> Last Thursday Sir Michael said that that had been the Crown's position throughout the remainder of the case and that he had never departed from that. But yesterday, in the light of a note of his final speech which junior counsel for O'Neill had taken and showed us, as it had been overnight to Sir Michael, it became plain that contrary to his original recollection he had used the words in his final speech suggesting that when O'Neill arrived at the house at 7 o'clock on the evening of 3rd December, it was 'a gathering of the clans'. Sir Michael very properly agreed that his first recollection must have been wrong. He then recalled that in view of what some of the defence witnesses had said, which of course was unknown to the Crown until they went into the witness box, he had challenged during O'Neill's defence, the bona fides of O'Neill's arrival at the house. In this respect he had departed from the attitude he expressed at the close of the case for the prosecution.[43]

This is extraordinary. During legal submissions in the absence of the jury, Havers had accepted that Patrick O'Neill had not gone to 43 Third Avenue to take part in any disposal of NG; he had gone there by arrangement with Anne Maguire so that his children could be properly cared for. In his closing speech to the jury Sir Michael Havers could not resist a slogan that would grip the imagination of the public and the attention of the press. The homing pigeon heading for Paddy Maguire's was there for 'a gathering of the clans'. In other words, he had gone to the house with the express intention of joining the group who were destroying and disposing of NG. I cannot find any evidence from either Patrick O'Neill himself or any defence witness that would enable Havers to change his stance completely and 'challenge the bona fides of O'Neill's arrival at the house'. Significantly, Lord Justice Roskill did not ask Havers to identify those witnesses or quote the detail of the evidence of anyone else.

So Sir Michael Havers first told the appeal court that he had never departed from the position he had adopted (accepting the innocent reason for going to 43 Third Avenue); then he had to backtrack because Patrick O'Neill's junior counsel, Antonio Bueno (now a QC), had made a note that Sir Michael Havers had told the jury in his closing speech that when Patrick O'Neill arrived there, it was 'a gathering of the clans'. Rather than admit he had made a serious error in retreating from his stated position, Sir Michael explained it by saying the unidentified evidence from defence witnesses justified that retreat. If Antonio Bueno had not made the note, kept it, then agreed it with other junior counsel and shown it to Sir Michael overnight, in accordance with legal ethics, then in the morning leading counsel had shown it to the appeal court judges, no one would have been any the wiser about how Sir Michael had changed his mind and his position.

Six of the Maguire Seven had their applications for leave to appeal against conviction and sentence dismissed on 30 July 1977. The decision surprised no one. Lord Justice Roskill did not agree with Edward Terrell QC, who described as 'morally offensive' Mr Justice Donaldson's comment that if he was merciful in sentencing his clients Vincent and Patrick 'there is an obvious danger that any mercy which may be extended to the two boys on the grounds of youth will encourage the use of young people and children for the commission of crimes of this nature.' Lord Justice Roskill said 'we endorse every word', adding, 'here were two children, old for their years, being used by their parents for participating in the handling of explosives which they must have known were for terrorist purposes'. There could be no leniency for the two boys on policy grounds. The attitude was, 'If we let these two off, we'll have to let others off as well.' Can that be right?

The seventh accused, Patrick O'Neill, had his sentence reduced from 12 years' imprisonment to eight on the ground that there was a possibility that he might have gone to the Maguire house for an entirely innocent purpose. That had been the prosecution's approach at one stage of the case and now the appeal court judges were accepting that was probably right. He later told the RTÉ *Today Tonight* team that he had lost everything, his family and his home. He was living out of a bag. Although he welcomed the substantial reduction in sentence, it was the fact that he went to prison at all that destroyed him and his family. It is known that he served some of his sentence in Parkhurst prison, the maximum-security establishment on the Isle of Wight. His present whereabouts are not known.

The truth could not, however, be suppressed forever. Sir John May published his Interim Report on the case on 12 July 1990, inviting the home secretary to review the case and send it on appeal for a second time. As *The Times* reported, Sir John said that 'crucial evidence in the trial . . . was mishandled and misunderstood by the trial judge, now Lord Donaldson of Lymington'.[44] On the same day the home secretary referred the case back to the Criminal Division of the Court of Appeal. On 26 June 1991 that court allowed the appeals against conviction, but only on the limited ground conceded by counsel for the DPP; that the prosecution had not disproved the possibility that the hands of six of the Seven had been innocently contaminated with traces of NG. And the possible source of that contamination? It could have been the towel in the bathroom on which Patrick O'Neill had dried his hands. But hadn't that been put forward as a possible source of contamination at the trial? And if it was contaminated, wouldn't the sniffer have detected NG on it? The prosecution scientists had ruled that out as a possible source of the NG, but if it was there the sniffer would have found it! The appeal court apparently disregarded that and raised the possibility that the towel was to blame. Did someone later put a contaminated hand into the drawer containing Anne Maguire's gloves? How was it possible for traces of NG to get under the fingernails of six of the seven people in the house, especially since the scientists from RARDE originally claimed that NG would not migrate under the fingernails simply by contact with another surface?

The judges accepted that it was highly improbable that all the Seven must have knowingly handled a bulk of explosives at the house. But in what was described as a 'damage limitation exercise' by their decision, a shadow of guilt lay over someone in 43 Third Avenue on 3 December 1974, quite wrongfully, as a result of the failure of the appeal court to face up to the truth.

Arrests at Balcombe Street

After the conviction of the Guildford Four, a difficulty might have arisen when four committed members of the Provisional IRA, Joseph O'Connell, Edward Butler, Harry Duggan and Hugh Doherty, were arrested by police after a siege at Balcombe Street in London on 12 December 1975. They admitted, in court and outside it, that O'Connell, Duggan and Butler had bombed Guildford. It was further admitted that O'Connell and Brendan Dowd (who had been arrested in Manchester on 10 July 1975) had bombed Woolwich, with others whom they refused to name. The police were told plainly and unequivocally that the Guildford Four were innocent.

Like the legal system, the police did nothing to try to establish the true facts. Voluntary admissions were disregarded while false and fabricated confession evidence, rejected by its makers, held the day. Perhaps most disquieting of all was that during the course of the trial of O'Connell and the others, the forensic scientist based at RARDE in Woolwich, Douglas Higgs, a supposedly independent and impartial witness, admitted that he had been instructed to tailor his evidence – and he did so.

What happened was this. The scientists decided to designate the IRA bombing campaign from August 1974 until January 1975 as Phase One. That phase concluded with the planting of seven time bombs in the London area on 27 January. Just under two weeks later the Provisional IRA announced a ceasefire. When that broke down the bombings continued. Phase Two of the IRA campaign began on 27 August 1975 with the placing of a time bomb in the Caterham Arms in Caterham, Surrey that injured 33 people, some of them critically. That incident, only 20 days before the trial of the Guildford Four began, would not have inclined anyone to believe the suspected bombers in that case, or to disapprove of the tactics used by the police to apprehend the actual bombers.

The arrest of the Guildford Four in December 1974 had not stopped the bombings. Douglas Higgs of RARDE admitted in evidence at the trial of Joseph O'Connell and his co-accused that he had prepared a list dated 26 January 1976 showing that he had examined four bombing incidents spread over two months which all had common features: the bombs all weighed about 5lb; they were all packed with a mixture of nails, bolts, nuts and washers (known to some as 'Belfast spaghetti'); they were all aimed at windows; and all had short non-mechanical fuses. That list included the throw bomb at the pub in Woolwich in respect of which Paul Hill and Patrick Armstrong had been convicted. He made a second list dated 17 June 1976, but this list excluded the Woolwich throw bomb. Asked why he had done that, he replied that he was instructed to do so by the police. Why he, as an independent and dispassionate witness, at least in theory, should have done what he was told and change his evidence, apparently without hesitation or question, will defy the comprehension of those who believe that the interests of justice are best served by the truth.

Mr Higgs also admitted that he had made two statements, the first in July 1975 and the second dated 10 October 1975, that linked the Guildford time bombs (as opposed to the throw bombs) with the other throw bomb incidents listed in Phase One. In his statement Mr Higgs said that the Guildford incidents were linked with the others by virtue of an NG-based explosive and the identification of many components from a Smith's pocket watch at the Seven Stars, and fractions of a similar watch bezel from the Horse and Groom. He concluded that all the incidents in Phase One were connected. The statements showing these links with bombings that occurred while the Guildford Four were in custody and therefore could not be responsible for them, were suppressed by someone on the prosecution side – for one reason only. To ensure that four innocent people would be convicted. That was shameful and the person responsible should be flushed out into the open and, if still alive, publicly identified.

On 9 February 1975 the IRA announced a ceasefire and, although there were a number of shootings, including the shooting dead of PC Stephen Dibble on 27 February, there were no further bombings in England until 27 August. As noted above, on that date a bomb exploded at the Caterham Arms in Surrey. The next day seven people were injured when a bomb exploded in a shop in Oxford Street; on the following day, one person was killed by a bomb at a shoe shop in Kensington Church Street, London.

The bombings from 27 August until the capture of the IRA team at Balcombe Street in December 1975 was designated Phase Two. After the Caterham pub bombing the Surrey Police told a press conference that it was too early to say who was responsible for that bombing but it was consistent in size, type and method with the explosions at the two Guildford pubs in October 1974. The Guildford Four could not have bombed Caterham, but the forensic links that proved that had to be concealed, and for a time they were. It suited the prosecution to present the Guildford and Woolwich bombings as isolated acts of terrorism committed by those three young men from Belfast and the young English girl sitting together in the dock at the Old Bailey, whereas in reality those bombings were part of a prolonged and sophisticated campaign carried out by members of the Provisional IRA.

In his final report into the Guildford and Woolwich bombings, Sir John May states that he did not think that Mr Higgs deserves criticism for the amendments to his witness statements.[45] Some may think otherwise. Counsel for Joseph O'Connell wanted to know why Mr Higgs had omitted the reference to the Woolwich bombing from his 17 June statement. He replied that he had been asked to do so by Det. Sgt Doyle of the Metropolitan police, who, he believed, was acting at the behest of counsel. He did not identify, and was not asked to do so, which counsel was involved. Whoever it was, I consider he was in fundamental breach of the duty which prosecuting counsel owes to the court and to the accused to ensure that a trial is fair.

Mr Higgs and his fellow scientists received less friendly treatment from the Court of Appeal in the case of Judith Ward, wrongly convicted in 1974 of murdering 12 people in the M62 coach bombing case. She spent 18 years in prison before her conviction was set aside by the appeal court. Judith was 25 years of age when she went to prison, and 43 when she came out. She was an extremely ill young woman who was a serial confessor to crimes related to the IRA that she had not committed. Her confessions were supported by the forensic evidence furnished by Mr Higgs and his RARDE colleagues. When her case went to the appeal court in 1993 the court said, 'we reject Mr Higgs' account as a deliberate falsehood . . . the consequence is that in a criminal trial three senior government forensic scientists deliberately withheld experimental data on the ground it might damage the prosecution case. Moreover Mr Higgs and Mr Berryman misled the court.'[46] Lord Justice Glidewell went on, 'three senior RARDE scientists took the law into their own hands, and concealed from the prosecution, the defence and the court, matters which might have changed the course of the trial . . . economical witness statements calculated to obstruct enquiry by the defence . . . and most important of all, oral evidence at the trial in the course of which senior RARDE scientists knowingly placed a false and distorted scientific picture before the jury. It is in our judgment also a necessary inference that the three senior RARDE scientists acted in concert in withholding material evidence.'[47]

If the jury who convicted the Maguire Seven in 1976 could have been aware of the comments of the appeal court judges about the professionalism and integrity of the scientists, especially Douglas Higgs and Walter Elliott, whose evidence formed the entire basis of the case against the Seven, and the criticism of them by Sir John May and Lord Justice Glidewell, they would never have reached guilty verdicts. Who, of all those involved in the case, is to blame for that?

In the light of those appeal court comments, few would be surprised if there was a prosecution against those whose misconduct helped convict yet another innocent. That, indeed, did not happen. In April 1993 the *Independent* reported that after a nine-month investigation by the West Yorkshire Police the CPS had decided that there would be no prosecution against Mr Higgs and his RARDE colleague Mr Berryman on the ground that there was 'insufficient evidence'. (The third RARDE scientist, Walter Elliott, was dead by this date.) I disagree with the decision of the CPS. There was more than enough evidence to put them on trial, but if that had happened, who knows what evidence against others involved in the prosecution of the Guildford Four might emerge from the shadows?

How fortunate for Judith Ward, and for three of the Guildford Four as well as the Birmingham Six, that capital punishment was no longer available to the state. Fourteen innocent people would undoubtedly have hanged for the enormity of the crimes, no fewer than 40 horrific murders, of which they had been convicted, but had not committed.

10   The Police on Trial

ON 19 OCTOBER 1989, after a long campaign headed by the late Cardinal Basil Hume and two former law lords, Lord Devlin and Lord Scarman, the appeal court quashed the convictions of the Guildford Four and they were set free. It was a very bad day for British justice to have to accept that the convictions in such a high-profile case were no longer satisfactory and could not be sustained. The prosecution had asked for the case, initially scheduled to start in January 1990, to be brought forward. The prosecution had previously indicated to the appeal court that they would contest the case. Something – initially no one knew what it was – had clearly happened to get the prosecuting authorities to change their mind.

On Tuesday 17 October 1989 Paul Hill was in Albany prison on the Isle of Wight when he was told by a prison officer he was being moved elsewhere. That had happened to him many times, on at least previous 43 occasions, in an effort to break him and his resistance to accepting the rightfulness of his conviction. He was taken by van to Brixton prison in London, where he met Patrick Armstrong, who told him that Gerard Conlon was also in Brixton prison. They knew something unusual was about to happen because Brixton is a remand prison that does not detain those serving life sentences, as these three men were. Later that day they found out what it was. BBC Radio announced, to the astonishment of many, that the Guildford Four were going to be released on Thursday 19 October. It was almost unprecedented that someone would be released from prison without a court hearing to establish the reasons for the decision. An official from the Irish Embassy, Jim Hennessey, arrived at Brixton. He seemed to Paul Hill to be in a state of shock, repeatedly saying, 'I can't believe it.' Neither could Paul, but it was true.[1] Arrangements were made to bring all four to court two days later.

At the special expedited appeal hearing at the Old Bailey in London, where the Four had been tried and convicted in 1975, the atmosphere in the courtroom was entirely different in 1989 from that of 14 years earlier. The office of the DPP had issued a statement saying that the prosecution would not oppose the appeal, so everyone knew in advance of the hearing that the convictions would be set aside. The presiding judge, Lord Chief Justice Geoffrey Lane, was said to be in a fury over the decision to allow the three Irishmen and the Englishwoman to have their liberty. He, among others, continued to believe in their guilt, and regretted that some unimportant lies by the police had undermined the safety of the convictions.

The *Sunday Times*, in a profile of Lord Lane, said:

Later, in the case of the Guildford Four, when the Director of Public Prosecutions finally threw in the towel and left him with no choice but to release them, Lane's distaste for his duty was equally shocking. Not a single word of apology for their years of wrongful imprisonment was uttered. No declaration of their innocence was made for the record. He swept them from the court, said one of the Four's lawyers, like an irritable publican getting rid of a bunch of unruly customers.[2]

The allowing of the appeal and the quashing of all the convictions meant trouble for someone; and in 1993 three former Surrey police officers ended up in the dock before Mr Justice William Macpherson of Cluny and a jury. I consider they were scapegoats.

Counsel for the Crown, Roy Amlot QC, began his address to the three judges, but more significantly to the world's press that had followed this case for years:

It is my onerous duty to have to inform the court that evidence of great significance had come to light. That evidence throws such doubt upon the honesty and integrity of the Surrey officers investigating this case in 1974 that the Crown now feels unable to say that the conviction of any appellant was safe or satisfactory. . . . The case against each appellant depended entirely upon confessions to the police. There was no other evidence. Each appellant was arrested and interrogated over a number of days. Each made more than one statement in writing. Each was interviewed by units of two or three officers from the Surrey Constabulary. A total of 12 Surrey officers were involved in the interview. Armstrong and Hill were also interviewed by officers of the Metropolitan Police about the Woolwich bombing, and Richardson made limited admissions to those officers about the Guildford bombings. In each case this occurred after they had already been interviewed by the Surrey officers and in each case the interviews took place during the period they were held at Guildford police station.[3]

Counsel continued: 'During the trial serious allegations were made against the Surrey interviewing officers by each appellant. There were allegations of brutality, threats, intimidation, inducements and the concoction of evidence. All these allegations were denied by the officers and it is clear that the jury acted upon those denials and relied upon the integrity of the officers involved.'

It should be noted that at no time during the hearing did Roy Amlot identify any police officer by name. Presumably this was done to avoid prejudicing any possible future legal proceedings.

But it is a matter of record that a detective inspector of the Avon and Somerset police had found some rough typed copies of notes of interviews between Patrick Armstrong and three Surrey police officers, DCI Style, Det. Sgt Donaldson and DC Attwell. These interviews were spread over three days, 4, 5 and 6 December 1974. These notes contained alterations, deletions and additional material, both handwritten and typed. Apart from some inconsistencies which were unimportant in the overall scheme of things, the finished product matched the handwritten notes which the three officers claimed were made during the interviews. If the handwritten notes were made then, what was the reason for the existence of the notes which were typed and then amended?

The detective inspector passed on the information she had found to the senior officer in charge of the overall inquiry, Det. Supt Brock. The suspicion arose that the handwritten notes used at the trial were not made at the time and in the way the police officers claimed. There was a meeting between Brock and his deputy chief constable, James Sharples. The investigating officers needed to tread carefully because a botched investigation might result in a flawed prosecution. It was decided that the three officers who had conducted the interviews should themselves be interviewed, not as suspects, so they were not cautioned and not reminded of their right to stay silent if they so wished.

In July 1989 all three officers agreed that the handwritten notes they were shown were the notes they claimed they made during the interviews held on three separate days with Patrick Armstrong. The officers claimed that the notes of interview were made either by Det. Sgt Donaldson or DC Attwell. To be more exact, Attwell told the Avon and Somerset officers that he took notes of an interview that started at 11.50 a.m. on 4 December and that he made notes of the third interview on 6 December commencing at 10.15 a.m. The second interview on 5 December starting at 11 a.m. was recorded by Det. Sgt Donaldson.

All three officers were interviewed by the Avon and Somerset police on various dates between 5 July and 5 September 1989. They were initially unable to give an explanation for the existence of the other set of notes. Det. Sgt Donaldson did not remember ever having seen them previously. DC Attwell said he thought he might have typed those notes 'to help the typist'. The only reason he and DCI Style could give was that they were given to the typists to enable them to understand the handwritten notes, which of course would be typewritten for use at the trial. Style, in an interview on 4 September 1989, suggested that the typewritten amended notes might have been used as a rough working copy.

When the three officers were interviewed under caution it was claimed, as Mr Justice Macpherson explained to the jury at the subsequent trial, first, 'that the rough typed notes may have been required for and indeed used for other investigations.'[4] Second, 'the material was there to be used . . . for Prevention of Terrorism Act applications.' Third, 'the preparation of 27th December 1974 statements required, so the defence say, some interpretation of Attwell's very bad handwriting and some assistance to be given to the typists.'[5] (It seems that efforts were made to interview former typists to ascertain whether they had any recollection of seeing these documents. No typist ever came forward to give evidence about how bad the handwriting was, in this case or, indeed, in any other, or whether they were assisted by the amended typewritten notes in the way suggested.)

Mr Justice Macpherson dealt with the absence of any such evidence very shortly and sympathetically: 'But in any event, even if there is no positive evidence of the use of the rough typed notes in these regards, say the defence, there should be no finding or conclusion that the rough typed notes could not have been so required or used if others in the big investigation had sought to use them.'

That statement to the jury in 1993 can be compared with Roy Amlot's submission to the appeal court in 1989 when he told the Lord Chief Justice that the explanation put forward was not regarded as satisfactory. In counsel's words, 'The inescapable conclusion is that no contemporaneous notes were made of each interview, as indeed was suggested by the defence at the trial, and that the officers seriously misled the court. None of these documents was disclosed to the Director of Public Prosecutions or to prosecuting counsel at the trial.'6

Amlot went on to describe how leading counsel for Patrick Armstrong at the trial, the eminent barrister John Leonard QC (later a High Court judge), had suggested that the first interview recorded by the police officers never in fact took place in the way recorded, but that there had been what was described as a 'softening-up' process followed by Patrick Armstrong's first statement under caution, which, contrary to what the officers claimed, was in the form of a question-and-answer session. That was denied by the police, who also denied all other suggestions put to them by Armstrong's leading defence counsel.

Lord Lane's observation on that issue was short and to the point. 'Either this typewritten document was a total invention or it was an amendment of some notes which had gone on previously, but in any event when the final version was produced as a so-called contemporaneous note, that was not true.' Roy Amlot agreed. He continued: 'The Crown says that not only did the officers, all three of them – and not just junior officers – mislead the court, but that because of the way the notes had been prepared and because of the statements that these officers made in 1974 for the purposes of the trial, it is clear that they agreed together to present their notes in this fashion.'7 Does this mean that they were acting together as a team with one common objective – to place a false picture before the court about whether they wrote the notes as events unfolded, or later in a typed version, which was amended from time to time in manuscript, in order to mislead the judge and the jury?

I fail to see the fundamental importance of the prosecution's approach to the note recording. Does it in the last analysis matter whether the officers wrote the notes at the time, in the course of the interview, or whether they pooled their recollections later in typewritten form, and then prepared their handwritten notes from the final amended typewritten version to use to refresh their memory in the course of giving evidence? Being a witness at a criminal trial involves not a test of memory, but a test of truthfulness. Police officers are often involved in more than one investigation at a time, and it is important for them to be able to refresh their memory of incidents, events and oral statements that they witness in the course of an investigation. They need to be able to avoid confusing one case with another. When they claimed they made a note during an interview, that is what they were encouraged to say at training school. But it wasn't always accurate and true and the courts seemed to know that too.

Roy Amlot QC then moved on to the officers who interviewed Paul Hill and obtained from him his alleged voluntary statements under caution. Hill made a total of seven such statements to the police: two on 29 November 1974 and one on each day from 30 November to 4 December. The four statements from 1 to 4 December 1974 were actually written down by Paul Hill himself. The first statement on 29 November 1974 was made to officers from the RUC investigating the murder of Brian Shaw, a former British soldier who had been shot dead in Arundel Street, Belfast. (Paul Hill's conviction for that murder was quashed in 1994.) The statement of 30 November 1974 was made to officers of the London Metropolitan Police.

The first statement on 29 November 1974 was written by DC McCawl and witnessed by Chief Inspector Cunningham, both RUC officers. It was properly timed in accordance with the Judges' Rules, but the heading is not in the usual format. It began at 4.30 p.m. and ended at 5.55 p.m. The second statement made on 29 November is not timed. Three officers were present: Det. Sgt Jermey, who actually wrote the statement; and Assistant Chief Constable C. Rowe and Detective Chief Superintendent Simmons, who witnessed it. The typewritten version is nine pages long.

The odd feature about these two statements is that on the detention sheet RB1/12/492 I can find no mention of either of the two RUC officers by name, but two visits to the cell were made, at 14.30 and 15.10 hours respectively. Then at 16.10 hours Chief Superintendent Simmons is mentioned with the words 'visit – to CID for interview'. This is odd because according to the RUC officers they were taking Paul Hill's statement from 4.30 p.m., which was 20 minutes later, until 5.55 p.m. In any event the next time noted on that detention sheet is 01.50 on 30 November. Did the Surrey officers take the second statement during that time?

Having drawn the court's attention to the conduct of the three unnamed officers whom he claimed had 'misled the court', Roy Amlot QC then moved on to examine the conduct of two other officers; again he did not identify either by name. He said that Avon and Somerset officers had found a set of manuscript notes relating to Hill. One of those two officers identified those notes. Counsel said:

The interview as revealed by the notes was never tendered in evidence and had not been disclosed to the Director of Public Prosecutions or to prosecuting counsel. It relates to relevant and significant matters. It is clear from the content of the notes that it took place two days after Hill had been charged . . . it is clear that these officers also seriously misled the court. The content of the notes bear no resemblance to the evidence given by the officers as to the way in which they claim Hill 'volunteered' to make his fifth statement. The inescapable conclusion is that the true interview was suppressed and a false version given by the officers to the court in order to circumvent the rule that a suspect once charged must not be interviewed except under special circumstances. Hill's fifth statement was of considerable significance in the trial because in it he was the first to name Carole Richardson. During the trial the officers denied the defence suggestions that there was an interview that day. The manuscript notes are inconsistent with that denial.[8]

The officers involved in taking this fifth statement from Paul Hill were DI Timothy Blake, the only Catholic police officer at Guildford police station (remembered, but not fondly, by Fr Paddy Carolan), and DC P.J. Lewis, whose police number was 236. (The same two officers had obtained another statement from Paul Hill the previous day, Monday 2 December, between 3.55 p.m. and 4.58 p.m.)

As Roy Amlot noted, Paul Hill was the first to provide the information identifying and leading to Carole Richardson in that fifth statement made between 3.50 p.m. and 5.30 p.m. on the Tuesday afternoon, 3 December; the day the Maguire Seven were supposed to be disposing of NG. As noted above, by 6.40 on that Tuesday evening the police were at Carole Richardson's mother's house in north London, where they asked Carole to accompany them to the police station. She went with them. In spite of her alleged IRA training in counter-interrogation techniques, Carole immediately told the police where they could find and arrest Patrick Armstrong at the Linstead Street squat. That is exactly what they did.

DC Lewis was interviewed by his police colleagues and asked to explain the circumstances in which that fifth statement from Paul Hill came into existence. He denied any wrongdoing in respect of it. He was not charged with any offence arising out of it. DI Timothy Blake is deceased. He was never charged with any offence prior to his death.

I consider that the most devastating disclosure that Roy Amlot QC made to the Lord Chief Justice was that 'the detention sheets for each appellant (*which do not appear to have been either required or made available at the trial*) . . .'[9] [emphasis added]. One is bound to ask why, since the number, times and content of the police interviews were of such importance and subject to such challenge and disagreement during the Guildford Four trial, did the defence of each of the Guildford Four not ask for the sheets to be handed over by the prosecution and subjected to detailed examination and analysis by the defence? And one may wonder, since the police could not have known whether or not the defence would ask for the detention sheets to be handed over, did they take a chance and allow evidence that damaged their sworn testimony to be available if asked for? Or did the police prepare for that contingency? I asked the CPS if there were two sets of detention sheets. Their response was 'no' but there were carbon copies of the original sheets. Patrick Victory, the now deceased former Assistant for Public Affairs to Cardinal Basil Hume, claimed in his splendid book about the case, *Justice and Truth*, 'There were two sets of detention sheets, the originals and a concocted set.'[10] He does not cite any authority or source for that proposition. I suspect there were two sets, but proof is lacking.

Roy Amlot QC continued with his submissions to the court, saying that the documents and records 'reveal a disturbing difference between the number and times of interviews according to the sheets, and the number and times of interviews according to the officers in evidence. Interviews are shown on the sheets which were never given in evidence or revealed to the Director of Public Prosecutions or prosecuting counsel. Interviews are shown on the sheets as taking place at markedly different times from those given in court by the interviewing officers, and the discrepancies apply to each appellant.'

I understand this to mean that every officer involved in interviewing each of the Guildford Four misled the judge and the jury by giving evidence of the timing of such interviews which was contradicted, or not supported, by the detention sheets. Were they falsifying the truth? What innocent explanation can there be for writing down one set of times and giving oral evidence that is different from the written record? Then, if this was the situation, why was the subsequent prosecution limited to only three officers, when on this version all those interviewers gave evidence at variance with their own documentary records? They did so for a reason. What was that reason? As far as the prosecution was concerned, Roy Amlot QC stated, 'it is the clear view of the Crown that the Armstrong and Hill notes show clear prima facie evidence that a total of five officers seriously misled the court in relation to the interviewing of two of the four appellants'. Why did he adopt this stance, limiting the prosecution to only five officers when it was apparent from his perspective that several others were also involved?

Whatever the answer, these allegations against the interviewing police officers do not stand alone. As noted above, two individuals, Lisa Astin and Frank Johnson, were important alibi witnesses for Carole Richardson's defence. She and they were interviewed by a total of four police officers. They claimed the notes of the respective interviews were made contemporaneously. ESDA analysis conducted for Avon and Somerset police indicates that the officers' notes were not contemporaneous but were written some time later.

Frank Johnson was interviewed by three officers first on 19 December 1974 in Newcastle. ESDA analysis tends to suggest that the notes of the interview were not contemporaneous as the officers claimed, and some additional questions and answers were apparently added in a rewritten version of the notes. The same three officers interviewed Frank Johnson again just over a month later, on 22 January 1975. There are differences between the manuscript record and the typed record of that interview, leading to the inference that the manuscript notes were not contemporaneous but were written after the typewritten record.

Lisa Astin was interviewed by two officers on 24 December 1974 at 8 p.m. Three pages of manuscript notes were said by those officers at the Guildford trial to be a contemporaneous note of that interview. ESDA tests on the first page, identified as RB1/9/230 revealed indented writing on it which is similar to the writing already on that page. This suggests that this record was not written contemporaneously. As for pages RB1/9/ 231 and RB1/9/232, they were written in a different ink from the first page, indicating that the notes were written in two parts at different times and could not therefore be a continuous, contemporaneous record. Does this evidence indicate that there was at least some prima facie evidence against those officers which would justify putting them before the court to see whether they had a case to answer?

The medical examination that Dr Makos carried out on Carole Richardson on 4 December 1974, when she allegedly made a remark amounting to an admission that she had been involved in bombing Guildford, has already been set out above. An ESDA test carried out on the witness statement made by the police officer who was present at the time of the examination showed it had been rewritten. The previous copy of the statement contained the words 'and I don't know anything about it' had been changed in the rewritten version to 'I've told the police a load of lies.' It is difficult to conjure up an innocent explanation for rewriting the witness statement and changing the text in that way.

Is it unreasonable therefore to consider that there was an abundance of prima facie evidence against an unspecified number of police officers involved in interviewing Patrick Armstrong, Lisa Astin and Frank Johnson?

But rather than prosecute those officers, when it was in the public interest to do so, the authorities chose the weakest case involving the weakest individual of the Guildford Four, Patrick Armstrong, whose health had broken down completely while serving his sentence. The Crown chose instead to scapegoat three retired officers, safe in the knowledge that the chances of conviction were virtually non-existent.

The three former Surrey police officers, Style, Attwell and Donaldson, were subsequently charged with conspiracy to pervert the course of public justice in relation to handwritten notes of interviews with Patrick Armstrong. Their trial eventually began at the Old Bailey in London on 20 April 1993. All pleaded not guilty. The long delay in starting the trial was apparently due to the commitment of defence counsel in other cases. The trial judge was Mr Justice Macpherson of Cluny. The three QCs appearing for the defence made up a formidable team.

None of the accused men gave evidence in their own defence. They were quite entitled to do that. The jury acquitted them after an 18-day trial. The defence tactic was simple: to put Patrick Armstrong on trial again, this time in his absence. Instead of concentrating on the activities of the police officers, the defence concentrated on the confessions, not only of Patrick Armstrong, but also of Paul Hill, Gerard Conlon and, to a lesser extent, Carole Richardson. Patrick Armstrong had not been asked to attend court as a witness and no subpoena requiring him to do so was served upon him.

Only four people knew the exact truth about the Armstrong confessions taken over three days in December 1974 and how they came into existence. The decision by the prosecution to run the case without him meant, in my view, that it was virtually certain that the three officers would be acquitted, simply because the jury would not hear from him his version of why he confessed in the way he did.

Defence counsel, from first to last, lashed Patrick Armstrong's reputation. One said, 'The innocent Patrick Armstrong does not exist. He is being created by the ill-informed, the mis-informed, and the not want to be informed.'[11] Another told the jury, 'The Horse and Groom was the worse peacetime outrage since 1945. The bombing was carried out by Patrick Armstrong. The jury that convicted him in 1975 had reached a just conclusion.'[12] The third said, 'In one word the allegation in this case is fabrication. The question you have to ask yourselves is, why fabricate the truth?'[13] At one stage during the trial, counsel suggested that Patrick Armstrong had been falling over himself to tell the truth to the police officers, and he sang like a canary.

In the course of researching material for this book and using the Freedom of Information Act 2000 I obtained from the CPS a document put in evidence by the defence at the trial of the three officers. It is headed 'Index to Defence Jury Bundle'. It lists 21 items, giving them each what is termed 'a Flag Number'. I found Flag 7 ('Extracts from 2 interviews of Carole Richardson'), Flag 8 ('6 statements under caution by Paul Hill, action dated 3/12/74 re; information given by Hill') and Flag 10 ('Extracts from Defence Brief of Mr Boxall') of considerable interest. Of equal interest are Flags 11 and 12, extracts from Conlon's pre-conviction confessions and extracts from Conlon's post-conviction confessions.

A number of questions arise from these existence of these documents put before the jury, apparently without objection from anyone, including the trial judge and the prosecution. First, since the test of admissibility of evidence is relevance, and the 1993 the jury had to consider whether the three officers had perverted the course of justice in relation to Patrick Armstrong, what is the relevance of the extracts from two interviews with Carol Richardson, the six statements of Paul Hill and the action taken in respect of information given by Hill, and the extracts from Conlon's pre- and post-conviction confessions? As far as I know, not one of the three officers on trial had anything to do with Richardson, Hill or Conlon in the course of the investigation into the Guildford bombings. That is separate and apart from the subsidiary question: who did the editing of the original statements so that they became 'extracts'? Did the editor select the material that he or she found most favourable to the police officers' defence? What part, if any, did the prosecution have in agreeing those extracts before they were shown to the jury? Whatever the answers to those questions might be, two matters are of fundamental importance. The first deals with the six statements of Paul Hill (Flag 8), the second with the extracts from Mr Boxall's brief (Flag 10). From the very outset, counsel for the prosecution Julian Bevan QC stressed to the jury one fundamental point. They were not concerned with the guilt or innocence of Patrick Armstrong but whether or not the handwritten notes were contemporaneous. He said, 'the foundation of the prosecution case rests on the existence of some rough typed notes that contained typewritten and hand written deletions and amendments. The allegation is that these three defendants manufactured and put forward notes of interviews at the trial which they asserted were contemporaneous. They were not contemporaneous at all but were written up at a later date.'[14] Even if Patrick Armstrong had bombed Guildford and Woolwich, that did not permit the police to fabricate evidence against him.

That being so, was the only purpose of putting in evidence the confessions of Conlon, Hill and Richardson as exhibits for the defence to prove that they, and Patrick Armstrong, were guilty as charged? If not, what was their relevance?

We've seen that at the Guildford Four trial Paul Hill made serious allegations of violent assault on him by unidentified Surrey police officers. He later claimed that a gun had been dry fired into the cell where he was being held at Guildford police station. The jury by their verdict totally rejected his allegations. Few people outside the courtroom believed him either; the public perception at the time was that the police simply do not behave in that way.

There is reason to believe, however, that it was common knowledge among Surrey police officers that an officer called Gerald Queen had been on duty at Guildford police station after the arrest of Paul Hill on 28 November 1974. When Hill's appeal against conviction for the murder of the former British soldier came before Belfast Crown Court in April 1994, a fellow Surrey police officer (later referred to as Witness B), who was allowed to conceal his identity for reasons I fail to understand, told the court that at Guildford police station 'he saw Constable Queen standing in front of a cell with his gun, which was a .38 Smith and Wesson revolver, pointing into the hatch of the cell door. Constable Queen's hands were outstretched and the gun was pointing into the cell . . . He turned and looked at the witness. He had an expression like a leer on his face. There were at least two clicks and there may have been a third click . . . the click which he heard was the fall of the hammer on an unloaded chamber. It was an unmistakable sound.'[15] He did not report what he saw because he 'believed the feeling within the station at that particular time was that they had arrested the people responsible for the Guildford bombings and he did not think that anything he said would be listened to'.

Another retired Surrey officer, referred to as Witness A, said in evidence that he was at Godalming police station in the charge room with at least three other officers when Constable Queen 'spoke about an incident with a revolver in Guildford police station, and indicated that he had drawn his gun, unloaded the bullets from it and had fired the gun dry at somebody in one of the cells'.[16] Although the prosecution authorities knew where to find Gerald Queen at the time of the appeal, for he was still a serving police officer with the rank of inspector (so terrifying a suspect in custody by dry firing a handgun at him is clearly not a bar to promotion in the modern police service), he did not appear as a witness in the Belfast appeal court to challenge or deny the allegations made against him by two former colleagues. The result was that the Belfast appeal court decided that 'we think it is very likely that an incident involving Constable Queen and his revolver did take place in the passage outside the cells in Guildford police station as described by Witness B.'[17]

I regarded it as a question of fundamental importance as to when the prosecuting authorities first knew of the evidence of Witness A and Witness B, so I asked the CPS when their statements came into their possession. In a letter dated 3 April 2008 a CPS lawyer replied, 'I am not able to say exactly when they were received by the Crown Prosecution Service but I can inform you that they were received under cover of a report from Avon and Somerset Constabulary which bears the date April 1991. In the circumstances, it may be possible to infer that it must have been received before the trial in April 1993.' This understates the case. It follows that for two years *before* the trial of the three Surrey officers the prosecution authorities had reason to believe that perhaps that some of the evidence in the Guildford Four case had been obtained in the most bizarre circumstances, at the point of a dry-fired gun. And if Witness B was telling the truth and had no motive to lie about a fellow officer, does it not follow that at least some, if not all, of the confession evidence against Paul Hill was worthless?

Did the CPS pass on to the prosecuting barristers in the police officers' trial the evidence from Witnesses A and B about the use of the gun and the boasts by their fellow officer? If they had done so, would those barristers have still allowed the defence to put in evidence the six confession statements of Paul Hill that appear at Flag 8?

My suspicion is that the CPS failed to inform prosecuting counsel about the evidence put forward by Witnesses A and B, but what is the explanation for allowing the confession statement made by Paul Hill which DI Timothy Blake and DC Lewis obtained from him after he was charged? As noted above, Roy Amlot QC had accused those two (unidentified) officers in open court on 19 October 1989 of giving false evidence, claiming that 'it is clear that these officers also seriously misled the court' and 'the true interview was suppressed and a false version given by the officers'. Why then were the jury that tried and acquitted the three Surrey officers allowed to see the fifth statement made by Paul Hill as if it had been lawfully and properly obtained, when the prosecution were alleging that it was not? Had Blake and Lewis falsified the truth? Surely the 1993 jury that tried the Surrey officers were entitled to know that the fifth statement was disputed in the way that it was.

In addition, I cannot find a single word which indicates that the 1993 jury were ever told, as Roy Amlot QC had told the Lord Chief Justice in 1989, that 'the detention sheets for each appellant . . . reveal a disturbing difference between the number of interviews according to the sheets and the number and times of interviews according to the officers in evidence'. Is that not a reflection on the truthfulness and integrity of those officers? It will be remembered that Roy Amlot went on to say, 'Interviews are shown on the sheets which were never given in evidence [does that mean that evidence was supressed by the police?] or revealed to the Director of Public Prosecutions or prosecuting counsel. Interviews are shown on the sheets as taking place at markedly different times from those given in court by the interviewing officers [which surely means that either the entry on the detention sheet is false, or the evidence of the officer involved is false] and the discrepancies apply to each appellant.'

So the entire case against each of the Guildford Four was tainted by the entries in the police documents, namely the detention sheets, or the evidence in open court and yet in 1993 the prosecution were not objecting in any way to the jury that tried the Surrey officers seeing statements which each of the Guildford Four made to the police in 1974. What had changed since October 1989, when Roy Amlot QC dissected the evidence which resulted in the release from prison of the Guildford Four? If I had been serving on the jury who tried and acquitted the Surrey officers, and had then been told in detail exactly what Roy Amlot QC told the appeal court in 1989 about Flag 7 (Carole Richardson's 'extracts'), Flag 8 (Paul Hill's confessions) and Flags 11 and 12 (Gerard Conlon's confessions), I would have wanted to know why the entire, unvarnished truth had not been disclosed to me to enable me to reach a true verdict on the evidence. I would also have liked to be told of the evidence that Det. Sgt Anthony Jermey gave to the court on the sixth day of the trial in 1975. According to the *Surrey Advertiser*, that officer said in his sworn evidence that 'he now realised that most of what the defendants had told the police was "a mixture of fact and fiction". He told Mr John Leonard QC, defending Mr Armstrong, that he had come to the conclusion most of what the statements contained were fairy tales.'[18] I consider it doubtful if that was ever mentioned at the 1993 trial. Nor was the evidence relating to Paul Hill's statements, when his counsel Arthur Mildon QC cross-examined the same witness, who told the court 'he thought the defendants put false circumstantial evidence into their statements to confuse the police. When he was asked whether a colleague of his, Mr Richardson, had brought a gun into Mr Hill's cell while he was being questioned, Sergeant Jermey strongly denied the suggestion.'[19]

I would have been surprised if, during the course of an investigation into bombings by a terrorist group, there were no armed police officers in the area where the suspects were being questioned. But the allegation of possessing a gun is quite different from an allegation of poking it through the flap on a cell door and dry firing it. Not only was there some evidence that that happened, but the prosecuting authorities knew of its existence and did not make use of it in 1993.

As for the three statements made by Patrick Armstrong to the three officers on trial, did the prosecution disclose to the jury the details, in relation to those statements, that Roy Amlot QC had revealed to the appeal court in 1989? (As noted above, the entries on the detention sheets related to him as well as the other three.) I consider the answer is probably not. When defence counsel were accusing Patrick Armstrong of 'singing like a canary' while in Guildford police station, was anyone who had been there at the time secretly smiling and wondering, will the discrepancies between the evidence of the officers and the recorded information in the detention sheets ever see the light of day? What will happen if defence counsel suddenly call for their production and examination in court?

There was of course no mention, probably on the grounds of relevance, of the fact that others – O'Connell, Dowd, Duggan and Butler – had confessed to bombing both Guildford and Woolwich. Nor was there any mention of the fact, I suspect, that Carole Richardson had confessed in detail to bombing the Seven Stars in Guildford, yet she could not, even on the prosecution's version of events, have done so. She was wandering around in bare feet with Lisa Astin in the Elephant and Castle area, yet no one noticed either of them on that Saturday evening of 5 October 1974 until she had her photo taken with the pop group at the polytechnic.

Some may have been surprised at the acquittals of the former officers, especially in the light of the observations of the Lord Chief Justice, Lord Lane, when the convictions of the Guildford Four were quashed in October 1989, that the officers seriously misled the court. In fact, they must have lied, he added. The jury that tried the three officers clearly did not think so. They returned their not-guilty verdicts after deliberating for over eight hours. 'When Mr Justice Macpherson told the officers they were free to leave the dock, all three smiled broadly and Mr Attwell mouthed "thank you very much" to the jury'.[20]

The reaction to the acquittal of the three officers was very mixed. Under the headline 'Joy and Fury at police acquittal', the *Belfast Newsletter* reported Home Secretary Kenneth Clarke QC as welcoming the verdict: 'I think the

British system in that kind of case is quite impeccable.' According to a report in *The Guardian*, he added, 'I am always glad to see innocent people acquitted, it enables everyone now to get that particular incident back in proportion. I hope we can now put this whole unhappy episode behind us.'[21] The Police Federation chairman Alan Eastwood said 'he was extremely delighted by the verdicts'. The *Daily Telegraph*, predictably but sadly, said, 'the acquittal of the three ex-policemen, and some of the new evidence heard in the course of their Old Bailey trial, suggests there are reasonable grounds that two of the Guildford Four, Mr Patrick Armstrong and Mr Gerry Conlon, might have been guilty after all. This raises the disturbing possibility that the real miscarriage of justice in their case occurred when they walked free'.[22] If one follows that approach, why not have more criminal trials in the absence of the accused, and with total disregard for the rules of evidence, under a benevolent judge? This begs the question: if the Four were guilty, why did the Crown not oppose their appeal against conviction in October 1989 instead of conceding that their convictions could not be sustained?

The *Irish News* headlined its report of the case with the words 'Armstrong still accused as lawyers allege guilt; Guildford Four outrage as policemen walk free'. Yet the *Sunday Times*, under the heading 'Travesty of Justice', commented, 'the law, which freed the Guildford Four by deciding the police had concocted the evidence, was now saying the police are not guilty either. Surely both verdicts could not be true?'[23] The responses of three solicitors in the case are worthy of note. Gareth Peirce, Gerard Conlon's solicitor, said, 'this case has been an object lesson in how anybody who does complain about the police can end up with their reputations being decimated in court'.[24] According to *The Guardian*, the officers' solicitor, Scott Ingram, on the other hand, said, 'my clients are obviously grateful to the jury for its verdict, the right verdict.'[25] The same newspaper, on the same date, noted the comments of Alistair Logan, solicitor for Patrick Armstrong and Carole Richardson: 'The only chance the police had to be acquitted was to put Armstrong and Conlon on trial, and that is what they have done. It was a whitewash from start to finish. It is a con-trick, a dirty lousy con-trick. It is an attempt to re-write history, an attempt to reconvict the Four.'[26]

The public struggled to understand the outcome of this case with the quashing of the Guildford Four convictions. In an attempt to explain at least one aspect of the case, the former appeal court judge, Sir John May, who had been appointed by the home secretary on 26 October 1989 to conduct a judicial inquiry into the cases of the Guildford Four and the Maguire Seven, where justice had plainly miscarried, said in his final report, published in

June 1994, 'the rule against the admission of hearsay evidence is commonly waived out of fairness to a defendant, whilst applied with full vigour to evidence against him.'[27] He considered that Patrick Armstrong and others of the Guildford Four would feel aggrieved that hearsay evidence had been used at the trial in order to discredit him and the other three in their absence, but, said Sir John, 'it seems to me to be an example of the lengths to which trial judges go to achieve fairness for defendants on trial before them'. I regard this as a mis-statement of an elementary principle in the law of evidence. I consider he is wrong about the admissibility of such evidence in order to be fair to a defendant, for as the appeal court said in *R. v. Turner*, 'the idea, which may be gaining prevalence in some quarters, that in a criminal trial the defence is entitled to adduce hearsay evidence to establish facts, which if proved would be relevant and would assist the defence, is wholly erroneous.'[28] Most first-year law students will be familiar with the 1964 Privy Council case *Sparks v. R.*[29] In that case a three-year-old child had been taken from an unlocked car where she had been asleep. Her abductor indecently assaulted her. Her mother asked her what the man who took her from the car looked like. The little girl said he was a 'coloured boy'. An American Air Force staff sergeant was charged with indecent assault. He was white. The victim was too young to give evidence in the case and the defence wished to have the mother's evidence before the court to show that her daughter had told her that her abductor was black. They were not permitted to do so. The child's statement, 'it was a coloured boy', was hearsay if it was repeated by the mother and could not be evidence of the truth of what was stated. The court ruled that the statement of the child to her mother could not be used to prove the guilt of an accused, and equally the defence could not use it to establish his innocence. Much of what follows on evidential matters also breaches the hearsay rule.

In the course of researching this case, I obtained a copy of the trial judge's summing-up in the Surrey officers' case. It is an intriguing document. It reveals some, but not all, of the truth about the evidence given at the trial. It does not, in my view, resemble anything like a fair, objective and impartial summary of the issues of fact to be decided by the jury, and matters of law to be decided by the judge. It would not have been out of place as part of the defence case. The first 19 pages are designed to show that Patrick Armstrong was guilty of the Guildford bombings. At page 3 the judge describes how a plan of one of the Guildford public houses was marked and signed by Patrick Armstrong as being the very spot where the bomb was planted. A photograph put in evidence by the defence enabled an explosive expert, Major Henderson, to describe that the explosion of that bomb vented the outside wall of the pub at exactly the spot where Patrick Armstrong had marked it. The judge was trying to indicate to the jury that there was independent evidence confirming the truth of Patrick Armstrong's confession. This overlooks the fact that not only did the actual bomber know the site of the bomb, so did the investigating police officers. In fact, Carole Richardson marked the exact spot on the plan where the bomb had been placed – but only at her third attempt. The first two attempts, according to Sir Michael Havers QC, were deliberate attempts to mislead. So what he regarded as true was accepted, but what he regarded as untrue was rejected.

Why did the prosecuting authorities decide not to call Patrick Armstrong as a witness for the prosecution without saying why they did not? Leading counsel told the court that Armstrong's value to the jury would have been 'less than zero'.[30] I regard that claim as completely misconceived. To sustain a conviction it was essential that the jury should see and hear his version of how and why the suspect handwritten and typewritten records of three interviews came into existence. He was there. He knew the truth. He should have been allowed to tell it.

Patrick Armstrong was released from prison in October 1989. Three months later the police asked his solicitor, Alistair Logan, whether Armstrong would make a witness statement. They gave no details. No mention was made of the three Surrey officers. The answer was yes: he would readily agree to an interview, subject to conditions imposed not by him or his solicitor but by two eminent doctors, a psychiatrist and a clinical psychologist. These doctors were treating Patrick Armstrong, whose mental health (now happily restored: he has since married and has a family) had broken down in prison. That frequently happens when an innocent person is convicted: a person who has no hope of ever receiving justice and faces a lifetime rotting in a lonely prison cell is unsurprisingly likely to have mental health issues.

The first condition was that the interview during which the statement would be provided should not take place in a police station. The reasons for such a condition are self-evident in the light of Patrick Armstrong's allegations about how he had been treated in Guildford police station. Second, such an interview should be video-recorded and either his solicitor or one of the doctors treating him, Dr James MacKeith, should be present throughout during the recording. Third, Patrick would be permitted to break off the interview if he felt he needed to rest.

The police refused, quite unreasonably in my view, to take a statement under these circumstances. Alistair Logan wrote to the DPP asking him to become involved, which he refused to do, saying it was not his function. The police sent a serious of questions which Logan described as 'anodyne', and suggested that Logan take a statement from his own client. He declined to do so, being totally unaware of what purpose that statement would be used for. He did not know what the police had discovered in the course of their investigation into the case, apart from what had been said in open court on the day the appeal was allowed. In the event Patrick Armstrong was never asked to be a witness in the trial of the Surrey officers. According to Logan, the police also wished to interview Carole Richardson. She too was ill as a consequence of her wrongful imprisonment. The two doctors required the same conditions relating to any proposed police interview with her. In addition, she felt unable to undergo an interview with a male officer and requested that any such interview should be carried out by a female officer. The police rejected these conditions and did nothing more to secure her attendance as a witness. Logan further claims that one of the defence counsel, Edmund Lawson QC, told journalists at court that the defendants' solicitors had been attempting to find Patrick Armstrong to serve him with a subpoena. Logan says that they could have contacted Patrick Armstrong through him at any time, but they made no attempt to do so. Armstrong was at that time living in Dublin but returning frequently to the UK and in contact with his solicitor. Contrary to this, a newspaper report said that 'the court heard that for nearly a year Avon and Somerset police tried to arrange an interview with him [Patrick Armstrong] and eventually posted him a witness form to fill in with his solicitor.'[31] Whichever version is correct, and I accept Mr Logan's, the result of the prosecuting authorities' decision not to ask Armstrong, or even compel him, to appear as a witness was twofold. First, the trial judge, Mr Justice Macpherson, was able to comment in the course of his summing-up on Patrick Armstrong's absence from the witness box. I wrote to the judge, now retired, and asked him why, since he had the power so to do, he did not call Armstrong as a witness himself. (The trial judge has the power to call any witness in a criminal trial. In the case of three innocent men wrongly convicted of the murder of the Cardiff prostitute in 1990,[32] Mr Justice Leonard called a witness when the prosecution and defence counsel declined to do so.) Mr Justice Macpherson, by then retired from the bench, replied on 6 July 2006 that he did not do so because he did not think that Patrick Armstrong would attend. Well, one never knows if one does not try. I consider that the interests of justice would have been better served if he had exercised his power to call Patrick Armstrong as a witness, rather than making repeated comments about his absence from the witness box.

At one stage of the trial an astute member of the jury sent a note to Mr Justice Macpherson asking whether the three accused officers would give evidence. At the time a trial judge had discretion to comment on the failure of the accused to give evidence, whereas the prosecution could not do so. But here the judge was faced with a specific question, which he answered. He told the jury, 'they have given or there is in the material before you some evidence from them in the statements under caution given in 1990'. In my view he failed to draw the distinction between those unsworn statements and evidence given on oath from the witness box in court. He went on to say, 'you must not, I direct you, hold against these men the fact that you have not heard from them in the witness box'. Did the jury consider that while Patrick Armstrong's absence from the witness box was sinister and a sign of guilt, the officers' absence was not sinister and had no evidential value one way or the other?

The trial judge could of course run the trial in any way he liked, subject to the rules of evidence and procedure, but was it right for him to tell the jury that they could not take into account the failure of the accused to give evidence? Should he simply have told them that the jury should not assume guilt from silence?

In addition, I consider that Mr Justice Macpherson might have been entering dangerous territory when he seemed to complain that, when quashing the convictions of the Guildford Four, the appeal court had treated the three officers unfairly, for he said, 'these three policemen were never called in that court to meet the matters raised here against them'.[33] Might the astute juror who sent the note to the judge have wondered, 'Well, now they have the chance to answer the matters raised against them; so are they going to?' In the event, the judge directed the jury, 'it would be wrong, and indeed I am sure you will understand unfair so to do and thus to suggest that silence might go one centimetre towards establishing their guilt'.[34] I do not disagree with that statement.

Did the jury draw the inference from the repeated observations about the absence of a material witness (for Armstrong and the three officers were the only individuals who knew the entire truth about the circumstances in which the interview notes had been written) that Armstrong stayed away because he had something to hide? That something, suggested the defence, was his guilt. However, it is a matter of record that Patrick Armstrong had gone into the witness box at his trial in 1976, had denied on oath that he had ever bombed Guildford or Woolwich, and had been cross-examined on his evidence at that time.

I consider that the judge encouraged the jury to draw that inference themselves, that being the purpose of his repeated comments on the absence from the witness box of one person, Patrick Armstrong, who must have known the truth about how the statements were obtained from him.

In doing this, I consider that Mr Justice Macpherson was breaching a fundamental principle of legal practice and procedure. At the outset of every criminal trial the jury are directed by the judge to decide the case only on the evidence given in court, and nothing else. In a trial in 2013 Mr Justice Saunders told the jury 'it is a central principle of our system of trial by jury that you decide your verdicts on the evidence and arguments you hear in court, and only the evidence and arguments you hear in court). If that is so, why did Mr Justice Macpherson say to the jury, 'there has been no clash as to the evidence as such; no ringing cross-examination. Things might have been different, you may think . . . if Patrick Armstrong had been here, but he was not.' He added, 'your conclusion will be based solely on what you have heard in this court and upon all the evidence which has been put before you on both sides'.[35] I do not find it easy to reconcile those two statements.

When the prosecution closed its case on the eighth day of the trial, as Ronan Bennett relates in his book *Double Jeopardy: Retrial of the Guildford Four*, not long before the end of the morning session the judge told the jury that they might have heard enough evidence to form a view about the case – as he certainly had, certainly about some aspects of it – 'Armstrong is not here, for example,' he said. Was that an invitation to stop the case, find the defendants not guilty on the grounds that they had heard no evidence, and would hear no evidence, from Patrick Armstrong? The judge invited the jury to send him a note if they wanted to dismiss the prosecution case against the three accused, and to do so at the start of the afternoon session. He might not have been greatly pleased when the jury did send him a note saying that they wanted to hear more evidence, and asking whether the accused officers would be going into the witness box to give evidence in their own defence.

By page 51 of the summing-up transcript the judge changed tack.

Perhaps it is at this point convenient just to refer again and to return to Armstrong's absence from the witness box. Mr Bevan [prosecuting counsel] you will recall, disarmingly says that because Armstrong would, for example, palpably be shown to be wrong in his original assertion that there was no interview on 4th December, thus he would contribute zero to the case. You will recall his submission about that. The defence argue, and with some force you may think, although it is entirely a matter for you, that this is not so because if he was here, you understand, he could have been cross-examined and who knows what gold, say the defence, might have been mined . . . I suppose it must be said that his evidence as to whether or not a note was made, and its form or look and content and how the note was made might have emerged; and might have, for all we know, emerged favourably for the defendants. It does seem to me his absence is of significance, but it is a matter for you to consider.

The point did not end there, lest the jury should have missed it. The judge went on, 'Members of the jury, we simply do not know . . . what might have emerged if he had been here. If the absence of Armstrong adds to the mystery and lack of knowledge of what actually happened in 1974 in connection with these interviews, why then you should, so it seems to me, regard his absence with some seriousness since it may add to the doubts about the case to which the defence point.'

In my view this amounts to nothing less than an open and repeated invitation to the jury to speculate on matters about which evidence had not been given, rather than remain true to their oath and act in accordance with the important legal principle, which lies at the centre of the criminal justice system, that cases are decided by the jury only on evidence they hear and see in the course of the trial. This is not a new concept of justice, but one of many years' standing.

For good measure the summing-up was not completed on Monday 17 May 1993 and the court adjourned until the following day. Mr Justice Macpherson directed the jury, for a second time, on the good character of the three accused officers – the three human beings as he called them, as if they could be anything else. (It will be remembered that Anne Maguire and the remainder of the Maguire Seven did not get a direction on good character once, let alone twice.) The judge added, 'acquittal of these men . . . I ask you to remember would have no bearing on the past. . . . What you are concerned about is what you have heard in this court, particularly about Armstrong and these three men. Armstrong was not here for you to see him and to see him tested in cross-examination.' What did the jury make of that? They were told on the one hand to deal with the evidence they heard in court, and then invited to speculate on what evidence might have been disclosed if Patrick Armstrong had been cross-examined. Were they confused by this, or did they get the message – Armstrong is absent because he is guilty?

My view is that the trial judge had formed a view on the facts of the case unfavourable to the prosecution. He showed his impatience with the prosecution at least once and he was prepared to put that view to the jury in a very subtle way, even though he introduced it with a fact that was totally irrelevant. He told the jury, 'If it should be of interest to you, I spent the weekend in Scotland and in Scotland it is possible to say that a case is not proven, but such a verdict is not open to you in the English courts and if a case is not proved, not proven so that you are not sure, the verdict must be not guilty. If you cannot at the end of the day be sure of guilt in each man's case then – I'm sure you understand – the verdict must be not guilty.'[36]

Much might depend on the tone of voice in which the judge said 'not proven' and 'not guilty'. Did he link them together in such a way that his meaning could not be missed?

No point was too small or insignificant for Mr Justice Macpherson's consideration if it could be used to undermine Patrick Armstrong's standing as a person and credibility as a witness. He told the jury in his summing-up, 'In 1990, the Court of Appeal was again faced with this case after the referral of the cases of the other three, *not of Armstrong*, but the other three to the Court of Appeal by the home secretary. The result of that referral was that all four cases were considered' [emphasis added]. Assuming that the transcript is accurate and correct, that is a totally false point. The then home secretary Douglas Hurd wrote in his memoirs, 'on 29 December, having worked through the papers again, I decided, despite the rebuff which they had given me over Birmingham, that I must refer the Guildford case to the Court of Appeal'.[37] He did so on 16 January 1989 in a written reply to a parliamentary question published in the House of Commons on that day. I cannot say whether Mr Justice Macpherson was misled, or he simply made it up, but in fact the home secretary referred *all four cases*, including Patrick Armstrong's, to the appeal court on 16 January 1989 and it is nonsense for anyone to claim that he did not.

As a matter of law, the non-appearance of Patrick Armstrong as a witness for the prosecuting authorities against the three Surrey officers, which I regard as a calculated and deliberate on their part, in my view allowed the defence to evade the Finality Rule in the law of evidence. That rule states that a party is obliged to accept as final the answer of a witness to a question that relates to a collateral matter. The reason for the Finality Rule is to confine the ambit of trial within proper limits and to prevent the true central issue from becoming submerged in a welter of detail. The central issue in the case against the three Surrey officers was whether the prosecution could prove beyond reasonable doubt that the notes they put forward as contemporaneous were not, and that they had lied when they claimed they were. The defence did not to have to prove anything, but they did raise a collateral issue, namely that they had no motive to fabricate or falsify evidence because Armstrong and his three co-accused were guilty as charged and the confession evidence was true. If Patrick Armstrong had gone into the witness box and denied bombing Guildford and Woolwich, as he would have done, since he is entirely innocent, my view is that the defence would have had to accept that answer as final, and could not give or call any evidence that he had done so. It should be noted that even if Patrick Armstrong was involved in the Guildford bombings (and he was not), that would not entitle a police officer to manufacture or fabricate evidence in order to obtain a conviction. In my view, the defence tactic of concentrating on the content of the confessions of each of the Four deflected the attention of the jury away from the prosecution case that the notes of interviews they put forward as contemporaneous were not. Did the jury wonder why, if the content of the interview evidence was true and each of the Guildford Four did confess to murder, did it really matter whether the police handwritten notes were made at the time or not?

Freedom of Information and Patrick Armstrong

There are a number of references in the summing-up to 'the defence jury bundle' of documents. I found that intriguing. I asked the CPS if I could see those documents. They refused. I was unable to understand why documents produced and examined in public in the course of a criminal trial would not be in the public domain. If I had attended the Guildford Four trial in person in 1976, would I not have listened to the evidence of what was set out in the documents on that list? Of course, by now, perhaps there was something to hide.

On 30 August 2006 the CPS told me that the bundle of documents was prepared and provided by the defence under the then disclosure rules. That cannot be exactly right because I knew from the content of the summing-up that among the documents, at the very least, were the confession statements made by Paul Hill and Gerard Conlon. These were provided to the defence by the prosecution, not the other way round. The defence may have put the bundle of documents together, but at least some of the content came from the prosecution.

On 18 October 2006 the CPS sent me a copy of the index to that bundle, with some deletions of names. It lists a total of 21 items.

I challenge the admissibility of some of the documents under the various Flag numbers. Flag 2 is listed as 'Michael Hill Q.C.'s trial brief copy of Donaldson's statement'. Hill was one of the prosecuting team. How his copy of a document, which may contain annotations, amounts to evidence defeats me. If someone considered it was admissible in evidence, why not provide a clean copy? We would then know for what purpose it was being tendered in evidence.

Flag 3 is equally controversial. It is said to be 'Note of Conference at 5 King's Bench Walk, 22/2/75'. This is presumably a note of what was discussed by the prosecuting barristers, a member of the DPP office and the police held on 22 February 1975 in the barristers' chambers. How can that amount to evidence in a criminal trial?

Flag 4 is also controversial. It is described as 'A complete list of prisoners at Guildford', which I understand to mean all those arrested as a consequence of what the police were told by Paul Hill and Gerald Conlon.

As previously noted, Flag 7 is 'Extracts from 2 interviews of Carole Richardson'. I claim first that this so-called evidence breaches the rule against hearsay. The criminal law is primarily concerned with relevant and direct evidence given orally from the witness box. The law allows the butler to say what he saw. It does not allow another witness to narrate what he says the butler saw, if the purpose of doing so is to prove that a fact asserted by the butler is true. The recitation of one witness, or statement in a document, of the testimony of another is hearsay if it is tendered for the purpose of proving the truth of that statement. The two criminal cases cited above establish that principle. If the defence wished to have Carole Richardson's evidence before the jury that tried the Surrey officers they should have called her as a witness. But was that the last thing they wanted to do? She would not have been well disposed to the prosecution or the police, who cost her some of the best years of her young life.

It is a matter of record that the Home Office instructed two distinguished doctors, James MacKeith and Gisli Gudjonson, to examine Carole Richardson at Styal prison in Cheshire on 30 April 1986. This was more than ten years after her conviction. Dr MacKeith told the Home Office in his report that Richardson had been abusing drugs heavily and was usually under the influence of them, as well as being psychologically and physically dependent. She had a vulnerable personality, with low self-esteem, poor self-confidence and an undue reliance on others' good opinion. From her own account, largely confirmed by the police doctor's statement, she was in an abnormal state of mind, probably suffering from an acute anxiety state, very distressed, frightened and desperate to be relieved of the stress of further interrogation. Dr MacKeith concluded that the statements that resulted in her conviction were very probably unreliable. That medical evidence did not hasten her release from prison, where she remained for another three years, and it did not feature in the case involving the Surrey officers. I cannot say if or when the Home Office provided this vital information to the CPS prior to the 1993 trial. The jury were simply told of the extracts from Carole Richardson's statements and no doubt were asked to rely upon them as representing the truth. In my view, that jury should have been aware of Dr MacKeith's professional medical assessment of Carole Richardson and should have been allowed to decide whether the extracts from police interviews with her were worth the paper they were written on.

Flag 8 consists of the six statements under caution made by Paul Hill in which he confessed to multiple murders. Would the jury have looked at them in a different light if they had known that at least one statement had been obtained after the terrifying incident at the cell door? It is my view that these statements also breach the rule against hearsay.

There is another related matter. As previously stated, if Paul Hill's defence team had called for the production of the detention sheets (the Detained Persons' Register), the defence barristers would have found that the detention sheet shows that on 30 November 1974 Paul Hill was taken from his cell at 1.15 p.m. by unidentified CID officers and returned at 7.50 p.m. No evidence was given by any police officer in any statement to account for this period of time, and no officer made any reference to it during the course of their evidence. Hill claimed in his evidence in 1975 that he had been interviewed on occasions other than those about which the police gave evidence. They denied his claim. Their own records prove the truth of his testimony and the falsity of their own.

It will be readily apparent what an enormous risk the investigating police officers ran in doing what they did. The defence should have asked for the detention sheets and sought an explanation if they were not produced. It is a matter of record that Paul Hill's detention sheets were available and used in cross-examination by his own counsel (the highly competent Northern Ireland barrister Michael Lavery QC) at his trial for murder in Belfast in June 1975, which was of course before the Guildford trial in London. Mr Lavery QC discovered, for example, that the time of Paul Hill's arrest had been wrongly recorded on the detention sheet. I can find no mention of the detention sheets and the evidential contradictions they clearly disclosed being made known to the jury that tried the Surrey officers.

Nor was that jury told what Lord Gifford QC told the Northern Ireland Court of Appeal during the hearing of Paul Hill's case to set aside his conviction for the murder of Brian Shaw. Under the headline 'English policemen lied at Hill trial, Belfast court told', *The Irish Times* reported:

> Lord Gifford QC alleged that lies were part of a cover up to conceal unrecorded interviews with Hill, including one by Sir Peter Imbert, later to become Commissioner of the Metropolitan Police. Hill's lawyer said that while he was being held at Guildford police station in 1974 about the pub bombings there and in Woolwich, three jailers had failed to record visits to him . . . during these unrecorded visits Hill was taken to a second floor room and questioned.[38]

Since Paul Hill told the jury (and presumably his lawyers) in 1975 that there had been visits by police officers at the time stated by him, it is incomprehensible that his lawyers in London did not call for the production of the detention sheet that proved (as first Michael Lavery QC and then Lord Gifford QC discovered) that at least one officer, Peter Imbert, was telling the truth in admitting the denied visits, which were not recorded as they should have been. Those two visits took place on 28 November sometime between 10.15 p.m. and 6 a.m., and at 11.30 a.m. on 29 November. That was not recorded either.

Flag 11 contains extracts from Gerard Conlon's pre-conviction confessions. Such evidence in my view again simply infringes the hearsay rule. He was not interviewed by any of the three Surrey officers in the dock. What he admitted doing was not evidence against Patrick Armstrong, and in any event I question the relevance of those confession statements to the issues the jury trying the officers had to decide; namely, if they had agreed together to put forward notes relating to interviews with Patrick Armstrong – not Gerard Conlon, not Paul Hill, not Carole Richardson. Those confessions proved nothing relevant to the police officers' trial, but they were gravely prejudicial in inviting the jury to think that they were.

Relevance seems not to have played much of a part in demolishing the reputations of the Guildford Four. A fact is relevant in a criminal case if it logically proves a fact at issue. When the judge reminded the jury, 'I add simply for completeness the fact that Paul Hill admitted and has been convicted of being involved in murdering an ex-soldier in Ireland in 1974. His appeal in that case remains unresolved',[39] one is bound to ask, to what issue in the case of the Surrey officers did that statement relate? It is highly prejudicial, but what does it prove? How were the jury helped in their deliberations on whether the prosecution proved that the officers rewrote their notes in relation to Patrick Armstrong's three interviews? Or whether they had any motive to lie in relation to him? That of course leaves to one side the fact that Paul Hill did not admit (as the transcript note records the judge as saying) murdering an ex-soldier in Ireland in 1974. He had pleaded not guilty and was convicted after a five-day trial in a non-jury Diplock court in Northern Ireland. If Mr Justice Macpherson did say to the jury that Paul Hill had admitted the murder, that was plainly misleading and wrong.

It should not be thought that the rule against the admissibility of hearsay evidence was completely ignored by Mr Justice Macpherson and counsel in the 1993 case. It was applied when it suited. Ronan Bennett attended the trial of the three Surrey officers and he relates what he saw and heard in his book *Double Jeopardy: Retrial of the Guildford Four*. During legal argument, carried out in accordance with the legal practice in the absence of the jury, it was disclosed that in the course of an interview on Wednesday 4 December 1974 Patrick Armstrong implicated a man called Paul Colman in breaking into a chemist's shop and stealing drugs on the Sunday before the pub bombings. The time of that allegation, according to the manuscript notes of DC Attwell, was 2.25 p.m. Paul Colman was in another part of Guildford police station being interviewed by DCI John Horton. That interview began at 1.12 p.m. It was common ground that the source of the information about the burglary of the chemist's shop was Patrick Armstrong. In the words of prosecuting counsel, 'Mr Horton was relying on information from Patrick Armstrong about the chemist shop job before Armstrong had uttered a word about it.' Horton seemed to be in possession of information one hour and fourteen minutes before the source, Patrick Armstrong, had provided it to another officer. The prosecution wanted this evidence shown as it tended to show that the notes made by DC Attwell might not have been contemporaneous. The defence objected, arguing that the prosecution had failed to call DCI Horton to prove the times, and this was an attempt by the prosecution to get inadmissible evidence in via the back door. The prosecution should have called Horton to give direct evidence of the timing of the interview and therefore any notes he made, not proved by him, were not admissible. They offended the rule against hearsay. The judge upheld that objection and the jury did not hear the evidence about one important point of conflict relating to times and the source of information.

Flag 12 in the defence jury bundle is even more interesting. Immediately after his conviction in 1975 Gerard Conlon was seen by Chief Superintendent Imbert and another officer in Wandsworth prison. He claims that it was made clear to him by the police that if he could help them with information about the IRA bombings, which of course were ongoing at that time, such information would help his father, Giuseppe Conlon, who was extremely ill at the time. Giuseppe died in custody on 23 January 1980, aged 56 years. He was returned to his family home in Belfast in a coffin.

Chief Superintendent Imbert took a long and detailed note from Gerard Conlon in prison. His state of mind was such that he would have confessed to anything. He provided names that were commonly known and details of incidents, some of which never happened. His information was worthless, and no help to Giuseppe. After the release of the Guildford Four in October 1989 someone began to hawk those notes around the media, such was the fury of some police officers that the Four's appeal had been allowed and they had been freed. They were helped, I have no doubt, by the *Daily Telegraph*'s report after the conclusion of the trial of the Surrey officers that their acquittal suggested there were reasonable grounds for suspecting that two of the Guildford Four, Patrick Armstrong and Gerard Conlon, might have been guilty after all. Initially no one in the media would touch the notes, but in March 1990 *The Guardian* published them. It was a further reprehensible attempt by some police officers to reconvict an innocent. The journalist involved, David Rose, later said that he deeply regretted what amounted to a grave error of judgement in publishing this material.[40] When the CPS, citing the provisions of the Freedom of Information Act 2000 and the Data Protection Act 1998, refused me access to the notes set out in Flag 12 they were wasting their time and mine, for those Acts do not, in my view, apply to information that is already in the public domain. Since I read *The Guardian* newspaper I know exactly what the Imbert notes contained. They are of very little worth.

The late Randolph Boxall was the junior defence barrister for Patrick Armstrong at the 1975 trial. Flag 10 contained extracts from his defence brief. The brief to counsel, containing the witness statements and the proof of evidence of his client, is delivered to him by the solicitors at the outset of the case and should normally be returned by counsel to the solicitors at its end. How extracts from Boxall's brief ended up as an exhibit at the Surrey officers' trial defies my comprehension. He died in 2001, so no explanation can be sought from him. Whatever the legal situation regarding who owns the documents, it is an incontrovertible fact that the ownership of the information contained in them is vested in the original defence solicitors and/or their client, Patrick Armstrong. They certainly do not belong to counsel in the case. The defence teams acting for the Surrey police officers and the CPS had, in my view, no lawful authority to be in possession of any extracts from Mr Boxall's brief.

I asked the CPS for access to the entire contents of the defence jury bundle on 14 June 2006. After they refused to provide anything other than the index and a copy of Flag 3 (the notes of a conference at 5 King's Bench Walk held on 11 February 1975) and Flag 14 (a handwritten note made by a Det. Sgt Carter as a day book of the 1975 trial), neither of which was of any interest to me, I appealed against their refusal to the Information Commission on 16 November 2006. I limited my request at that stage to: Flag 6, extracts from two interviews of a person whose name had been redacted; and Flag 9b, a statement under caution dated 4 December 1974 and a witness statement dated 19 December 1974 from a person whose name had also been redacted. This evidence clearly emanated from someone who had been arrested on suspicion of involvement in the Guildford bombing who later became a potential witness. I contend that all this so-called evidence breached the rule against hearsay and was not admissible. I also asked to see Flag 10.

By 30 July 2008, some 18 months later, I still had not received any decision on my appeal. On that date I spoke to the case worker dealing with the case at the Information Commission. I told him that I would be content to limit my request for access to Flag 10 only. I hoped it would expedite the resolution of the case.

On 2 September 2008 the Information Commission sent me an email saying 'I can confirm that the CPS has allowed me to inform you of the following in relation to item 10 [Flag 10] of the withheld information from the Defence Jury Bundle in *R. v. Attwell* and others: "Item 10 is the recollection of an interview conducted by two police officers with a suspect of Guildford bombing on 5 December 1974. The document contains handwritten notes/annotations by an author that the CPS is unable to confirm, and consists of four pages".' I regard this as being at variance with the description of the document in the index, namely that it was extracts from Boxall's brief. I regard the term 'recollections of an interview' as being devoid of any legal meaning. At the relevant time in 1974 interviews in police stations were not tape-recorded. It was the practice of the police to compile a note in their notebook either during the currency of the interview or immediately afterwards, while the questions and answers were still fresh in the officer's memory. Such a note could be used, with leave of the trial judge, as an aide-memoire, to refresh the witness's memory. Before giving leave the judge had to be satisfied that the notes were contemporaneous, made either at the time or immediately after the interview.

According to their witness statements and the evidence at the 1975 trial, DC Attwell said that he took notes of an interview with Patrick Armstrong that commenced at 11.50 a.m. on 4 December 1974. Det. Sgt Donaldson said he made notes of an interview with Armstrong that started at 11.00 a.m. on 5 December 1974. DC Attwell said that he took notes immediately after an interview with Armstrong that started at 10.15 a.m. on 6 December 1974. Those three interviews formed the subject of the prosecution case against them in 1993.

The officers could not explain at initial interviews how their witness statements were identical to the contents of the altered typescript. It was admitted, however, that Attwell did the typing, and Donaldson and Style made the handwritten amendments on the typed copies. When they were interviewed under caution it was claimed first 'that the rough typed notes may have been required for and indeed used for other investigations'.[41] Second, 'they say that the material was there to be used, if required, for Prevention of Terrorism Act applications, in particular in connection with Colman'.[42] Third, 'And of course, the preparation of 27th December 1974 statements required, so the defence say, some interpretation of Attwell's very bad handwriting and some assistance to be given to the typists.'[43] As we saw above, no typist ever gave evidence about how bad the handwriting was, and when, if at all, they were assisted by the amended typewritten notes in the way suggested. The judge dealt with the absence of any evidence in a way that must have greatly pleased the three accused men. 'But in any event, even if there is no positive evidence of the use of the rough typed notes in those regards, say the defence, there should be no finding or conclusion that the rough typed notes could not have been so required or used if others in the big investigation had sought to use them.' I regard this as an invitation to decide an issue in favour of the three officers on which there was no evidence to support a tentative suggestion made on their behalf as to the possible uses to which the notes might perhaps be put. That is not the way in my view to decide contested issues of fact in a criminal trial.

None of this was of any real interest to the Information Commission because, as they set out in their Reply dated 16 March 2009, the Tribunal is not the correct forum in which to air general views about the admissibility of evidence of the conduct of criminal proceedings. I agree with that. The Information Commission and Tribunal is concerned simply with the interpretation and application of the law set out in the 1998 Data Protection Act and the Freedom of Information Act 2000.

In the event the Information Commission decided on 20 January 2009 that the contents of Flag 10 relate to identifiable individuals and contain sensitive personal data on the interviewing officers, the interviewee and the persons referred to by both. The material, they ruled, need not be disclosed. The complaint against the CPS was not upheld. I lodged notice of appeal to the Information Tribunal against that decision. I particularly wanted to know whose privacy, which particular individual, was being protected by this refusal to disclose the information I sought relating to the four-page document that made up Flag 10.

I knew that that Randolph Boxall had endorsed a document with words indicating that Patrick Armstrong had admitted to him that he gave most of the answers attributed to him by his interviewers. Was this the document at Flag 10? I knew also that Mr Justice Macpherson had made reference to Boxall's notes, indicating that they were at Flag 14 of the defence jury bundle.[44] I consider that either there was a slip of the tongue on the judge's part or the stenographer made an error either in hearing or transcribing what he said. He really meant Flag 10. It will be remembered that Flag 14 is Det. Sgt Carter's day book of the 1975 trial, in which he kept a running record of events. The CPS gave me a copy of that record. There would be no reason whatsoever for a junior defence barrister to have access to that day book, still less to endorse it with any observation made by his lay client Patrick Armstrong. A barrister would on the other hand have every reason to endorse a witness statement with the answers to questions he put to his client about the content of that statement. If Boxall did not endorse a note or observation on Flag 10, which document did he endorse?

There are two further pointers to the fact that Boxall would have taken instructions on the so-called recollections of an interview from Patrick Armstrong and recorded those instructions on the papers upon which the police recollections were written and that was Flag 10. First, Mr Justice Macpherson reminded the jury of 'Mr. Boxall's own copies of annotated witness statements which appear at Flag 2 and 10 of the defence jury bundle, in order to reconstruct what occurred'.[45] Second, he told the jury, 'First and foremost the defence argue that *it is proved before you* that Armstrong did say to these officers everything or substantially everything that he is reported to have said, and that everything he did say or was reported to have said, did in fact happen' [emphasis added]. Since the defence did not give or call any evidence, when and by whom was it proved that Patrick Armstrong did say everything he is reported to have said? It would not be necessary in my view to look any further for that proof beyond the note/annotations on Flag 10. What better proof could there really be than the fact that these were written by Patrick Armstrong's own counsel, recording his instructions?

On 26 March 2009 I amended the grounds of appeal to the Information Tribunal to seeking access only to the handwritten annotations on Flag 10 and indicated that I had reason to believe that these were made by Randolph Leonard Boxall of counsel and were to the effect that Patrick Armstrong had admitted to him that he gave most of the answers attributed to him by this interviewers.

On 28 April 2009, in preparation for the tribunal hearing, a telephone conference was held between all three parties, the CPS, the Information Commission and myself. It was chaired by the deputy chairman of the tribunal, Murray Shanks. During the course of the conference Mr Shanks disclosed that the person referred to as 'a suspect' in Flag 10 was in fact Patrick Armstrong. I was astonished by this. Armstrong was not a suspect in the case but a defendant, and I accuse the CPS of being less than truthful in according him the status of 'suspect' when they prepared their case for non-disclosure of Flag 10. He may have been a 'suspect' at the time of the interview; he certainly was not in 2009.

The CPS was ordered by Mr Shanks to serve a statement of their position in relation to the contents of Flag 10 and they did so in a 16-paragraph document on 21 May 2009. This time they decided to tell part of the truth. They still would not admit that the handwritten annotations were made by Boxall. But in paragraph 2 they amended the definition of Flag 10, saying that it 'represents four pages which are extracts from the statements of two police officers which sets out their recollections of an interview they conducted with the defendant'. In paragraph 6, they reveal that the police officers who recorded their accounts of the interviews that took place were Donaldson and Attwell. This is astonishing, and I find the use of this document at the trial of the Surrey officers most bizarre and unprecedented and an obstruction of the truth. If the defence wanted the jury to hear the recollections of these two officers of an interview with Patrick Armstrong, why did the prosecution (and the trial judge) allow the document to be put in evidence, rather than requiring the officers to give evidence on oath from the witness box? Was this interview the same one they say took place on 5 December 1974, or another? If the latter, did the officers mention it at the original trial? And if not, why not? In any event, who prepared and authored this summary? Who decided what should be left in and what should be taken out of this supposed interview?

(Mr Shanks was unable to understand why I did not wish to access the content of the interview, as opposed only to the annotations/notes endorsed on them, saying that it would not be easy to understand the annotations without reference to the text. I did not accept that. I have little or no interest in discovering what Donaldson and Attwell recollected. If it was important and incriminating it should have been given at the trial in 1975 in their oral evidence. I question whether the content of the document would be more helpful than harmful to Patrick Armstrong; I doubt whether the two police officers were giving him a reference of good character, or that the interview was a discussion of the weather or the state of the economy.)

Most fundamental of all, however, is this question: why did the defence need to extract the papers from Randolph Boxall's brief if the purpose of the exercise was to tell the jury only what the officers remembered about that interview? The answer may, of course, be simple. I consider that Mr Boxall noted on a statement somewhere the fact that his client admitted to him that he gave most of the answers attributed to him by his interviewers, and that was the proof that I consider Mr Justice Macpherson had in mind when he made that point to the jury. What better way to destroy Patrick Armstrong's credibility than to use what he told his counsel against him? It may only be a short step from drawing the conclusion that if Armstrong admitted the answers attributed to him then what he said to his own junior barrister was the truth. Wasn't that a step the lawyers representing the police officers wanted the jury to take? Why fabricate the truth? That was a question that was repeated again and again by defence counsel. If I had been serving on that jury and I saw a written statement by defence counsel that his client had told him that he made admissions attributed to him by the police, I would regard the question of whether the police made a contemporaneous note or rearranged their notes as unimportant, as long as they accurately reflected what the defendant said. In such circumstances I would not regard the officers as being involved in a conspiracy to pervert the course of justice.

At the Surrey officers' trial the prosecution refused to say whether it was their case that Armstrong's confession evidence was false. That is hardly surprising since the prosecuting authorities had spent the entire trial in 1975 forcefully claiming that it was the whole unvarnished truth, rather than anything but the truth.

There was of course no mention before the jury trying the Surrey officers that Patrick Armstrong's case at his trial was that he confessed because he had been punched and kicked by police officers. That he had been told about the dismembered bodies of the victims of the Guildford pub bombing with the threat that he would face the same fate if he did not confess. That he claimed in evidence that at the time of his arrest he was high on drugs, barbiturates, Tuinal and speed. That he accused DC Attwell of putting a gun to his head when he arrested him, telling him not to move or he would empty the chamber into him.

The jury that tried and acquitted the three Surrey officers heard none of that because the prosecuting authorities decided not to invite, or compel, Patrick Armstrong to appear as a witness for the prosecution. One jury had heard the allegations of ill-treatment and rejected them. The jury trying the officers never knew that the allegations had been made.

For the purposes of the appeal to the Information Tribunal the CPS maintained that Flag 10 contains sensitive personal data relating to a number of people that should not be disclosed. The Information Commission submitted two responses: an open response that was served on me; and a closed response that was seen only by the tribunal. Even in the midst of a search for information, the authorities prefer secrecy to openness.

I regarded my appeal both to the commission and the tribunal as weak on legal grounds because the 1998 Act and the 2000 Acts are so carefully and craftily drafted that a third party seeking information about another individual is most unlikely to be able to access that information on the basis of what is, in effect, personal privacy.

Under Section 40(2) of the Freedom of Information Act, information is exempt from disclosure if it constitutes personal data. This is defined as data relating to a living individual who can be identified from that data. Sensitive personal data is defined in Section 2 of the Data Protection Act 1998 as information that relates to matters such as racial or ethnic origin, political opinions or personal religious beliefs, mental or physical health, membership of a trade union, sexual life, and, of more practical application to this case, any commission or alleged commission by the person of any criminal offence.

The commission ruled that because Flag 10 contained sensitive personal data of the defendants in the trial, disclosure of its contents would be unfair to them. What I wanted to know, however, throughout this case, was whose privacy was being protected.

The tribunal made its decision on 14 September 2009.[46] The appeal was dismissed. A copy of the ruling is at Appendix 1. The information sought is covered by Section 40(2) of the Freedom of Information Act. The CPS and those directly involved in the trial of the three Surrey police officers may welcome the result, but in my view they will not be pleased at one particular finding of fact. The tribunal has seen the document at Flag 10. I have not, but I contend for reasons set out above that the annotations/notes were written by Randolph Boxall. The tribunal notes, 'The document bears some manuscript notes. Although the CPS is unable to tell us the name of the author of the notes and the Tribunal cannot say for sure, it seems more likely than not from the surrounding circumstances that they were made by Mr Boxall (as the Appellant contends) and that they record instructions Mr Boxall was given by Mr Armstrong in 1975 relating to what was said in the typescript recollection.'

I regard this as proof of the point I was making. On the balance of probabilities it seems to follow from this that at the trial of the Surrey officers in 1993 the prosecution and the defence, together with the trial judge, allowed the jury to see, and no doubt act upon, evidence that was clearly covered by legal professional privilege and therefore not admissible for that reason alone. The principle is set out in the criminal lawyers' 'bible', Archbold's *Criminal Pleading, Evidence and Practice*, as follows:

> Legal professional privilege attaches to confidential written or oral communications between a professional legal adviser and his client, or any person representing the client, in connection with and in contemplation of, and for the purpose of legal proceedings, or in connection with the giving of legal advice to the client. The common law right to consult legal advisers without fear of the communication being revealed is a fundamental condition on which the administration of justice rests; once established no exception should be allowed to its absolute nature. Consultations with lawyers should take place in a manner which favours full and uninhibited disclosure.[47]

No one would seriously suggest that this principle did not apply here. If Mr Boxall had been alive at the time of the 1993 trial of the three Surrey officers, does anyone consider that he could have been called into the witness box by the defence and asked to tell the jury what instructions Patrick Armstrong gave him in relation to the content of Flag 10? He would have been bound to claim legal privilege, which is vested not in him but in his client, and refuse to disclose confidential information.

The Information Tribunal noted for good measure 'that it seems to us that the information sought by Mr O'Connell must have been subject to legal professional privilege in favour of Mr Armstrong at some stage'[48] and other sections of the Freedom of Information Act could have been pleaded to exclude disclosure. The CPS could not have done that without admitting that the annotations/notes on Flag 10 were written by Boxall, and this they are not prepared to do. The words themselves might indicate that he wrote them. The one person who can claim a legal right to see Flag 10 is, of course, Patrick Armstrong himself. I doubt if he ever will and I do not blame him in the slightest. He is an innocent man, falsely imprisoned for almost 15 years by the state in reliance on false and fabricated confession evidence. He was then forced to stand by and say nothing as the legal system put him on trial again in 1993 and reconvicted him in his absence. His reputation was lashed again and again and he was branded with the false label of being an IRA bomber who murdered innocent people. Now the state purports to protect his privacy, under the Freedom of Information Act, by the non-disclosure of a document that may reveal the truth.

Postscript

Leading counsel for the prosecution of the three Surrey police officers was Julian Bevan QC. I wrote to him in connection with my research on 14 June 2006 asking him a series of questions relating to the defence jury bundle in that case. First, why did he agree to the statement dated 3 December 1974 made by Paul Michael Hill being included in that bundle when the Appeal Court had been told on 19 October 1989 that the handwritten notes of the interview that preceded the taking of that statement bore no resemblance whatsoever to the evidence given in court by the two police officers who obtained it? I asked: 'why was that tainted statement allowed in evidence at the trial you prosecuted in 1993 when either you knew or ought to have known how it was obtained?'

Second, when, if ever, did he discover that at least two former Surrey police officers had made statements describing the conduct of their colleague Constable Gerard Queen in pointing a gun through the flap of a cell door and dry firing that gun at one of the Guildford Four, namely Hill?

Third, I asked who obtained the notes of Patrick Armstrong's junior defence counsel, Mr Boxall, and why they were not covered by professional legal privilege; and would he explain how they became admissible in evidence (presumably not to advance the prosecution case against the former police officers, but to undermine the evidence of the client for whom Boxall had been acting at the trial in 1975)?

I received no reply to my letter to Julian Bevan QC. Accordingly I wrote to Nigel Sweeney, who had been junior counsel for the prosecution, not only at the successful appeal court hearing on 19 October 1989 of the Guildford Four, but also at the trial of the three Surrey police officers. He knew better than most every detail of the case that led to the quashing of the Four's convictions. I asked him only two questions: did he agree with the decision to put before the jury that tried Vernon Attwell, John Donaldson and Thomas Style the tainted confession statement made by Paul Hill on 3 December 1974? And if he did, why? I received no reply from him either.

As noted above, the CPS informed me on 3 April 2008 that they had received in April 1991, under cover of a report from the Avon and Somerset Constabulary, copies of the statements of two police officers, one of whom had witnessed PC Queen dry firing the gun in Guildford police station, and the other had heard him boasting to colleagues about what he had done. This begs the question: was this information passed on to Julian Bevan QC and Nigel Sweeney; and if not, why not? If it was, why did they allow the jury that tried the Surrey officers to see the six statements made by Paul Hill without indicating the circumstances in which at least one of those confession statements was obtained?

The matter does not end there. These two distinguished barristers would not have been much wiser but they would have been much better informed if they had read (and there's no evidence they did) the article by David Rose, the home affairs correspondent of the *Observer*, dated 14 October 1990. It is headed 'Gun-threat Guildford officer still in police'. According to Mr Rose, 'a police officer said to have threatened Paul Hill of the Guildford Four with a gun as he lay in his cell is still serving as an inspector with the Surrey Constabulary. Details of the allegation are included in a report delivered by Avon & Somerset police to the Director of Public Prosecutions 10 days ago.' (This article was published just over a year after the release of the Guildford Four, and it conflicts with the statement to me from the CPS that the information was received by them in April 1991.)

The article goes on to claim that two retired officers, a former detective chief superintendent and a woman detective constable had been questioned about the results of the ESDA tests on original papers in the case.

The DPP's report states the tests revealed tampering with notes of interviews with Miss Richardson and her two alibi witnesses, Lisa Astin and Frank Johnson. The Avon & Somerset investigation had disclosed a passage of the police typescript of an interview with Mr Johnson in January 1975 which does not appear in their original handwritten notes, suggesting they could not have been accurate or contemporaneous . . . two pages of an earlier interview with Mr Johnson are also said to have been inserted at another time. The changes to the interview with Miss Richardson appear innocuous in themselves . . . But according to the report, a different pen was used to record the final seven pages of her interview records. Because the change came midway through the interrogation, and corrections to the first part were made later with a second pen, the report says, the notes could not have been contemporaneous.

Two extracts from interviews with Carole Richardson appear at Flag 7 in the defence jury bundle. Did they represent the truth, or did these documents conceal more than they disclosed? Why were just three Surrey police officers selected for prosecution when it was widely known that others, perhaps less innocent than they, had a case to answer before a criminal court? The families of the seven people who died at Guildford and Woolwich have the right to know who killed their loved ones. Did the state conceal the truth at any subsequent trial rather than face up to it? Was material evidence withheld from the jury trial in 1975 and in the appeal court in 1989? For example, were there two copies of each of the detained persons registers? The police and the prosecution at the original Guildford Four trial could not possibly have known whether the defence would have called for their production in evidence before the jury that tried the Four in 1975. If the defence had done so, would they have discovered that the entries and the police evidence simply did not match? How would the police have explained that? Did they prepare other false copy documents that would have concealed the truth and produced them if called on to do so?

These unanswered questions cast a shadow over the criminal justice system that will not be lifted unless and until the entire unvarnished truth is told about the wrongful convictions of four innocent young people, two of whom (Carole Richardson and Gerard Conlon) have now died long before their time. That is never likely to happen. Too many reputations depend upon its concealment rather than its full disclosure. It was ever thus.

11 Covering up the Truth

THE BRUTAL MURDER in February 1989 of Belfast solicitor Pat Finucane was one of the worst of the Troubles. It is most unlikely that any member of the security forces who plotted his murder will ever be called to account. Such a prosecution might provide the key to establishing who, without actually pulling the trigger, snuffed out his life in such horrific circumstances, and for what purpose.

During the Standing Committee debate on the Prevention of Terrorism (Temporary Provisions) Bill, which became an Act of Parliament in 1989, Lord Hailsham's son, Douglas Hogg MP, the parliamentary under-secretary of state at the Home Office, made a statement that caused immense apprehension among those lawyers in Northern Ireland who were prepared to stand up to the state and its security apparatus to ensure fair treatment and due process for their clients in criminal cases. One such lawyer was the solicitor Patrick Finucane. His family had been forced out of Belfast by loyalists at the outset of the Troubles in 1969. He was then 20 years of age. Unlike Gerard Conlon, Paul Hill and Patrick Armstrong, he did so well at school that he won a place at Trinity College, Dublin, and qualified as a solicitor in 1979. During the last ten years of his life he proved to be a formidable, fearless advocate. He was mainly responsible for bringing a High Court action on behalf of the families that required members of the RUC to give evidence about the killing of Gervaise McKerr and other 'shoot to kill' cases outlined in Chapter 12.

Pat Finucane was shot dead in front of his wife, Geraldine (who was wounded by the gunman), and his three young children, Michael, Katherine and John, in the family home in north Belfast on 12 February 1989. The gun used was a 9mm Browning semi-automatic pistol, a standard issue firearm in the British army since 1967.

On 12 December 2012 the prime minister David Cameron told the House of Commons that following a review by Sir Desmond de Silva QC of the circumstances of Pat Finucane's murder it would be up to the police to decide whether to open fresh criminal proceedings into the case. The 829-page review disclosed, as the prime minister accepted, a 'shocking level of collusion between Special Branch agents and Loyalist paramilitaries' and state engagement in a 'relentless attempt to defeat the ends of justice'. Politicians were exonerated of being involved in a conspiracy to murder, but army officers were later found to have lied to investigators and frustrated police inquiries. Mr Cameron admitted that areas of collusion set out in the review included identifying, targeting and murdering Pat Finucane, supplying the murder weapon, facilitating its later disappearance and thereafter deliberately obstructing subsequent investigations. It can hardly get worse than that, one may think.

Was it the state that wanted Pat Finucane dead, or was it simply a band of bloodthirsty loyalists? My view has always been that the security forces in Northern Ireland, consisting mainly of RUC officers, allied with their counterparts in British military intelligence, planned the murder and then covered it up. Those responsible have not been publicly identified and called to account, and they never will be. The UK does not punish those who do its dirty work, openly or in secret.

On 24 November 1988, about seven weeks after the inquest into the deaths of three members of the IRA shot dead in Gibraltar by the SAS in March of that year, Douglas Hogg MP went to Belfast to meet senior officers of the RUC. Among them was Sir John Hermon, the chief constable, not greatly liked by those under his command when he chided them for being over-influenced by 'the three Ds' – drink, debt and dames. The suicide rate among his officers was unacceptably high: in 1996 the RUC disclosed that 55 police officers had committed suicide since 1970, 47 of them using handguns issued by the force for their personal protection.[1] For many of them, especially uniformed officers in the front line, their main objective in life seems to have been simply to avoid being murdered or seriously injured by those they considered enemies of their country. No fewer than 302 police officers met violent deaths during the Troubles. It is a very distressing number on any view.

The purpose of Douglas Hogg's visit to Belfast was to be briefed by the RUC. He was responsible at that time for shepherding the Prevention of Terrorism (Temporary Provisions) Bill through the House of Commons. This was not a novel piece of legislation. Similar terrorism-related Acts had been passed between 1973 and 1984. When the bill became law it was intended that it would apply not just to England and Wales, but also to Scotland and Northern Ireland. At the time Douglas Hogg went to Belfast there was an air of anticipation of further deadly violence. According to the book *Lost Lives* by David McKittrick *et al.*, during the previous year, 1987, 106 people met violent deaths; 16 of them were RUC officers. Of the 105 people killed during 1988, six were police officers. Clearly this killing spree could not be allowed to go on.

I consider that some members of Margaret Thatcher's government were not enamoured by the search to establish the truth at the Gibraltar inquest by Paddy McGrory, the Belfast solicitor who represented the families of the deceased. Skilful though he was, McGrory did not discover – because it was carefully concealed – that a so-called 'independent' witness, Gibraltar police officer Constable James Parody, the only witness to support the SAS claim that they had called upon Danny McCann and Mairead Farrell to surrender, might not in fact have been entirely independent. He claimed that while relaxing in his apartment on Winston Churchill Avenue he had seen and heard the confrontation between McCann and Farrell and the soldiers who shot them. What he did not disclose was that his brother Harry was an undercover police officer who was actually present at the scene at the Shell petrol station where both IRA members died. Did that not impinge, even slightly, on his 'independence' as an eyewitness? The soldiers who shot the three IRA members were, so they claimed, told that one or all of the three would be carrying a device calculated to trigger the explosion of a car bomb planted in the Convent area. Not only was there no such device in their possession, there was no bomb either.

Watching the proceedings in the public area of the Gibraltar Supreme Court building was a member of the IRA, Seamus Finucane, a brother of Pat Finucane. He had been interned without trial in 1972 and imprisoned for the unlawful possession of a gun in 1977. He heard evidence that one of the three deceased, his fiancée, Mairead Farrell, had been shot at close range. Two bullets hit her in the head. Burn marks on her clothing indicated that the firearm that killed her had been discharged first into her head and her face, and further shots were fired from only three or perhaps two feet away from her back, pulping her heart and her liver. Was Seamus Finucane's presence at that inquest made known to the politicians, including Douglas Hogg, who were in Belfast in November 1988? Was his name linked to that of his brother Pat, the solicitor practising law in Belfast?

Douglas Hogg was accompanied on his visit to Belfast by his private secretary. She made a detailed note of the discussion between the minister and the RUC officers:

> The RUC referred to the difficulties caused by the half dozen or so solicitors who are effectively in the pocket of terrorists, and who made good use of their right to insist on access to documents. This was put rather nicely, I thought, by the argument that such solicitors are defending the organisation rather than the individual.[2]

This means, and was intended to mean, that solicitors were putting the interests of the Provisional IRA above those of their clients, and defending one when they should have really been defending the other. I know of not one single case, let alone a single prosecution, against any solicitor in Northern Ireland over the 30 years of the Troubles, where such an allegation was ever publicly made, let alone proved. They have acted with the utmost propriety and courage in discharging their legal obligations to the court, their clients and their profession.

Later, on 13 January 1989, Douglas Hogg was provided with 'profiles' of Patrick Finucane and another Belfast solicitor, Oliver Kelly. It is suspected, but not proved, that these two names may have been given to Hogg at the meeting in November, although it was not until 28 November 1988 that the senior assistant chief constable asked the head of the RUC's Special Branch to prepare a note on these two solicitors' family connections with members of the Provisional IRA.

However that may be, it is clear that information about solicitors was given to Douglas Hogg, and it may be that Finucane and Kelly were actually mentioned by name. What is in dispute is whether the comments about the solicitors should have been made public. The chief constable, Sir John Hermon, was 'adamant that he had specifically asked Mr Hogg NOT to disclose that information. . . . [he] had asked the Head of Special Branch to look at the problem of solicitors in particular the fact that they may have involved themselves in terrorism. Mr Hogg was told of these concerns but I personally asked him not to tell MPs/Parliament but to keep it to himself.'

Douglas Hogg does not agree with that. He claimed, 'I was there to brief myself in connection with a Bill for which I was responsible member and going to speak in the House of Commons. The idea that I had been told this stuff and would not use it in the House of Commons is bizarre.'[3]

In his report, Sir Desmond de Silva accepted Douglas Hogg's version of events, stating, 'On the basis of the documents I have reviewed, I am satisfied that it was understood by all concerned that Mr Hogg wished to refer to the issue of solicitors in Northern Ireland during the course of the forthcoming debates in the House of Commons.'[4]

Douglas Hogg needed further information and asked for a concrete example of solicitors being in the pockets of terrorists. According to the Cory Collusion Inquiry Report by retired Canadian judge Peter Cory presented to the House of Commons on 1 April 2004, the RUC's Special Branch sent Hogg documents identifying Patrick Finucane on 6 January 1989. The documents claimed that Finucane came from a staunchly republican family, and two of his brothers (both unnamed in the report) had served terms of imprisonment for terrorism offences. The documents continued, 'Finucane has continued to support the Republican cause using his expertise in an advisory capacity and associating closely with PIRA/PSF [Provisional Sinn Féin] personnel'. An attachment to the documents set out an analysis of Pat Finucane's 'Relatives with PIRA connections'.

Those documents led Judge Cory to comment, 'Yet there is nothing in the document that indicates that Patrick Finucane was a terrorist or that he belonged to a terrorist organisation. From a review of the documents it could be inferred that RUC SB tended to identify a solicitor with his clients.'[5] If Judge Cory could reach that conclusion, which is really self-evident, why could not Douglas Hogg have done so?

In the event, on 17 January 1989, during a debate on the Prevention of Terrorism Bill, Douglas Hogg said, 'I have to state as a fact, but with great regret, that there are in Northern Ireland a number of solicitors who are unduly sympathetic to the cause of the IRA.' There was an interruption as some MPs expressed their disbelief at such a sweeping and dangerous statement. Mr Hogg would not give ground: 'I repeat that there are in the Province a number of solicitors who are unduly sympathetic to the cause of the IRA. One has to bear this in mind.'[6] He went further: 'I am advised as a Minister that those are the facts. I believe them to be true and I state them as facts on advice I have received.'

His remarks were met with an immediate response from Seamus Mallon, the deputy leader of the SDLP. He said he believed that Douglas Hogg was a patsy who had been told to say this, and that he had been fed information and conned into making a statement 'which, because of his own honesty, I believe that he will regret'.[7]

Mr Mallon told the House of Commons, though his remarks were directed to a wider constituency:

[T]his was a remarkable statement for the minister to make about members of the legal profession who have borne much of the heat in a traumatic and abnormal situation. Such words should not be said without the courage to support them. I find it appalling that the Minister should make an accusation with such emphasis, and without, it seems, the intention of substantiating it. . . . I have no doubt that there will be lawyers walking the streets or driving on the roads of the North of Ireland who have become targets for assassins' bullets as a result of the statement that has been made tonight. Following the Minister's statement, people's lives are in grave danger . . . it will be on the head of this Minister and government if the assassin's bullet decides to do, by lead, what this Minister has done by word.[8]

Pat Finucane must have been told of the content of Douglas Hogg's statement, which must have delighted many of those in the police who hated him. He took no precautions for his personal safety, no doubt believing that others would accept that he was only doing for his clients what they would have done for themselves if they had the knowledge, training and ability to defend themselves. But he must have known of the bitterness and hostility that consumed so many in the RUC, especially the Special Branch, who attacked him not because of who he was, but because of what he did. He was particularly loathed because of his legal challenges in the courts against legislation being introduced from Westminster that did not conform to international standards of due process and fair trials. The Special Branch of the RUC had him in their sights because when he sought disclosure of information about the investigation of his clients, rather than disclose it, they would abandon the prosecution and his client would walk free. But it wouldn't end there, because Finucane would perfectly properly follow up with a civil action against the RUC claiming damages for false arrest and wrongful imprisonment. In the main those actions were almost always settled by paying compensation to avoid disclosing the Special Branch's tactics.

The three cases (McKerr, McGeown and Brian Gillen) that perhaps sealed his fate were decided in November 1988. On 14 November the inquest in Craigavon began into the deaths of three members of the IRA, Sean Burns, Eugene Toman and Gervaise McKerr. They had been shot dead by the RUC in County Armagh in 1982. Patrick Finucane argued on behalf of Gervaise McKerr's family that the unsworn evidence of the police officers involved was not admissible. The coroner, James Elliott, thought otherwise. The lawyers representing the families of the other two deceased had their instructions withdrawn and withdrew from the case, but Finucane continued with his legal submissions. On 17 November the coroner adjourned the inquest indefinitely while Finucane made an application to the High Court for a ruling on the admissibility of the contested evidence. On 25 November Mr Justice Carswell ruled in the High Court in Belfast that the coroner was correct in his ruling on admitting unsworn statements from the police. Patrick Finucane immediately lodged a Notice of Appeal against that ruling.

On the very same day, Henry Maguire and Alexander Murphy were returned for trial, charged with the horrific murder of two British army corporals, Derek Wood and David Howes. They were in plain clothes and had strayed, accidentally or otherwise, into the funeral procession of Kevin Brady, who had been shot dead by a loyalist gunman, Michael Stone, in Milltown cemetery on 16 March 1988. Kevin Brady, a 30-year-old Belfast taxi driver, had been at the cemetery for the funeral of the three people shot dead by the SAS in Gibraltar on 6 March 1988 when he was killed.

A third man, Patrick McGeown, who had also been charged with the murder of the two soldiers, was set free. There was no evidence against him. That was a ruling as a matter of law. His solicitor in the case was Patrick Finucane. Patrick McGeown was a long-standing member of the Provisional IRA who had been convicted of the unlawful possession of explosives, for which he was sent to prison for 15 years. In prison, he had taken part in the blanket protest – the refusal to wear prison clothing. He had spent 42 days on hunger strike until his family authorised medical treatment for him while he was in a coma. He was released from prison in 1985. He spent several months in custody in 1988 awaiting a decision of the court on the merits of his case prior to his release. During that time his two-year-old son died of meningitis.

As he left the Crumlin Road courthouse in Belfast he was photographed walking side by side with Patrick Finucane. That photograph was given to the vicious criminals who killed the solicitor, partly for visual identification, but more probably as a justification and explanation for the planned murder of a family man in front of his wife and children. Was Finucane's murder a penalty for daring to suggest that there might be insufficient evidence against a man with a criminal record for terrorist offences?

On 29 November 1988 the European Court of Human Rights ruled that the UK had breached the European Convention on Human Rights by detaining individuals for seven days under the terrorism legislation. Can there be any doubt about the fury that ruling caused among Britain's ruling elite? There was little doubt who they would blame for it.

In fact in all these three cases Patrick Finucane was acting in a professional capacity, appearing in open court in the presence of the press and the public, making legal submissions and arguing issues of fact on behalf of clients for whom he was acting and from whom he was taking instructions. He was not the decision-maker in these cases – decisions and rulings on matters of law and questions of fact are made by the judge – he was the advocate doing his best for his client. He was bound by the rules of professional conduct in acting for his client, and argued rules and principles of criminal law and the law of evidence, to each of which the prosecution had the right of reply.

His loyalist killers, however, were encouraged by the police to brand Patrick Finucane not just as an accomplice of terrorists but a terrorist himself.

On Sunday 12 February 1989, 26 days after Douglas Hogg's scurrilous statement, two masked men burst through the unlocked front door at the Finucane family home in North Belfast and shot Patrick Finucane 14 times in the head and the body from close range. He had no chance to defend himself or his young family, who watched him die in what should have been the safety of his own home. It took 15 years to bring one of his killers to justice.

The Irish Times of 16 February 1989 had an elegant approach to Douglas Hogg's public pronouncements, which were undoubtedly linked directly to Patrick Finucane's cruel murder. Under the heading 'Words and Bullets' the newspaper said, 'murder gangs do not, as a rule, consult political oracles. But to present them with excuses or endorsements or what can be taken for either is at best an act of folly, or at worst hideous responsibility'. It is my view that Douglas Hogg's inflammatory words gave the green light to those loyalist killers, in concert with some members of the RUC and the army, who were waiting for some kind of signal from the authorities to murder a man some considered an enemy of the state. Sir Desmond de Silva wrote in his report, 'the real importance, in my view, is that a series of positive actions by employees of the State actively furthered and facilitated his murder and that, in the aftermath of the murder, there was a relentless attempt to defeat the ends of justice.'[9]

According to the BBC news broadcast on 17 April 2003, Douglas Hogg, on learning of the murder of Patrick Finucane, issued a statement saying, 'This is clearly, like so many others, a tragic and wicked killing. As to its cause, that must be a matter for the RUC. I very much hope those people responsible will be arrested, and sentenced to extremely long terms of imprisonment.' So at the same time as this patsy politician was expressing the hope that there would be arrests for a hideous murder, state employees were making relentless efforts to ensure that no one would ever be called to account for what they had done.

The same news report reveals that the senior police officer Sir John Stevens, who carried out an investigation into collusion, concluded that a branch of British army intelligence and some police officers in Northern Ireland actively helped a paramilitary group to murder Catholics in the late 1980s. He said, 'My inquiry team also investigated an allegation that senior RUC officers briefed the parliamentary under-secretary of state for the Home Department, the Rt Hon. Douglas Hogg QC, MP, that some solicitors were unduly sympathetic to the cause of the IRA. Mr Hogg's comments about solicitors' support for terrorism made on 17 January 1989 aroused controversy. To the extent that they were based on information passed by the RUC, they were not justifiable and the inquiry concludes that the Minister was compromised.'

I find this approach regrettable. Why not use plain English? Doesn't this mean that the information passed to the minister was untrue and he was misled by it?

When Sir John Stevens' conclusion was conveyed to Douglas Hogg, as it must have been, did he not consider, as any ordinary, normal human being would have done, that he should make a full and public apology to Patrick Finucane's widow and his three children, who had suffered such a dreadful tragedy? Could he not simply have said, 'I am so sorry for putting information forward in the House of Commons which I had been given and which misled me, and which in the event turned out to be untrue. I deeply regret that the publication of this untrue information led to the dreadful murder of your husband and father'? But sadly this will not happen.

Just for the record, a senior police officer investigating Patrick Finucane's murder told his inquest, 'we have no evidence to suggest that Patrick Finucane was a member of PIRA'. The presiding coroner confirmed that: 'the police refute the claim that Mr Finucane was a member of PIRA. He was just another law-abiding citizen going about his professional duties in a professional manner. He was well known both inside and outside the legal profession. He was regarded in police circles as very professional and he discharged his duties with vigour and professionalism.'[10]

In the aftermath of the most high-profile murder of the Troubles in

Northern Ireland, the truth of which I consider will never be made public, two notable events happened. At Easter 1990, Douglas Hogg was admitted to the front rank of the legal profession and was appointed a QC; a deliberate and calculated slap in the face for those lawyers whose criticism of Douglas Hogg remains undiminished to this day.

The second noteworthy event was the UN's Basic Principles on the Role of Lawyers, unanimously adopted by the Eighth UN Congress on the Prevention of Crime and the Treatment of Offenders on 7 September 1990. Those basic principles are considered a fundamental precondition to fulfilling the requirement that all persons have effective access to legal services. Principle 18 restates a long-established convention that 'lawyers shall not be identified with their clients or their clients' causes as a result of discharging their functions'. That is what happened in Northern Ireland, and it led to the death of a decent and honourable lawyer. Too many in the security forces there chose not to understand that concept, with fatal consequences for one family. It also damaged the reputation of the British political and legal system, perhaps beyond repair.

The bill that Douglas Hogg was shepherding through parliament at the time became the Prevention of Terrorism (Temporary Provisions) Act 1989, 'An Act to make provisions in place of the Prevention of Terrorism (Temporary Provisions) Act 1984; to make further provisions in relation to powers of search under, and persons convicted or scheduled offices within the meaning of, the Northern Ireland (Emergency Provisions) Act 1984; and to enable the secretary of state to prevent the establishment of new explosive factories, magazines and stores in Northern Ireland.' The Act has seven parts, 28 sections and nine schedules. I cannot find anywhere in the Act any provision that would affect the duties and obligations of solicitors in dealing with their clients in police custody or anywhere else. In fact the legislative provisions of the Northern Ireland (Emergency Provisions) Act 1987 include, in Section 14, the right of suspects to have someone informed of their detention under the terrorist provisions, and Section 15 sets out the right of the detained person to have access to legal advice and the circumstances in which that access might be delayed. Nothing like that appears in the 1989 provisions. Although the government claimed that there might be opposition to the Bill that became the 1989 Act from the Labour Party, which was allegedly going 'soft' on terrorism, I am unable to see any compelling reason why the RUC should have made the outrageous allegations against Northern Ireland solicitors in connection with this bill. I can find nothing in the Act that indicates that information was needed for briefing Douglas Hogg about the two Belfast solicitors, Patrick Finucane and Oliver Kelly, for the purpose of getting the bill through parliament. I have been told that there might have been a proposed opposition amendment to the bill seeking to permit a solicitor to have limited access to documents in certain circumstances. I cannot find any evidence of such a proposed amendment. My view is that access to documents is governed by the disclosure provisions in these cases, and where appropriate the prosecution can apply to a judge for an order not to disclose those documents in the public interest or in the interest of national security.

Did some senior officers in the RUC take advantage of the situation to make it appear that the state complied with the disposal of a difficult member of the public who happened to be a solicitor? In his Third Report Sir John Stevens said that he had uncovered enough evidence to lead him to believe that the murder of Patrick Finucane could have been prevented. He further believes that the RUC investigation into his murder should have resulted in the early arrest and detection of his killers. There was, he said, collusion involved in his murder and in the circumstances surrounding it. Evidence was withheld; and agents of the Crown were involved in the murder.[11]

On 12 December 2001 Billy Stobie, a 51-year-old loyalist paramilitary member of the UDA, and a former soldier in the British army, was shot dead outside his home on the Glencairn estate at the top of the Shankill Road in Belfast. He had another interest in his life beyond his role as a loyalist foot soldier: he had been recruited by Special Branch to act as an agent, for which, it is said, he was paid the sum of £20 a week. According to a newspaper report he had been put on trial 11 years previously on a charge of unlawful possession of a firearm. His defence was that he was being framed by his Special Branch handlers. According to the newspaper report, 'he instructed his solicitor to tell the Crown lawyer privately he would tell all he knew about the Finucane case if he was convicted. Minutes later, a policeman made a mistake in the witness box, by referring to previous convictions, and the judge declared a mistrial. In 1991 the charges were dropped and a not guilty verdict was recorded.'[12] This is a classic method, not infrequently used, of ensuring that a trial is aborted. Mentioning the accused's previous convictions in the course of a trial is forbidden, save in exceptional circumstances, and is deemed to be so prejudicial as to deprive the accused of the possibility of a fair trial.

On two separate occasions Billy Stobie had been put on trial on a charge of aiding and abetting the murder of Pat Finucane. It was claimed by the prosecution that he had provided the killers with the gun used to murder him. Both trials collapsed, as they tended to do in Northern Ireland when someone felt that the truth, a very scarce commodity there, was about to be disclosed. The reason advanced in court was that the main witness for the prosecution, a journalist to whom Stobie had allegedly confessed, was too ill to give evidence. The second trial had ended only two weeks before Billy Stobie was himself murdered. He knew the truth about the solicitor's death, but he would never be allowed to tell it. He had gone so far as to appear on Ulster Television supporting the call of the Finucane family for a public inquiry into the solicitor's death. An organisation calling itself the Red Hand Defenders claimed they had killed him because he had committed crimes against the loyalist community. That was a cover name for the UDA, which was not declared an illegal organisation until 10 August 1992. It was known that some members of the UDR, the largest infantry regiment in the British army, were members of the UDA before it became a proscribed organisation.

On 16 September 2004 one of the two masked men involved in murdering Pat Finucane pleaded guilty to his murder. He was Ken Barrett, then aged 41, a member of the West Belfast Brigade B Company of the UDA, who had for some time been a Special Branch informer. He achieved national prominence when the television journalist John Ware tape-recorded him confessing to the murder. That confession featured in the BBC *Panorama* television programme *Licence to Murder*, broadcast on 23 June 2002. After that, did the RUC have any alternative but to charge him with murder?

The other masked man, known only as 'Davy', then aged 25, had been a member of the UDA for ten years. He was arrested several times on suspicion of the murder, but never charged with it. Ken Barrett is described by the authors David Lister and Hugh Jordan as a man 'with a growing reputation as an eager assassin who would shoot just about anybody if he was given a gun and pointed in the right direction'.[13] One of the authors claims that 'Davy' confessed to him that he had murdered Finucane. He said it was quite clear that 'they didn't shoot dead a solicitor. They shot Pat Finucane, the IRA man.' That this man was a practised and accomplished killer may be established by the fact that he freely admitted the murder of three other Catholics in August 1986, May 1988 and September 1988. He has never been convicted of any of those offences.

On 13 September 2004, at Belfast Crown Court, Ken Barrett admitted the murder and 11 other charges. He was sentenced to life imprisonment by Mr Justice Weir, who recommended that he serve not less than 22 years before he could be considered for release. The judge knew, and said so, that under the Northern Ireland (Sentences) Act 1998, which came into law following the Belfast Agreement, certain prisoners may apply to the Sentence Review Commissioners for a declaration of release under the provisions of that Act. Because he was transferred to a prison in England for his own safety, it is questionable whether the provisions of the Act applied in his case. However, he did apply to the commissioners and they decided that the Act did apply to him. He was released from prison on 23 May 2006, having served less than three years in custody. He cut all ties with Northern Ireland that same day. Unlike Billy Stobie, he wanted to go on living.

This case is not closed and it never will be. Members of the Finucane family say that a number of police road blocks that had been in place along the nearby Antrim Road on the Sunday evening an hour before Patrick Finucane was murdered were quietly withdrawn, allowing the gunmen's car safe passage to the crime scene. Those road blocks were not far from the family home on Fortwilliam Drive. Who ordered their withdrawal and who ordered the terrible murder are questions that call for answers. The then Labour government promised a full judicial public inquiry into Patrick Finucane's murder if Judge Peter Cory recommended one should be held. He did so recommend. The new coalition government broke that promise and substituted the review conducted by Sir Desmond de Silva. That review was based entirely on written documents, so no witnesses were called to give evidence and be cross-examined. Sir Desmond was only allowed access to documents that the state thought he should be allowed to see. Try though he did, he failed to uncover the truth. Will anyone? Ever?

12 Unlawful Killing

MICHAEL ARGYLE WAS a pillar of the legal establishment. Educated at Westminster School and Trinity College, Cambridge, he became a barrister in 1938 and was appointed a QC at the exceptionally young age of 36. He was interested in politics, and fought two general elections as a Conservative and Unionist candidate, in 1950 and 1955, losing on both occasions. He caused an outcry when he claimed that there were 5 million illegal refugees in the UK. It could be said that his political views were several miles to the right of Ghengis Khan.

He enlisted in the armed forces at the outbreak of the Second World War, serving with the 7th Queen's Hussars with distinction in India and Italy, where he was awarded the Military Cross for bravery. He ended the war with the rank of major, a title he reassumed when his judicial career ended in July 1987 after he told a group of Nottingham law students that judges should be allowed to impose the death penalty in cases where the maximum punishment for an offence was more than 15 years. His comment attracted a severe reprimand from the Lord Chancellor, Lord Havers, and within two months he indicated he would retire in the July of the following year.

His first part-time judicial appointment was as Recorder of Northampton, and then as Recorder of Birmingham, where he attracted much publicity by threatening long sentences of imprisonment for those who vandalised and stole from public telephone boxes. There was an immediate drop in the commission of those offences in Birmingham; but there was a substantial increase in the vandalisation of phone boxes in neighbouring Coventry, so it may be that those responsible simply moved on to another city.

He was then appointed a circuit judge and then, in 1970, an additional judge, sitting at the Old Bailey. He frequently welcomed controversy, courting journalists, and warning them in advance when he was about to deliver an explosive quote.

On 22 June 1971 he presided over the *Oz* magazine obscenity trial. Three young men – two Australians, Richard Neville and former barrister Jim Anderson, and the magazine's co-editor, Felix Dennis – were charged with conspiracy to corrupt public morals and with sending indecent objects through the Royal Mail. All three were acquitted of the most serious charge but imprisoned on a lesser charge that would normally have been punished by the imposition of a financial penalty. But Judge Argyle had a custodial sentence in mind. Richard Neville was sent to prison for 15 months and recommended for deportation back to his native Australia. Jim Anderson was imprisoned for 12 months, and Felix Dennis for nine. The *New Law Journal* called the sentences 'indefensibly severe'. The three convicted men appealed against conviction and sentence.

In November 1971 the appeal court was told by counsel that the trial judge had misdirected the jury no fewer than 87 times in the course of the summing-up, which they described as 'highly prejudicial'. That court agreed and quashed the convictions because of 'serious and substantial misdirection'.

On 26 August 1994, under the heading 'Judge's terrorist comments trigger fury', the *Nottingham Evening Post* said the former Old Bailey judge Michael Argyle QC had urged that Northern Ireland security forces be allowed to come out with all guns blazing to deal with terrorists. He had written an article entitled 'Let our guns speak' and submitted it to the *Belfast Telegraph*, but they had declined to publish it. Argyle, who lived in Fiskerston in Nottinghamshire at the time, then apparently decided to publicise his views in his local paper instead and they printed some, if not all, of what he had written.

His description of himself in the article is self-explanatory: 'A Conservative and Unionist who was defending the actions of the security forces in the Province.' He wrote: 'The terrorists are the enemy' – in itself not a very profound statement – but he added:

[T]here are not many of them and they must be met, fought upon their own ground, if necessary by using their own methods, beaten and crushed. The terrorists could not long survive without the active support of their womenfolk. These women who applaud and congratulate their men and their supreme courage in murdering children, nurses, ex-servicemen, OAPs and so on are also every bit as much the enemy as their men, and must be treated as such.

What he meant was clear: shoot to kill any woman in Northern Ireland who could be regarded, presumably by him and others like him, as supporters of terrorists. So much for the rule of law in his simplistic view of life.

When Alex Atwood, at the time the SDLP councillor for West Belfast, was told of these comments he said that Argyle was 'ignorant, dangerous and reckless'. Although Atwood had never met Argyle, he seems to have summed him up very well. As a judge and a lawyer Michael Argyle should have known better – the penalty for soliciting one person to murder another is life imprisonment. The families of the innocent women brutally shot in Northern Ireland in the circumstances described by Argyle might well agree with Alex Atwood's description of him.

Máire Drumm was 57 at the time of her murder. She was the mother of five children, one of whom, Marie Teresa, then aged 20, had been sent to prison in November 1975 for the unlawful possession of a revolver. Máire Drumm held strong political views that caused her to serve prison sentences on no fewer than four occasions. She shared those views with her husband, Jimmy. She had at one time been the vice president of Provisional Sinn Féin and was a strong believer in community politics. When, at the outset of the Troubles, the British army, acting without any legal authority, imposed a curfew on a large part of the Lower Falls Road area in west Belfast from 10 p.m. on Saturday 3 July 1970 until 9 a.m. the following Monday, in order to carry out house-to-house searches, Máire Drumm marched down the Lower Falls Road at the head of a procession of hundreds of women carrying food, mostly bread, piled up in prams. The soldiers, not knowing what to do, simply looked on as the curfew was broken. It is widely accepted now that the violent and vicious conduct of some elements of the army over that first weekend in July, especially the Black Watch regiment, which brought to Northern Ireland all the violent sectarian loathing and hatred that surrounded and sustained them in their native Scotland, was a very serious error. From that weekend, the British army lost the sympathy and support of the Catholics and nationalists in Belfast and throughout Northern Ireland.

On 10 December 1974, almost three weeks after the Birmingham bombings, Máire Drumm and other republicans had taken part in a meeting in Feakle, County Clare in the Irish Republic, with eight Protestant clergymen who had put forward a plan to end the violence throughout the island of Ireland and in Britain. Máire spoke in terms of reconciliation, calling for a Council of Ulster, saying that those who lived there should provide the solution rather than waiting for others from outside to do so. She said that there was no reason why Catholics and Protestants of the

North should not work together to solve their long-standing problems. She claimed that Sinn Féin supported the policy of a federal Ireland in which the province of Ulster would be one of four self-governing provinces. She recognised that in Ulster the Protestant community would still be in the majority and their position would be protected by a central federal government. The President of Sinn Féin, Ruairí Ó Brádaigh, said that he and his party wanted to see a peace that would endure and be based on justice. However, that meeting broke up in some disarray when the Special Branch of An Garda Síochána arrived at the scene. Although the personal contacts were found to be useful, no agreement was reached about anything.

About two years later, sometime in 1976, Máire was told that she was in urgent need of medical treatment on cataracts in both her eyes and that failure to receive it would result in the loss of her sight. She sought a visa from the American government to travel to the United States to receive the required treatment there. It is said, without any hard evidence, that the British government lobbied against her being granted a visa, and in the event it was refused.

Although she was fearful of entering any hospital in Northern Ireland, but even more fearful of the consequences if she did not, and no doubt with a sense of foreboding and apprehension, she decided first to make her will. She then went into the Mater Hospital on the Crumlin Road in Belfast. Late in the evening of 28 October 1976 a British army unit that had been surrounding the hospital was discreetly withdrawn. The officer in charge of that unit was later posted to Aden, where he was reportedly killed in action. No explanation for the withdrawal of that protective army unit has ever been given.

Just before 10.30 p.m. Mrs Drumm was in a small room next to Ward 38 on the second floor of the hospital when two men wearing white laboratory coats and armed with a revolver entered the building. They knew exactly where to find their victim. It is now known that a member of the UVF who had served in the British army worked as a security officer in the Mater Hospital. Did he tell the killers where they would find their defenceless victim? It is likely that Máire Drumm never saw her killers; one of them shot her three times in the chest from point-blank range. Efforts to save her were in vain. She died almost immediately in the hospital's operating theatre.

According to the journalist David McKittrick, one of those involved in the killing was a man who was detained in 1983, tried, and then ordered to be detained at the secretary of state's pleasure when a finding of guilt was recorded against him. He was only 16 years old at the time of the murder. The court was told that he had been initially chosen to carry out the murder himself but a change of plan meant that he handed over the weapons and then disposed of them afterwards.[1]

There was not a hint of condemnation of the conduct of those cold-blooded killers anywhere in the British press. One newspaper, the *Daily Mirror*, headlined its account with the words 'Hate Granny Shot Dead', and went on to describe her murderers as 'an execution squad'. Were they carrying out the orders of the state?

Was this the kind of conduct the former judge Michael Argyle had in mind when he wrote 'let our guns speak' in the *Nottingham Evening Post*? When Máire Drumm was buried in Belfast, the *Sun* published a picture of her two weeping daughters, with the caption, 'The bitter harvest of hate that was sown by Máire Drumm is reaped by her two grieving daughters'. There cannot be too many occasions when the victim of a horrific murder is blamed for the grief of her surviving family.

Another woman shot dead in equally horrific circumstances was Miriam Daly, a lecturer in social and economic history at Queen's University Belfast. Considering the discriminatory policy of that university, exercised over many years and costing the British taxpayer many thousands of pounds in compensation when those discriminated against won damages at various tribunal hearings, it is a tribute to her immense talent that she was employed there at all: not only was she a Catholic and a republican, she was also a woman.

Miriam was born in 1939 in County Kildare in the Republic of Ireland. She met her first husband when they were both lecturers at University College Dublin. He died unexpectedly at a very young age and some years later she married again. Her second husband, James Daly, was English, with family connections in Ireland. He also worked at Queen's. They were frequently photographed together at rallies calling for the restoration of political status for those detained in the H-blocks at the Maze prison. On one occasion they received a bullet through the post, and they had a number of anonymous phone calls threatening them with violence, even death.

In 1980 the UDA, which had been formed in Belfast 1971 to co-ordinate a violent campaign against the nationalist population in that city and elsewhere in the province of Ulster, drew up a list of targets for sectarian assassination. Those on the list were considered to be advocates and supporters of the political campaign surrounding prisoners detained in the Maze prison's H-blocks. Miriam Daly was high on that list, as was Bernadette

Devlin McAliskey. It is believed that the senior loyalist in the UDA, John McMichael, ordered that Miriam Daly, a member of the National H-Block Committee, should be 'taken out' where she least suspected she would be harmed – her own home. Daly had argued that the abolition of Special Category Status for prisoners in 1976 was the British government's way of criminalising those who regarded themselves not as criminals but as freedom fighters. She was also under suspicion in some quarters as having at least known of the plans to murder the Conservative politician Airey Neave on 30 March 1979. There was no evidence of that. Neave, a close confidant of Margaret Thatcher, and her shadow secretary of state for Northern Ireland, died when a bomb exploded in his car as he drove out of the car park at the Palace of Westminster in London.

It was not admitted, but not forcibly denied either by his acquaintances, that John McMichael had contacts in the UDR and the RUC, contacts who would be useful in planning a sectarian murder. He is thought to have provided essential information for those planning and carrying out summary execution of the innocent. (John McMichael eventually proved, to some, that he knew too much, perhaps because he was colluding with the RUC and the army, and his murder was arranged by his loyalist accomplices, who provided cover for members of the Provisional IRA to construct, place and detonate the car bomb that killed him outside his own home.)

Miriam Daly lived in a predominately Catholic area of west Belfast, and on the day of her death she was alone at home; her husband James was in Dublin and could easily be followed and warnings given as he returned home.

On the afternoon of 26 June 1980 Mrs Daly received word that the security forces were engaged in a sweep though the nationalist area of Andersonstown in west Belfast, where the family lived. Was that a planned operation to ensure cover for the murder? Since her husband was away from home all that day, and because of the political tension at the time on account of the increasing efforts of the National H-Block Committee to obtain political status for prisoners in Long Kesh and elsewhere in Northern Ireland, Miriam decided to return home to be there when her children (Donal and Marie, then only ten years of age) returned from school. She was known to be alive at about 2 p.m. when she called at a shop to buy a loaf of bread. Just after three o'clock Marie came home to find her mother lying face down in the hallway. There was blood everywhere. Miriam's hands and feet had been tied, probably to a chair. A pillow had been used to deaden the sounds of the six shots fired into her face and head at point blank range. The gun used was a 9mm semi-automatic pistol, the standard-issue small firearm used by the British army. The telephone line had been manipulated so that it could take incoming calls, but it was not possible to make an outgoing call, so if Miriam had wanted, or even been able, to seek help, she could not have done so. No one ringing the house would have known that anything was wrong.

Rumours that British intelligence was involved in these two assassinations refuse to go away. The killers were able to enter, and then leave, a predominately Catholic and nationalist area where even the most brazen loyalist killers would hesitate to go, unless assured of safe passage to and away from the victim.

It must take a special kind of deep pathological hatred to kill a defenceless woman in the circumstances in which Máire Drumm and Miriam Daly died. In both cases the killers arrived at, and departed from, the death scene where only a short time previously the security forces had been present in some numbers, yet they apparently saw no one or heard nothing in connection with either murder.

The third violent loyalist attack against a woman was directed at Bernadette Devlin McAliskey. She was born in Cookstown, County Tyrone into a staunchly Catholic family. Her father, a carpenter, was branded a political suspect and was unable to get work. She was one of the new generation of people in Northern Ireland who received a university education at Queen's University in Belfast as a result of the Education Act 1944. She was a high-profile political figure in the civil rights movement, inspired by Martin Luther King, which sought parity of esteem and equality of treatment at the hands of the state.

In 1969, at the age of 21, she was elected to the House of Commons as the Independent Unity MP for Mid Ulster. Her political philosophy did not endear her to her parliamentary enemies, of whom there were many, and not always to her friends, of whom there were few. She remained in the House until her defeat in the general election in February 1974.

On the morning of Friday 16 January 1981 she was at her home in Derryloughan near Coalisland in County Tyrone, getting her three young children ready for school, when three men broke down the back door with a sledgehammer. They were armed with a .38 revolver and a 9mm semi-automatic pistol. One man shot her husband, Michael, four times as he tried to bar their progress in the kitchen. Another went to the bedroom, where Bernadette was dressing the children. She moved the three children to the far wall of the bedroom and faced her attacker without flinching. He fired eight shots at her at point blank range, not stopping until the magazine was empty. The three children, in a state of shock, were screaming and crying as they witnessed the savage attack on their mother only feet from where they were crouching, covering their ears against the noise of the gunfire.

All three men, Andrew Watson, aged 25, Thomas Graham (38) and Raymond Smallwood (31), ran from the house towards a waiting car. They never reached it; they ran straight into the arms of four members of the SAS who were waiting for them outside. On seeing the soldiers the three men threw down their weapons and lay on the ground. Not a shot was fired during the arrests. It later emerged that the four soldiers had been dug into a hide in a copse near the house. An explanation later advanced was that they were there to find out who was vising the McAliskey home. Does it really take four heavily armed members of the SAS to carry out such a simple act of surveillance? The soldiers left the scene quickly with their captives. They claimed their radios were inoperative and as the telephone wires at the house had been cut, they were unable to summon help for the grievously wounded couple. In the event, soldiers from the locally based Argyll and Sutherland Highlanders arrived shortly afterwards. They summoned medical help that saved the lives of Michael and Bernadette McAliskey.

In her book *Biting the Bullet*, Jenny Simpson describes her husband, an SAS soldier, being ordered from Belfast to County Tyrone the night before the attempted murders to cover Bernadette Devlin McAliskey 'because the police had been given a tip off that Loyalist paramilitaries might be planning to make a move on her'. That may account for the presence of the soldiers at the time, but it does not explain why they did not detain the three gunmen before they entered the house, rather than when they were leaving it. Not a single shot was fired by any of the soldiers at the three men, two of whom were carrying guns, as they were scooped up into military custody. In almost every case, in dealing with the nationalist people of Northern Ireland, the SAS opened fire first and asked questions afterwards. The four soldiers held their fire in this instance. Was it because they knew in advance the political persuasion of those they were about to capture?

The journalist Liz Curtis gives an interesting insight into the media treatment of the shooting of Michael and Bernadette. She notes in her book *Ireland: The Propaganda War* that the 'British papers showed relatively little concern about who the attackers were, and were more interested in Bernadette McAliskey's character and in portraying the British troops who arrived at the scene in a heroic light. The *Daily Mirror* wrote, "just a few hours before her condition worsened, fiery Republican Bernadette had vowed to fight on. She said as she lay in her hospital bed: "I am not dead yet and I will never give up the struggle. I have been expecting this for a long time. I knew that I and my family have been at risk. Now they think they have got me.'"' Ms Curtis records, 'the entire quote was a fantasy. Bernadette McAliskey was in fact unable to speak for some two weeks after the incident.'[2]

Andrew Watson, one of the men involved in this attempted double killing, was a former member of the UDR. When he left the UDR is not known, but it was often the practice for someone in his position to leave immediately before he was apprehended for a terrorist crime, to enable the authorities to claim that he was a former soldier, rather than a serving one. He was sentenced to life imprisonment. Raymond Smallwood, the driver of the car that took the would-be killers to the scene, was jailed for 20 years. Following his release from prison after serving half his sentence, he was shot on 11 July 1994 by the Provisional IRA in front of his wife at their home in Lisburn. He died in the ambulance on the way to hospital. The third member of the loyalist death squad was Thomas Graham. He was sent to prison for 15 years. All three men gave a clenched fist salute as they were led from the dock in the courtroom. The UDA commander John McMichael was in court to see his comrades in arms sentenced.

According to Bernadette, who was also present in court with her husband to see the loyalist gang being sentenced, the presiding judge Mr Justice MacDermott said during his homily on sentence that he understood why the attempt had been made on her life. This was offensive in the extreme. How is it possible to understand the gunning down of a defenceless woman in front of her children? This comment was outrageous and it would have been better for the reputation of the judiciary in Northern Ireland, where public confidence in the criminal justice system among the nationalist community was almost non-existent, if that view had never been expressed. But it also called into question the competence, fairness and impartiality of the judge himself.

It would be idle to suggest that the nationalist community in Northern Ireland gave their wholehearted support to the criminal justice system, which was regarded as neither even-handed nor fair. The reviews of the system conducted by Lord Diplock, Gerald Gardiner QC and Sir George Baker started from the basic proposition that the entire judiciary were impartial and trustworthy. It would be interesting to know what these three public servants thought of the homily of the Lord Chief Justice Lord Lowry on sentencing a number of men connected to the RUC in June 1980. The Chief Justice seemed to show a degree of sympathy and understanding somewhat similar to that expressed by Mr Justice MacDermott.

On 6 June 1976, Michael McGrath, aged 56, was enjoying a quiet drink in the Rock Bar in Keady, County Armagh, a predominately Catholic area. He did not know it but four rogue police officers were cruising the area in an official police car intent on violent conduct. They were using the police and army frequency on the car radio to avoid any police or army patrols.

On arriving at the Rock at about 10.40 p.m., one of the officers left the police vehicle and placed a 10lb gelignite bomb against the door of the public house. To make the 17 people inside the Rock think that they were safer inside than outside the building, RUC Reserve Constable William McCaughey fired gunshots through the windows. The purpose was obviously to cause maximum casualties inside the bar when the bomb exploded. The device itself failed to explode, although the detonator ignited.

Michael McGrath was leaving the bar at the very time the police car arrived. He was shot twice in the stomach by RUC Reserve Constable Laurence McClure. Some of the police officers fired at him as he lay wounded on the ground. He was taken to hospital for treatment. The police investigated this terrorist outrage but made no progress until they arrested William McCaughey for abducting a Catholic priest in 1978. He and Laurence McClure, who was arrested shortly afterwards, implicated two other serving police officers, Ian Mitchell and David Wilson.

Michael McGrath was told of the arrest of the four officers and was given a number of dates on which to attend court. The dates were changed. He was told he would be contacted. He was not. He learned the outcome of the case on the radio.

McCaughey, McClure and Mitchell were charged with attempting to murder Michael McGrath, wounding him with intent to do so, attempting to murder the 17 occupants inside the Rock Bar, and possession of firearms and explosive substances with intent to endanger life. McCaughey pleaded guilty to wounding Michael McGrath and was sentenced to seven years' imprisonment. McClure was sentenced to two years' imprisonment for causing an explosion, possession of an explosive substance with intent, and possessing firearms and ammunition with intent. That sentence was suspended for three years, which meant that he left court on the day of the sentence and would only be back in court if convicted of another criminal offence carrying a term of imprisonment. Some might consider his act of terrorism just as evil as those carried out by men not wearing the uniform of the Crown. Mitchell and Wilson (who admitted withholding information) also received suspended terms of imprisonment for their crimes. Mitchell's offence was that he knew of the intended attack on the Rock Bar and did nothing to prevent it. For reasons never explained, the DPP gave no legal or factual grounds for his refusal to proceed on the outstanding charges that the men denied. Was the reason that if there had been a full trial in open court the truth might not have been welcome to those fighting a dirty war in Northern Ireland?

As for Lord Lowry, his homily on sentence included the following sentiments addressed not only to the men in the dock but to all other members of the security forces, especially those in the RUC:

> It does not seem realistic to believe that after they have endured – some with their career in ruins, others with their careers in jeopardy – that they require much by way of deterrent or by way of reform, and no proper sentence which I pass will make an impression on terrorists while other members of the police force are no doubt already embarrassed, sufficiently embarrassed and shocked by what has happened in these cases and been seen to happen to their colleagues . . . I must remember that whatever sentence is just it would follow that it would be imposed on a different and lower scale from that appropriate to terrorists, no matter whichever side, whose aim is to achieve their political ends by violence and to attack the very fabric of society.

This quotation is extracted from the case of *Michael McGrath v. The United Kingdom*, European Court of Human Rights, Application no. 34651/04, so it cannot be impeached in any way.

The case arose because Michael McGrath alleged that there had been no adequate investigation into allegations of collusion and/or involvement by security forces in his being seriously injured. His claim was upheld and he was awarded damages.

This court hearing did immense damage to the reputation not only of the RUC but also of the criminal justice system: the most senior judge in Northern Ireland seemed to accept that these officers had acted out of a sense of frustration, when in fact what these rogue officers were seeking was revenge and retribution. Was he applying a double standard in implying that uniformed security force gunmen and bombers had some justification for their shooting and bombing, whereas other gunmen and bombers who sought the overthrow of a sectarian state had no just cause and no justification for doing so and therefore attracted condign punishment? Was Lord Lowry accepting that the RUC officers were taking the law into their own hands and turned to terrorist-like tactics because of the inaction of the criminal justice system?

Lord Lowry did a great disservice to the law when he indicated that the convicted officers should face lesser punishment than other offenders who committed the same type of crime because their motives were more worthy. Was he right when he said, 'it is a matter of admiration that the RUC had resisted the temptation to resort to violence when friends, colleagues and neighbours had been killed'? Is that not the very same argument put by young men in nationalist areas who saw their families, friends and neighbours gunned down without pity and without punishment, when they considered joining the Provisional IRA? Did the judge not appreciate that when those who take an oath to uphold the law, and are trusted by society to do so, betray that trust, undermining public confidence in the police, that calls for greater, not lesser, punishment?

What Lord Lowry probably did not know at the time is the fact that the gun used to shoot Michael McGrath was the same weapon used to murder the three Reavey brothers in County Armagh in January 1976. (See Chapter 11.) That provides a link between these accused officers and the notorious Glenanne gang, thought to be responsible for some 58 murders in that area during the 1970s. No member of that gang was ever called to account for those crimes. Some if not all had a licence to kill, provided by the state that ensured their protection and their silence.

On 27 January 1999, the Rev. Ian Paisley, who spent almost his entire life posing as a Christian while preaching the politics of hate, added insult to injury to the still-grieving Reavey family. In a statement covered by parliamentary privilege, meaning that he was protected against any claim for defamation, Paisley told the House of Commons, 'it is interesting to note that a police dossier carefully prepared on the Kingsmill massacre has recently come to light. It shows that the police did thorough work, had definite evidence and could, if they had been encouraged, have got men into courts; but that did not happen . . . According to the dossier, Eugene Reavey, a well known republican, set up the Kingsmill massacre.' He went on to name another group of individuals who, he said, carried out that horrendous crime (see below).[3] Paisley made no suggestion about who had failed to encourage the RUC to get the men before the criminal court. Nor did he explain how this was allowed to happen.

In fact, the former chief constable of the RUC, Ronnie Flanagan, denied that such a file ever even existed. Who was lying – the police officer or the preacher? In the event, Paisley put the life of Eugene Reavey and the others named in mortal danger, so much so that they required police protection. Eugene's mother Sadie Reavey asked Paisley on several occasions to withdraw that false accusation and to meet her to apologise for the immense grief he had caused her and her family. Paisley ignored her pleas. Mrs Reavey died on 28 July 2013 at 92 years of age.

The British government of whatever colour, red or blue, was unable to deal effectively with Paisley, described in a 'Secret' document dated 8 April 1981 and disclosed by the Public Record Office of Northern Ireland, as:

> A thorn in our flesh . . . his gift is to foment and focus negative emotions and views, he is a destructive critic, unable to create even a party which is more than a vehicle for himself. And if he were to try to be constructive, he would most probably not be able to maintain his political position. In sum, were Paisley to disappear overnight, a major obstacle to reconciliation and progress would have vanished with him . . . to allow Paisley to make trouble until we judge his antics too destructive to be let continue . . . we may find that this point is never reached. But if Paisley were to stir up another major new strike, for example, or foment paramilitary activity, it would be difficult for HMG [Her Majesty's Government] not to be seen to take action against him.[4]

I regard this as proof positive that it was widely known and accepted in government circles, even at the highest level, that Paisley had the power to influence policy by the threat of using loyalist paramilitaries to maintain his loudly stated position of 'No Surrender'. It took many years of wasted lives of those who served prison sentences following and supporting Paisley's brand of constitutional refusal before it was apparent that the only word of any relevance in Paisley's vocabulary was 'No!'

In 1988, Lord Lowry, who was so understanding of the criminal conduct of frustrated police officers, was appointed a Lord of Appeal in Ordinary in the highest criminal and civil court in the United Kingdom. The politician responsible for his appointment was Margaret Thatcher. Clearly Lord Lowry was, in her famous phrase, 'one of us'.

Other offences were alleged against Laurence McClure, one of the officers involved in the attack on Michael McGrath. The DPP came in for more severe criticism for his failure to give any reasons for dropping charges against McClure for his involvement in the attack on Donnelly's Bar in

Silverbridge, County Armagh on 19 December 1975. On that date a car drew up outside the bar and shots were fired and a bomb thrown into the premises. Three people in the bar died and many more were injured. One of the dead was Michael Donnelly, aged 14, the son of the owner of the bar. There had been allegations of collusion between the security forces and loyalist paramilitaries operating in that area. It was alleged that McClure was the driver of the car involved. Does not the public have the right to know why the case against Laurence McClure was not proceeded with, and in whose interest it was that on this occasion he walked out of court without any further punishment being imposed upon him? Did someone fear the truth?

The office of the DPP found itself under public scrutiny again when it failed to give reasons why there was no prosecution against members of the RUC who were alleged to have killed Nora McCabe on 9 July 1981. She died after being hit in the head by a plastic bullet fired at her from an RUC vehicle. That shot was unjustified and unlawful.

On that date the atmosphere throughout Northern Ireland was highly charged, and there were fears for the complete breakdown of law and order. For some time past the Provisional IRA and its political wing Sinn Féin had used the idea of a hunger strike by prisoners to effect political change. The tradition of the hunger strike has been very long in the history of Ireland, involving as it does a vocation to self-denial and sacrifice. No fewer than 22 republican prisoners have died on hunger strike since 1917, perhaps the best known being Terence MacSwiney, Lord Mayor of Cork, who died on 25 October 1920 after 75 days without food whilst detained in Brixton prison.

Those members of the Provisional IRA involved in the armed struggle did not regard themselves as common criminals. Others took the opposite view. From June 1972 convicted paramilitaries had been given special privileges. This special-category status ended for those convicted after 1 March 1976, whatever their crime. In order to seek a return to special-category status as political prisoners the Provisionals decided to make five demands of the state to achieve that objective. Those demands were as follows:

1. The right not to wear prison uniform.

2. The right not to do prison work.

3. The right to free association and access to education.

4. One visit, one letter, one parcel per week.

5. Full restoration of remission of sentence lost through the present protest.

The Provisionals said that a failure or refusal to accede to those demands would result in prisoners going on hunger strike.

The first hunger strike in the H-Blocks began on 27 October 1980. A month later the Northern Ireland secretary Humphrey Atkins mentioned in the House of Commons the statement of Cardinal Hume, the Cardinal Archbishop of Westminster, who had condemned the hunger strike. The cardinal said that it was a form of violence against one's own body that could not be condoned as being in accordance with God's will. He stressed, however, that this was his personal view. Atkins clearly wanted the cardinal's view to be followed by all Catholics in Northern Ireland. It wasn't.

After the second hunger strike began on 1 March 1981 Cardinal Hume went to Northern Ireland and on his return issued a statement that the hunger strikers were committing suicide. My understanding is that he repeated that view when he met some of the family members of those on hunger strike who asked him to intervene with Thatcher and urge her to settle the conflict. My further understanding is that the cardinal's theological position was that if a person embarks on a course of conduct which he foresees will result in a prohibited consequence, he will be deemed to have intended to bring that consequence about.

When the Primate of All Ireland and leader of Irish Catholics, Cardinal Tomás Ó Fiaich, said, after the death of hunger striker Raymond McCreesh (whose brother is a Catholic priest), that he would never have been in prison but for the abnormal political situation in Northern Ireland, and posed the question, 'Who is to pronounce him a murderer or a suicide?', he received a reply from Sir Peter Rawlinson QC, a former attorney general in the Tory government of Edward Heath. Sir Peter, who had long cherished ambitions of being appointed the first Catholic Lord Chancellor since Thomas More, said that he was ashamed and distressed by Cardinal Ó Fiaich's statement. The prisoners had killed themselves, he said; it was suicide, and that was, as Sir Peter understood it, a mortal sin. (Sir Peter never did achieve his political ambition because Thatcher disliked him immensely and he could expect no promotion to the bench while she was prime minister.

On 10 May 1981, during the course of an interview with RTÉ, the widely admired bishop of Derry, Dr Edward Daly, said that he would not describe Bobby Sands' death as suicide. Bishop Daly could not accept that. He did not think Bobby Sands intended to bring about his own death. I agree with the bishop on both legal and moral grounds. As a matter of law, if a person embarks on a course of conduct intending to bring about a prohibited consequence, he has deliberately and intentionally brought that consequence about. Where Cardinal Hume and Sir Peter Rawlinson went wrong was to confuse foresight of a consequence with intention.

If I am standing on the bank of a fast-flowing river, and I see a distressed young person placing a newborn baby into the water, I will realise that the child will almost certainly drown unless someone attempts to save her. I can swim, but not very well. I foresee that if I go into the river it is possible, perhaps even probable, that I will drown in an attempt to save the baby's life. Even so, I could not in all conscience stand by and do nothing. So I go into the river. My aim, my object, my purpose in going into the water is to save the child, not to bring about my own death. I might foresee the consequence that I would lose in my life in doing so, but I do not intend to bring that consequence about. In the same way, the hunger strikers wanted to achieve their five demands. They foresaw that going on hunger strike to achieve that purpose might possibly, even probably, result in their own deaths. That was not their aim, object or primary purpose. To die was the last thing they wanted; it certainly was not their main objective.

I hesitate to disagree with Cardinal Hume, whom I regard as one of the great Christian leaders of the twentieth century, and I give thanks and pay tribute to him for his immense support, both morally and intellectually, for those wrongly convicted of the Birmingham and Guildford pub bombings. I share his distaste for those in the criminal justice system who whisper in the shadows that they were all guilty as charged. I regret the propaganda circulated by the Northern Ireland Office that he tried to prevent the appointment of Tomás Ó Fiaich as a cardinal in 1979. That was totally untrue. I consider the falsehood damaged Cardinal Hume's reputation, for no apparent reason and without just cause. But on this point I consider that the cardinal's view, and that of Sir Peter Rawlinson QC, that the hunger strikers were committing suicide was entirely wrong.

Ever since the death of Bobby Sands, the first republican hunger striker of the Troubles, on 5 May 1981, there had been an upsurge in the threat of civil disorder and violence that the Westminster politicians were determined to resist. The response of the police as deaths followed in quick succession was the use of plastic bullets as a means of crowd control. Literally thousands were fired on the streets of Northern Ireland during that month. There were bound to be casualties. Among them was Julie Livingstone, aged 14, hit in the head by a plastic bullet near her home in west Belfast. That round was fired from an army personnel carrier. She was walking past a peaceful anti-H-block demonstration when she was hit. The army claimed there was a riot going on; local people said there was not. A second hunger striker, Francis Hughes, had died on 12 May and some women and children were banging dustbin lids on the road in the Lenadoon area of west Belfast in a protest against his death. Julie died the next day. An inquest jury found that she was an innocent bystander who had not been rioting.

On 21 May two hunger strikers, Raymond McCreesh and Patsy O'Hara, died. The following day 11-year-old Carol Anne Kelly died after having being hit by a plastic bullet three days earlier. She had been walking home from a shop carrying a carton of milk. Local people said there was no rioting until after Carol was hit. The army, one of whose soldiers fired the plastic bullet, claimed otherwise. It is a matter of record that on the day she was fatally injured, five soldiers of the Royal Green Jackets were blown up and killed in a massive car bomb explosion in south Armagh. Was the death of this child an act of revenge against an unseen enemy, and was it a case of anyone would do, provided they were Irish?

After the death of the fifth hunger striker, there was another killing. Nora McCabe, aged 33, a married woman with three children aged from three months to seven years, was hit in the head by a plastic bullet, causing fatal injuries. Her family have always claimed that she was murdered.

On the morning of 8 July 1981, Nora McCabe left her Belfast home in Linden Street, which is adjacent to Clonard Street. It was about 7.45. She intended to go to a shop on the Falls Road, a comparatively short walk from where she was living. There was much noise and apprehension in the air because a prisoner, Joe McDonnell, after 61 days without food, had died on hunger strike at about five o'clock that morning. A woman called Joan Mooney was walking nearby. She claimed she saw an RUC Land Rover turn into Linden Street and stop only about ten feet away from Mrs McCabe. There was a bang as a plastic bullet was fired from the Land Rover. Mrs McCabe was hit on the head and collapsed in the street. She was taken to the Royal Victoria Hospital, but surgeons were unable to save her life. She died the following day. At the inquest into her death in November 1982, five RUC officers gave sworn evidence that there were two petrol bombers and a number of youths rioting in the area before an order was given to fire one plastic bullet. The officer who actually discharged that round apparently did not appear at the inquest to give evidence. The senior officer who was present and had given the order to fire said no baton round was fired into Linden Street or at its junction with the Falls Road. That was where Nora McCabe was found dying.

At first blush this seemed like the usual conflict of versions of the same incident: local eyewitnesses claiming one version, the army and the RUC another. But the situation was entirely different because of the worldwide interest in the lives and deaths of those on hunger strike. The solicitor acting for the McCabe family at the time, Pat Finucane, discovered that a Canadian television crew had filmed the local area and the fatal incident. That information might not have been welcomed with open arms by the RUC officers who had been in the Land Rover. A senior RUC officer went to Canada to interview the film crew and watch their film. He told the resumed inquest in November 1983 that the first of two Land Rovers had reached the junction of Linden Street and had fired one plastic bullet. He conceded that there was no evidence that any petrol bombs had been thrown. In its verdict the jury described Mrs McCabe as an entirely innocent party.

The state dealt with the case thereafter in its usual practised and accomplished fashion. It totally denied liability for Nora McCabe's death, while accepting at the same time that she died of injuries consistent with having been hit by a plastic bullet. It offered damages by way of compensation to her family for her untimely death. It was a condition of the offer of payment, however, that the family sign a 'gagging order' that prevented them from speaking to the media or publicly about the terms of the settlement. The department of the DPP, even after seeing the Canadian film, decided there was insufficient evidence to prosecute anyone for the unlawful killing of Nora McCabe. Her family challenged that decision in the High Court in Belfast.

At the hearing before three judges in January 2009, counsel for the family, Barry MacDonald QC, told the Court that there could be a prima facie case of police officers plotting to pervert the course of justice. The claim, relied on by the DPP, that there was rioting and general disorder in the area was not supported by the Canadian film. Counsel played the film to the court, saying, 'this film discredits completely the accounts made under oath by the five police officers and the account given by Witness A.' Witness A was the officer who did not appear at the inquest, but had fired the fatal baton round. There was no sight of the 'petrol bombers' anywhere on the film. Counsel claimed that when the officer did what he did, he intended to kill or cause Nora McCabe serious injury, something which the DPP said could not be proved by the existing evidence.

In dismissing the application, the presiding judge said that based on all the evidence available in 1983 the decision not to prosecute was open to the DPP and that decision could not be condemned as irrational. However, the learned judge did point out that there was no evidence that the DPP had ever considered bringing a prosecution against the police officers for perjury or perverting the course of justice at a time when they should have been aware of the conflict between the evidence of the police officers and the facts established by the Canadian film. I regard this as a serious failing on the part of the prosecuting authority. Why, in the light of that film, was there not a realistic prospect of conviction of the police officers for giving false evidence at the inquest and making up their witness statements preparatory to it? And why was it not in the public interest to bring that prosecution at the time the film became available?

The judge concluded the case by expressing the sympathy of the court for Mr McCabe's 'sense of powerlessness and frustration that no one had been made amenable for his wife's death'. No one ever will. The police officer who ordered the firing of the baton round is now dead. So is the officer who fired it. They knew the truth. Did they tell it?

13 The Killings Go On

B<small>ETWEEN</small> 1969 <small>AND</small> 1991, 21 members of the security forces were prosecuted for killings using firearms while on duty in Northern Ireland. Nineteen were found not guilty. One was convicted of manslaughter and given a suspended prison sentence. Just one – a soldier – was convicted of murder. Although given a life sentence, he was released after serving two years and three months of his sentence and reinstated in the army.[1]

It is often said that the death of a child is every parent's worst nightmare. But that is a scenario that no fewer than 141 families from the Catholic/nationalist/republican community in Northern Ireland had to endure during the Troubles. For them, there is no respite from their grief, most especially if they have been denied truth and justice at the hands of the state.

In the early hours of Wednesday 28 February 1973, Corporal Francis William Foxford, a soldier in the Hampshire Regiment, shot and killed a 12-year-old schoolboy, Kevin Heatley. Kevin, his parents and five brothers and sisters lived on the Derrybeg estate in Newry, County Down. He attended St Joseph's secondary school, where he was immensely popular. He was four feet ten inches in height.

The prosecution case against Corporal Foxford was that he was the leader of a nine-man patrol that entered the Derrybeg housing estate in Newry at about midnight on 28 February. He detached himself from his patrol, walked some 15 yards along a footpath, stopped, raised his rifle to hip or waist level, and fired a single shot along the road. The shot hit Keven Heatley, who was innocently standing on the same footpath about 130 yards away from him. The bullet entered the upper part of the centre of Kevin's forehead, causing fatal brain damage. The calculation of distances, and the height of the deceased child, were given in evidence and appear in the law report of the case.[2]

The corporal's defence was simple. He claimed he lawfully fired his rifle at Kevin Heatley in self-defence and in defence of members of his patrol because the 12-year-old schoolboy was armed with a handgun, from which he had immediately before discharged a low-velocity shot at the accused and his fellow soldiers. No handgun or low-velocity weapon was found by the army on the body of the deceased, or at the scene, which was searched shortly after the shooting. I can find no information about the street lighting in the area, and it was, of course, dark. For a 12-year-old boy to fire a handgun from an open, rather than concealed, position at a soldier who was further than the length of a football pitch away from him was a very ambitious undertaking. If that happened.

Within five days of the shooting the MOD in London had sufficient information to answer in written form a question put down in the House of Commons by Ken Maginnis MP, who asked 'the Minister of State for Defence if he will give details of the shooting of Mr. Kevin Heatley at the Derrybeg Estate, Newry, County Down, on Wednesday 28 February 1973'.

The minister, Peter Blaker MP, replied:

At about 11.20 p.m. on 27 February a routine army patrol in the Derrybeg Estate, Newry, was attacked by a group of people throwing bricks, bottles and other missiles. A man was arrested and the patrol withdrew to allow the situation to calm; but when it returned at about 11.50p.m. the crowd had grown and was more hostile than before.

As the patrol was leaving the area again, the soldier bringing up the rear saw a male person of short stature appear round a corner, and adopt a standing position with his right hand outstretched at waist level. The soldier clearly saw a muzzle flash in the person's hand and he heard a pistol shot, accompanied by the sound of a bullet passing near him.

The soldier returned one shot and he saw the person fall but, because of the crowd, the patrol was unable to see what happened to him after that. Reinforcements were called and they cordoned off and then searched the area, but nothing was found. The troops had completely left the area by 02.00 a.m. 28 February. As allegations had already been made that the soldier who had returned fire had been under the influence of alcohol at the time, he was medically examined on returning to base but no evidence was found to support the allegation.

I understand that at 12.41 a.m. 28 February Kevin Heatley, aged 13 [*sic*], was admitted to hospital in Newry with single gunshot wound to the forehead. He was later certified dead. I have received no specific evidence to show how or by whom he was conveyed to hospital.

It may be worthy of note that there was no expression of sympathy from the Tory minister for the bereaved parents.

That information about the sequence of events, was clearly based on the evidence provided by the soldier who shot and killed the boy. The hospital to which he was taken, by local people in a van, was Daisy Hill Hospital in Newry.

At the trial the prosecution called nine witnesses, some of whom the trial judge regarded as being reliable and impressive. The accused gave evidence in his own defence. He relied on his good character as a ground why his evidence should be believed, and on the description of him by his commanding officer that he was a good and competent soldier. Both are important points for the defence in a criminal trial. He maintained on oath that he was fired at, and returned fire. He heard the bullet from a low-velocity weapon pass close to the left of his head. He said the person who fired the shot was small, and that as well as hearing the noise of the discharge he saw the muzzle flash of the weapon, which seemed to be about the middle of the firer's body. He then, from a standing position, fired an aimed shot from his shoulder at the firer, the effect of which he could not see.

Three military witnesses then gave evidence. Soldier D said he heard a low-velocity shot from directly behind him and he heard Corporal Foxford return fire. Private L also heard a low-velocity shot and then he heard a high-velocity shot. Private Morgan, the radio operator with the group, said he had no doubt that two shots were fired and the first in time was a pistol shot followed by an SLR shot. It appears that none of these soldiers saw the person, some 130 yards away, who, according to Corporal Foxford, fired the handgun.

The trial judge, the former attorney general, Mr Justice Basil Kelly, sitting without a jury in the newly created Diplock courts, convicted Corporal Foxford of manslaughter on the basis of gross negligence. The judge said he found his evidence 'unreliable and unacceptable in very many matters . . . I felt generally that the evidence he gave was fundamentally untrue on the crucial issues and I feel that those soldiers who supported his evidence to the extent that they did, did so from motives of loyalty and sympathy.'[3]

The corporal had committed an unlawful and dangerous act when he discharged his rifle without taking proper aim into a street where members of the public might be, and in this case actually were. This was a case of negligence of the grossest kind. The judge said, 'I can find no evidence to support the allegation of the accused that Kevin Heatley had a gun and fired a shot at the accused and his patrol and I am quite satisfied that this was not the case. Nor do I accept that the accused believed at any time the deceased had a gun or had fired a gun. I think it is was extremely doubtful if he even saw Kevin Heatley at all.'

That being so, a murder charge would not have been appropriate, for there was no intention on the part of the accused to kill the boy. In his homily on sentence, the judge said, 'it was a momentary lapse in your normally high standard of discipline and restraint'. The sentence of the court was that the accused was sent to prison for three years. That would be within the lower range of sentences imposed at that time for manslaughter by gross negligence. The judge did find as a fact that Corporal Foxford had had a small quantity of beer, but he was at all times sober and alcohol played no part in his actions on that night.

That was on 15 March 1974. Corporal Foxford was immediately transferred to England to serve his sentence, no doubt on the grounds of his own safety. Within a week he was granted bail pending appeal. That in itself was a highly unusual procedure; the appeal court had said time and time again that only in the most extreme and unusual circumstances should bail be granted pending an appeal, because the judiciary were reluctant, in the event of the appeal being rejected, to send an accused back to prison after he had been released from custody on bail.

In fact, a note attached to a letter dated 2 April 1974, written by Adrian Carter, the private secretary in the Northern Ireland Office, to the prime minister, Harold Wilson, says that members of the security forces accused of scheduled offences would be tried in the non-jury Diplock court in Belfast. However, any such person convicted in that court was specifically excluded from the restrictions on the admission to bail of those charged with, or convicted of, such offences. Unlike any other private individual, therefore, members of the security forces were in a privileged position because they fell within the common law rules when applying for bail and it was within the discretion of a judge of that court whether to grant bail or not. In practice they always did. The reasoning was simple. In the House of Commons it was decided that 'it was undesirable to confine members of HM Forces in custody with members of the very terrorist organisations they were expected to combat'. The Northern Ireland judiciary simply adopted that approach. In fact, no member of the armed forces released on bail in this way had absconded.

In a covering note to the prime minister, Lord Tom Bridges stated that the Foxford case had attracted a certain amount of public attention, and it had been reported that 'The feelings in Ulster amongst the Catholic population that release on bail in these circumstances would not have been permitted to one of them . . . but . . . This very question was debated at some length in Committee Stage during the passage of the Act [the Emergency Provisions Act] and the release on bail thus corresponds with the vote of the British Parliament.' That was the very point on which Harold Wilson had sought to be informed, for it had been suggested to him that there was some resentment among the Catholic population of Northern Ireland on the grounds that a Catholic civilian accused of a similar crime would not be released pending an appeal. Two points arise from this. First, the civil service in London, as well as the politicians, were in 1974 talking of the 'Catholic' population rather than the nationalist people of Northern Ireland; and second, parliament had always intended that different procedural rules should apply in criminal cases to the security forces than to everyone else.

As he was entitled to do, Corporal Foxford appealed to the Court of Criminal Appeal on 28 May 1974 against his conviction and sentence. Lord Chief Justice Lord Lowry presided over the court. Lord Justice Curran and Lord Justice Jones sat with him. Leading counsel for Corporal Foxford, John Creaney QC, one of the most experienced and formidable members of the Northern Ireland Bar, ran the appeal on the basis of prosecution errors in the conduct of the case, and wrong decisions flowing from that on the part of the trial judge. The defence claimed that the trial judge permitted Crown counsel to conduct the trial in a manner which was irregular, oppressive and unfair. At the beginning of the case, prosecuting counsel had told the trial judge that he intended to call as prosecution witnesses Soldier D and Soldier L, indicating that they would say they heard the low-velocity shot before Corporal Foxford fired his rifle. Why he decided to do that is incomprehensible in the light of what followed, but having said he would, he then changed his mind, without telling the defence team that he was doing so. He simply closed the case for the prosecution and sat down without calling those two witnesses. As a matter of law at that time, the prosecution must have in court the witnesses whose names were on the back of the indictment (the written form of accusation setting out the charge the accused faces). The names of the two soldiers were on the back of the indictment. However, the prosecution could decide whether to call them and, if they called them, whether to examine them or merely tender them for cross-examination by the defence. Where the witness's evidence is capable of belief it is the duty of the prosecution to call him, even if the evidence he is going to give is inconsistent with the case sought to be proved. The discretion of the prosecution must be exercised in a manner calculated to further the interests of justice and at the same time to be fair to the defence. If the prosecution appear to be exercising their discretion improperly it is open to the judge to interfere and in his discretion to invite the prosecution to call the witness.[4]

In the event, the two soldiers went into the witness box after Mr Justice Kelly directed the prosecution to call them and tender them for cross-examination by the defence. The judge had the power to call the witnesses himself, but did not do so. The prosecution called each witness into the witness box, identified them and left it to defence counsel to adduce their evidence. Then the prosecution purported to re-examine their witnesses, but in reality cross-examined them for the sole purpose of showing that their evidence was suspect and unreliable. This cannot properly be done in the re-examination of a witness. Moreover, was this really a case of the prosecution cross-examining their own witness? This is not permitted: a party cannot cross-examine their own witness except in circumstances where the witness proves to be hostile, and even then the leave of the court is required before this can be done. All this could have been avoided if the trial judge had called the witnesses himself, and then left it to both sides to cross-examine the witnesses he had called.

Worse was to follow. When Corporal Foxford gave evidence, the prosecution produced a statement about the incident that he had made at 4.40 a.m. on 28 February, shortly after the patrol returned to their base. The prosecution had not adduced that statement in evidence. It was not admissible. The purpose of doing this was presumably to compare and contrast the content of that statement with his evidence on oath before the trial judge.

In the course of the appeal hearing Lord Lowry referred to the RUC Force Order in operation between September 1970 and September 1973, under which if an offence against the ordinary criminal law was alleged against military personnel in Northern Ireland, the interviewing of military witnesses and the alleged offender himself was conducted exclusively by military personnel. Lord Lowry said that this practice had been discontinued, 'but we deprecate this curtailment of the functions of the police and hope that the practice will not be revived'. His hope was in vain; the practice did continue from time to time. Should he not have made it clear that such practice and procedure must never be revived and that it was the responsibility of the police and not the army to investigate crime, no matter who was the alleged offender? In the end, however, because the person who took that statement did not identify himself as the recorder of it and therefore he could not be found and called as a witness, that meant it was not admissible in evidence in chief as part of the prosecution case. The defence complained that the statement had not been previously produced, had not been properly proved or shown to the accused or his legal team at any time prior to Foxford giving evidence. On all those points the defence were correct.

However, there remains this question. Did the defence not know of the written answer in the House of Commons that was clearly based on the statement made by Corporal Foxford? The army had possession of this statement until they handed it over to the prosecution, and that seems to have been some time after the case had commenced. Why was that? Why was it not properly disclosed well in advance of the trial? Is it seriously suggested that at the same time as they handed it over to the prosecution the army failed to tell Corporal Foxford and his legal team that they had done so? He knew what was in that statement, because he made it. Did he not tell his legal team that he had done so? Did they ask him whether he had done so? Where the prosecution went wrong, in my view, was the failure to tell the defence that they had the statement in their possession, that they intended to use it, and to set out arguments addressed to the trial judge why they should be allowed to use it in the way they did.

It may be worthy of note that the civilian defence witnesses in the case made their witness statements not to the RUC but to a private individual who was not a police officer. Lord Lowry called that 'an unorthodox procedure'. He did not inquire into the reason. Perhaps he knew it already. The people of Newry simply did not trust officers of the RUC and avoided any contact with them, even in a case like this. In fact, when the relevant eyewitnesses gave their statements they made them not to the police, but to Paddy O'Hanlon, whom Lord Lowry referred to, in what I regard as a disparaging way, as 'a certain Mr O'Hanlon'. In fact he was the independent nationalist MP for South Armagh, a founder member of the SDLP, and later a barrister in both Northern Ireland and in the Irish Republic.

Not only were the RUC not trusted, but the Hampshire Regiment were particularly hated in that part of Northern Ireland. There had been rioting on the estate on that Tuesday evening before the fatal shooting, but when the nine-man patrol returned there local residents claimed they had been drinking, were noisy and abusive, sounding loud whistle blasts as they went through the housing estate looking for trouble. Anyone who considers that a 12-year-old boy should be at home in bed while that was going on clearly has no insight into the effect of this behaviour, if it happened, on all the residents of that housing estate.

Corporal Foxford's appeal against conviction and sentence was allowed and he was set free. He clearly did not have a fair trial. The trial judge and the prosecution made a number of wrong decisions that went to the heart of the case and that might have resulted in the wrongful conviction of an innocent man.

But for the people of Newry in particular, and the nationalist people of Northern Ireland in general, the legal system in which they had little or no faith or confidence had failed again, and the brutal killing of a young schoolboy had gone unpunished. They had no faith either in the impartiality of Lord Lowry, a former officer with the Royal Irish Fusiliers. The Provisional IRA tried on three occasions to assassinate him. In 1982 a gunman barely missed shooting him at Queen's University Belfast when he was there to give a lecture at the law school. The lecture went ahead. Whatever other criticisms may be directed against Lord Lowry, there can be no doubt, in my view, that in this case the reasoning, logic and application of legal principles by Lord Lowry were entirely right in law.

In this case, as in many others, no reference was made to the fact that in the week before Kevin's death, three young soldiers of the Coldstream Guards, Robert Pearson, Malcolm Shaw and Michael Doyle, had been shot dead by the Provisional IRA in Belfast. Did the deaths of those soldiers affect in any way the behaviour of the nine-man patrol in the Derrybeg housing estate on that fateful night?

Around lunchtime on that same Wednesday, 28 February, a sniper shot and killed a 20-year-old soldier, Lance Corporal Alan Kennington of the Light Infantry, in the Ardoyne area of north Belfast. He had just left a shop where he had bought some chocolate. The girls working in the shop later remarked how polite and friendly the soldier had been as he made his purchase. He could not have known that would be the last thing he ever did. The Provisional IRA issued a statement saying that the shooting was in retaliation for the killing of Kevin Heatley. Would it have been any source of consolation for Kevin's parents as they made preparations for his funeral to know that across the Irish Sea two other parents in a small village in Somerset were also making arrangements to bury their own young son? Does the grief of one family exceed that of another in such heartbreaking cases? Can anyone seriously think that the murder of Alan Kennington advanced the political cause of the Provisional IRA to bring about the reunification of the island of Ireland?

The pain was not over yet. In November 1974 Desmond Heatley, Kevin's father, drowned himself in the Newry Canal. He had never recovered from the trauma of the sudden and tragic death of his own little boy.

On 30 October 2012 the Historical Enquires Team announced in the media that they intended to investigate Kevin Heatley's killing. The result of such an inquiry is given to the family, not to the press; so how it progressed and what, if any, conclusion it came to has not been made known.

Still the killing of soldiers and children went on. On Tuesday 3 August 1976, 20-year-old Private Alan Watkins of the Hampshire Regiment was shot dead in the street while on patrol in the town of Dungiven in County Derry. He was hit by a shotgun bullet fired from point-blank range.

The Killing of Majella O'Hare

Eleven days later, on Saturday 14 August 1976, a 12-year-old child was shot twice in the back by a soldier from the Parachute Regiment in the grounds of St Malachy's church in Ballymoyer, Whitecross, near Newry. She was on her way to visit the church with a group of children, seven girls and two boys. The youngest child was three years old, the eldest 16. About 150 yards away, a local man, James O'Hare, was cutting the grass in the schoolyard, where he was the school caretaker. The children were walking in his direction and he could see them clearly. There were three groups of soldiers around the church and its grounds. One group was armed with a general-purpose machine gun that was protecting a vehicle checkpoint on the nearby road. James O'Hare saw the children walk past one of the groups and he recognised his daughter, Majella, among them. She was holding the three-year-old girl's hand.

Suddenly a gun was fired. The children started to scream. One of the children fell, mortally wounded. James O'Hare ran towards the group of children intending to give whatever help he could to the injured child. He described what happened next in a witness statement he made to the late Fr Denis Faul on 26 August 1976. He heard a bang, then:

I saw a child fall. Immediately I ran towards the children, about 150 yards. When I got to the point it was my own little girl. She was lying on her left side with her head against the brow of the hill. On my way up I noticed the child try to get up on two occasions. On the second time she went down with a bang. I went down on my hunkers and held her up in my arms and the blood pouring from her left side. The other children were hysterical . . . shortly after a paratrooper approached and said 'what the fucking hell are you doing here?' 'I said I was the girl's father and the next word he said was 'close your fucking mouth'.

Another child, aged 13, gave a slightly different and perhaps more comprehensive eyewitness account of what she saw: 'At this time Majella's father was upholding her in his arms and he was saying things to her, and one of the soldiers who was applying a field dressing said "shut up". Jim said "she is my daughter" and the soldier replied "I don't give two fucks who she is, take your fucking hands off her."'

A short distance away, near the churchyard, was a nurse, Alice Campbell. That Saturday, 14 August 1976, should have been her wedding day. Her fiancé, Brian Reavey, aged 22, had been murdered in his home in Whitecross, South Armagh on 4 January, together with his two brothers, John, aged 24, and Anthony Reavey, who was only 17 years of age. Before Anthony died he was able to describe how two gunmen, both dressed in khaki and wearing black masks, walked into the house and opened fire with a submachine gun. The killers were believed to be members of the UVF. No one has ever been convicted of those killings.

Some ten minutes after the attack on the Reaveys, another group of murderers descended on the home of the O'Dowd family in their home some 15 miles away at Ballyduggan, near Gilford, County Armagh. There were 12 children in that family, eight sons and four daughters. By some good fortune, their mother, Sadie, had taken some of the children to visit her sister, leaving her husband, Barney, her two sons, Barry, aged 24, and Declan (19), with their uncle Joseph in the house. Three masked gunmen, dressed in combat jackets, burst into the house and shot Joseph, Barry and Declan dead. Barney was gravely injured but survived the attack. The family are related to John O'Dowd, a minister in the Northern Ireland Assembly.

The pitiless killings did not end there. Jimmy Reavey, the father of two dead sons, soon to be joined in death by the third, appealed that there be no retaliation for the murder of his sons. That appeal fell on deaf ears. The very next night, Monday 5 January 1976, the Provisional IRA murdered ten men as they returned in a minibus from their place of work in a textile mill at Glenanne. Their bus was stopped by a group of armed men wearing combat jackets. Each man was taken from the bus and asked his religion. Only one, Richard Hughes, was a Catholic. The gunmen told Hughes to move away and run down the road. His fellow workers, thinking he had been selected for assassination, tried to protect him. The gunmen then opened fire, killing the ten Protestant workmen. An eleventh, Alan Black, was shot 18 times but survived. When the police arrived they described it as 'a scene of indescribable carnage'. A group calling itself the South Armagh Republican Action Force claimed responsibility for these ten murders, known as the Kingsmill massacre.

There was no proper and effective police investigation into the six murders of the members of the Reavey and O'Dowd families. In the Northern Ireland Assembly on 30 June 2010, the SDLP assembly member Dominic Bradley said during an adjournment debate:

> [A] group comprising loyalist paramilitaries who acted in collusion with members of the police force, the RUC Reserve and the UDR known as the Glenanne gang, was responsible for at least 18 gun and bomb attacks, in which 58 people were murdered. That group had its headquarters at the farm owned and run by James Mitchell [at one time an RUC Reservist], who is now deceased. It was situated just outside the village of Glenanne, around two miles from where the Reavey family lived. One of the gang's members, former RUC sergeant John Weir, confessed to his part in the gang's activities and exposed the gang's members . . . The gang was responsible for the murder of the Reavey brothers, the O'Dowds, and many others.

These were allegations of the most serious kind. They deserved full investigation, but was there any investigation at all? In spite of this incriminating first-hand evidence, not one person identified by their accomplice John Weir was ever put on trial for any criminal offence. The reason is not hard to find. The Glenanne gang was being run by British intelligence, whose capacity to suppress the truth is unlimited. John Weir was sent to prison for life for murder. He did not stay silent, but he was seldom listened to.

It has long been my view that the Glenanne gang, particularly one member, Robin Jackson (now deceased), murdered, among others, Sergeant Joseph Campbell outside Cushendall police station on 25 February 1977. Sergeant Campbell, who was 49 at the time of his death, was married with eight young children. He was murdered because it was feared he was about to expose the activities of some rogue RUC officers who were carrying out robberies in his area and who were directly or indirectly involved in importing firearms by sea from Scotland into the Red Bay area near Cushendall. Campbell was lured into a trap at the police station by the second of two phone calls made to his home. A gunman was waiting for him as he locked the police station gates. He was hit in the head with one shot from a high-velocity weapon. That was a planned, deliberate and well-executed murder by a trained marksman who knew exactly what he was doing.

Initially, and no doubt to the surprise of many outside of Northern Ireland, RUC officers displayed little interest in tracing the murderer of their colleague. The rotten and corrupt system in Belfast that had protected the murderer of Patricia Curran in 1952 was alive and well 25 years later in the Glens of Antrim, protecting those who considered they were striving, by any means available, to save their country from 'Rome Rule'.

An RUC detective sergeant, Charles McCormack, was later charged with Sergeant Campbell's murder, but he was acquitted after a trial in April 1982. The prosecution evidence came from that officer's double agent Anthony O'Doherty, a former member of the IRA whose cover name was Agent 294, following an attempt on his life. He apparently believed his allies in the RUC had been responsible for his attempted murder, so to save himself, he went to the authorities in Belfast and told all. At trial, Agent 294 was an unsatisfactory witness, but that did not mean he was not telling the truth. However, such witnesses are easy to discredit by an expert cross-examiner, and he was.

Rosemary Campbell and her children, especially her son Joseph Jr, continued to seek the truth. In 2009 the Police Ombudsman of Northern Ireland began an inquiry into the murder. On 4 March 2009 Charles McCormack, then 72 years of age, was again arrested on suspicion of murdering Sergeant Campbell. There must have been new evidence found to provide reasonable grounds for arrest. This was permitted after the abolition of the double jeopardy rule by the Criminal Justice Act 2003. That rule, which has its origins in the Fifth Amendment of the US Constitution, prevents a second prosecution of a defendant for an offence of which he or she has been previously acquitted or convicted. Part 10 of the Act enables the DPP to consent to an application by a prosecutor to the Court of Appeal to quash an acquittal of a qualifying offence and order a retrial. (A qualifying offence is one that carries a maximum sentence of life imprisonment. There are 30 such offences, including, of course, murder, under the Act.) The DPP must be satisfied that there is new and compelling evidence against the acquitted person in relation to the qualifying offence, that it is in the public interest for the application to proceed and that any retrial would not be inconsistent with the UK's and Northern Ireland's obligations under Articles 31 and 34 of the Treaty on European Union. The Court of Appeal has the power to quash the acquittal and order a retrial only if the court is satisfied that there is new and compelling evidence against the acquitted person in relation to the qualifying offence, and that it is in the interests of justice to make the order.

In the event the DPP decided there was insufficient new and compelling evidence that would justify him asking the Court of Appeal to set aside the acquittal and order a new trial. Charles McCormack's reaction to that information is not known. What is known is that he died in July 2014 at his home near Ballymena in County Antrim.

Returning to the events in south Armagh, it is self-evident that unless strenuous efforts are made by the police in linking pieces of relevant evidence obtained at an early stage of an investigation, there is little chance of proving guilt beyond reasonable doubt.

Cathal Boylan, the Sinn Féin Member for Newry and South Armagh, during the same adjournment debate in the Northern Ireland Assembly, made the startling claim that the gun used in an attack on the Rock Bar in Keady, County Armagh, on 25 June 1978 was the same weapon used to kill the three Reavey brothers. That tied those involved in the Rock Bar attack in with three horrific murders. Rather than search for the truth, the police concealed it, not wanting to know the answer to a very compelling question: did the person who fired the gun on one occasion also fire it on the other?

Nurse Alice Campbell, aged 22, was placing flowers on Brian Reavey's grave near the church when the firing started. She realised that Majella had been hit. She wanted to go to the little girl's aid, but a soldier would not let her. Eventually, after about five minutes, he relented and went with her to where Majella was lying on the ground. That soldier was shouting for bandages and began to help Alice. In her statement made to Fr Denis Faul on 26 August 1976, she related, 'The child was lying on the road. Someone had taken the father to the side. The child was lying on her back. A wound was visible on her abdomen – an exit wound. I tried to deal with this. She was semi-conscious and groaning. I was tilting her chin with my hand to give her more air, and she pushed my hand away and muttered "don't do that". The soldier who was assisting me kept saying, "this is your fucking Provos for you".'

The parish priest from Whitecross, Fr Peter Hughes, arrived at

St Malachy's church a few minutes before noon that day. He drove to where the soldier, Alice and the little girl were. The first thing the soldier said to the priest was, 'isn't this a terrible thing, to see a little girl shot by an Armalite rifle?' The attempt at covering up the truth was beginning there and then.

A military helicopter arrived. James O'Hare was in such a state of grief and shock he was unable to walk to it. Someone carried him over to the stationary craft and placed him inside. Alice Campbell described how 'the girl was put in head first with her legs dangling out, the wrong thing to do as it cut off her air supply . . . there was very little room for me . . . With the help of the father I tried to get her head up. I thumped the soldier on the back and told him to bring the child's legs in and he did so. He said "it'll only take five minutes. We have a doctor standing by". I started to give her the kiss of life in the helicopter and I told the father to start saying the Act of Contrition.'

James O'Hare was in the helicopter beside his dying daughter. His recollection was, 'Majella had her hand in her long hair on her left side, and I could see her moving her hand which I thought she was trying to ease herself. She was hurting. Eventually she took it up to my chest near my right shoulder, and she says, "Daddy, Daddy" in a very faint voice . . . and to me she just died . . . I said to Nurse Campbell, "she's dead". Nurse Campbell said "no" and gave her the kiss of life about one minute before we landed at the hospital.' It was the same hospital where Kevin Heatley had died from gunshot wounds in February 1973.

Majella's mother, Mary O'Hare, was told her daughter had been shot and taken to Daisy Hill Hospital in Newry. She rushed to the casualty department of the hospital and was taken to a side room. There Alice Campbell told her they were doing all they could for Majella. Then Mary saw Fr Hughes. He was weeping, openly and unashamedly. Mary knew then that all was lost. 'I asked him if she was dead, and he said yes.'

Majella was pronounced dead at 12.10 p.m. No less than four minutes later the army press office in Lisburn issued a statement saying that a gunman had opened fire at an army patrol and a 12-year-old girl had been hit. The statement went on, 'at 11.15 a.m. two or three shots from an automatic weapon had been fired at a foot patrol who had not returned fire, and a young girl had been injured.' That statement was short and to the point. It was also untrue.

After that initial statement the army's explanation changed quite substantially. They said they had returned fire; then came a variation – fire *may* have been returned. The next explanation on that Saturday appeared after 2 p.m. Now the army believed that the soldiers *had* returned fire, and a child was caught in the crossfire. It was a neat piece of footwork so far: originally the soldiers had been fired on, they had not returned fire; then they may have done; then they actually did fire, but it was not admitted that the returned fire had hit the child. By 3.30 p.m. the army press office said that it was certain that the army had returned fire, but had failed to hit the gunman. Majella O'Hare had died in the crossfire. Was this a partial admission that a soldier may have shot Majella? It was not denied that this may have happened.

The next day, after the post-mortem on Majella's body, the RUC issued a statement 'confirming that the fatal bullets probably came from an army weapon. Reports that the army came under fire is still under investigation.' In the event, no other bullets or cartridge cases were found in the area where the little girl was fatally wounded. Surely that proves there was no other gunman at the crime scene.

On 22 August 1976 the *Sunday Times* journalist David Blundy wrote, 'there are still serious doubts about the army's claim that the patrol was fired on by a gunman. Eyewitness reports do not confirm this claim, and, unofficially, police investigating the case refer to the army's phantom gunman.'

In April 1977, Private Michael Williams appeared before Lord Justice Maurice Gibson charged with the unlawful killing of Majella O'Hare. He pleaded not guilty. He had initially been charged with murder, but when he appeared in court the charge against him, which he denied, was now one of manslaughter.

In his evidence Williams claimed that he had aimed at a gunman in a hedge. He was covering other soldiers mounting a checkpoint when he heard a 'crack'. He said he did not see the children in front of him when he fired his weapon. He was adamant that he had seen the gunman in the hedge. He said there was no way his gun could have discharged accidentally. 'I cocked the weapon and fired it,' he admitted.

Williams was acquitted. The judge chose to believe his evidence about seeing the gunman, whom few, if any, others saw, and ruled that an honestly held belief, even if mistaken, that he was firing at a gunman would amount in law to a defence to the charge. No one on the nationalist side in Northern Ireland was in the least surprised at the verdict.

As part of its review of past cases the HET examined the evidence in this case. They found no evidence to suggest there had ever been a gunman. Some may find this surprising because there has been criticism in the past that the team adopted a different approach to killings by the security forces than it did in other cases. They called on the army to apologise for killing Majella O'Hare.

However, on 9 February 2012 the secretary of state for Northern Ireland, Owen Patterson, met Majella's brother, Michael and her two sisters, Marie and Margarita, in London and handed to them a letter of apology written by the defence secretary, Liam Fox. Mary O'Hare, now aged 88 years, was not well enough at that time to travel to London but on 28 March 2011 she did meet Mr Patterson in Hillsborough Castle in Belfast.

The letter said:

> I apologise for Majella's death and offer you my heartfelt sympathy. Although many years have passed I have no doubt that your grief and that of your family has not diminished . . . both the initial investigation by the RUC and the more recent review have concluded that it was unlikely that there was a gunman in the area when the soldier opened fire and struck Majella, as he claimed. The soldier's actions resulted in the loss of a young and innocent life, causing sorrow and anguish for those who knew and loved Majella. On behalf of the government, I am profoundly sorry that this tragic incident should have happened.

Mary O'Hare had long sought that apology from the army and the government. Now she has it. When Private Williams was leaving court after his acquittal she had approached him and asked him, 'Why did you do it?' Other than shrugging his shoulders, he made no reply.

Michael O'Hare has spoken of his wish to speak to Michael Williams to see whether there is a genuine regret for what happened. I undersand that the HET tried to talk to Williams but got no further than his lawyers. 'They said that he was contrite about what happened, but he would never be able to give evidence in the state he was now in.' His defence, that he saw the gunman but did not see the children before he fired, convinced Lord Justice Gibson of his innocence. Would others have been so easily convinced?

An inquest into Majella's death was opened in October 1977. Neither Williams nor any of the other soldiers present at the killing scene attended to give oral evidence to the coroner. In a written statement presented to the court, Williams again claimed that he had fired at a man in a hedge. An open verdict was returned.

Subsequent to that the Northern Ireland Office paid the sum of £1,500 to Majella's family. In Northern Ireland the payment of compensation is regarded as an admission of liability and wrongdoing on the part of the state. Majella had been the youngest daughter in a family of four children. James O'Hare died on 5 December 1992. He had never really recovered from the death of his youngest child.

The Law and the Military: A Special Case?

Researchers from the Pat Finucane Centre have discovered a number of documents in the National Archives showing that senior army officers were allowed personally to lobby the attorney general not to prosecute soldiers and to seek preferential treatment in other ways.

Included in the confidential documents is a diary of a meeting attended by J.M. Parkin, the head of the C2 Division at the British army headquarters in Northern Ireland, outlining the suggestion that the courts should be allowed to take evidence from 'sensitive' witnesses on commission. That means taking evidence on oath from a witness whose attendance at court can for good reason be dispensed with. This procedure conceals the identity of the witness, something the military and the police would find very appealing.

As an alternative (clearly to avoid the risk of conviction if soldiers were to be prosecuted in a criminal court), it was suggested that new legislation should be brought in so that prosecutions against soldiers, including private prosecutions brought by individuals and not by the state, would be heard not by a criminal court but before a tribunal, which could hear cases quickly and informally. The members of the tribunal would be permitted to take evidence in camera (i.e. in the absence of the press and the public) and the parties would not be allowed to cross-examine the other's witnesses. This might have suited the army very well, but it was hardly in accordance with the rules of due process and the principle of equality before the law.

The memorandum then recorded events on Wednesday 1 December 1971 when there was a meeting with the attorney general, Basil Kelly QC, MP, a member of the Stormont government. That memorandum, dated 6 December 1971, states that the head of the C2 Division at the British army headquarters in Northern Ireland, J.M. Parkin, recorded after a meeting with the attorney general in Belfast:

> I have no doubt that the attorney general is doing all in his power
> to protect the security forces against criminal proceedings in respect

of actions on duty. He must however preserve an impartial approach and is worried about the possibility of private criminal proceedings should he fail to act in cases where inactivity could hardly be justified. Given his delicate position this is understandable. I am however satisfied that there is no need to remind him of the danger to morale inherent in prosecutions of soldiers or police.

This is astonishing but not surprising. Is it really the role of the first law officer to the Crown to protect soldiers and police officers from the consequences of their conduct? Is it not the responsibility of the legal process to apply the presumption of innocence until proved guilty, and to ensure they receive a fair trial? Was it the case that the attorney general decided to prosecute in cases where he feared that if he did not a private citizen might bring a prosecution because the evidence was sufficient to justify the test, namely there were grounds for believing that there was a realistic prospect of conviction? What lies beyond and behind the words 'danger to morale'? Is it an implied threat that the security forces might become dangerous if their members were prosecuted?

Events move on to 17 January 1974. By this date direct rule from London had been imposed on Northern Ireland. The post of attorney general of Northern Ireland had been abolished. (Basil Kelly had been the last holder of that office.) Sir Peter Rawlinson QC was the attorney general in Edward Heath's Conservative and Unionist government. He had a meeting with Lieutenant General Sir Frank King of the British army headquarters in Lisburn, County Antrim and the director of army legal services on 8 January 1974. In a letter dated 17 January to General Sir Cecil Blacker at the MOD in London, King said, 'the attorney general assured me that he himself carefully reviews every serious allegation against a soldier and that the final decision whether to prosecute in such cases is made by him only after close and anxious consideration of all the evidence and the requirements the public interest.' Some may find this strange because the post of DPP for Northern Ireland had been in place since 1972 and it was thought, certainly by me, that it was the DPP who made the decision to prosecute in these cases, though he might consult the attorney general in exceptional or difficult cases if he wished to do so.

The letter continues: 'He assured me in the plainest terms that not only he himself but also the DPP and senior members of his staff, having been army officers themselves, having seen active service and knowing at first hand about the difficulties and dangers faced by soldiers, were by no means unsympathetic or lacking in understanding in their approach to soldier prosecutions in Northern Ireland.' I pose this question: When, as may have happened, criminal trials take place in front of judges sitting alone without a jury, would a judge who had served in the military have exactly that same type and level of sympathy for the soldier in the dock? Would justice be impartial, objective and fair in those situations?

The next sentence is sinister: 'Rather the reverse, since directions not to prosecute had been given in more than a few cases where the evidence, to say the least, has been borderline. The case of the shooting of Joseph McCann, a well known IRA leader, in April 1972 was cited as an example.' McCann had been shot dead in the Markets area of Belfast by a soldier from the Parachute Regiment. He was unarmed at the time of his death. At his inquest a soldier gave evidence that he expected Mr McCann to be carrying a weapon (a variation on the theme of 'I thought he had a gun that he was going to fire at me'). It would be of interest to know who at the meeting described this as a 'borderline' case. Was it Sir Peter Rawlinson QC?

Paragraph three of the letter reads: 'The attorney general indicated that the figures showed that less than ten per cent of all cases submitted to the DPP, dealing with shooting incidents involving soldiers and with allegations of assaults by soldiers, resulted in prosecutions. No soldier was ever prosecuted in this type of case, he said, unless there was evidence of brutality or callousness on the part of that soldier or evidence that the soldier had clearly, unjustifiably and substantially overstepped the mark in the use of force.' The figure of nine out of ten cases referred being refused prosecution speaks for itself. Does it appear that the question of guilt or innocence was being decided not by a court, but by someone else, who was neither impartial nor fair?

In paragraph six of the letter Lieutenant General King wrote: 'In addition the attorney general has now undertaken to invite my views on the public interest aspects of the prosecution of a soldier arising out of an operational shooting incident before any final decision in the case is reached.' I regard this as compromising the independence of the attorney general, who left himself open to arguments from a biased and partial source, when he should not have done. The status and identity of the accused should not be taken into account when deciding whether to prosecute.

In constitutional theory prosecutors are required to act at all times in accordance with high ethical standards and in the best interests of justice. That does not include the interests of the government of the day, or the army or the police, not even the interests of the victims. Factors to be considered by prosecutors that might be described as public interest factors include: how serious is the offence; what is the suspect's culpability; what was the harm caused; was the suspect under 17 years of age at the time of the offence; is a prosecution a proportionate response; and are there sources of information that require protection? In weighing up all or any of these factors, why would the attorney general require, or benefit from, the view of the head of the British army in Northern Ireland in deciding to prosecute a serving member of that army? The decision to bring a prosecution is his alone and cannot be shared with anyone else.

The matter did not rest there. The army made its position clear in a letter dated 3 April 1974 from Sir Frank King to the new attorney general in the Harold Wilson Labour government, Samuel Silkin QC. Sir Frank continued to press his view that a court-martial trial for soldiers was a more appropriate forum than the ordinary court procedure. He may not have spelled it out, but if he got his way that would allow the army to choose the judge advocate, the military members of the panel to whom he was legal adviser, as well as the officer from the army legal services who would conduct the prosecution. All very cosy.

What is most significant, however, is his statement:

> I believe I am right in saying that when you left us I was in no doubt about the extent of my problem and my deep concern about the way in which the situation is likely to deteriorate unless action is taken. My apprehension is that if a series of prosecutions of soldiers in the civil courts arising out of operational incidents, were to result in several soldiers being convicted and sent to prison, the effect on operational efficiency and morale of the army in Northern Ireland would be extremely serious. It would not be overstating the position to say that the whole method of operations of the army in the Province would need careful reappraisal. The public interest considerations in such event are clear.

If this is not a threat it is difficult to know what is. Does it not mean, and is it not intended to mean, that if there were to be more prosecutions and convictions of soldiers, resulting in a prison sentence, the army would have to re-examine its role in Northern Ireland? This is an outrage. Has there ever been an occasion in the past when senior army officers have considered it was their responsibility to decide what role, if any, the army should take in carrying out its military duties and obligations in another country outside the UK? Is it not the responsibility of the army to accept and act upon the orders and directions of the democratically elected government in power? Surely it was not within the province of the army to decide where and how they should operate in the field?

14   Killing Without Question?

THERE HAS BEEN much discussion whether, in the course of the Troubles in Northern Ireland, the UK government acted fairly, reasonably and lawfully. Or did they act unlawfully, just as they allegedly did in Kenya in 1956, by training soldiers specifically to target identified individuals and assassinate them? This question arises because in May 1984, following allegations of a 'shoot to kill, don't question' policy levelled against the RUC, the political and legal establishment appointed, at the invitation of Sir John Hermon, the chief constable of the RUC, another police officer, John Stalker, to investigate the allegations. When it became apparent that Stalker, then deputy chief constable of the Greater Manchester Police, was determined to find out what had happened during some five weeks at the end of 1982, when six men were shot dead by the RUC, someone decided to defame him and have him removed from the inquiry rather than let him disclose the truth.

It is a long-established legal principle in the common law of England, Wales and Northern Ireland that where a suspect peacefully submits to the authority of a person making a lawful arrest, the use of force by the arrester is not justified. But where arrest is resisted, either by force or by flight, reasonable force may be used to effect the arrest. The arrester is entitled to increase the amount of force in proportion to the resistance met and may ultimately be justified if the suspect is killed. Similarly it may in certain instances be lawful to kill a fleeing suspect. But in order to justify the use of force in such circumstances, there must exist an actual right of arrest, and the force used must always be reasonable in the circumstances.

By the time of these incidents the 'rules of the Yellow Card', which governed the conduct of the security forces in Northern Ireland, had been changed and reissued in 1980. (The Army Code remained the same.)

Under the heading 'Instructions for Opening Fire', Rule 1 stated, 'in all situations you are to use the minimum force necessary. FIREARMS MUST ONLY BE USED AS A LAST RESORT.' Rule 2 stated, 'your weapon must always be made safe; that is, No live round is to be carried in the breech'; and Rule 3, 'a challenge must always be given before opening fire unless: (a) to do so would increase the risk of death or grave injury to you or any other person.'

The RUC Force Instructions were substantially the same as the Yellow Card. In one case, Chief Justice Lord Lowry said that the Yellow Card was intended to lay down guidelines for the security forces but did not define the legal rights and obligations of those members under statute or common law. But, he added, on reading the Yellow Card one might conclude that in some ways the security forces are intended to be more tightly restricted by the instructions they are given than by the ordinary law.[1]

It was thought that until 1967 the common law in England and Wales was broadly identical to Article 2 (the Right to Life) of the European Convention for the Protection of Human Rights and Fundamental Freedoms, but that line of thinking may now have changed.

Under Section 3(1) of the Criminal Law Act (Northern Ireland) 1967, 'A person may use such force as is reasonable in the circumstances in the prevention of crime, or effecting or assisting in the lawful arrest of offenders or suspected offenders or of persons unlawfully at large.' Some lawyers regard this section as so vague and ambiguous that it does not provide any legitimate grounds for departing from the principles of international law or common law.

However, since that Act was passed before the army was deployed in Northern Ireland, it is questionable whether the use of deadly force by the security forces in that province needed to be more precisely and carefully defined to enable the police and the military to understand fully when it was open to them to shoot to kill. Vagueness and uncertainty in the drafting and interpretation of the law is highly undesirable.

I have never regarded the RUC as a part of the normal police service within the UK; it was rather an armed paramilitary organisation tasked with a peacekeeping role at a time of violent civil unrest, and which operated without the consent or support of a large proportion of the nationalist population of Northern Ireland. It was, in the words of the journalist Chris Ryder, a 'force under fire'.

It is a matter of record that 302 police officers were murdered in the course of the Troubles, and about 9,000 injured, mostly by the Provisional IRA. Tragically, about 70 officers took their own lives; 1,183 were forced to move house for their own and their families' safety. For many it was a continuous struggle simply to stay alive and uninjured. It could not have been easy to cope with such continuous pressure, either professionally or personally.

In the last two months of 1982 a number of killings by the RUC in north Armagh led to allegations that the police were operating a 'shoot to kill' policy.

On the evening of 11 November 1982 three members of the IRA, Eugene Toman, Sean Burns and Gervaise McKerr, were shot dead. Thirteen days later 17-year-old Michael Tighe was shot and killed; he had no connection with any paramilitary organisation. His companion Martin McCauley was wounded in the same incident. On 12 December 1982 Seamus Grew and Roderick Carroll, both members of the INLA, were shot dead. All the deceased were shot by a specially trained undercover unit of the RUC.

Events really began in the early afternoon of Wednesday 27 October 1982 when three police officers died together in the course of their duty. Sergeant Sean Quinn, aged 37, was a Catholic, married, with three young children; Constable Alan McCloy (34) was married with two young children; and Constable Paul Hamilton (26) had been married for one month. The three men were murdered in a bomb explosion at Kinnego embankment near Lurgan in County Armagh. They had been lured into a trap by a telephone call, allegedly from a farmer complaining that a thief had stolen a battery from his tractor. He had made that call under duress and no such theft had taken place. The area to which the officers was called was said by John Stalker in his book *Stalker* to be 'out of bounds': it was dangerous to police officers and they required special permission to enter the area. Some may find it surprising that this permission was given and that the incident happened in respect of what appears on the face of it to be a minor criminal offence.

The officer who gave permission for the incursion knew that the RUC had at the beginning of September, following a tip-off from MI5, allowed a unit of the IRA to store a large quantity of explosives in a hayshed at the rear of a house, 12 Ballynerry Road, on the outskirts of Lurgan. A very sophisticated listening device had been placed in the roof of the barn by a specialist MI5 officer. That would enable the police to hear not only the conversations inside the hayshed, but any other noises that might indicate that the explosives were being moved. It was hoped that an IRA bombing team would be arrested when they returned to collect the explosives. The RUC claimed they did not know the intended target, nor did they know the identities of the members of the IRA bombing team.

However, unknown to anyone, the IRA bombing team did return to the shed and remove the explosives. The listening device had failed, probably because of adverse weather conditions. The explosives, thought to be about 1,000 lb, made up the bomb that killed the three RUC officers at the Kinnego embankment.

The armoured Ford Cortina car in which the three uniformed officers were travelling at the time was found almost totally destroyed in a crater some 14 feet deep and 40 feet in diameter. All three officers must have died instantly. A police informer named four local men as being responsible for their murders. Three of the four would be dead within a fortnight. They were Sean Burns, aged 21, Gervaise McKerr (31), Eugene Toman (21) and Martin McCauley (19). Apart from the informer's unsubstantiated claim, for which he is alleged to have been paid £20,000, there was no evidence against any of the four named men.

At about 9 p.m. on Thursday11 November 1982, Burns, McKerr and Toman were shot dead by RUC officers at Tullygally East Road, near Lurgan. The original version of events put out by the RUC press office was that there had been a vehicle checkpoint at which an officer carrying a torch and accompanied by a colleague had tried to wave down and stop a Ford Escort on the carriageway. The driver stopped momentarily, then suddenly moved forward, colliding slightly with the torch carrier, and drove away very quickly. The occupants of another patrol car, which happened by chance to be parked nearby, saw what had happened and pursued the Escort over a distance of some 500 yards. Those officers claimed that they were fired at from inside the vehicle and they returned fire, killing the three men in the car. At least 108 bullets were fired by the police at the men from a submachine gun, Ruger rifles and a handgun.

As John Stalker discovered, the truth was quite different. He found that the three deceased men had been under surveillance for hours that day and the RUC had planned to detain them at an entirely different place. There was no waving down of their vehicle by the torch carrier. No police officer was struck by the Ford Escort. As for the claim that the pursuing RUC officers were fired upon, not one of the three deceased men was armed with a weapon of any kind.

More detail about the case can be found in the judgment of Mr Justice Stephens handed down on 31 January 2014 in the application for a judicial review brought by Hugh Jordan, whose son Patrick Pearse Jordan had been shot dead by the RUC while he was running away from a stolen car in Belfast on 25 November 1992.[2] The Judge was a highly experienced criminal practitioner who had been appointed to the High Court bench in

2007. The judge related, with reference to the deaths of McKerr, Toman and Burns, 'Police opened fire on the fleeing vehicle and a chase ensued involving police officers who were members of a uniformed unit within Special Branch called the Special Support Unit (since renamed as Headquarters Mobile Support Unit [HMSU]). During the pursuit the SSU officers discharged further shots at the vehicle, which failed to negotiate a slip road and crashed into a grass bank. SSU officers again opened fire on the suspect vehicle. All three occupants . . . were shot dead. No firearms, explosives or other materials of significance were discovered in the vehicle.'

The judgment continues, 'Following the shooting, the SSU Officers involved, together with other members of the unit, including Officer V [in the Jordan inquest] who was the head of the unit, took part in a debriefing prior to their interviews with the CID Officers tasked to investigate the shootings. At that debriefing, senior Officers required the SSU Officers involved not to disclose the involvement of Special Branch or the fact that the interception of the suspect vehicle had been a planned operation. Alternative explanations for the involvement of the police at the scene were suggested by those senior officers. All the officers involved made false statements in accordance with the cover story.'

Was this proof, in the plainest language possible, of a conspiracy on the part of police officers in the service of the state to pervert the course of justice by concealing and fabricating material information? If the officers who shot the three deceased were acting lawfully, why falsify the truth?

In the event the DPP, Sir Barry Shaw, received a report of an internal investigation into the fatal shooting from an RUC chief superintendent recommending that no action be taken against the three police officers. Objective observers would not be surprised by that decision. There the matter lay for some time. There had been some disquiet when the car in which the three deceased men were travelling when they were shot dead was shown to the press. They counted between 20 and 30 bullet holes in and around the driver's door and a further ten entry marks on the boot of the vehicle, consistent with the vehicle being fired upon from the rear. One newspaper reported that it was evident that several bullets had passed through the windscreen and windows. Only the front passenger side window had been left intact.[3] Does this not challenge the police statement that the car had been fired on from the back? Does that evidence suggest that the car had been fired on after it had stopped?

Any public sympathy there might have been for the three deceased men, who had been shot so many times that they were barely recognisable, faded when they were given an IRA funeral, with an escort party wearing black berets and black gloves, and all three coffins draped in the Irish tricolour.

On 7 March 1993 the family of Gervaise McKerr lodged an application with the European Court of Human Rights claiming a breach of Article 2 of the Convention in that McKerr had been unlawfully killed and there had been no effective investigation by the RUC into the circumstances of his death. On 4 May the court handed down its judgment that there had been a lack of independence of the investigation carried out by the RUC; there had been a lack of public scrutiny and information to the victim's family concerning the investigation by John Stalker and Colin Sampson. That included not providing reasons for the failure to prosecute any police officer for perverting or attempting to pervert the course of justice.

With regard to the inquest, the court ruled that the procedure there did not allow verdicts or findings which might play an effective role in securing prosecutions in respect of any criminal offence that might be disclosed. Moreover, there had been no advance disclosure of witness statements at the inquest. (That effectively deprived the family's legal team from knowing beforehand that they needed to prepare cross-examination and perhaps arrange for the attendance of other witnesses.) The issue by the state of Public Interest Immunity Certificates (preventing the disclosure of evidence) had the effect of preventing the inquest examining matters relating to outstanding issues. The court also noted that the police officers who shot Gervaise McKerr could not be compelled to attend the inquest as witnesses and give evidence on oath; the inquest proceedings did not start promptly (it was not opened until 4 March 1984); neither those proceedings nor the Stalker/Sampson investigation proceeded with reasonable expedition. (The responsibility for that could not be attributed to either officer – they were deliberately obstructed at every turn by the RUC in Belfast and elsewhere in Northern Ireland.)

The Court held unanimously that Article 2 of the Convention had been violated by failure to comply with the obligation, implicit in the article, to hold an effective official investigation when an individual has been killed by the use of force. Despite this ruling the British government refused to take any further steps to conduct a full, adequate and independent criminal investigation into the death of Gervaise McKerr.

Death in the Hayshed

The next incident involving allegations of a shoot-to-kill policy involved Martin McCauley, then aged 19. He had been named by the informer as the fourth man involved in the deaths of the three RUC officers on 27 October 1982. Twenty-eight days after that incident, on Wednesday 24 November 1982, he was shot and seriously wounded by officers of the RUC.

For reasons unknown, and never likely to be known to the authorities, he had gone with 17-year-old Michael Tighe to a hayshed, known locally as Kitty's Hayshed, on the outskirts of a republican area adjoining the town of Lurgan. McCauley later claimed that he had been asked by the elderly widowed owner of the house and the hayshed to look after them while she was away. He saw that a window in the shed was open; it should not have been. The two young men went inside. The listening device installed by MI5 that had failed previously had been replaced and the new one was fully operational. It was 4.30 in the afternoon.

Seven members of the SSU approached the hayshed. They claimed that they challenged two armed men inside the shed and, on being confronted by them, they opened fire in self-defence, killing Michael Tighe instantly and gravely wounding Martin McCauley.

The SSU officers were debriefed before being interviewed by detectives. As Mr Justice Stephens noted in his judgment, 'At the debrief a cover story was formulated, purportedly to conceal aspects of Special Branch involvement. All the officers involved made false statements in accordance with the cover story.' Could it have been easy to induce seven police officers to conceal the truth and tell outright lies? If they were acting lawfully, why falsify the truth?

The original false story claimed that the officers had been on routine patrol when one of them saw a man with a gun go from the cottage into the nearby hayshed. One officer claimed he heard muffled voices and the sound of a firearm being cocked. The most senior officer present, a sergeant, called out 'Police. Throw out your weapons.' There was no response and he said it again. Looking through into the shed the sergeant saw Martin McCauley point a rifle at a fellow officer, a constable. The sergeant fired 14 rounds and the constable fired three rounds at Martin McCauley. Almost immediately that constable and another saw Michael Tighe pointing a rifle, and they shot him. In total, three RUC officers discharged their firearms that afternoon. One of the officers admitted firing no fewer than 33 rounds of ammunition at the two young men. Martin McCauley was later to claim that a police officer held a handgun against his head and talked about 'finishing him off'. This was denied by the police.

A search of the hayshed by the police found three First World War Mauser rifles. There was no ammunition. No shots had been fired at the police.

The survivor, Martin McCauley, was charged with two offences:

possessing the rifles with intent to endanger life; and possessing them in suspicious circumstances. He appeared at Belfast Crown Court before Mr Justice Basil Kelly, a former attorney general in the Unionist government in Northern Ireland before direct rule, sitting alone without a jury in a Diplock court.

Before the trial began the police officers were given the opportunity by the office of the DPP to lay out the truth in advance of the court hearing, when their evidence would be on oath and subject to cross-examination by defence counsel. They then admitted that in fact their presence in the area was not a routine patrol and that they had not seen a gunman move from the cottage to the hayshed. Apart from that they stood over their previous version of events.

In cross-examination by Arthur Harvey QC, the sergeant denied inventing the story about the gunman outside the shed. Instead, he said, it had been provided to him by senior officers in order to conceal the source of the information as being the Special Branch, and its purpose was to protect an informant whose life might otherwise be at stake. He claimed he was reassured that even though he lied about the circumstances, he was protected by the Official Secrets Act from any consequence of doing so. That is simply not true; there is no such protection.

As Mr Justice Stephens noted in his judgment in 2014, 'At the subsequent trial of Martin McCauley, the trial judge, Lord Justice Kelly, declined to rely on the evidence of Officer M and other police officers at the scene. He acquitted Martin McCauley of possession of firearms with intent to endanger life' (in other words the trial judge rejected the evidence that he had pointed the rifle at any police officer), but 'convicted him of possession of firearms in suspicious circumstances. He imposed a sentence of three months imprisonment suspended for two years.' (That may be a typographical error – the actual sentence was two years' imprisonment, suspended for three years.)

What the trial judge did not know, and neither did the prosecution and defence lawyers, or the seven police officers at the crime scene, was that the events of that afternoon were being recorded by the MI5 listening device inside the hayshed. Moreover, a transcript of the content of the tape existed. John Stalker discovered this and asked for access to the material, which would confirm that the two warnings were given by the police to McCauley and Tighe, and show that no threat had been made to finish McCauley off with the handgun as he had claimed. Of course, if the tape showed otherwise, what then would be the consequence for those who fired the fatal shots? Had they killed without warning and thus without justification?

While he awaited access to the tape recording John Stalker delivered an interim report in September 1985. He included in that report his findings relating to the shooting of the three men at Tullygally and the killing of Seamus Grew, aged 31, and Roderick Martin Carroll, aged 22. Only the important evidence relating to the tape recording in the hayshed remained to be resolved and for decisions to be taken on the basis of his findings.

The Killing of Seamus Grew and Roderick Carroll

Seamus Grew and Roderick Carroll were both members of the INLA. That organisation had claimed responsibility for the bombing of the Droppin' Well pub near the military base in Ballykelly, a town about 15 miles east of Derry city. The pub was known to be a favourite of soldiers from the base.

Sometime in the evening of Monday 6 December 1982, a courting couple placed a 10 lb bomb near the support pillar, which, when it exploded, brought down the pre-stressed concrete roof on the dance floor, where about 150 young people were enjoying themselves that evening shortly before Christmas – the season of goodwill. Eleven soldiers died in the explosion. Six civilians, four of them women, were also killed. Seventy people were injured. It was a terrible atrocity.

In the House of Commons the next day the prime minister Margaret Thatcher said: 'This is one of the most horrifying crimes in Ulster's tragic history. The slaughter of innocent people is the product of evil and depraved minds and the act of callous and brutal men.' She spoke for many when she said that. Did someone thereupon decide to strike back, and were Seamus Grew and Roderick Carroll selected for assassination in retaliation for those brutal murders? There was no evidence to show that either man was involved in the fatal bombing incident.

On the evening of Sunday 12 December 1982 the two men were in a yellow Allegro car owned and driven by Seamus Grew and heading for McGrew's family home in Mullacreevie Park, Armagh city, where he lived with his wife and eight-year-old son. He had served a prison sentence for terrorist offences and had been released earlier that year. He was clearly a marked man from the day he left prison. (This is apparent from evidential material provided to the author by a private individual in Northern Ireland.)

On that Sunday evening an unmarked police surveillance vehicle stopped the Allegro. A police constable emerged from his vehicle. He was said to be armed with a pump-action shotgun and a machine pistol. He shot and killed both occupants of the car. No firearms or explosives were found in the car. That constable was at that time allegedly stationed in Belfast. He had been brought from there to County Armagh, a place he had never policed and about which he knew nothing except for the briefings given by RUC senior officers prior to this operation.

Within less than five weeks in November and December 1982 police officers had shot dead six men, and wounded a seventh, claiming they were shooting at persons armed, dangerous and intending to kill the officers, so that the police had to shoot to kill in order to live.

In reaction to these killings the deputy leader of the SDLP, Seamus Mallon, called on the chief constable of the RUC, Sir John Hermon, on that Sunday, 12 December, to deny that the police were operating 'SAS-style' patrols with a licence to kill.

No admission to this effect was ever made by the chief constable. The police had other problems to deal with. Less than three months previously a member of the security forces, Private Geoffrey Edwards of the UDR, at that time the largest infantry regiment in the British army, had tried to murder Seamus Grew. On Wednesday 22 September 1982, at about 10.20 p.m., Edwards, wearing a mask that concealed his face, approached the front door of Grew's house in Mullacreevie Park, forced his way in and fired a shot at Seamus Grew, who was lying on the floor, behind a door, covering the body of his young son with his own. That shot missed. Private Edwards fired again, this time at Maureen Grew and her friend Teresa, who were drinking coffee in another room. Someone outside the house fired a pistol shot through a window. All shots missed their intended target. The two gunmen fled in a car driven by a third man. The police arrived about an hour later.

If the RUC had managed to arrest Edwards for attempted murder they might have saved the life of Peter Corrigan, who was shot dead by Edwards on 25 October 1982 as he walked along the street in Armagh city with his 16-year-old son Martin. Peter was the father of 11 children.

When he was eventually arrested in December 1983 Private Edwards was charged with murder and six counts of attempted murder. In all he admitted 19 terrorist offences. In January 1985 Mr Justice Murray sentenced him to life imprisonment for murder and six concurrent sentences of 20 years for attempted murder. Asked to name his accomplices in the UVF he refused to do so, or to indicate the location of weapons used by him and others, saying it was more than his life was worth to do so. His barrister told the judge that it was the failure of the security forces to obtain sufficient evidence to convict those suspected of murder that led him to commit the offences. Edwards claimed that he had 15 friends in the regiment who had been murdered in the previous seven years. Counsel at the sentencing hearing said it was 'a case of a misplaced sense of duty'.

Roderick Carroll was 22 years of age when he died. He had been arrested and detained with Seamus Grew for three days between 14 and 17 November 1982. Both men were questioned about the murder of two police reservists, Constables Ronald Irwin and Snowden Corkery. Corkery was the father of three children, the eldest of whom was only five years old. The two men were brutally shot down in the late afternoon of 16 November 1982 in Newry Street in the town of Markethill, County Armagh. A gunman fired about 45 shots at the two officers before escaping in a car. Both Carroll and Grew denied any involvement in the double murder and no evidence was ever found to show that they were involved.

On his release from custody Roderick Carroll wrote a letter of complaint dated 20 November 1982 to the Complaints and Discipline Branch of the RUC stating that while detained he had been threatened that he would be killed by the security forces. He was, on 12 December. Eleven days later the RUC Complaints and Discipline Branch wrote to him, acknowledging receipt of his letter of 20 November and saying, 'The subject will receive attention'.

Seamus Grew also complained to the police that he had been threatened while in custody that 'he would be in his box before Christmas'. Someone had decided that he was going to die.

According to the assistant state pathologist for Northern Ireland, Dr James Press, Seamus Grew was struck by seven bullets, most of which could have come from behind and to his left. One bullet had entered the left side of the back of his head and had passed to the right, fracturing the skull and lacerating the brain before exiting on the right side of the scalp.

Roderick Carroll was shot by at least seven or possibly nine bullets, according to Dr Press, most of which appeared to have come from behind and to his right. One bullet entered the right side of the back of the scalp and passed forwards to the left side, lacerating the brain and brain stem before lodging in the left side of the base of the skull. When a Catholic priest, the Rev. Patrick McDonnell, Administrator of St Patrick's Parish in Armagh, arrived at the killing scene, he counted 13 bullet holes in the passenger door of the car. He found Roderick Carroll slumped forward in the driver's seat. He went around to the passenger side and found Seamus Grew not in the vehicle but lying outside it, on the road. He was lying face upwards and appeared to have been shot in the back of the head. According to the pathologist the bullets were 9mm parabellum. The appearance of the entrance wounds indicated that the bullets had struck some object such as a car door before hitting Roderick Carroll.

Within hours the RUC press office issued a statement claiming that officers in uniform were manning a road block at Girvans Bridge, five miles from the centre of Armagh, when a car broke through, knocking down a policeman. The car was identified as belonging to a known terrorist. The police at the roadblock radioed for help and another police car which was in the area gave chase. The police car forced the terrorist car to halt in Mullacreevie Park. The terrorist car then reversed at speed. The officers were revealed in its headlights, shouting to the driver to stop. Believing they were about to be fired on, they opened fire themselves and killed Seamus Grew and Roderick Carroll. There was a problem with that statement: almost every word of it was untrue.

More is known now than was known at the time about the police units involved in these three fatal shootings. In 1982 the top-secret sections of the RUC were grouped into five offices. One of the groups was Echo Four – E4. One of E4's special tasks was close surveillance of individuals who were targeted for special observation. A particular section within that group had prime responsibility for such operations; this section was known as the Technical Support Unit, Echo 4 Alpha – E4A. The unit comprised serving RUC officers under the command of a Special Branch inspector. Members of the group almost always operated in civilian clothes rather than in police uniform.

E4A operated closely with two SSUs – sometimes referred to as Headquarters Mobile Support Units – to which it passed intelligence gathered in the course of its own operations. The SSUs operated in unmarked vehicles, known as 'Q cars'. There were about 48 members in total in the two groups. All were members of the police service, but many were former soldiers in the British army who had served both in Northern Ireland and elsewhere. All were volunteers who had been specially selected for the units. They were trained by the SAS.

All this begs the question: when and by whom was it decided on policy grounds that the state should abandon the traditional police concept of the use of minimum force and replace it with the use of maximum and lethal force?

The hallmark of their training was 'firepower, speed and aggression'. They were trained to put people permanently out of action, rather than incapacitate them and take them alive. They were issued with rapid-fire weapons which were not standard-use weapons in the RUC.

Their existence became more widely known when the DPP in Northern Ireland decided to prosecute three officers for the murder of Eugene Toman, and one officer for the murder of Seamus Grew.

The first officer to be put on trial in Belfast Crown Court was Constable John Robinson. He appeared before the non-jury Diplock court presided over by Mr Justice MacDermott in March 1984. Constable Robinson's first version of events, obtained from him about a week after the incident, was untrue. The usual police approach regards the first hour after a killing as 'the golden hour' when the best available evidence should be gathered and safeguarded. There was no golden hour in Northern Ireland in 1982, at least not in cases involving the security forces. Asked to explain his untruths, he said that senior officers had told him and other members of his unit to protect an informer and to conceal the fact that they were taking part in a planned operation, not a random stop and search. He was apparently led to believe that the Official Secrets Act might be breached if he told the truth.

On the face of it the prosecution case against Robinson appeared to be strong. If anything it was stronger as the accused officer gave his evidence on oath from the witness box, knowing that he would be subjected to cross-examination by prosecuting counsel testing his credibility and his conduct. It is clear that he did not intend to stand alone and say nothing. He said a lot, perhaps too much for some people's liking.

He said he had left the police vehicle after stopping the Allegro by waving his police cap. He recognised Seamus Grew as the driver. He went to the passenger side of the Allegro. The driver began to rev the engine and the officer called on the occupants to stop. The passenger door was opened and then shut. The officer heard a loud bang. Thinking he had been shot at and his life was in danger he fired 15 shots into the passenger door, emptying the magazine. He was about 10 or 15 feet away from the car. He had killed Roderick Carroll. He said he then reloaded his Smith and Wesson revolver and ran around to the other side of the Allegro – which meant that he was lit up by the headlights of the car – and then fired four shots at the driver's door from a distance of about ten feet. He then opened the driver's door with his left hand. Seamus Grew fell out of the car onto the road. He was dead. A woman who lived nearby on the estate heard the gunfire and ran to the scene. There she noticed three men in dark clothing, carrying handguns. It is not known who these men were, and what part, if any, they had in this incident. Were they eyewitnesses who declined to tell anyone what they had seen?

A forensic examination of Seamus Grew's parka jacket showed there were two entry holes in the upper back, around which were particles of unburnt propellant. That seemed to indicate that the muzzle of the pistol that caused the death was fired from a distance of between 30 and 36 inches from the back of the deceased. When asked to explain this evidence, which suggested that Seamus Grew had not been shot through the door of the car, Robinson replied, 'my recollection is that I fired four rounds through the door'. When he did that, he claimed, he was acting as a police officer and in self-defence. 'I fired to kill', he said in evidence, 'because I believed they were trying to kill me'.

The prosecution rejected that. They argued that the evidence proved that this was a deliberate shooting carried out in circumstances where it must have been clear that the deceased was not carrying a weapon.

During his evidence the prosecution wanted to test whether Constable Robinson was being truthful and accurate in his version of events and more particularly the cover story, which seemed to change from time to time. Mr Justice MacDermott stopped the questioning in its tracks, ruling:

> I am not in this case conducting an inquiry into why the officers who advised, instructed or constrained the accused acted as they did. Neither the police as such, nor these officers in particular, are represented in these proceedings or charged with anything. My task throughout has been to decide whether or not the accused is guilty as charged . . . the true facts should be ascertained, if that be possible, as quickly as possible, and that a person who may have to face a charge of murder (or indeed any charge) should not be required to tell a false story . . . if his statement contained secret or operationally important matters then arrangements for editing, if appropriate, could have been made.

Does that mean that the cover-up was totally unnecessary and could and should have been avoided?

What the learned judge ought to have considered, however, was this very fundamental point: how is it possible to believe entirely the evidence of a witness who admits that he had lied previously because he was ordered to do so? Would it not have been in the interests of justice for Mr Justice MacDermott to have given a judicial ruling whether it was correct or not for one police officer to tell another that in disclosing the truth he might be in breach of the Official Secrets Act? How can this possibly be so, since the essence of such offences under that Act is to prevent the disclosure of specified information to a person who is not authorised to receive it? Obviously a police officer is authorised to receive information imparted to him in the course of a criminal investigation.

Yet again this begs the question, which perhaps the learned judge ought to have posed: why was it necessary to falsify the truth? It was readily apparent almost from the very outset that the police were acting on information provided by an informer. Once that was known, what was there left to hide? Only the identity of that person, something which the court would not have compelled the police to disclose: it was not relevant to the issue the court had to decide; and its non-disclosure would not hinder or prejudice the parties to the case, and more especially the accused, in any way.

On 3 April 1984 Mr Justice MacDermott ruled that John Robinson was not guilty of the murder of Seamus Grew. He said, 'while police officers are required to work within the law, they are not required to be supermen and one does not use jeweller's scales to measure what is reasonable in the circumstances . . . I am satisfied that the accused honestly believed he had been fired at and that his life was in danger.' The learned judge therefore chose to believe Robinson's evidence that he was acting lawfully when he shot Seamus Grew dead. It is a principle of English law that the accused in a case such as this where a police officer (or soldier) fires a weapon on the basis of a factual assessment which was mistaken, that accused must be judged against the mistaken facts as he believed them to be. This is regardless of whether, judged objectively, his mistake was reasonable. Constable Robinson was acquitted because the trial judge accepted that his honestly held mistaken belief that the two deceased men were armed and had put his life in danger was a full defence to the charge of murder.

Putting it another way, if an accused has acted in good faith, his conduct is excusable and he will not be convicted. As Justice Cardozo expressed it in the American case of *Brown v. United States*, 'detached reflection cannot be demanded in the presence of an uplifted knife'.[4]

The learned trial judge in Belfast had in addition to bear in mind the approach adopted by Lord Morris of Borth-y-Gest in the case of *Palmer v. Regina*, in the Privy Council on appeal from the Court of Appeal of Jamaica.[5] Lord Morris said:

> If an attack is serious so that it puts someone in immediate peril then immediate defensive action may be necessary. If the moment is one of crisis for someone in imminent danger he may have to avert that danger by some instant reaction . . . if there has been no attack

then clearly there will have been no need for defence. If there has been an attack so that defence is reasonably necessary it will be recognised that a person defending himself cannot weigh to a nicety the exact measure of his necessary defensive action. If a jury thought in a moment of unexpected anguish a person attacked had only done what he honestly and instinctively thought was necessary that would be most potent evidence that only reasonable defensive action had been taken.[6]

That is why the verdict in the case of Constable Robinson cannot be impeached. It is accordance with established legal principles.

It should be noted, as a matter of law, that if in another criminal case the accused's alleged belief was mistaken and the mistake was an unreasonable one, that might be a very good reason for deciding that the belief was not honestly held and should therefore be rejected. If, however, the accused used lethal force under a mistaken and unreasonable belief that he was entitled to do so, he will not be convicted if he genuinely laboured under this belief.

After the verdict the SDLP politician Seamus Mallon issued a statement. He had seen at first hand the horror of sectarian assassination; he and his young daughter were nearby when the two police reservists Constables Ronald Irwin and Snowden Corkery were shot dead on 16 November 1982 in Markethill in County Armagh. He had helped the officers in their dying moments as they lapsed into unconsciousness where they had fallen. He was no supporter of violence on any side. He said the case 'was a deadly blow to the hope that justice will ever be fairly administered in Northern Ireland' and asked whether the chief constable would be taking any action against the officers named in court as part of the cover-up allegations. I have found no evidence that Sir John Hermon ever did take action.

To the regret of some, Mr Justice MacDermott is reported to have praised Constable Robinson for his sharp shooting.[7] Nothing like that should ever have been said. It caused great offence not only to the families of Seamus Grew and Roderick Carroll, but also to those who consider that while justice may be imperfect, it should also be impartial.

On 7 April 1984 Sir John Hermon issued a statement at the conclusion of the trial and acquittal of Constable Robinson, who had been told he was at liberty to return to his police duties. In his statement the chief constable denied any cover-up by the RUC regarding events leading to the deaths of Seamus Grew and Roderick Carroll, but admitted that two unarmed RUC men had crossed the border into the Republic for observation purposes in December 1984. It is a fact that the Austin Allegro car driven by Seamus Grew, accompanied by Roderick Carroll, had entered the Irish Republic. The police claimed they had information that they intended to pick up a terrorist named Dominic McGlinchey and bring him over the border to County Armagh. In fact, as they discovered, the two men travelled into the Republic to attend the funeral of Roderick Carroll's grandfather at his parish church in Magherafelt, County Derry. He was buried in the cemetery at Desmartin near the church. No mention of that funeral was ever made during the court case. Nor was it disclosed that after the funeral the two men had driven Roderick Carroll's sister Irene back to their family home in Callanbridge in Lurgan. On arrival their car was surrounded by about eight soldiers from the UDR. That was a matter easily proved one way or the other. In spite of the allegation that Grew and Carroll were terrorists, no attempt was made to arrest them. For one simple reason: there were no legal grounds for arresting them. The two RUC officers who were following them that day must have seen and noted all of this. The officers must have known that when they entered the Irish Republic they had no lawful authority to be there in their professional capacity.

The two men and Irene left the family home to drive Irene back to her own house in County Monaghan, which, although it is in the province of Ulster, is in the Republic of Ireland. Then the Allegro was driven back to the Grew household in Mullacreevie Park.

None of this latter information seems to have been provided to anyone concerned in the trial of this case and one is bound to ask why not. To add to public unease about the truth surrounding the case, six Catholic priests in the Armagh parish issued a statement describing how on 19 November 1982 a message had been received that Seamus Grew and Roderick Carroll were being threatened with death at a UDR vehicle checkpoint. One of the parish priests went to the checkpoint, verified the threat and, seeing their distraught state, stayed for about 20 minutes until a UDR officer ordered him to leave the scene. The priest assured Seamus Grew and Roderick Carroll that they were safe because he had recorded that interview with the UDR officer.

This was only 23 days before the two men were shot dead. If they were dangerous terrorists, why were they not detained on 19 November, interrogated, charged and put on trial?

As for Sir John Hermon's denial of any cover-up, one need look no further than the judgment of Mr Justice Stephens referred to above to see how wrong that denial actually was.

The learned judge stated, 'On 12 December 1982, nine members of the HMSU were deployed in the Armagh area on an anti-terrorist operation'. He describes the alleged pursuit into Mullacreevie Park housing estate, the stopping of the car, the shooting of the two men and the fact that no shots came from within the car. No firearms or explosives were found in the car. He then says:

> The HMSU Officers involved in the shootings were debriefed prior to interview by the CID Officers tasked to investigate the incident. At the debriefs, attended inter alia by Officers V and M, first at Gough Barracks and then the following day at HMSU HQ at Lisnasharragh, a cover story was formulated, purportedly to conceal aspects of Special Branch involvement in the incident. All the officers involved made false statements in accordance with the cover story, which involved, inter alia, fabricating an account of the deceased breaking through a fictitious police check point, injuring a police officer (who had in fact been injured in a collision involving an Army surveillance vehicle) and then driving away from the scene at speed. It also involved an officer who had in fact been on leave being inserted into the account in order to take the place of another Special Branch Officer whose involvement and role it had been decided to conceal altogether. This required the officer to make a false claim for overtime.

As will be seen, this fraudulent officer, who was not present at the incident but was prepared to say that he was, is now known to be Constable David Brannigan.

The judgment goes on: 'At the inquest, Officer V accepted that he told the Stalker Sampson team that his role was to "plug" holes in the cover story as and when they appeared. He accepted that he and the other officers involved in that episode had weaved "a web of deceit" and that, in relation to the "build up and what happened afterwards", he was "one of the main weavers of this web of deceit".'

Is greater proof than this needed to show that rather than tell the whole unvarnished truth about the killing of Seamus Grew and Roderick Carroll, the RUC were prepared to go to any length to falsify the truth? Just why was it necessary to go to these incredible lengths to conceal the presence of one police officer and replace him with another – one who wasn't even on duty on 12 December? In order to ensure continuity in this tissue of lies

Constable Brannigan was prepared to make a fraudulent claim for money, which he received and accepted. One senior officer asked about this said he thought that Constable Brannigan would give the money to charity. He didn't.

The Prosecution of Police Constable Brannigan

Constable Brannigan entered the narrative again in June 1984 when he appeared before Lord Justice Maurice Gibson, sitting alone in the non-jury Diplock Crown Court in Belfast, charged with the murder of Eugene Toman. He was the officer who had actually fired the shots at the deceased, who was found half in and half out of the passenger door of the car on the Tullygally East Road near Lurgan, as outlined above. It was thought that he might have been alive, attempting to get out of the motor vehicle, before he was fatally shot. The state pathologist, Professor Thomas Marshall, considered that in his professional opinion Eugene Toman had been shot in the back. If that was so, and if he had been wounded, did this unarmed man present any danger or threat to anyone? Moreover, if Eugene Toman had been shot dead during the car chase, why was he found partly inside and partly outside the Ford Escort? The explanation put forward in court was that he had fallen against the inside door handle and this dead weight had pushed down the handle, causing the car door to open.

It seems a matter of regret that no evidence was put before the court that in that particular model of the Ford Escort the door handle was a small plastic lever which was pulled *outwards*, towards the passenger, not downwards, out of a moulded niche. Would that not have advanced the prosecution case?

In the dock with Constable Brannigan, and jointly charged, were Sergeant William Montgomery and Constable Nigel Robinson. They pleaded not guilty. Sir John Hermon had resisted their prosecution, saying that they would not be convicted. He was right. They were acquitted by Lord Justice Gibson on 5 June 1984. He ruled at the close of the prosecution evidence against them that in spite of the fact that they had shot dead three unarmed men they had no case to answer. They were not required to give evidence of what they knew, what they did and what they said before they fired. Although it is said in their defence that they were trailing the three IRA men on the night they died because the officers believed they were on their way to kill a member of the security forces, no evidence was given by them or anyone else to support that suggestion. Perhaps most astonishing of all is the disclosure by the television journalist Chris Moore, in a BBC Northern Ireland programme broadcast in 1988, that MI5 and MI6 had electronically bugged the car used by the three men, something John Stalker never discovered. It was claimed that the security forces involved in the surveillance operation were able to listen to the conversation in the car. If that bugging device was transmitting (and recording), would the conversation inside the car have indicated what the three men were doing, where they were going and what they intended to do when they got there? If they were planning a murder, and discussing it, why not disclose the existence of the device and any recording made by it? That would have been evidence very favourable to the police officers and would have supported their defence. If they were not planning a murder, why were they shot dead?

Lord Justice Gibson, who knew nothing of this, castigated the DPP for bringing the case on what he called 'such tenuous evidence'. He said, 'there never was the slimmest chance that the Crown could have hoped to secure a conviction.' He said that the accused officers 'knew of the suspicion that the three were on their way to commit murder, of the probability that they were armed, and that they were dangerous terrorists who had let it be known that they would not be arrested alive'. One is bound to ask, upon whose evidence was that last point based? When and where had they said, jointly or individually, that they would never be taken alive?

The learned lord justice displayed his anger at the way the prosecution had commenced the case at the committal hearings in the lower magistrates' court, saying, 'The prosecution's failure at the preliminary inquiry to disclose information at its disposal . . . had left the presiding magistrate . . . with a very partial picture, and I do not think I am putting this too far if I say it was a false picture, of the circumstances of the shooting.' Was that anger misplaced? The cover-up of the truth that began at the crime scene was obviously continued at the police station. For whose benefit? Why does not the suspicion of false and contrived evidence contaminate the entirety of the case? Why falsify the truth?

Had the law been misused in this case? Was this the ideal written about, and perhaps longed for, by the British army officer Brigadier Frank Kitson in 1971, in his book *Low Intensity Operations*? He had written, 'the law should be used as just another weapon in the government's arsenal, and in this case it becomes little more than a propaganda cover for the disposal of unwanted members of the public. For this to happen efficiently, the activities of the legal service have to be tied into the war effort in as discreet a way as possible.' Had someone in a position of power decided that

Gervaise McKerr, Sean Burns and Eugene Toman were unwanted members of the public to be disposed of? Did a senior judge solemnly give what appeared to be a stamp of approval to that disposal?

Lord Justice Gibson went on to make a statement that caused an uproar in Ireland and elsewhere. 'I wish to make it clear that, having heard the entire Crown case, I regard each of the accused as absolutely blameless in this matter. That finding should be put on their record along with my own commendation as to their courage and determination for bringing the three deceased men to justice, in this case, to the final court of justice.' He added, in words likely to cause considerable dismay, 'The case is going to have a more widespread effect among other members of the security forces . . . When a policeman or soldier is ordered to arrest a dangerous criminal, and on the basis of that order to bring him back dead or alive, how is he to consider his conduct now?'

Is this tantamount to judicial approval of a 'shoot to kill' policy? Shortly afterwards, Lord Justice Gibson issued a statement explaining that he did not endorse any such policy. But it must be said that such a remark undermined confidence in the judiciary, who must remain impartial and independent of the state that appoints them.

To add to the controversy, the republican newspaper *An Phoblacht* described the judge as being 'thoroughly representative of the North's colonial judiciary; a Unionist, bigoted and biased against Nationalists, who constantly used the law to prop up British rule in the Six Counties'.[8]

This criticism fails to take into account the fact that he knew, and other members of the judiciary knew, that the fears of the security forces of being shot first were both real and justified. A split-second decision had to be made in very many cases, especially in the Armagh area. Less than two years before the three 'shoot to kill' cases in the Lurgan area, there had been a tragic accident in the nearby town of Forkhill. On 1 January 1980 Lieutenant Simon Gregory Bates, aged 23, and his signaller, Private Gerald Hardy, aged 18, both of the 2nd Battalion of the Parachute Regiment, were shot dead by their fellow soldiers. It was 1.30 a.m. An ambush had been set and, breaking standard procedures, the two soldiers became detached from the six other paratroopers and then walked forward to join them. As they did so, the other soldiers saw the two armed men, failed to recognise them, and opened fire without challenge or warning, killing them both. This illustrates the ever-present risk of armed men, even when they are highly trained, being placed in such hostile surroundings that their instant responses lead to tragedy.

In revenge against the judge for his injudicious remarks when he acquitted Montgomery, Robinson and Brannigan, on 27 April 1987 the IRA murdered Lord Justice Gibson and his wife, Cecily. She was driving their car on a journey from the Irish Republic back to the North. They had been on a continental holiday. Shortly after they crossed the border a bomb explosion killed them both. The explosion was so massive it totally destroyed their car and their bodies were so badly burned that they were only identified by dental records. To add to the tragedy, some nine years after his acquittal by Lord Justice Gibson, Constable Brannigan committed suicide by shooting himself.

When Mr Justice Stephens referred to the murder of Eugene Toman and the acquittal of the three police officers, he noted, as mentioned above, that members of the SSU had been told by senior officers to stick to a cover story.

Taken together, these findings of Mr Justice Stephens indicate a calculated and determined cover-up in all three fatal shootings on the part of the police. Would uniformed officers really repeat lie after lie to deceive their colleagues in the detective branch of the same police service, in order to conceal the activities of MI5? Or was there a more sinister reason?

John Stalker had no doubts why the prosecutions against the four officers failed. He wrote in his book, 'the files were poorly prepared and presented. We had expected a particularly high level of enquiry in view of the nature of the deaths, but this was shamefully absent. The files were little more than a collection of statements, apparently prepared for a coroner's inquiry. They bore no resemblance to my idea of a murder prosecution file. Even on the most cursory readings I could see clearly why the prosecution had failed'.[9]

So was there a tissue of lies in each case, followed by an incomplete and incompetent investigation? For example, it was known that 108 shots had been fired at the car containing the three deceased men. There had been a pursuit, allegedly, over 500 yards. Had the driver not been disabled until the very last moment? How had he continued to drive for so long and so far? John Stalker considered that as many as 20 cartridge cases were removed from the scene. He presumed this was to mislead the forensic scientists and to hide the true nature and extent of the shooting. He went on: 'I had to regard the investigation of the matter as slipshod, and in some aspects woefully incomplete.'[10] This is bound to lead to the question: was anyone really interested in establishing a true version of how the three men died in that car?

John Stalker was never allowed access to those recordings or transcripts. He was removed from the inquiry in June 1986. He could not be relied upon to suppress the truth. His replacement, Colin Sampson, did not gain access to that material either. According to the investigative journalist Peter Taylor in his book *Stalker – the Search for the Truth*, notes were taken of the material transmitted from the listening device, and a copy made of the tape itself, but Colin Sampson never saw either. If those who appointed him regarded him as a poodle who would lie down and roll over, they were dramatically wrong. In 1988 he recommended to the DPP that no fewer than 11 members of the RUC should be charged with criminal offences arising out of the three separate fatal incidents in November and December 1982. Among those offences must surely have been listed the offence of wiping the audio tape recording from the transmitter installed in the hay barn. Whoever wiped that tape had least a case to answer for obstructing and perverting the course of justice. It is thought that the person involved was not a police officer but a member of MI5. Of course, no member of the RUC was likely to stand in his way in doing that, since the consequences of disclosure might be substantial.

The Stalker/Sampson recommendations must have placed the DPP, Sir Barry Shaw QC, in a difficult position. He had previously brought prosecutions against four members of the RUC and had been heavily criticised for doing so when they failed.

The office of the DPP had come into existence when direct rule from Westminster was imposed in Northern Ireland in 1972. Sir Barry Shaw was the first appointment. He was a barrister of many years' standing, with a distinguished military record; he had served in the Royal Artillery during the Second World War. He and his staff were highly regarded by the legal profession in Northern Ireland for their integrity and professionalism. The DPP was responsible for bringing prosecutions for the most serious criminal offences and especially those that were tried in the non-jury Diplock courts.

After he received the recommendations in March 1987, Sir Barry Shaw decided there was sufficient evidence to bring a prosecution involving the perversion and obstruction of justice, and in his view prosecutions should be brought. He was under a statutory obligation, however, to consult the attorney general, then Sir Patrick Mayhew QC, regarding the public interest in bringing such prosecutions against as yet unknown and unidentified individuals.

On 25 January 1988 Sir Patrick made a statement in the House of Commons.[11] Some may regard it as a simplistic survey of facts in chronological order, but it disguises, and was calculated to disguise, lying by police officers on an industrial scale. The statement recited the three shooting incidents in which six people died and one was wounded; the CID investigation; and the submission of files to the DPP. The deceased and the wounded man were named. The acquittals of the four police officers were noted.

Mayhew then said, after reference to the fact that in certain of the statements of evidence furnished for his consideration, material and important facts had been omitted, and that matters that were untrue and misleading in material and important respects had been included. He went on, 'In consequence of this, on 11 April 1984, the Director formally exercised his statutory power to request the Chief Constable to ascertain and furnish to him full information with regard to the circumstances in which false or misleading evidence was provided by any member or members of the RUC. He also required him to investigate whether there was evidence to suggest that any person was guilty of an offence of perverting, or attempting or conspiring to pervert, the course of justice, or of any other offence in connection with the investigation of the three shooting incidents.'

That request had been handed to John Stalker on 24 May 1984 after he had agreed to conduct the inquiry. He delivered his interim report to the chief constable on 18 September 1985. It is thought that he recommended the prosecution of 11 police officers for offences of conspiracy to pervert the course of justice and perjury. For reasons never explained, but which call for an explanation, instead of forwarding the report forthwith to the DPP, Sir John Hermon sat on it for five months, finally sending it, with his observations, to the DPP on 13 February 1986. It only took the DPP three weeks to decide that further investigations needed to be undertaken.

Not by John Stalker, however. In the delicate phrase used by Sir Patrick Mayhew, 'on 29 May 1986, Mr Stalker ceased to have responsibility for the investigation he had undertaken'. Someone more curious than the MPs who had to listen to this might have wanted more details of how and why John Stalker had 'ceased to have responsibility for the investigation' and further wondered what, if anything, his interim report had said about the lies and false and misleading evidence he had been asked to examine.

As Sir Patrick told the House, Colin Sampson delivered three reports to the DPP on 22 October 1986, 23 March 1987 and 10 April 1987. (This time there were no delaying tactics because Sampson sent copies of the reports straight to the DPP on those same dates.) His recommendations about prosecutions have been set out above.

After considering all the evidence, the DPP decided there should be no further prosecutions in any of the three fatal shooting incidents. That decision should surprise no one. The unenthusiastic RUC police officers who investigated them had not even made their best efforts to get a prosecution on its feet and after the passage of time there was no hope of ever being able to obtain cogent and admissible evidence to put before a court.

The attorney general's statement in the Commons went on: 'The Director has, however, concluded that there is evidence of offences of perverting or attempting or conspiring to pervert the course of justice, or of obstructing a constable in the execution of his duty, and that this evidence is sufficient to require consideration of whether prosecutions are required in the public interest, and he has consulted me accordingly.'

From the legal standpoint, under the Prosecution of Offences (Northern Ireland) Order 1972, the DPP is required to discharge his functions under the direction of the attorney general and to be subject to the directions of the attorney general in all matters. The attorney general's responsibilities also include deciding whether it is 'in the public interest' to initiate a prosecution. The attorney general is a politician, the leader of the Bar, and legal adviser to the government of which he is a member. He (or she) attends cabinet meetings but is not a member of the cabinet. He is independent of the prime minister who appointed him and he is expected to apply legal principles in the decision-making process, irrespective of the political consequences.

Sir Patrick announced his decision. After saying that he had considered matters concerning the public interest and in particular considerations of national security, he said, 'I have informed the Director fully with regard to my consultations as to the public interest, and in the light of all the facts and information brought to his notice, the Director has concluded, with my full agreement, that it would not be proper to institute any criminal proceedings.'

This placed the responsibility for taking no action against anyone firmly on the shoulders of the DPP. But hadn't he told the director that it wasn't in the public interest to prosecute, when that was a decision the director was expected to make himself before deciding whether to launch a prosecution?

The director had decided that the sufficiency of evidence threshold had been passed; so that left the second criterion – the public interest. What would have been the situation if the director had considered it was in the public interest to proceed, on the basis that a cover-up had been discovered and in order to maintain public confidence in the impartial administration of justice, but the attorney general had declined to accept that decision?

In addition, what issue of national security was involved in these three cases?

The folly and absurdity of the whole approach adopted by Sir Patrick

Mayhew is to be found in his next statement. 'The Director has arranged to discuss with the Chief Constable and Deputy Chief Constable of the RUC safeguards to ensure that, in the future, facts and information reported to the Director are in all respects full and accurate, whether or not any security interest is involved.' Does that mean that there would be a discussion that in the future a case sent to the DPP should be properly and fairly prepared by the police, without lies or cover-up, and this should apply even in those cases involving the security of the state, which meant virtually every serious case in Northern Ireland? Why discuss that? Why not direct the police that any file submitted to the DPP for consideration for prosecution must contain statements that are accurate and true, and nothing less than that would be acceptable?

At the conclusion of the attorney general's statement, Kevin McNamara replied on behalf of the Labour opposition. He mentioned the growing concern not only in Northern Ireland, but also in Britain and the international community about the cases. He said, 'Six men died in 1982. A coroner resigned. A deputy chief constable began an inquiry and then found himself the subject of an inquiry. We have allegations of RUC cover-ups, of perjury by police officers, of illegal incursions by members of the security forces in the Republic of Ireland. Some questions have been raised about the RUC Special Branch, about the roles of the headquarters mobile support units, about the involvement of MI5 and about the withholding of information from police inquiries by members of the security forces.'

McNamara said he found it incredible beyond belief that the government had come to this conclusion. Was he right about that? Was this a decision not just of the attorney general but of his ministerial colleagues in the Conservative and Unionist government? He went on to mention that Article 8 of the Anglo-Irish Agreement talks about achieving confidence in the administration of justice in Northern Ireland and how it would be damaged by the Mayhew statement. That confidence would be greatly shaken and, worse still, it had undermined all the efforts to achieve acceptance of the RUC among the nationalist community.

'We must ask,' he continued, 'what the grounds of national security are? What are the grounds of public interest which could shield members of the police force, against whom there was evidence of perjury, of conspiracy to pervert the course of justice, of impeding a police officer in the execution of his duty. All this, and yet we are to be denied knowledge of the reasons why the government had come to this conclusion.' He spoke of the need to know whether there was a 'shoot to kill' policy, and he personally wanted to know from the government what its attitude was to 'the use of the lethal force, necessary force and reasonable force'. He made reference to the allegation that before the Stalker inquiry began Stalker faced delays, evasions, lies and refusals to act from members of the RUC who were bent on obstructing his work.

He asked, 'will the attorney general therefore publish both the Sampson Reports, so that we can form a judgement?' He then added the telling observation, 'Quite honestly, on this matter we do not trust the decision of Mr Attorney . . . all this undermines confidence in the forces of law and justice. It is a grave blow to peace in that area.'

In response, Sir Patrick Mayhew said, 'I have been asked if there is a shoot to kill policy, and I was told, "we will never be told". It is plain from my statement that no offence has been disclosed, apart from possible cases relating to the perversion of the course of justice. That means that no evidence has been disclosed of any offence – such as incitement to murder – such as would be comprised in what has been loosely called a shoot to kill policy.'

I consider that Kevin McNamara was right to criticise the attorney general in the way he did, and to express his lack of trust in him. If the only criminal conduct discovered in the course of the inquiry into the six fatal deaths was possibly perverting justice, was that just the lies and cover-up stories fabricated after each deadly incident? If so, what issue of national security was involved that enabled the participants to avoid prosecution?

The Labour MP Ken Livingstone accused Sir Patrick Mayhew of reducing himself and his office 'to the level of accomplice to murder'. When Livingstone refused to withdraw that comment, the Speaker suspended him from the House.

That same afternoon, the Lord Chancellor, Lord Mackay of Clashfern, read to the House of Lords exactly the same statement that the attorney general was reading to the House of Commons. In response the former Labour attorney general and thereafter Lord Chancellor Lord Elwyn Jones, a lawyer of very substantial experience, referred to 'the grievously worrying background of allegations which must inevitably put the standing and reputation of the Royal Ulster Constabulary in some danger of being adversely viewed by the public . . . I cannot think of any other episode in our criminal law which is quite as complex and unhappy,' and he called for a judicial inquiry into the whole matter.

He was not likely to get that. The public examination of events that were concealed in the midst of carefully co-ordinated lies was the very last thing that the authorities in Belfast and London would voluntarily agree to.

The government hoped that the joint statements in parliament would conclude discussion of the events of November and December 1982. For a time they were correct.

At the end of the trial of the three police officers who were acquitted on 5 June 1984 of killing Eugene Toman, an inquest was opened later in that same month and adjourned to await completion of the Stalker/Sampson investigations into that case and others. The inquest resumed in May 1992 but was later adjourned. On 31 January 1994 the inquest was closed and the jury discharged. It was reopened with a fresh jury on 22 March 1994. The coroner, John Leckey, ruled that the public had a proper interest in knowing whether any further relevant information into the killings had come to light. He issued a subpoena for the production of the reports prepared by John Stalker and Colin Sampson. The House of Lords had previously ruled that the police officers involved in the incidents could not be compelled to give evidence to the inquest if they did not wish, so the evidence of eyewitnesses would not be available to the inquest jury.

On 5 May 1994 the secretary of state for Northern Ireland issued a Public Interest Immunity Certificate stating that the disclosure of the Stalker/Sampson report would cause serious damage to the public interest. The court upheld that decision on the ground that it was not relevant to the coroner's inquiry and in any event it was not in the public interest to allow the report's production. On 8 September 1994 the coroner abandoned the reopened inquest. He could not hope to achieve his purpose in the light of these legal rulings and decisions.

Twenty-five years later to the day, on 25 January 2013, the CCRC announced that it had referred the conviction of Martin McCauley to the Northern Ireland Court of Appeal. He had applied to the commission to review his case in November 2005. Why it took the commission more than seven years to refer his case seems inexplicable. He had been arrested in Colombia in 2001 with two other men, Niall Connolly and James Monaghan, accused of training rebel FARC guerrilla forces in the use of explosives and bomb-making equipment. He was originally cleared of the charges, but in 2004 the appeal court convicted him and sentenced him to 17 years in prison. He went to the Republic of Ireland in 2005, having absconded from Colombia. If he returns to Northern Ireland he faces extradition to South America.

The decision to refer the case on appeal was based on information obtained by the commission that was not known to the trial judge and that raised a real possibility that the appeal court would quash the conviction.

The information on which that assessment was based is 'sensitive' and consequently the commission could only supply Martin McCauley and his legal advisers with a summary of the reasons for the referral. The commission did, however, supply a full account of those reasons in a confidential annex both to the court and the Public Prosecution Service (formerly the Department of Public Prosecutions), and left it to the court to make a decision on disclosure of the information concerned. Clearly Martin McCauley's lawyers will find it difficult to construct their arguments based on material they have not been allowed to see.

In the event the DPP, Barra McGrory, came to the conclusion that the appeal should not be resisted and he invited the appeal court to exercise their inherent discretion to quash the conviction on the basis that to do otherwise would undermine public confidence in the criminal justice system.

In giving the judgment of the court on 10 September 2014 the Lord Chief Justice, Sir Declan Morgan, noted that at the original trial Mr Justice Basil Kelly had expressed considerable doubt about the allegation that Michael Tighe and Martin McCauley each held and pointed a rifle in the direction of the police officers from inside the hay barn. That judge knew that the evidence was that the rifles were unloaded, without ammunition. The police evidence was that Michael Tighe and Martin McCauley both reappeared, each holding and pointing a rifle, a second time after the police had fired into the hayshed. He found it difficult to accept that they would have reappeared in exposed places with their unloaded rifles after a burst of gunfire had been directed towards them. Mr Justice Kelly thus excluded the police evidence on the ground it was unreliable. He only convicted the two accused because he did not believe one word of the explanation advanced by them. He thought they had entered the hayshed for the joint purpose of handling or working at those rifles.

The Lord Chief Justice noted that the eavesdropping operation carried out at the hay barn prior to the fatal shooting on 24 November 1982 had been set up by the RUC Special Branch, with technical expertise provided by MI5. The existence of the operation was disclosed to the DPP, but not to Mr Justice Kelly or the defence teams.

What the DPP was not told, however, was that the eavesdropping operation produced audio recordings of the events immediately before and during the fatal killing of Michael Tighe. Those who heard one tape recording recollected that no warnings were shouted by the RUC officers before they opened fire on the hayshed. They had sworn that such warnings had been given.

Very soon after that recording was made, certainly during the month of November, a senior RUC officer destroyed what he believed was the only copy of the tape. He did so because he considered it potentially damaging to the RUC. In fact it went much further than that: did it not prove that the incident at the hay barn involved a 'kill, don't question' approach by the police to the two young men inside the hayshed? But in fact there were other copies of the tape and there also existed transcript copies of its content. These were held by MI5.

Worse was to follow. In the course of its investigations the CCRC discovered a memo dated 25 November 1982 from an officer who said that he had learned that the RUC officers had exceeded their orders and shot the alleged terrorists without giving them the chance to surrender. That, of course, was not disclosed to the trial judge or to the defence. If it had been, would the prosecution have been able to get their case under way at all? In furtherance of this cover-up, the deputy head of the Special Branch of the RUC had both the tapes and the monitor logs destroyed. He did this apparently because of the deep embarrassment the disclosure of this evidence might cause. Did he not realise that such conduct might be unlawful, amounting to the obstruction of justice?

The Lord Chief Justice, Sir Declan Morgan, then recited the fact that an unauthorised copy of the hayshed tape had been made by the army. When and why is not known. It ended up in the possession of MI5, who kept it until someone decided to destroy it, sometime in the summer of 1985. It follows from that that this evidence existed at the time of the original trial of Martin McCauley. It should have been disclosed to his defence but it was not. Justice was again obstructed. Such evidence would have supported his case and undermined the case for the prosecution.

Sir Declan Morgan indicated that there were three grounds upon which the appeal would be decided. First, did the misconduct of the RUC in destroying their copy of the eavesdropping tape and MI5 failing to disclose their copy when they knew that Martin McCauley's trial was pending mean that he did not have a fair trial? The court decided that he had been deprived of a fair trial.

Second, did the conduct of the authorities amount to an abuse of process? The lord chief justice noted that the police officers involved in the shooting lied to the investigating officers when providing their original statements – and this was at the direction of senior officers. The fact that officers at the scene had been briefed prior to making their witness statements was 'entirely inappropriate'. The destruction of the tape could well amount to the perversion of justice. The DPP was initially misled by not being told of the existence of the eavesdropping device; even when, no doubt reluctantly, its existence was disclosed, he was not told either of the recording or the transcription of the recording, in spite of the request for that material. Sir Declan Morgan said that 'the failure of the Security Service to disclose the tape to Mr Stalker and to provide it to the prosecution was reprehensible.' All these matters amounted to grave misconduct and were so prejudicial as to deprive Martin McCauley of a fair trial.

Third, such was the misconduct in this case that it would be contrary to the public interest in the integrity of the criminal justice system to uphold the conviction. The conviction was set aside.

The truth was only established in this case, in the face of repetitive lies of police officers and senior members of MI5, because there was sufficient material available to prove that lie followed lie, involving many individuals, from the outset of the incident to the end of the original trial of Martin McCauley. If, as was intended, he had been shot dead without warning alongside Michael Tighe, the truth would have been buried with them. 'Dead men tell no tales.'

As noted above, the CCRC did not share the results of their investigation with the lawyers acting for Martin McCauley, preferring to leave the amount and extend of the disclosure of the truth to the appeal court.

This is not the first time the CCRC has acted in this secretive way, which is contrary to the principle of open justice. It did exactly the same in May 2008 in the case of Danny Morrison, the former publicity director of Sinn Féin.

On Friday 5 January 1990, Alexander 'Sandy' Lynch left his home in County Derry to attend a meeting in a house in the New Lodge district of north Belfast. He had been summoned to attend by the Provisional IRA. His interrogator was to be Alfredo 'Scap' Scappaticci, regarded by some as a ruthless psychopath, who was a senior figure in the Provisionals' internal security unit, known colloquially as 'the Nutting Squad'. That group existed to find and eliminate informers within the IRA. It is now believed that Scappaticci was an agent, code-named Stakeknife, for the army and MI5. The price of betrayal in his case gave him an income said to be £80,000 a year. He is suspected, with Denis Donaldson, of giving away the movements of three IRA members who were on a bombing mission in Gibraltar in March 1988. It is believed by some that Alfredo Scappaticci has lodged, and left untouched, his money from his trade in treachery in a bank in Gibraltar.

Sandy Lynch, also an agent run by the army and MI5, had been told by his handlers that he would be 'invited' to the meeting to be questioned about being an informer; that he should go to the house, where he would be under police surveillance; and that he would be protected against all harm. He agreed to this. The carefully prepared trap was set.

Danny Morrison went to the house in north Belfast intending to organise a public press conference, at which it was expected that Sandy Lynch would confess to being an informer recruited by the army. Morrison entered the house. Scappaticci had already left and was far away. A combined police and army unit descended on the area and arrested Danny Morrison, together with seven others. They charged him with aiding and abetting the abduction and false imprisonment of Sandy Lynch. Although Freddie Scappaticci's fingerprints were found in the house, he was not charged with any offence. That might have aroused some suspicion about his involvement, not with the abduction, but with the arrival of the army and the RUC. Strangely, no one seems to have been suspicious.

When Danny Morrison appeared in court in 1991 he watched as Sandy Lynch gave evidence against him, not knowing at that time of the involvement of his pal 'Scap' from the 'Nutting Squad'. But the defence had some useful information with which to cross-examine the alleged victim, namely that four years previously, in 1987, he had shot and wounded a man in County Down. He denied that, but accepted that if it were true it certainly damaged, if not destroyed, his credibility as a witness. In the event Danny Morrison was convicted and sent to prison for eight years.

On the day of Danny's conviction Sandy Lynch was shown on the television news. A man called Peter Duggan recognised him. He told Danny Morrison's solicitors and the police that the man on the television was the man who had shot him in 1987 in County Down. Duggan wanted the police to help provide him with a new identity and money to find a safe house where his rather chequered past on the periphery of terrorism in Northern Ireland would not catch up with him.

On the basis of that information, among other matters, Danny Morrison decided to appeal against his conviction and sentence in 1992. It was expected that Peter Duggan would be a compelling witness. He failed to appear. Had he been warned off by someone, or had he voluntarily stayed away? The appeal was dismissed and Danny Morrison served his time in prison.

There the matter rested until May 2003 when an undercover agent, Kevin Fulton, who had worked for MI5 after leaving the army, is said to have threatened to expose Scappaticci as an agent unless the MOD gave him a retirement pension and a resettlement package. He apparently got neither. Someone then, and it is not known who, unmasked Freddie Scappaticci in the media. He suddenly left Northern Ireland, returning a few days later to give a press conference in Belfast denying his alleged treachery, but thereafter silently and swiftly disappeared. His present whereabouts are not known to anyone but a select few. His fate was sealed when in 2004 a journalist, Greg Harkin, and a former army intelligence army officer, Martin Ingram, who had worked in the deeply feared Force Research Unit of the British army, published a book, *Stakeknife: Britain's Secret Agents in Ireland*, naming him as an informer. Nothing has been seen or heard from 'Scap' for some time. He will almost certainly live under constant state protection for the rest of his life. He is reputed to have left a set of documents naming those who were involved in his treachery and betrayal, as an insurance against a sudden death.

When this astonishing version of events became public, representations were made to the CCRC to invite them to send the case of Danny Morrison and his co-accused back to the appeal court to see whether their convictions should be allowed to stand. In 2008 the Commission agreed to do so.

On 24 October 2008 the convictions of all eight men were quashed. The Chief Justice, Sir Brian Kerr, said in the course of his ruling that the CCRC had forwarded a report to the court with 'confidential annexures'. Counsel on both sides invited the chief justice, with Lord Justice Higgins and Lord Justice Coghlin, to read those documents and they did so, separately. All three arrived at the same conclusions: first, that the convictions could not be regarded as safe and would accordingly be quashed; second, that they could deliver an 'open' decision because there was nothing in those documents that would infringe the public interest or the interests of justice if the information that led to the convictions being set aside was disclosed.

For reasons not given then or later, counsel for the Crown invited the appeal court judges not to do that, but to allow further argument why the reasons should *not* be disclosed to the public. The Crown's lawyers were instructed by the state to oppose the disclosure of what? Was it the truth? Who fears the truth? The Crown sought a 'closed' judgment, i.e. one in which the reasons for quashing the convictions were not explicitly stated. The judges agreed. Two *ex parte* applications were heard, at which neither Danny Morrison nor his co-accused nor any of their lawyers were allowed to be present.

The following January Sir Brian Kerr delivered the judgment of the court.[12] Material and information which in October 2008 would not harm the interests of justice nor the public interest suddenly needed to be concealed. His Lordship said: 'Two private hearings were held. As a consequence of material and information received by us in the course of the hearings we have concluded that it is not possible to disclose all of the reasons that led to the quashing of the convictions. The judgment that follows contains as much information as we feel able to give in the light of the constraints that we now recognise ourselves to be under.'

The chief justice then proceeded to read four paragraphs that can be easily summarised. Material evidence had not been disclosed to the DPP by the police. He was deprived of the opportunity to decide whether there should be a prosecution at all, and furthermore he could not tell the defence, as he would have been bound to do, what that withheld information actually was, because he had not seen it. If there had been full disclosure resulting in the case being run against Danny Morrison, he and his co-accused could have submitted to the trial court that there had been an abuse of process of the court. 'Abuse of process' was judicially defined in the House of Lords in 1992 as 'something so unfair and wrong with the prosecution that the court should not allow the prosecution to proceed with what is, in all other respects, a perfectly supportable case.' The chief justice considered that submission would have succeeded, but if it had not and the trial went on, then the giving of that undisclosed evidence would almost certainly have led to the acquittal of all those charged before the original trial court.

In the final paragraph of his judgment Sir Brian Kerr put on record that the DPP would ask the chief constable of the PSNI to investigate evidence arising out of the CCRC's report, because that might uncover certain matters involving criminal offences being committed by someone. It is not difficult to surmise who that might be, or what that evidence might comprise.

At the time of writing in 2016 I could find no evidence that anyone has been called to account for any criminal activity in the course of investigating or presenting Danny Morrison's case that led to his wrongful conviction.

If there had been a fruitful investigation, might the public have been told why a protected witness like Sandy Lynch did not face prosecution for shooting and wounding Peter Duggan? Even more important, some may wish to know when, how and why Alfredo Scappaticci was recruited by the army's Force Research Unit. It is suspected by some that not only did that unit know of his role in the IRA's 'Nutting Squad', but it made no attempt to stop him interrogating, then torturing and killing suspected informers in the IRA at a time when he was being paid handsomely by the state that so carefully and cleverly concealed the truth.

His name is, however, not completely out of the frame. He is being sued, jointly with the MOD and the police, by Margaret Keeley, the former wife of Kevin Fulton. She wants damages against those three parties for unlawful arrest and wrongful imprisonment. Her claim states that she was detained at the infamous Castlereagh police station in 1994 for three days before being released without charge.

After her release she says that she and her former husband were taken to premises in the New Lodge area of Belfast and there interrogated by, among others, Freddie Scappaticci.

In June 2014 lawyers for the MOD and the chief constable of the PSNI (the successors of the RUC) sought to persuade a High Court judge to hold the proceedings not in open court but in secret session, coupled with an Order for Closed Material Procedures, which would prevent Margaret Keeley's lawyers from seeing certain evidence in the case. The court order was made under the provisions of the Justice and Security Act 2013. All very convenient for those who might wish to hide the truth.

According to *The Guardian*, Barra McGrory, the Northern Ireland DPP, had instructed the chief constable of the PSNI to open an inquiry into up to 20 killings by the IRA that may be connected to Freddie Scappaticci. The director said that the Northern Ireland police ombudsman 'has carried out a comprehensive analysis of material emanating from three investigations carried out by Lord Stevens into allegations of collusion. A common link across a significant number of potential crimes, including murder, was the alleged involvement of an agent of military intelligence code-named Stakeknife.'[13] Allegations have surfaced that the price of treachery, perhaps not unsurprising in these inflationary times, has grown from the 30 pieces of silver paid to Judas Iscariot to £80,000 a year paid by the British government to Scappaticci into a bank account in Gibraltar, where it awaits his collection. He left Northern Ireland in May 2003 and his present whereabouts is a closely guarded secret. It is doubtful if he is spending more time with his money in Gibraltar.

In June 2016 the chief constable of Bedfordshire Police, Jon Boutcher, was invited to investigate allegations of murder and collusion made against Scappaticci, in which no current or former members of the RUC, the PSNI, the MOD or MI5 will be permitted to take part. He told the media on 9 June that his 'principal aim in taking responsibility for this investigation is to bring those responsible for these awful crimes, in whatever capacity they were involved, to justice'. That will not happen. I predict that inquiry will go nowhere. The state has too much to hide.

But one is bound to ask: has the principle of open justice, that is justice being done, and being seen to be done, been abandoned? Justice in secret, behind closed doors, is no justice at all. Not only that: does not secret justice lead to injustice and the conviction of an innocent, whilst the guilty walk free?

Appendix

Decision of Information Tribunal 17 September 2009

Tribunals Service
Information Tribunal

Appeal under section 57 of Freedom of Information Act 2000

Information Tribunal Appeal Number: EA/2009/0010
Information Commissioner's Ref: FS50142499

Determined on papers	**Decision Promulgated**
14 September 2009	**17 September 2009**

BEFORE

CHAIRMAN

Murray Shanks

and

LAY MEMBERS

Anne Chafer and Henry Fitzhugh

Between

MIICHAEL O'CONNELL

Appellant

and

INFORMATION COMMISSIONER

Respondent

and

CROWN PROSECUTION SERVICE

Additional Party

Subject areas covered:

Freedom of Information Act 2000:
Personal data s.40

Data Protection Act 1998:
Personal data s.1(1)
Sensitive personal data s.2
Principles, Sched 1
Processing of sensitive data, Shed 3
Processing of Personal data, Sched 2

Cases referred to:

Durant v FSA [2003] EWCA Civ 1746

Tribunal's determination

The appeal is dismissed and the Information Commissioner's decision notice is upheld for the reasons set out below.

Reasons for Determination

Background facts

1. The notorious Guildford bombings took place on 5 October 1974. On 22 October 1975 the Guildford Four (including Patrick Armstrong) were convicted of murder. As is well known the convictions were based on evidence of confessions made to the police. On 19 October 1989 the Guildford Four's appeal against conviction was allowed and they were released.

2. In April 1993 three Surrey police officers involved in the investigation of the bombings (namely Vernon Atwell, John Donaldson and Thomas Style) were tried for conspiracy to pervert the course of justice in relation to Mr Armstrong. At their

trial various documents were put before the jury on their behalf, including, at item 10 of the Defence Jury Bundle, a document described as "Extracts from the Defence Brief of Mr Boxall". Mr Boxall (who we understand is now deceased) had acted as junior counsel to Mr Armstrong at his trial in 1975.

3. This appeal concerns item 10. The Tribunal has seen the document and been given some information about it by the CPS in the course of the appeal and we can say this much about its contents. It consists of four typed pages extracted from a larger document which sets out the recollection of DS Donaldson and DC Attwell of an interview they conducted with Mr Armstrong on 5 December 1974. The document bears some manuscript notes. Although the CPS is unable to tell us the name of the author of the notes and the Tribunal cannot say for sure, it seems more likely than not from the surrounding circumstances that they were made by Mr Boxall (as the Appellant contends) and that they record instructions Mr Boxall was given by Mr Armstrong in 1975 relating to what is said in the typescript recollection.

4. The Appellant, Mr O'Connell, was an English barrister from 1966 until his retirement in 2006 and was also a member of the Irish Bar from 1977. He states that he is "...researching the area of confessions in police custody and the response of the state when convictions are set aside by the Appeal Court...". Whatever the exact scope of his research it is apparent that he has a keen interest in and detailed knowledge of the whole affair, which, needless to say, remains one of great public interest.

5. On 14 June 2006 Mr O'Connell made a request under the Freedom of Information Act 2000 for a copy of the entire Defence Jury Bundle from the CPS. Following an internal review of an earlier decision the CPS informed him on 18 October 2006 that they would not supply him with (among other things) item 10 in the bundle because it was exempt under section 40(2) of the Act ("Personal information"). The Commissioner upheld the CPS's decision on item 10 in a decision notice dated 20 January 2009 and Mr O'Connell appeals to this Tribunal under section 57 of the Act on the basis that the decision notice is "not in accordance with the law". In the course of his appeal Mr O'Connell has made it clear (initially in a letter to the Tribunal dated 26 March 2009) that he accepts he is not entitled to see the

typescript comprising the police officers' recollection and he seeks only to see the manuscript notes.

The issues

6. Based on the submissions of the parties and the terms of section 40(2) of the 2000 Act and the relevant provisions of the Data Protection Act 1998, the Tribunal understands the issues to be as follows:

    (1) Whether and to what extent the manuscript notes constitute "information" at all for the purposes of the 2000 Act;

    (2) Whether they constitute the "personal data" of any person(s) and, if so, who the data subject(s) is and whether the data is "sensitive personal data" for the purposes of the 1998 Act; and

    (3) If so, whether the disclosure of such information to a member of the public would contravene any of the data protection principles and in particular whether such disclosure would be a fair processing of the information and satisfy one of the conditions in Schedule 2 to the 1998 Act and in addition (if the data is sensitive personal data) one of the conditions in Schedule 3.

Issue (1)

7. There is no doubt that some of the manuscript notes taken in isolation are likely to be of limited value and potentially misleading. The Commissioner has submitted that some of them (identified in his closed response) do not even constitute information. We do not accept this submission: in our view however tenuous and potentially misleading the material sought may be, it still constitutes information, even if it is only information to the effect that certain marks have been made on certain sheets of paper held by the public authority.

Issue (2)

8. We are quite satisfied that item 10 contains information about the alleged involvement of Mr Armstrong and a number of other named individuals in the

Appeal Number: EA/2009/0010

Guildford bombing and that it therefore contains "sensitive personal information" relating to those individuals for the purposes of the 1998 Act (see in particular section 2(g)). We are also satisfied that the manuscript notes in isolation (which, as we have said, appear to reflect Mr Armstrong's instructions on the typescript) also constitute his "sensitive personal data" and contain such data relating to at least one other named individual. Mr O'Connell submits that because Mr Armstrong's conviction was quashed by the Court of Appeal and the Prime Minister issued a public apology to him and ten others in 2005, information about his alleged involvement in the Guildford bombings is no longer sensitive personal data; there is nothing in the 1998 Act which points to such a conclusion and section 2(g) expressly refers to information "...as to...the commission or *alleged* commission by [the data subject] of any offence."

9. The CPS have also submitted that the document "contains the personal data of the police officers who have recorded their accounts of the interviews...[ie] DS Donaldson and DCI Attwell". We reject that submission. The document contains no information about them save for the fact that they interviewed Mr Armstrong and their recollection of that interview, which presumably they recorded as part of their duties as police officers. That information does not in our view therefore satisfy either of the tests (namely "privacy" and "focus") identified by the Court of Appeal in *Durant v FSA* [2003] EWCA Civ 1746.

Issue (3)

10. Given our conclusion in paragraph 8 above that the information Mr O'Connell seeks constitutes the sensitive personal data of Mr Armstrong, it is clear that it could only be disclosed if one of the conditions in Schedule 3 to the 1998 Act was met (see Schedule 1 para 1(b)). We cannot see that any of those conditions have been met. In particular, so far as we are aware no-one has sought, and Mr Armstrong has not given, his explicit consent to disclosure (para 1 Schedule 3) and the information in question was not made public as a result of steps deliberately taken by him (para 5 Schedule 3) (though the latter may well have applied in relation to the police officers had the information in question constituted only their personal data). It follows that the information sought by Mr O'Connell was exempt under section 40(2) of the 2000 Act.

Conclusion

11. Since section 40(2) provides an absolute exemption, that conclusion means that the appeal must be dismissed. We do not need to and will not comment on what we may have concluded in relation to the balancing exercise required by para 6(1) Schedule 2 to the 1998 Act had we needed to carry it out but we do note in passing (a) that it seems to us that the information sought by Mr O'Connell must have been subject to legal professional privilege in favour of Mr Armstrong at some stage (so that section 42(1) of the 2000 Act may have been relevant) and (b) that section 32(1)(a) and/or (b) of the 2000 Act may also have applied.

12. Our decision is unanimous.

Signed:

Murray Shanks
Deputy Chairman

Date: 17 September 2009

ENDNOTES

Introduction

1 The FOI request was dated 29 December 2012.
2 *The Irish Times* 3 January 2002.
3 *Ibid.*
4 BBC News Channel, February 2005.
5 Hansard. House of Commons Debates (HC Deb hereafter). Standing Committee B. 17 January 1989 at col 509.

1 Past Events

1 Letitia Fairfield (ed.), *Notable British Trials.*
2 *Ibid.*, p. 238.
3 *Ibid.*
4 Peter Taylor, *Loyalists*, p. 126.
5 Hansard HC Deb, 20 December 1956 vol. 562 cols 1456–63.
6 Command Paper 814, 1959.
7 *The Guardian,* 9 April 2011.
8 *The Guardian,* 9 April 1993.
9 Supreme Court judgment: *Keyu & Anor v Secretary of State for Commonwealth Affairs*, para. 204.
10 *Ibid.*, para. 21.
11 *Ibid.*, para. 24.
12 *Ibid.*, para. 26.
13 *Ibid.*, para. 40.

2 Justice for Iain?

1 Cited in Ludovic Kennedy, *Thirty-Six Murders and Two Immoral Earnings, p. 69.*

3 The Fourteen Hooded Men

1 Her Majesty's Stationery Office (HMSO) Cmnd 4823.
2 4 June 2014.
3 Compton Report, para. 88.
4 *Ibid.*
5 *Ibid.*, para. 64.
6 *Sunday Times,* 17 October 1971.
7 *Daily Telegraph,* 19 January 1978.
8 *Observer,* 21 November 1971.

[9] Compton Report, para. 105.

[10] Parker Report, HMSO Cmnd 4901.

[11] Compton Report, para. 49.

[12] *Ibid.*

[13] *Ibid.*, para. 64.

[14] *Ibid.*, para. 62.

[15] *Ibid.*, para. 84.

[16] *Ibid.*, para. 78.

[17] *Ibid.*, para. 80.

[18] *Ibid.*, para. 119.

[19] *Ibid.*, para. 18.

[20] *Ibid.*, paras 297–300.

[21] *Ibid.*, para. 300.

[22] *Ibid.*, para. 256.

[23] HMSO Cmnd 4901.

[24] *Ibid.*, para. 35.

[25] *Ibid.*, para. 37.

[26] *Ibid.*, para. 20.

[27] Lord Gardiner's Minority Report, para. 14(b)(i).

[28] *Ibid.*, para. 21(2).

[29] *Ibid.*, para. 10(d).

[30] Report of Sir William Gage, Baha Mousa Inquiry, HC 145.

[31] *Ibid.*, para. 2.52.

[32] *Ibid.*, paras 2.1409 and 2.1410.

[33] 8 September 2011.

4 The Window Cleaners

[1] Cited by Michael Mansfield, *Presumed Guilty*, p. 121.

[2] *Independent*, May 1993.

5 The Troubles and the Truth

[1] Para. 7.13.

[2] Peter Taylor, *States of Terror: Democracy and Political Violence*, p. 120.

[3] William Whitelaw, *The Whitelaw Memoirs*, p. 176.

[4] Fenton Bresler, *Reprieve: A Study of a System*, p. 251.

[5] Cameron Report, HMSO Cmnd 532, para. 177.

[6] Scarman Report, HMSO Cmnd 566.

[7] Devlin is a native of Cookstown, County Tyrone. She entered politics while a student at Queen's University, Belfast. She was elected to the House of Commons in April 1969, making her the youngest ever female MP when she took the parliamentary seat for Mid Ulster from the Unionist Party. She did not stand for re-election in 1974. Bernadette is a passionate believer in the promotion of unity among the people of Ireland and she sought justice and truth on their behalf.

[9] *R. v. Foxford* (1974) Northern Ireland Law Reports, p. 194.

[10] Saville Report, Vol. 1, para. 3.35.

6 Can You be Irish and Innocent?

[1] Hansard HC Deb 25 January 1989 cols 1156–7.

[2] *Ibid.*

[3] See Tom Davis, 'ESDA and the analysis of contested interview notes', *Forensic Linguistics* 1 (1994), 71–89.

[4] Tim Kaye, *Unsafe and Unsatisfactory?*

[5] *Independent*, 24 April 2001.

[6] *Birmingham Evening Mail*, 23 April 2001.

[7] *Ibid.*

[8] Bob Haywood, Special Report, *Sunday Mercury*, 29 April 2001.

[9] *Ibid.*

[10] *Ibid.*

[11] *Sunday Mercury*, 24 October 2012.

[12] Louis Blom-Cooper, *The Birmingham Six and Other Cases*, p. 42.

[13] Paddy Joe Hill and Gerard Hunt, *Forever Lost, Forever Gone*, p. 67.

[14] Criminal Appeal Reports 1991, vol. 93, p. 306.

[15] *Ibid.*

[16] *Independent*, 8 October 1993.

[17] Paddy Joe Hill and Gerard Hunt, *Forever Lost, Forever Gone*, pp 78–79.

[18] Hansard HC Deb 11 November 1991 vol. 198 col. 343.

[19] Hansard HC Deb 12 December 1991 vol. 200 col. 1221.

7 Defending the Innocent: the Guilford Four

[1] 13 December 1990.

[2] Bob Huntley, *Bomb Squad*, p. 165.

[3] *Ibid.*, p. 166.

[4] Sir Robert Mark, *In the Office of Constable*, p. 130.

[5] David Rose, *In the Name of the Law*, p. 12.

[6] *Ibid.* pp. 39–40.

[7] May Report, paras 10.53 and 10.54.

[8] Court of Appeal transcript, p. 48.

[9] 17 September 1974.

[10] 39th edn, 1976, para 442.

[11] *Dallison v. Caffery*, Vol. 1 Queen's Bench 364 at 369, in the Court of Appeal.

8 Defending the Innocent: the Maguire Seven

[1] Yorkshire Television *First Tuesday* 'Aunt Annie's Bomb Factory', aired 6 March 1984 and Gerard Conlon's statement to the police dated 3 December 1974.

[2] Page 64 of the transcript of the summing-up.

[3] 1 September 1991.

[4] Criminal Appeal Reports vol. 6, p. 11.

[5] Bob Huntley, *Bomb Squad*, p. 169.

[6] *Ibid.*

[7] 5 May 1976.

[8] Court of Appeal transcript, p. 42.

[9] All England Law Reports, vol. 3, p. 480.

[10] May Report, para. 7.3.

[11] 24 May 1991.

[12] May Report, para 11.29.

[13] May Interim Report, para. 11.33.

[14] *Ibid.*

[15] 23 May 1990.

[16] 25 March 2014.

9 The Judiciary on Trial

[1] Court of Appeal hearing transcript, p. 47.

[2] Twibell *et al.* 1982.

[3] *Independent* 18 May 1991.

[4] Transcript of the 1976 trial.

[5] *Ibid.*

[6] *Ibid.*

[7] *Ibid.*

[8] Summing-up at the 1976 trial, p. 28.

[9] Transcript of the 1976 trial.

[10] *Ibid.*, pp. 43, 44.

[11] *Ibid.*

[12] May, Second Report, Para. 5.10.

[13] *Ibid*, para. 5.8.

[14] Transcript of the summing-up.

[15] *Ibid.*

[16] *The Times* 15 January 1976.

[17] Summing-up at the 1976 trial, pp. 55, 56.

[18] *Ibid.* p. 73.

[19] *Ibid.*

[20] *Ibid.* pp 66–7.

[21] Home Office Circular 31/1964.

[22] *Ibid.*, pp. 77, 78.

[23] Anne Maguire, *Why Me?*, p. 16.

[24] Summing-up, p. 76.

[25] *Ibid.*

[26] Summing-up, p. 79.

[27] Bob Woffinden, *Miscarriages of Justice*, p. 266.

[28] *Ibid.*

[29] Summing-up, p. 81.

[30] Sir John May's Interim Report, p. 25.

[31] *Ibid.*, p. 50.

[32] Adrian Zuckerman, 'Miscarriages of justice and judicial responsibility', 492.

[33] Summing-up, pp 65–6.

[34] Trial transcript, p. 84.

[35] Transcript of the summing-up, p. 89.

[36] *Ibid.*

[37] *Ibid.*, pp 89–91.

[38] Statistics from Hansard HC Deb 4 March 1993 vol. 220 cols 177–84W.

[39] 5 March 1976.

[40] Court of Appeal transcript, p. 49.

[41] *Ibid.*, p. 50.

[42] *Ibid.*, p. 46.

[43] *Ibid.*, p. 47.

[44] 13 July 1990.

[45] Para. 15.48.

[46] Criminal Appeal Reports 1993, vol. 96 p. 49.

[47] *Ibid.*, p. 51.

10 The Police on Trial

[1] Paul Hill, *Stolen Years*, p. 245.

[2] 17 March 1991.

[3] Submission to the court, p. 4.

[4] Transcript of his summing-up to the jury, p. 55.

[5] *Ibid.*

[6] Transcript of Roy Amlot's submission, p. 17.

[7] *Ibid.*, p. 19.

[8] *Ibid.*, pp. 19–20.

[9] *Ibid.*, p. 22.

[10] *Justice and Truth*, p. 187.

[11] *Independent*, 20 May 1993.

[12] *The Times*, 20 May 1993.

[13] *Daily Telegraph*, 20 May 1993.

[14] *Irish Press*, 21 April 1993.

[15] Extract from the Northern Ireland appeal court judgment of Lord Hutton, p. 14.

[16] *Ibid.*, p. 15.

[17] *Ibid.*, p. 17.

[18] 24/25 September 1975.

[19] *Ibid.*

[20] *Belfast Newsletter*, 20 May 1993.

[21] *The Guardian*, 20 May 1993.

[22] *Daily Telegraph*, 20 May 1993.

[23] *Sunday Times*, 23 May 1993.

[24] *Belfast Newsletter*, 20 May 1993.

[25] *The Guardian*, 20 May 1993.

[26] *Ibid.*

[27] May Report, para. 122.

[28] Criminal Appeal Reports 1975, vol. 61, p. 88.

[29] All England Law Reports 1964, vol. 1, p. 727.

[30] Cited in Ronan Bennett, *Double Jeopardy*, p. 23.

[31] *Belfast Newsletter*, 20 May 1993.

[32] There were two trials. The first was in 1989. The judge died during that trial so it had to be abandoned. It was during the second trial in 1990 that the judge called the witness.

[33] Transcript of the summing-up, p. 13.

[34] *Ibid.*, p. 33.

[35] *Ibid.*, p. 24.

[36] Transcript of the summing-up, p. 31.

[37] Douglas Hurd, *Memoirs*, p. 354.

[38] *The Irish Times*, 24 February 1994.

[39] Transcript of the summing-up, p. 8.

[40] David Rose, *In the Name of the Law*, p. 346.

[41] Transcript of the summing-up, p. 55.

[42] *Ibid.*

[43] *Ibid.*

[44] *Ibid.*, p. 5.

[45] *Ibid.*, p. 36.

[46] Tribunal Service website, ref. EA/2009/0010 or FS50142499.

[47] Archbold, *Criminal Pleading, Evidence and Practice* (2008 edn), para. 12–7.

[48] Information Tribunal's Decision, para. 11.

11 Covering up the Truth

[1] Chris Ryder, *The RUC 1922–1997*, p. 448.

[2] De Silva Report, para. 14.9.

[3] *Ibid.*, paras 14.16 and 14.18.

[4] *Ibid.*, para. 14.23.

[5] Cory Report, para. 1.259.

[6] Hansard. House of Commons. Standing Committee B. 17 January 1989 at Col 508.

[7] *Ibid.*, col. 520.

[8] *Ibid.*, col. 519.

[9] De Silva Report, para. 115.

[10] Cory Report, para. 1.13.

[11] Stevens Inquiry, Third Report, paras 4.6 and 4.7.

[12] *The Guardian*, 13 December 2001.

[13] David Lister and Hugh Jordan, *Mad Dog*, p. 53.

12 Unlawful Killing

[1] David McKittrick *et al.*, *Lost Lives*, p. 684.

[2] Liz Curtis, *Ireland: The Propaganda War*, p. 101.

[3] Hansard HC Deb, 27 January 1999, col. 380.

[4] Memorandum written by D.E.S. Blatherwick, Political Affairs Division.

13 The Killings Go On

[1] Amnesty International, *Political Killings in Northern Ireland*, p. 15.

[2] Northern Ireland Law Reports 1974, p. 181 (report of the trial); p. 195 (report of the appeal).

[3] *Ibid.*, p. 193 (trial report).

[4] Archbold, *Criminal Pleading, Evidence and Practice* (1973 edn), para. 444.

14 Killing Without Question?

[1] *R. v McNaughton*, 1975.

[2] [2014] Northern Ireland Queen's Bench (NIQB) 11.

[3] *The Irish Times*, 13 November 1982.

[4] 256 US 335 (1921).

[5] All England Law Reports 1971, p. 1077.

[6] *Ibid.*, p. 1088.

[7] *New Statesman*, 15 June 1984.

[8] 30 April 1987.

[9] John Stalker, *Stalker*, p. 40.

[10] *Ibid.*

[11] Hansard HC Deb 25 January 1988 vol. 126 cols 21–35.

[12] *R. v Morrison & Ors*, 2009, Northern Ireland Court of Appeal 1 (9 January 2009).

[13] 21 October 2015.

Bibliography

Books

Amnesty International. *Political Killings in Northern Ireland* 1994.

Archbold, J.F. *Criminal Pleading, Evidence and Practice*, 39th edn, 1976.

Ashmal, Kadar. *Shoot to Kill?* Mercier Press 1985.

Barker, Alan. *Shadows: Inside Northern Ireland's Special Branch*. Mainstream 2004.

Barton, Brian. *From Behind a Closed Door: Secret Court Martial Records of the 1916 Rising*. Blackstaff Press 2002.

Bennett, Ronan. *Double Jeopardy: Retrial of the Guildford Four*. Penguin Books 1993.

Black, John. *Killing for Britain*. Frontline Noir 2008.

Blom-Cooper, Louis. *The Birmingham Six and Other Cases: Victims of Circumstance*. Duckworth 1997.

Bourke, Richard. *Peace in Ireland*. Pimlico 2003.

Bowyer Bell, J. *The Irish Troubles*. Gill & Macmillan 1994.

—. *The Secret Army*. Academy Press 1974.

Boyle, K., Hadden, T. and Hillyard, P. *Law and State: The Case of Northern Ireland*. Robertson 1975.

Brandon, R. and Davies, C. *Wrongful Imprisonment: Mistaken Convictions and their Consequences*. Allen & Unwin 1973.

Bresler, Fenton. *Reprieve: A Study of a System*. Harrop & Co. Ltd 1965.

Brown, Johnston. *Into the Dark: Thirty Years in the RUC*. Gill & Macmillan 2005.

Bruce, Steve. *The Red Hand*. OUP 1992.

Cadwallader, Anne. *Lethal Allies*. Mercier Press 2013.

Callaghan, Hugh and Mulready, Sally. *Cruel Fate*. Poolbeg 1994.

Carver, Michael. *Britain's Army in the 20th Century*. Pan 1999.

Casey, J. *The Irish Law Officers*. Round Hall Sweet & Maxwell 1996.

Clarke, Sister Sarah. *No Faith in the System.* Mercier Press 1995.

Cobain, Ian. *Cruel Britannia.* Portobello 2012.

Cole, J.S.R. *Irish Cases on Criminal Law.* Golden Eagle 1975.

Conlon, Gerry. *Proved Innocent.* Hamish Hamilton 1990.

Conway, V., Daly, Y. and Schweppe, J. *Irish Criminal Justice.* Clarus Press 2011.

Coogan, Tim Pat. *On the Blanket.* Roberts Rinehart 1997.

—. *The IRA.* Palgrave 2000.

—. *The Troubles.* Palgrave 2002.

Curry, Austin. *All Hell will Break Loose.* O'Brien Press 2004.

Curtis, Liz. *Ireland: The Propaganda War.* Pluto Press 1984.

Cusack, Jim and McDonald, Henry. *The UVF.* Poolbeg 2000.

—. *The UDA.* Penguin Ireland 2004.

Darbyshire, Neil And Hilliard, Brian. *The Flying Squad.* Headline Book Publishing 1993.

Davis, Tom. *ESDA and the Analysis of Contested Interview Notes.* Forensic Linguistics 1994.

Dewar, Michael. *The British Army in Northern Ireland.* Arms and Armour 1996.

Dillon, Martin. *The Dirty War.* Hutchinson 1990.

—. *The Enemy Within.* Doubleday 1994.

English, Richard. *The Armed Struggle.* Macmillan 2003.

Fairfield, Letitia. *Notable British Trials.* William Hodge 1953.

Foreman, Freddie. *The Godfather of British Crime.* John Blake Publishing. 2009.

Geraghty, Tony. *The Irish War.* Harper Collins 1998.

Gillard, Michael and Flynn, Laurie. *Untouchables, Dirty Cops, Bent Justice And Racism In Scotland Yard.* Cutting Edge Press 2004.

Hellawell, Keith. *The Outsider.* Harper Collins 2002.

Hamill, Desmond. *Pig in the Middle: The Army in Northern Ireland 1969–85.* Methuen 1986.

Hamilton, Claire. *The Presumption of Innocence and Irish Criminal Law.* Irish Academic Press 2007.

Hill, Paddy Joe, and Hunt, Gerard. *Forever Lost, Forever Gone.* Bloomsbury 1995.

Hill, Paul and Bennett, Ronan. *Stolen Years.* Doubleday 1990.

Hillyard, P. *Suspect Community: People's Experience of the Prevention of Terrorism Acts in Britain.* Pluto Press 1993.

Huntley, Bob. *Bomb Squad.* W.H. Allen 1977.

Ingram, Martin and Harkin, Greg. *Stakeknife: Britain's Secret Agents in Ireland.* O'Brien Press 2004.

Jordan, Hugh. *Milestones in Murder.* Mainstream 2002.

Kaye, Tim. *Unsafe and Unsatisfactory?: Report of the Independent Inquiry into the Working Practices of the West Midlands Police Serious Crime Squad.* Civil Liberties Trust 1991.

Kee, Robert. *Trial and Error.* Penguin Books 1989.

Kennedy, Ludovic. *Thirty-Six Murders And Two Immoral Earnings.* Profile Books, 2002.

Kitson, Brigadier Frank. *Low Intensity Operations.* Faber & Faber 1971.

Larkin, Paul. *A Very British Jihad.* BTP Publications 2004.

Lister, David and Jordan, Hugh. *Mad Dog: The Rise and Fall of Johnny Adair and 'C Company'.* Mainstream 2003.

McGladdery, Gary. *The Provisional IRA in England.* Irish Academic Press 2006.

McGuffin, John. *Internment.* Anvil Books 1973.

McKee, Grant and Franey, Ros. *Time Bomb.* Bloomsbury 1988.

McKittrick, David, Kelters, Seamus, Feeney, Brian, Thornton, Chris and McVea, David. *Lost Lives: The Stories of the Men, Women and Children who Died as a Result of the Northern Ireland Troubles.* Mainstream 1999.

Maguire, Anne, and Gallagher, Jim. *Why Me?* Harper Collins 1994.

Maguire, Patrick and Gebler, Carlo. *My Father's Watch.* Fourth Estate 2008.

Mansfield Q.C., Michael. *Presumed Guilty.* William Heinemann Ltd 1993.

Mark, Sir Robert. *In The Office of Constable.* William Collins 1978.

Mullen, Chris. *Error of Judgment.* Chatto & Windus 1986.

Murray, Raymond. *The SAS in Ireland.* Mercier Press 1990.

—. *State Violence.* Mercier Press 1998.

Ní Aoláin, Fionnuala. *The Politics of Force.* Blackstaff Press 2000.

Nobles, Richard and Schief, David. *Understanding Miscarriages of Justice.* OUP 2002.

O'Brien, Justin. *Killing Finucane.* Gill & Macmillan 2005.

Rees, Merlyn. *Northern Ireland: A Personal Perspective.* Methuen 1985.

Robertson, Geoffrey. *The Justice Game.* Vintage 1998.

Rolston, Bill. *Unfinished Business: State Killings and the Quest for Truth.* BTP 2000.

Rose, David. *In the Name of the Law: The Collapse of Criminal Justice.* Vintage 1996.

Ryan, E.F. and Magee, P.P. *The Irish Criminal Process.* Mercier Press 1983.

Ryder, Chris. *The RUC 1922–1997: A Force under Fire.* Methuen 1989.

Sanders, Andrew and Young, Richard. *Criminal Justice.* Butterworth 1994.

Simpson, Jenny. *Biting the Bullet: Married to the SAS*. Harper Collins 1996.

Stevens, John. *Not for the Faint-hearted: My Life Fighting Crime*. Weidenfeld & Nicholson 2005.

Stalker, John. *Stalker*. Harrap Ltd 1988.

Target, G.W. *Bernadette: The Story of Bernadette Devlin*. Hodder & Stoughton 1975.

Taylor, Peter. *Stalker: The Search for the Truth*. Faber & Faber 1987.

—. *Brits: The War against the IRA*. Bloomsbury 2001.

Thorpe, D.R. *Supermac: The Life of Harold Macmillan*. Chatto & Windus 2010.

Victory, Patrick. *Justice and Truth*. Sinclair-Stevenson 2001.

Walker, Clive and Starmer, Keir. *Justice in Error*. Blackstone Press 1993.

—. *Miscarriages of Justice*. Blackstone Press 1999.

Ward, Judith. *Ambushed: My Story*. Vermilion 1993.

Whitelaw, William. *The Whitelaw Memoirs*. Aurum Press 1989

Williams, Glanville. *Textbook of Criminal Law*. Stevens 1978.

Woffinden, Bob. *Miscarriages of Justice*. Hodder & Stoughton 1987.

Archives

National Archives, London

Public Record Office of Northern Ireland

Hull History Centre

Government Publications

Aitken, Brigadier Robert. Report of an Investigation into Cases of Abuse and Unlawful Killing in Iraq in 2003 And 2004. Ministry of Defence 25 January 2008).

Cameron Report: Disturbances in Northern Ireland: Report of the Commission appointed by the Governor of Northern Ireland. HMSO, Cmnd 532, 1969.

Compton Inquiry: Report into Allegations against the Security Forces of Physical Brutality in Northern Ireland Arising out of Events on 9 August 1971. Sir Edmund Compton. HMSO Cmnd 4823.

Cory Collusion Inquiry Report. HC 470. London: Stationery Office 2004.

de Silva Report: Report of the Pat Finucane Review. Rt Hon. Desmond de Silva QC. HC 802–I. London 2012.

Gage Report: The Baha Mousa Public Inquiry Report by Sir William Gage. HC 1451–2).

Information and Advice for Prisoners about Grounds of Appeal and the Appeals Procedure. (Royal Commission on Criminal Justice Research Study No. 18. HMSO. London 1993.

May Report: Interim Report on the Maguire Case. Rt Hon. Sir John May. HC 556. London 1990.

May Report: Second Report on the Maguire Case. Rt Hon. Sir John May. HC 296. London 1992.

May Report: Final Report on the Guildford and Woolwich Bombings. Rt Hon. Sir John May. HC 449 HMSO 1994.

Miscarriages of Justice. Home Affairs Committee 6th Report. Session 1981–82. HC 421. HMSO 1982.

Office of the High Commissioner for Human Rights (1990).

Basic Principles on the Role of Lawyers Adopted by the 8th United Nations Congress on the Prevention of Crime and the Treatment of Offenders. Havana, Cuba.

Parker Report: Report of the Committee of Privy Counsellors Appointed to Consider Authorised Procedures for the Interrogation of Persons Suspected of Terrorism. Lord Parker of Waddington. HMSO, Cmnd 4901.

Philips Report: Royal Commission on Criminal Procedure. Cmnd 8092. HMSO 1981.

The Role of Forensic Science Evidence in Criminal Proceedings. Royal Commission on Criminal Justice, Research Study No. 11. HMSO 1993.

Royal Commission on Criminal Justice, Research Study No. 18. HMSO 1993.

Runciman Report: Royal Commission on Criminal Justice. Cmnd. 2263. HMSO 1993.

Saville, Lord Mark. The Report of the The Bloody Sunday Inquiry. Gov. UK. 15 June 2010.

Scarman, Lord Leslie. Report of Inquiry into Violence and Civil Disturbances In Northern Ireland In 1969. HMSO 566.

Tucker Report: Report of the Tucker Committee on New Trials in Criminal Cases. Cmnd. 9150. HMSO 1954.

Journal Articles

Baldwin, J. and McConville M. 'Allegations against lawyers: some evidence from criminal cases in London'. *Criminal Law Review* 1978. (p. 741)

Bennion, F. 'Propositions of law in conviction appeals'. *Criminal Law Review* 1984. (p. 282)

Bridges, L. and McConville, M. 'Keeping faith with their own convictions'. *Modern Law Review* 1994. (p. 75)

Brownlie, I. 'Police questioning, custody and caution'. *Criminal Law Review* 1960. (p. 298)

Coleman, R.F. and Walls, H.J. 'The evaluation of scientific evidence'. *Criminal Law Review* 1974. (p. 276)

Greer, S. 'Miscarriages of justice reconsidered'. *Modern Law Review* 1994.(p. 58)

Hill, P. 'Finding finality'. *New Law Journal* 1996. (p. 146)

Howard, M.N. 'The neutral expert: a plausible threat to justice'. *Criminal Law Review* 1991. (p. 98)

Humphreys, Christmas. 'The duties and responsibilities of prosecuting counsel'. 1995. *The Criminal Law Review* 1955. p. 739

Inman, M. 'The admissibility of confessions'. *Criminal Law Review* 1981. (p. 461)

Jackson, J.D. 'Two methods of proof in criminal procedure'. *Modern Law Review* 1988. (p. 549)

O'Connor, P. 'The Court of Appeal: re-trials and tribulations'. *Criminal Law Review* 1990. (p. 615)

Ormrod, R. 'Scientific evidence in court'. *Criminal Law Review* 1968. (p. 240)

Reiner, R. 'Investigative powers and safeguards for suspects'. *Criminal Law Review* 1993. (p. 808)

Smith, John, 'Criminal appeals and the Criminal Cases Review Commission'. *New Law Journal* 1995. (p. 145)

Thornton, P. 'Miscarriages of justice: a lost opportunity'. *Criminal Law Review* 1993. (p. 926)

Tregilgas-Davey, M. 'Miscarriages of justice within the English legal system'. *New Law Journal* 1991. (p. 141)

Twibell, J.D., Home, J.M., Smalldon, R.W. and Higgs, D.G. 'Transfer of NG to hands during contact with commercial explosives'. *Journal of Forensic Sciences* 27 (1982) 783–91.

Walker R.J. 'The Criminal Appeal Act'. *New Law Journal* 1966. (p. 116)

Zander, M. 'Legal advice and criminal appeals'. *Criminal Law Review* 1972. (p. 132)

Zuckerman, Adrian. 'Miscarriages of justice and judicial responsibility'. *Criminal Law Review* 1991. (p. 492)

Index